The Nature of Shamanism

The Nature
of Shamanism

Substance and Function
of a Religious Metaphor

Michael Ripinsky-Naxon

STATE UNIVERSITY OF NEW YORK PRESS

Published by
State University of New York Press, Albany

For information, address State University of New York Press,
State University Plaza, Albany, N.Y. 12246

Production by Cathleen Collins
Marketing by Nancy Farrell

Library of Congress Cataloging in Publication Data

Ripinsky-Naxon, Michael, 1944–
    The nature of shamanism: substance and function of a religious
metaphor / Michael Ripinsky-Naxon.
        p.   cm.
    Includes bibliographical references and index.
    ISBN 0-7914-1385-3. — ISBN 0-7914-1386-1 (pbk.)
    1. Shamanism. 2. Experience (Religion) 3. Metaphor—Religious
aspects.   I. Title.
BL2370.S5R52   1993
291.1'4—dc20   92-5415
                                                                          CIP

10 9 8 7 6 5 4 3 2 1

TO MY WIFE, AGATA,
Who Understood, Encouraged, and Believed,
in the Sun above the Aegean Blue
and the California Desert.

Contents

Illustrations   *ix*

Acknowledgments   *xi*

1   Introduction: A Personal Dialectic   *1*

2   Shamanism and Culture: Configurations of a
     Religious Metaphor   *13*
          Cultural Ethos and Mysticism   13
          Hunting Magic   23
          Master of the Animals—The Lady of Wild Things   25
          The Spiral and the Labyrinth   33
          Shamanism and Ancient Egyptian Religion   37
          Shamanistic Metaphors, Techniques,
               and Appurtenances   42
          Mongolian Shamanism   56
          The Celtic Religion   59
          The Role of the Shaman   62

3   Substance and Function of Shamanism   *69*
          Definitions and Problems   69
          "Answering the Call," Initiation, and
               Shamanic Enlightenment   71
          The Shamanistic Experience   92
          Shamanism and Psychopathology   101

4   The Psychotropic Universe: Cosmology of the
     Spirit World   *105*
          Cosmic Transformations   105
          Corresponding Realities and Otherworlds   112
          Numerical Potencies   121
          Rock Crystals and the Hexagonal Universe   123
          Reason and Order   127

5   The Ritual Drug Complex: Ethnobiology of
     Heaven and Hell   *131*
          The Drug Ceremonial   131
          Psychoactivity and Mechanisms of Hallucinations   142
          Phosphenes   148

6   The Botanic Experience: Hallucinogens in
     Archaeology and Ethnohistory   *151*
          The Old World   153
          The New World   166
          *The Quest for Magical Plants and the
               Origins of Cultivation   184*

7   The Power of Metaphors: Phenomenology of
     Symbolic Forms   *187*
          Language, Perception, and Reality   187
          Metaphor, Myth, and Transcendence   192
          Visionary Experiences and Art   197
          Phosphenes and Shamanistic Symbolism   202
          Shamanistic Parallels and Survivals   204

Notes   *209*

Bibliography   *257*

Index   *273*

Illustrations

1.1 The animal-headed, Greek St. Chrisophoros   *3*

2.1 A trance ceremony of the Rufaim in Upper Egypt   *17*

2.2 A floor plan of a tent belonging to an Evenk shaman   *25*

2.3 A Northwest Coast Indian shaman's mask   *26*

2.4 An Ainu shaman-priest at a bear-cult ritual   *29*

2.5 The Egyptian god Osiris, enthroned   *38*

2.6 The Siberian shaman Tulayev of the Karagass   *47*

2.7 Costume of a Tungus shaman. (Detail)   *48*

3.1 Mexican curandero's *botanicas* and power objects   *71*

3.2 A Precolumbian mushroom stone with a toad (a toad-stool)   *98*

3.3 *Banisteriopsis caapi* (yajé) in an old botanical   *100*

4.1 A Precolumbian ceramic figurine depicting a person with a spirit counterpart   *116*

6.1 Shamanistic rock painting from Tassili n'Ajjer, Algeria   *152*

6.2 A rock carving of a shamanic figure in the Camonica Valley   *156*

6.3 A Bronze Age Greek figurine of a *kourotrophos*   *158*

6.4 The Little Metropolitan Church in Athens, with poppy or opium pods on an ancient edifice   *160*

6.5 Diagrams of the Maya and the Navajo cosmos   *171*

6.6 A Maya World-Tree from Palenque as a cosmic axis   *172*

6.7 *Amanita muscaria* illustrated in *Codex Borbonicus*   *175*

6.8 A Mochica, Peru, vessel in the form of a human head and *Amanita muscaria*   *180*

Book Cover: Rock painting of a shamanic figure in Tassili n'Ajjer.

Acknowledgments

I AM INDEBTED TO many in Europe, North Africa, Southwest Asia, and the Americas for their suggestions, help, patience, and hospitality: to them I extend my profound gratitude. In particular, however, I wish to express my thanks to Professor Gérardo Reichel-Dolmatoff, whose extensive knowledge of the subject not only made his comments valuable and his words of encouragement meaningful, but expanded my own horizon by prompting me to reflect more intensively on these aspects of shamanism that he considers important, both as epistemological and dynamic factors in the cultural process. To my longtime friend, Ilya Kakitelashvili, I owe uncountable hours of animated discussions and provocative exchanges of ideas in New York and Los Angeles. Last, but never least, I am grateful to my wife, Agata, from whom I received thoughtful stimulation and the benefit of helpful interest.

1

Introduction:
A Personal Dialectic

EVERY SERIOUS BOOK, I was apprised, needs an erudite introduction. The potential reader feels reassured by "shamanistic" guidance in the initiatory encounters with the ephemeral world of ideas. I found out rather quickly that the task of writing such a book, without an adequate preamble (read as "another book") chartering the topographic domains, could not be accomplished judiciously to the mutual satisfaction of the initiated and the neophytes, alike. How can one discuss meanings and symbolic forms of a phenomenology without first looking into its function and substance?

The decision to write this book was reached in Vravrona (ancient Brauron, sacred to Artemis), on the east coast of Attica, our home during a lengthy stay, overlooking haze-covered islands of the proverbial Mediterranean. After a sojourn in the Italian Alps during the earlier part of 1989, particularly to the sites in the Camonica Valley, rich in ancient rock art abounding with shamanistic themes, I returned to Greece determined to apply myself, with enhanced fervor, to the book that I had been writing at the time. In the meantime, my renewed energy had been generating a noticeable impact. However, instead of strengthening my current enthusiasm, it took a subversive course, making my writing task more arduous: the process of fermentation of an idea for the present book was begun. Thus, what was to become an ordinary preamble has been "shamanistically" transformed into a book—hopefully less ordinary.

The interim months ushered in an Aegean summer, hot and not so idyllic. We set out to explore the little known, and almost uninhabited, southern part of the Cycladic island of Naxos. With a four-wheel-drive vehicle parked in the belly of a fuel-burning leviathan, we put out to sea for this isle of Dionysos and Ariadne. Once we penetrated the desolate interior of Naxos, our path consisted of a grievous dirt-and-rock trail, climbing and descending through the mountainous terrain until it unfolded onto the coast. We stopped along the way at an ancient stone windmill, dating to about fourth century B.C. and could not resist the opportunity to explore the surrounding grounds. Near some bushes, we discovered recent heapfuls of hooved goat legs, cut off below the knee, and stains of blood. In certain areas of the world, animal legs have been attached to shamans' vestments and paraphernalia, and the animal skin body coverings worn by the ancient Greeks and by the present-day shepherds did not go for want of limbs either.

Although Greek Orthodoxy is descended in a direct line from the Byzantine Church, one can find surviving remnants of the ancient folk religion in the interior countryside. I had witnessed such living relics on several other occasions, including sacrificed goats tied with a wire to high poles on the island of Syros. All these happenings were not new to me, by any means; they only further confirmed my belief that the antecedents of ancient Greek religion had had shamanistic beginnings and that many of these elements survived in the Bronze Age and during later periods. A few of these still exist today, not only in the beliefs of the country folk, but also in the Greek Orthodox Church. To wit, the priest assumes the obvious shamanistic aspect of a psychopomp by ritually extricating the soul of the deceased, which otherwise will remain bound to the body, or, for that matter, witness the animal-headed St. Chrisophoros. In any case, soon after returning to Attica, the urge grew stronger, I gave into it, put off work on the other book, and began writing this one.

I have attempted here an integrated examination of the substantive aspect of shamanism as a phenomenology of religious experience and of its cultural function as a metaphor in myth, religion, art, and language. These, to me, represent both the dynamic factors and products of the ongoing hominizing process. I have also endeavored, in part, to confront the transformational forms and processes involved in the development of the precognitive, unconscious, magico-religious responses and their gradual transformations into cognitive experiences, which, through a maze of verbal and nonverbal symbols, such as ritual behavior, result in the articulation of mystical states, as well as in the ultimate numinous essence. However, a full study of the meanings and configurations of shamanistic metaphors in human cultures will have to wait for a

Figure 1.1 The Greek St. Chrisophoros. Vestiges of his shamanistic aspect are indicated by his animal-headed form. (Author's archives).

subsequent volume. My concerns with such themes, though, ensue from a long-standing interest in the phenomenology and philosophy of cultural metaphors and symbolic forms.

The challenge of scientific progress serves as an open invitation for dialectic interpretations and speculative reconstructions of the metaphoric and abstract forms within the physical and symbolic terrain of culture, since the "speculative and subjective are part of the scientific process."[1] As long as man remains capable of symbolic thought and behavior, the historical time-frame will be viewed through the lens of the present: one symbolic mode of thought trying to uncode the symbolic process of another. Is it intellectually wrong?—I think not. Such an attitude only upholds Einstein's belief that all great ideas in science (here meant a disciplined intellectual process) are products of the "pure mind" (ideologically non-dogmatic and open to innovative concepts). After all, the psychological satisfaction and romance associated with such inquiries have always been connected with the pursuit of the unknown and speculative.

A productive method to such ends not only recommends the adoption of a structural approach to re-weaving the symbolic fabric deduced from a particular cultural mode, but it also requires the scrutiny of the arbitrary, analytic constructs thus imposed, since undoubtedly the latter will influence the overall outlook perceived by the investigator. We are confronted by a situation where perception (output) is modified by conception (input). This is not a novel idea in physical sciences. Werner Heisenberg's Uncertainty Principle, which fulfills a pivotal condition in quantum physics, offers good theoretical and experimental parallels: The observer or the experimenter will inadvertently modify, to varying degrees, the behavior of the perceived phenomenon by virtue of the very process of the inquiry. Therefore, the observation of any phenomenon in its *true* mode is precluded, altogether. Hence, there will always exist a discrepancy between the way things really *are* and how they *appear* to be. This "differential" is accounted for by the Uncertainty Principle, and performs a critical function in any major equation dealing with the structure and behavior of phenomena. In fact, in the words of Stephen Hawking, one of the most illustrious physicists alive today, "Heisenberg's uncertainty principle is a fundamental, inescapable property of the world."[2]

In 1920, Sigmund Freud published *Beyond the Pleasure Principle*, which, being tinted with unaccustomed—for Freud—metaphysics, frightened away many of his disciples. In this new treatise, Freud reaffirmed his belief in the unity within the living world by advancing a theory that conjectured the existence of a life force together with a death wish in *all* living things. Death occurs when Thanatos overwhelms Eros: both the wish and the will being expressions of an instinctive force.

Two years later, through his work with the chacma baboons, Eugène Marais formulated a novel hypothesis about the human mind. He postulated in *The Soul of the Ape* (written in 1922, but not published until 1969, posthumously) that the development of the intellectual and reasoning faculties in man had screened out the real psyche—the original primitive mentality based on instinct—and had delegated it to another realm in the brain, where it has survived as our subconscious mind. It would have been extremely satisfying to have Freud's views on Marais's ideas pertaining to the origins of the human subconscious. The conflict suggested by the latter, between reason and the instinctive psyche, bears profound implications for the genesis of religion, the birth of the *Magna Mater*, and shamanism.

During this time, the world was undergoing important ideological and economic shifts, witnessing the rise of fervent pragmatism agitated, on one hand, by the Marxist dialectic of cultural materialism in the Old World and, on the other, embellished with the naiveté of the utopian materialism of surplus wealth in the capitalist New World. The new socioeconomic perspectives created an impact on the theoretical objectives in many academic disciplines, notably in the cultural and behavioral sciences, wherein the uprising social trends came to be reflected in the aims and the theoretical methodology displayed in many areas of study. In psychology, the new school of behavioralists and environmentalists revived the *tabula rasa* concept by proclaiming humans to be solely a product of their environment. In other words, regardless of genetic composition, personal predisposition, and preferences, an individual could be, from an early age, molded into becoming whatever was planned and designed for him or her. Such theories were received by an enthusiastic audience, for they offered the much needed "scientific" confirmation to the economic and political dogmas of social pragmatism. Thus, the *conception* of social reality helped mold the *perception* that humans created of themselves.

This situation became evident, as well, in the plight of the student of culture and comparative religions, as it ensued from the inherent difficulty to identify logical principles leading to the formulations of axioms, theories, and laws which could be used in predicting, with some degree of consistent accuracy, the dynamics of a cultural process and the human responses thereto. Much time and energy were invested into refutations of the various forms of evolutionism (Tylor, Frazer, White, etc.), diffusionism (Wisser, Childe), relativism (Boas), functionalism (Malinowski, Radcliff-Browne), organicism—regular and super (Durkheim, Kroeber), structuralism (Lévi-Strauss), and a host of other

-isms, which ultimately brought with them a discord and a rigidity of thought manifested in the plethora of academic writings of the *genre* in the last three decades or so.

There were, of course, notable exceptions, particularly one offspring known as cultural ecology. This infant wrestled with the philosophical concept (still no theory) of systems that were believed to exist intrinsically in the interplay between Culture and Environment. The new credo dispatched its believers after a holy grail emanating cues and signs as an expression of a dynamic, adaptive balance between the two principle forces. More often than not, the zealous acolytes confused functionalism with adaptation, by failing to realize that a cultural trait or a complex that displays merely a functional purpose does not qualify automatically for the platinum rating of one that has earned the considerable rank by actually developing an adaptive survival value. The result of this loose thinking could be witnessed in the endless lists of publications offering little more than descriptive, analytical profiles of cultures posed against the background of their physico-biotic environments.

Still, notwithstanding these worthy efforts by certain pioneers braving the *terra incognita*, when compared to the bulk of published studies, only a small number—very small, indeed—actually ascended beyond the descriptive, functionalist treatments. Ironically, those involved in the studies of the different facets of human culture, their visions obliterated when it came to "universal" categories, ultimately placed themselves in a very frustrating corner. A new philosophical system was sadly lacking. If "universal" features can be admitted into existence, then cultural metaphors and other symbolic forms are their cognitve reflections. Claude Lévi-Strauss expended much intellectual energy on devising analytic strategies that could isolate symbols as structural units within a cultural system. However, instead of attempting to arrive at some purview of the metaphor as a cultural idiom embodied in its own phenomenological form (epiphany, so to speak), he was content to tie it to a cultural mythology. There is absolutely nothing paltry with his approach, except that it does not enlarge adequately our comprehension of the metaphor as a phenomenon possessed of its own intrinsic substance and structure.

It ought to be, therefore, of little surprise that our preconceptions should affect the way we perceive not only the physical world about us, but the way we perceive cultural metaphors and other forms of symbolic manifestations—including the reflection of our own conceptions in what we make out shamanism to be. The cultural characteristics that a specialist anticipates to find will not only influence the formulation of his hypothesis regarding their patterns and interrelationships, but will also affect the final picture that is perceived. The question of how closely such a cultural portrait approximates the actual cultural experience falls within the realm of *uncertainty*. And sharp differences between one portrait and another of the same culture are often based, to borrow John Bintliff's eloquent phrase, on a "hypothetical distinction."

Thus, when in 1935, the German cultural philosopher Oswald Spengler published his provocative views on the flourishing Minoan civilization, his explanations about its cultural demise were syncretic with the sentiments and the mood of the times.[3] In Europe, the atmosphere before World War I and during the period between the two World Wars prompted a sense of passive fatalism and a peculiar feeling of helplessness in respect to the chain of events imbued in the historical process. The decline and doom of all civilizations were regarded as an existential phenomenon, a part of an unalterable cycle through which all advanced cultures must pass. Whatever cause might have actually been responsible for the disappearance of the Minoan palace civilization, it was considered and interpreted in the context of a "natural" decline within the irrevocable cycle of history.

The remarkable thing about Spengler's observations is to be seen in his perception of the Minoan monuments and finds at Knossos and Phaistos as sacred enclosures, each forming a religious complex that functions as a city of the dead, or a necropolis, rather than a habitat for the living. The absence of true fortified walls, coupled with his keen understanding of Bronze Age religious beliefs surrounding death and the life hereafter, led Spengler to conceive the possibility that the walls around Knossos and Phaistos had been originally intended for the protection of the sanctity and peace of the deceased, lying within their precinct, rather than for the defense of human lives against the invading forces arriving from without. His critical analysis of the problem made him posit an important question: "Were the 'palaces' of Knossos and Phaistos temples of the dead, sanctuaries of a powerful cult of the hereafter? I do not wish to make such an assertion, for I cannot prove it, but the question seems to me worthy of serious consideration."[4]

Oswald Spengler was the first to recognize the fallacy imbedded in the interpretations advanced by Sir Arthur Evans, the discoverer of Knossos and the Minoan civilization. Sir Arthur's stubborn preconceptions and arbitrary conclusions about the special position occupied by the Minoans in the historico-cultural arena enjoined him from taking a sober look at the archaeological evidence, which included thousands of written records. Evans proceeded to formulate ideas about ancient Crete that were, to a large extent, results of his idealization of a civilization that he loved almost with a blind passion, one binding a parent to a child. His belief in the premature, catastrophic demise of the allegedly peace- and art-loving Cretans blinded him to the possibility of finding cultural ties between his pet protagonists and other Greeks. He characterized the former as having developed a unique form of culture, borne of independent roots, dissociated from any other. Consequently, in his supreme task to decipher the writings of the Minoan palaces, Evans's exceedingly biased mode of thought led him not to success, but to a veritable failure. He simply refused to entertain any notion of a plausible connection between the language of Bronze Age Greece and the one spoken in ancient Crete. This strong conviction—or rather a personal sentiment—inherent in the conceptualization, distorted his perception, affecting not only the outcome of his reconstruction of the Minoan society, but also rendering his paramount efforts to decipher its language utterly futile.

Spengler, however, was prevented from pursuing further clues to this intriguing question. He died one year following the appearance of the aforementioned book. The curious aspect about Spengler's remarks lies in the fact that they remained unnoticed for many decades until the publication, in 1972, of *Wohin der Stier Europa trug* (English version, 1974, titled *The Secret of Crete*)[5] by the late Hans Georg Wunderlich, who held the chair of geology and palaeontology at the University of Stuttgart until his death. Perhaps the insufficient notice drawn by Spengler's last book can be attributed to the overwhelming impact produced by his earlier, seminal, and extremely influential work, *The Decline of the West*.

The case of Sir Arthur Evans and the Minoan civilization does not stand alone in the annals of scholarship, instead it has analogues in each and every period or epoch. In comparison with Heisenberg's Uncertainty Principle, this syndrome is an "inescapable property" of the social/ behavioral sciences and humanities. Consequently, any interpretation or analysis that has as its subject a facet of culture is bound to be speculative and defined by a "hypothetical distinction."

When one studies the development of a cultural process, whether from the viewpoint of anthropology or comparative religions, one cannot build an intellectual framework without noting the connecting links between one culture trait and another. Culture growth, abstract or material, does not occur independently of other processes within the particular culture's context. To examine the content of a religious impulse among mankind, not as a series of changes in a chain of historical vignettes but as a phenomenological process, will take us back tens of thousands of years to a time when *Homo sapiens*, with their subspecies, had shared analogues of numinous experiences in their awareness of the great procreative force, manifest in the cyclical birth and death of nature, probably as the Great Mother or a close kindred. Most likely, these human creatures had not shared a set of *beliefs*, as much as they shared in the pool of common emotional and "religious" *experiences*—the transcultural (or should I say pan-human?) experiences of the existential quest for meaning. From this fertile soil, nourishing a common existential root, sprouted another, a new universal system, the *Ur*-religion, where mankind's role became less passive and more articulate. This system can be viewed as the first systematic attempt to understand and modify phenomena falling within the domain of human experience. It is known as *shamanism*.

The basic elements of shamanism describe multiple functions reflected in the roles of its practitioners, the shamans. As individuals specializing in the performance and the enactment of rituals, they are also the tribal timekeepers, or custodians of the calendar. In hunting magic, the shamans foster and consolidate a vital relationship with Master of the Animals, or an equivalent figure, thus, assuring consistent bounty for their people. As healers, they employ various methods prescribed by the cultural norms, including the ability to see the causes of disease and augur the future. Not less important is the shaman's function as a guide, or a psychopomp, for the souls of the dead, ascertaining that these do not become dispersed in the universal vastness, but are assured proper passages to their respective destinies in the spirit realms. Last, but definitely not least, is the underscored importance of the extensive and vital role played by hallucinogenic plants in shamanistic rituals and imagery, and as crucial factors in cultural dynamics. The experience acquired in drug-induced visions and integrated through socially-approved cognitive channels is a major key to culture change. This force of shamanistic phenomenology constitutes a pervasive note in this book.

Moreover, the shaman's intellectual abilities are of real social consequence, particularly as they apply to issues involving the culture-environment system. Equipped with an impressive corpus of empirical knowledge (ethnoscience) and a profound grasp of human behavior, the shaman fulfills the vital role of a psychocultural adaptive mechanism, not merely as a healer of diseases, but as a harmonizer of social and natural dysfunctions and imbalance. In view of his ecological significance, the shaman's role as an agent in transcendental and existential realities tends to be underplayed by those who regard cultures as systems of more pragmatic and functional configurations. The importance of the latter two is undeniable in its own right; however, to de-emphasize symbolic (religious, spiritual, etc.) considerations is to fail in the understanding of the full integrative potential inherent to shamanism as a dynamic factor in the cultural process. Therefore, in a book, bearing the subtitle *Substance and Function of a Religious Metaphor*, the keynote should be, it seems to me, justifiably placed on the aspect of shamanism as a mythico-religious idiom rather than on its pragmatic-ecological values.

The essence of sociocultural existence is centered around mythic imagery, which lends to human life an existential dimension. Pure, rational thought is no more an objective reality than the myths wherefrom such a concept is derived. Myths make up the fundamental responses to the basic human need for meaning. This need is an inescapable condition of human existence, pervading all areas of interactions: from techno-mechanical and sexual to highly symbolic and creative. In effect, myths often become cultural expressions for religious and ethical codes. At the same time, they are of paramount importance to the enactment of shamanistic rituals. Thus, many such rituals and the corresponding techniques, found all over the world, are validated by aetiological mythologies and cosmic paradigms. The significant place occupied by myths in the shaman's repertoire becomes apparent to anyone who has devoted some time to this subject.

In his article on "Shamanism," for the fifteenth edition of the *Encyclopedia Britannica*, Diószegi included mythic traditions among the nine characteristic features of this religious complex.[6] Eliade, in *Shamanism: Archaic Techniques of Ecstasy*, recognized the fact that the shamans' "ecstatic experiences have exercised, and still exercise, a powerful influence on the stratification of religious ideology, on mythology, on ritualism"[7] Joseph Campbell, too, stressed this point repeatedly.[8] The core of any religious practice, shamanism not exempted, is to be found in the experiential framework that lends to its spiritual character. Ancient and classic shamanism was not characterized by a common object of worship (e.g., a Buddha), or a codified body of dogmas. Instead, it comprised specific techniques and ideology by which spiritual issues could be addressed.

To ensure survival, human beings learn and devise cognitive meanings. These can be found in the parallel extensions formed by the antipodal worlds, and available through the diverse techniques utilized by the shamans. It is the shaman's task to organize and impart coherence to the inveterate journey of existential quest, thus affording ideological purpose and ecological possibilities to the human condition. Shamanistic states of consciousness are not regarded as extraordinary occurrences, neither are these alternate states viewed as separate realities. It is all part of a larger monistic whole: in contradistinction to the well-established western myth (a philosophico—scientific metaphor), developed by Descartes through dialectic logic, demonstrating the existence of dichotomous systems, that is, a "real" disparity between the antipodal cosmic entities—mind and matter.

The quest for the existential metaphor, in the mythico-religious realm, conditioned human society along the lines that can submit to interpretations in terms of a cognitive approach—a model—germinal in a theoretical design. The attempts to understand the worldviews and daily dramas of aboriginal cultures must take into account the roles of the diverse factors exerting an impetus on the developmental process. The success of such an understanding does not lie so much within the selected area of study, inasmuch as it stems from the methodology embedded in the intellectual strategy that can be applied to different problems. It is an intellectual adventure, as yet unquantifiable, paving the route to a better understanding of our past and the human condition in general.

I have encountered a raised eyebrow, on an occasion or two, in response to my use of certain reference sources. I am quite aware that several authors (e.g., Sir James G. Frazer) to whom I refer are considered to be outdated and not in vogue; used, primarily, for their historical curiosity. Nevertheless, in spite of the apparent obsolescence of these individuals, some of them managed to articulate stimulating ideas. Thus, by citing them, I do not necessarily adopt their methodologies or theoretical perspectives, but, instead, retrieve what I feel may be applicable and worth notice. (How and where, for instance, can we possibly obtain, today, the field experiences of such observers as Knud Rasmussen with the Eskimos, or Leon Sternberg with the Gilyaks?) Henceforth, to the charge of this particular criticism, I submit that even an outdated concept or theory may contain kernels of enlightening observations: A good methodology is not defined by the material we use, but rather by how judiciously we use it. As a parting point, here: the Huxley-Zaehner debate on mystical experience can obviously go on *ad infinitum*, standing unresolved and locked in this status quo for a very long time, if not forever. *Sufficit!*

The early materials on shamanism tend to lean towards the esoteric, while later scholarly materials are scattered in specialized, and often obscure, publications. One earlier pivotal synthesis of this subject was Mircea Eliade's *Shamanism: Archaic Techniques of Ecstasy* (original French edition, 1951; English translation, 1964). It confined itself, primarily, to the category of a documentary sourcebook, employing a historico-textual approach, which, unfortunately, did not address the subject matter in the appropriate cultural context. Neither did it deal with its theme as a phenomenology proper. Moreover, Eliade's *Shamanism* conveys a touch of personal bias, which, all in all, makes the book somewhat outdated. In spite of its apparent shortcomings, it nevertheless provides a useful starting point for some purposes. Still, like every work, it sets its own scope and limitations. On the other hand, an important contribution to the ethnographic study of shamanism was made, among others, by Gérardo Reichel-Dolmatoff's classic work, *Amazonian Cosmos: The Sexual and Religious Symbolism of the Tukano Indians?* Although a more extensive list will be found in the reference section, it befits to mention a few additional persons whose works have contributed to our understanding of shamanism: A.E. Anisimov, Vilmos Diószegi, Carl-Martin Edsman, Anna-Leena Siikala, Louise Bäckman and Åke Hultkrantz, Weston La Barre, Peter T. Furst, Michael J. Harner, and Johannes Wilbert.

2

Shamanism and Culture: Configurations of a Religious Metaphor

Cultural Ethos and Mysticism

IN THE LAST QUARTER of the nineteenth century, a Lamaist adept made his way to the Tibetan capital of Lhasa. He was a Buryat Mongol, born in Azochozki, to the east of Lake Baikal, a region that has remained, to this day, one of the primary shamanistic centers. His peers knew him as Ghomang Lobzang. Later he came to be known under the name of Akohwan Darjilikoff, and in Tsarist Russia as Hambro Akvan Dorjieff, a Russianized rendition of the Tibetan cognate for "thunder." Dorjieff was to become a recognized figure in twentieth-century metaphysics and the occult, albeit still under a different name. His influence, felt in various American and European circles, included Germany before World War I and during the period between the two World Wars. It has been duly intimated that he was visited by Karl Haushofer, professor of geopolitics at the University of Munich, on several occasions between 1903 and 1908. Haushofer became, in due time, the founding father of the esoteric and occult Thule Group, established in 1923, and modelled on a version of Eastern mysticism. The Group enlisted in its ranks the likes of Hitler; Himmler; Hitler's personal physician, Morell; Goering;

and the Nazi party ideologue, Rosenberg. Meanwhile, Dorjieff's reputation reached the West in the guise of his more familiar name as Georg Ivanovich Gurdjieff.[1]

According to the metaphysics espoused by Gurdjieff,[2] *this* reality consists of a quasi-dream, and consequently, human existence is in a slumber state. To break this sleeplike condition, one must learn self-awareness, or self-remembering, and introspection. The accomplishment of these is a prerequisite to genuine spiritual growth and change. He practiced techniques of Yoga, involving strenuous physical movements, such as dancing and breath control, which, he claimed, would harmonize the mental, emotional, and physical facets of humans. The yogin, like the alchemist, promulgates changes in the substance, which in India are believed to be the deeds of an archetypal magician. Gurdjieff's role in modern society can be compared, by analogy, to the function performed by a shaman in a tribal setting. Whether genuinely spiritual or a "rascal-master," as Alan Watts described him in his autobiography,[3] Gurdjieff occupied an important position in his capacity as a practitioner of the occult. The views he expressed had a considerable impact on the ideological orientation of not only Adolf Hitler and the Third Reich, but on many western intellectuals, as well, among them D.H. Lawrence. In assuming a counterpart role, which could be superficially compared to a shaman-priest,[4] Gurdjieff led his disciples through the rigors of physical and mental strains toward a so-called spiritual journey via trancelike abandonment.

Regardless of the phase of cultural development, the power of crowd psychology promulgates an individual and a social need—an emotional niche, so to speak—demanding the satisfaction of its desire for the magical, or the symbolic. Ceremonial and mystical acts have a way of fulfilling this condition. Hence, any kind of ritual specialist, addressing herself or himself to such a need, may find acceptance within the mores of any given sociocultural configuration—be it an Asiatic shaman, Gurdjieff, or Hitler. Inasmuch as culture influences social behavior, social needs give rise to cultural forms.[5] Therefore, under these terms, shamanism may be viewed as a substantive content of a religious transformation and phenomenology, effecting in ritual techniques that aim at satisfying pre-existing psychosocial conditions.

Hence, for example, the belief system of the Mehinaku Indians of the Upper Xingu river in Brazil allows for individual innovations and creations of new supplementary cults and the corresponding shamanistic rituals. Thus, when a Mehinaku tribesman originated, not so long ago, the new Deer Spirit cult, he was able to implement it, as Gregor assesses perceptively,[6] owing not only to his psychological predisposition, but also to his cognizance and understanding of the dynamics operating in the social situation. One of the most interesting aspects of the cultural dynamics in this process is, unquestionably, evinced by the flexibility of the social modalities that allow a very rapid integration of a personal experience into the larger religious context of indigenous culture. This leads to the very plausible inference that several other spirits and their associated cults had been authored by certain Mehinaku individuals who had been subject to visionary experiences or some other forms of imagery-visualization, or who were, at times, just contriving inventors of rituals for purposes of status gain and political influence. However, an important point to bear: A new ritual, to be successfully integrated, must follow an established norm.

There is only a very fine line separating two extreme facets of a personality structure. Sometimes the extremes are so pronounced that they appear as an anomaly. When the celebrated American traveler W.B. Seabrook visited the awesome Sultan Pasha Atrash at his home, in the mountains of the Druzes of the Gebel, he observed a peculiar quality about his host: "meekly gentle as a lamb," and yet when the Sultan Pasha rode his horse to a real battlefield, he did so "with the unmistakable gleam of the fanatical, born 'killer' in his eyes. I came finally to the conclusion that he was of the abnormal 'inspired mystic' type."

> Few men become legendary figures within their own lifetime, but the tales I had heard of this man—the warlord of the Druzes—in the European clubs of Beirut and the tents of the desert, were fabulous beyond belief. Miracles of ferocity and meekness were equally attributed to him. He fought with the savageness of an insane tiger, and returned from battle to weep and pray for the souls of the men he had hacked to pieces with his scimitar. His old mother had to restrain him from giving away all their goods to the poor. He was a devil, mad with bloodlust. He was a holy saint. He was a sort of Mad Mullah. He was a sort of Christ.[7]

What befits a Uralo-Altaic shaman or a Middle Eastern mystic describes, just as well, a ritual practitioner from the South Pacific. Sometime between A.D. 300 and 400, the first Polynesian colonizers of Rapa Nui, or Easter Island, arrived in a canoe under the banner of an *ariki mau*, or a Big Chief called *Hotu Matu'a*. He was vested, through inheritance, with secular and religious authority. Possessed of immense "spiritual powers," capable of invoking and communicating with the ancestral spirits and deities who were frequently consulted when guidance was needed, the *ariki* embodied, in fact, the Polynesian equivalent of a shaman. The contact with the Otherworld was often sought at public gatherings in the ceremonial plaza by means of propitiatory offerings and sacrifices, and, not to be overlooked, by the consumption of a narcotic potion known as *kava* (*Piper methysticum*). The exact symptoms provoked by *kava* ingestion by the settlers of Easter Island are not known to us, but its continued ritual use for many centuries thereafter suggests hallucinogenic properties. As the influence of the shaman-chief subsided, a class of priesthood probably evolved on the island, with elaborate ceremonies, including possible human sacrifice and cannibalism.[8] The archaeological evidence, in conjunction with oral tradition and ethnographic material from the island, corroborates this account. Here, too, we have an allusion, if perhaps only allegorical, to a journey performed by a shaman-type figure, who, in response to prompts by the supernatural beings encountered on one of his *kava*-induced trips, collected his kinsmen into a canoe for an ocean voyage in quest of an envisioned island.[9] Since, however, the characteristic feature of Polynesian ecstatic religions is possession by supernatural entities, this particular element has given rise to a vast number of "inspired" individuals, medicine men, priests, and healers—all anxious to effect preternatural cures.

Fear and apprehension evoke the imagination. They have been, among others, kinetic elements in the creation of basic religious forms. The instinct of fear induces the imagination to engender a system of beliefs whereby the anxiety evoked by fear can find an outlet, thus reducing the stress factor. At the same time, the primal and archetypal desires for wholeness (oneness) and a "state of bliss" have transformed into causative energies, since the time of primeval existence, resulting in an impetus focused on the quest for methods and metaphors promising the recovery of these conditions, as they might have hopefully existed for "primordial man." The religious awareness of the mystical is tightly interwoven with the idea, or the sense, of the Holy, which according to Rudolf Otto, borders almost on the precognitive, that is, not being derived experientially, but "issues from the deepest foundation of cognitive apprehension which the soul possesses," and plants "its independent roots in the hidden depths of the spirit."[10] Jane Harrison's observation assumes an amplified meaning with her remark that in ancient Greece "The highest divinities of the religion of fear and riddance became the harmful bogeys of the cult of 'service'. The Olympians, in their turn, became Christian devils."[11]

Yet, to the ecstatic Whirling Dervishes, one of the orders comprising the Sufi sect, mysticism aims at comprehension of truths—truths more profound than any expounded by reason or apprehended by logic—and it seeks to attain this higher state of consciousness through the channels of contemplation and ecstasy. Its ideological objective may be construed

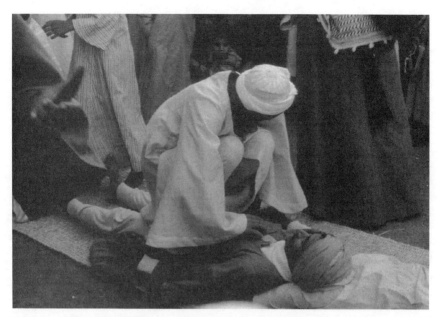

Figure 2.1 One of the Rufaim, or the Howling Dervishes, is squatting on a sword placed across the abdomen of a man lying down in a trance. A village near Thebes, Upper Egypt. (Photograph by the author).

as a mystical sacrament, leading to oneness with the divine essence, by way of an alchemical transmutation of the soul. It is understood, at the same time, that varied mystical orders developed their own techniques to achieve the ecstatic state. The Rufaim, an ascetic and a distinct order of Dervishes,[12] recognize pain and fasting as an expedient method in this direction. Others, like the Mevlevi, a Turkish name for the Whirling Dervishes, believe in the divinity of body and soul: the latter being necessary for the flourishing of the other, like a stem upholding a flower. Reflections, in a Platonic image, of divine beauty and harmony—this inarticulable condition of spiritual unity—are to be glimpsed by exposing the senses to the many dimensions of beauty, especially to something as "perfect" as the trance-inducing rhythms of music and dance. The thirteenth-century Sufi poet-sage, Jelal ed-Din, who established the Mevlevi order, wrote of the inseparable, coexistent qualities that we identify as Truth, Beauty, and God. Christian mysticism has, likewise, found expression in the pens of those seeking God in beauty. Regardless of their religious backgrounds, mystics the world over would generally concede that Divine Trinity coalesces the universal aspects bespoken by the Sufi philosopher. Of course, exceptions are duly acknowledged;

yet, it should be remembered that what may appear, at a first glance, to be differences in doctrine may, on closer scrutiny, translate into matters of conceptual definition.

One of the more enlightening statements on Sufi mystical doctrines—and mysticism, in general—across which I have come, one that is appealing for its obvious simplicity and perplexity alike, was the exhortation by Sheikh Shefieh el Melewi,[13] the paramount religious leader—sort of a pontif—among the Whirling Dervishes. The venerable Sheikh cautioned of hidden dangers lurking along the paths of the unprepared—the uninitiated—particularly, of the "weak minds." When "the fool" is dosed by flashes of illumination, he proclaims, "I am God!" and consequently suffers annihilation[14] on account of this distortion. At the same time, it is neither improper nor unsafe to utter, "God is I." He alluded, here, to the founder of their order, Jelal ed-Din, who had written that when Allah is being adored, it is Allah who is adoring himself. Sheikh Shefieh concluded with a sentiment, which we find expressed independently, over and over, in different places and by different sources at different times—whether it is an Eskimo shaman or the Swiss writer, Hermann Hesse—that the ultimate secret of existence cannot be imparted through words from one person to another. God is the divine harmony that permeates all things, and consequently all paths lead in this direction. Each individual must start on the journey that seems best suited to that person.

Existential quest for meaning is a common experience shared by all cultures. This process is structured, and "more or less formalised in all societies or, at least, in some of its leading members."[15] The techniques and mechanisms employed to achieve this goal can be found throughout the world and display remarkable methodological conformity: meditation and altered states of consciousness, which are induced by external agents, such as drugs, or by internal means, such as fasting, sensory deprivation, breath control, immolation of the body, and so forth. Hence, the publication of Aldous Huxley's book, *The Doors of Perception*, became an important landmark for the study of phenomenological mechanisms in religion, particularly in the field of visionary experience. It was not only a daring, personal exposition of a courageous intellect, but was artistically illuminating and thought provoking, as well. As soon as the book made its appearance, it was confronted by an educated, albeit uncertain and antagonistic, public. But even the behavior of an educated public has a tendency to conform to the norms of crowd psychology— predisposed, on the whole, to hostile reactions when it comes to matters challenging religious issues and anything else that has to do with "the great unknowns," such as altered states of consciousness, hallucinogens, and even classic mysticism. The main charges brought up against Huxley proclaimed that he had reduced all preternatural experiences to a mono-phenomenology, disregarding the qualitative differences between the mystics throughout the world, and thus robbing the preternatural states of their mystery, mysticism, and profound meaning—namely, the *numen*.

The late R. C. Zaehner, then Spalding Professor of Eastern Religions and Ethics at Oxford University, disagreed vehemently with the thesis expressed in Huxley's book. In fact, Zaehner attributed the impetus for writing his own book, *Mysticism: Sacred and Profane*, and for his experiments with the chemical mescalin, to the reaction he had experienced as a result of reading Huxley. Furthermore, he felt that the premise expounded in *The Doors of Perception* impoverished religion by divesting it of all the richness to be found in transcultural diversities of mysticism. Yet, at the same time, Zaehner failed to account for the impact exerted by a specific cultural context on the experience of a mystic, irrespective of the primary causes for such an experience. As a matter of fact, not too many qualified persons have addressed, in a meaningful depth, the vital question posited by the undefined role that a given culture plays in shaping the nature of a preternatural experience, regardless whether such a mystical state is considered to be plainly biochemical, gloriously supernatural, or both. The rich diversity of mystical states that are encountered result not only from the psycho-logical and neurophysiological predispositions of the subject, but also from the social environment created by the enculturation process and acting upon the subject.

Zaehner pointed his finger at this specific state of consciousness, which to Huxley had become "as evident as Euclid," accusing the latter of "enthusiastic exaggeration...of his experiences when under the influence of mescalin...."[16]

> Huxley did not seem to be merely advocating yet another variety of religious 'indifferentism'; he was, simply by equating his own drug-induced experiences with the experiences of those who approach their goal by more conventional means, striking at the roots of all religion that makes any claim to be taken seriously.[17]

Thus, Zaehner voiced his disapproval of Huxley's efforts to adduce a comparison between "what he experienced under mescalin... to the highest concepts of religion which the mystic claims to realize at least in part." Furthermore, he rejected adamantly the notion that "the natural [biochemical, that is] mystical experience" could be a manifestation of the "holy" and that such an experience could have anything to do with "the direct experience of God," as exemplified by the Beatific Visions of some Christian mystics, who perceived "God in His unutterable holiness." Such a conception would be at odds with the idea of religion as defined by Christianity.[18] It is discomforting to think of a reputable scholar attempting to formulate an objective claim for "the highest concepts of religion," and professing to have the knowledge (a belief would be more appropriate) of the essence comprising the true "means" to a path of an authentic or "sacred" religious experience, and, at the same time, intimating that his way is, by far, the preferred one and superior to others. Whereas, such philosophical attitudes are manifestations of faith, and not of an impartial scholarship, the actual implications detected in Zaehner's discourse, indeed, suggest that his personal faith modified his conception, and consequently influenced the choice. But, then, this is neither dispassionate analysis nor an objective quest for truth.

Mircea Eliade seems to share in Zaehner's opinion favoring the more "conventional" methods in the attainment of a mystical state. According to an erroneous belief held by Eliade, the use of psychedelic substances reflected a degenerate and profane technique in a visionary experience, particularly in shamanism.[19] At the same time, he has convincingly demonstrated that shamanism has definite links with certain Yoga doctrines. These especially hold true in cases showing evidence of healers and magicians, whose functions invoke the universal trait of rainmaking, as well as the taming of wild beasts (a parallel to the shaman's all-important role as Master of the Animals), no lesser than the tiger, which acts as the neophyte's mount in trances induced at shamanistic initiations.[20] Other traditions and legends of India, such as the cycle of *Matsyendranath*, contain vivid shamanistic themes of initiatory death—encountered almost universally—which consist of killing, disembowelling, skinning, and washing of the initiate's entrails. All such ordeals are, in some way, characteristic of the symbols and rites of initiations in general, but particularly of those pertaining to shamanism.[21] The shamanistic interpretations of these and related themes—as, for example, embryogenesis, insemination, sickness, and death—afford valuable insights and are of great interest in themselves.[22] The prominent role occupied by the drum in Tantric and Tibetan Buddhism is, in itself, a strong feature attesting to old shamanistic roots. In the Shinto rituals and temples of Japan, drumming is used as a device to effect altered states of awareness, as it is also in contemporary Japanese youth movements.[23]

However, still earlier, Christopher Dawson had anticipated Eliade when he had noted with a profound insight, in the Gifford Lectures on *Religion and Culture*, delivered at the University of Edinburgh in 1947,[24] that the shaman is "the social organ of inspired utterance," and thus rendered with the role of a seer, or the equivalent of a prophet, he is just as "important as an ascetic and a 'holy man' who has acquired, by training, the mastery of spiritual techniques." As such, the shaman runs in close analogy to the spiritual master, especially in India, where the two seem almost indistinguishable. Their link, according to Dawson, is suggested by the *Vanaprasthas*, in which the "meditation on the ritual becomes more important than the rite itself." The last clause may ring true in the case of an Indian *guru*, but is stretched out of proportion for a shaman, who, by virtue of his function, has to be a master of technique and not merely of mystical abstractions. Consequently, his objective is mainly teleological, whether directed to pragmatic or spiritual ends, rather than remaining purely transcendental. Therefore, it is not surprising to find the prevalence of a belief that certain techniques known to the mystic adepts—but particularly to the shamans—will lead to the development of spiritual abilities in those who manage to uncover them.

In the summer of 1962, Carlos Castaneda entered a forest with his teacher, Don Juan, a Yaqi Indian shaman, in search of magical plants. After the necessary preparations and ritual, Castaneda ingested, under the guidance of Don Juan, some quantity of the substance, whereby he began having hallucinations in which the peyote god, Mescalito, appeared to him all green. Green is the color of vegetation deities to be found throughout the world. In the Arthurian legend, for example, the Green Knight represents a pagan survival symbolizing such a divinity.

The shamans' domain is the dark and thick forest, or another remote area, where he can isolate himself to accommodate his needs for solitude and trance. As a result, the shamans generally practice their craft alone, a fact which sometimes creates misconceptions between the interests of the community and those of the shamans. Clearly, there are some who have abused their positions, just as there are shamans who do not act solely for personal gains, but who go about their functions without regard for material or political considerations. Sieroszewski, who had spent quite a long time with a Siberian tribe, provided the following observation in the *Twelve Years among the Yakuts*:

> The duties undertaken by the Shaman are not easy: the struggle which he has to carry on is dangerous. . . . The wizard [a shaman] who decides to carry on this struggle has not only material gain in view but the alleviation of the griefs of his fellow men; the wizard who has the vocation, the faith and the conviction, who undertakes his duty with ecstasy and negligence of personal danger, inspired by the high ideal of sacrifice, such a wizard always exerts an enormous influence over his audience. After having seen once or twice such a real Shaman, I understood the distinction that the natives drew between the "Great," the "Middling," and the "Mocking" or deceitful Shamans.[25]

Such "an enormous influence" has been, nonetheless, manipulated and usurped, at times, by others in power. In A.D. 802, the Khmer ruler, Jayavarman II, compelled a Brahmin priest, "skilled in magic science," to initiate rites that would transform the monarch into a *devaraja*, or a god-king, thus consolidating sovereignty in one divine ruler, and establish *Kambuja* (Cambodia) independent and free of a tributary allegiance to Java.

Unfortunately, the poor understanding of the phenomenology of shamanism in the past years prompted many specialists of ethnohistory and comparative religions to issue statements depriving shamanism of its socially transcendent character, and even of its vital role in the dynamics of the cultural process. In the same Gifford Lectures in 1947, Dawson[26] assured his listeners, with a dose of ethnocentricity, that very little value was to be gained by comparing "the primitive Shaman" to a "mystic or the Vedantist philosopher," since, unlike the priest or the prophet, the shaman was to be found in the "lowest levels of culture." Although holding on to the idea of the "very primitive," as far as religious systems were concerned, Dawson, probably leaning on Emile Durkheim and Max Weber, correctly assessed the significant role of shamanism, alongside other types of beliefs, in the formation of various social institutions, including the rise of specialized hierarchies within a stratified social organization. Yet, more importantly, he realized that, regardless of the popularity or mystical appeal of any religious institution, once it has managed to influence the social order, it, in turn, becomes integrated and bound by the norms of social behavior.[27]

In this rather enlightened notion, we can discern the rudiments of the conceptual fonts to be found, for instance, in Reichel-Dolmatoff's extremely significant observation that the shaman's prolific imagination and his intellectual knowledge must be counted as crucial factors in cultural dynamics.[28] Others recognize also the shaman's role as an agent of culture change: Hultkrantz's recent publication, dealing with the visionary quests among the Shoshoni Indians,[29] demonstrates aptly the validity of such a perception. In spite of the basic importance conveyed by this idea, the role of the shaman's characteristics, as seminal agents of cultural force, was, for the most part, underestimated considerably and left outside the limelight. Effective religion furnishes the building blocks for different institutions that make up the social structure. To be efficient, however, it must confine itself to the maze of mutually interdependent cultural norms and assume the function prescribed by the external order that it helped create, and from which it draws its communal, or public, authority.

Hunting Magic

As the size of a social unit increased, so did the need for intensified food procurement, leading inadvertently to a deepening desire to control the outcome of the hunt. Of the group activities that can be said to best illustrate shamanism, hunting magic undeniably comes first and is also tied directly with animistic and totemic beliefs. It is apparent that shamanistic beliefs, in some form or another, have flourished in hunting societies, ancient and contemporary alike.[30] This practice, as has been pointed out, does not appear to fully manifest efficient traits for a functional adaptation to a cultural system with agrarian ethos, or, as Hultkrantz observed from an evolutionary viewpoint, for those "with a higher level of technological and social complexity"[31] than the hunters. In a close comparison with my earlier statements, pertaining to the arid regions of Southwest Asia and Australia, that ecological considerations are to be viewed as dynamic factors in social organization,[32] Hultkrantz argues correctly that the interplay within a culture-environment system produces an impact on the organizational pattern of religious institutions. He writes, perhaps too deterministically at first glance, that ". . . similar ecological conditions have created similar intensified shamanistic systems in the whole Arctic area."[33]

The Mundari tribesmen, neighbors of the Dinka in the semiarid region by the White Nile, forge very strong ties with their animals. In fact, they have established very-well defined sociocultural niches, which govern their interactions with the animal world. One need not stress the obvious intimacy, including a form of eroticism that developed as a result of particular closeness, and totemic relationships, which the Mundari share with their animals. These tribesmen do not differentiate linguistically between natural and supernatural qualities; consequently their shamanistic practices, especially as they relate to hunting magic, are thought not to contain any supernatural attributes. There is nothing supernatural about magic; it is as real as anything else in this World or in the Other. When a Mundari shaman dies, he cannot be buried in a grave, but instead, like the animals that his magic helped to kill, he is laid down on the ground surface in the bush. It is said that not a single vulture will ever bite off the flesh of a dead Mundari shaman, who has been left unburied to blend and fuse into the savannah landscape.

The mystery and the enigma of death comprise the central metaphor in hunting rituals, both before and after the killing of the prey. A pygmy hunter, who in the early hours of the day draws his chase game on the ground before setting out to hunt, returns later in the day to pour the blood and place the hair of the killed animal on its image. The next morning, the hunter returns to erase the drawing in the belief that the creature he killed had made a successful soul-journey to the Otherworld. In order to expedite such a journey, the shamanistic practice involving hunting rituals calls for an offering of returned blood in the belief that the animal spirit will thus be able to complete its journey to the Master of the Animals. Knud Rasmussen was offered a most perceptive explanation for this concept from a shamanistic standpoint: "The greatest peril of life lies in the fact that human food consists entirely of souls. All the creatures we have to kill and eat, all those we have to strike down and destroy to make clothes for ourselves, have souls, as we have."[34]

In Central Australia, on the other hand, the functional value of totemic systems can be noted:

> Totemism has enabled the Walbiri to feel and be in unity with nature. A regard for animal life is expressed by an intrinsic control on unrestricted hunting: one tends to be benevolent towards the totem animals of one's relatives, and only under abnormally severe environmental conditions will a man kill an animal of his own totem. Prior to the European settlement of Australia, there existed an island-wide equilibrium between the population and the food resources.[35]

The sacred experience induced by the drinking of *Datura* (only once in a person's life), during the puberty rites of the southern Californian Luiseño, generally brings about the visions of an animal that teaches the initiate his sacred mythical chant. The person will not kill, thereafter, any individuals belonging to the species of the animal seen in the vision. A spiritual alliance is forged, from this time on, between the initiate and the animal. Alfred Kroeber surmised that "It is clear that the concept of the vision corresponds exactly with what among certain primitive tribes has been unfortunately denominated the 'personal totem'. . . . The similarity to shamanism is also obvious; but it would be misleading to name the Luiseño institution outright 'shamanistic' or 'totemic.'"[36]

Totemism still plays a role among the trenchantly shamanistic Evenks of Siberia. Its pronounced theme is evidenced in the belief that their ethnogenesis is derived from a bear, while the Evenk shamanistic World Tree, *turu*, is located in the totemic domain of the shaman's clan, and connected by several paths with the three worlds of the universe. Likewise, totemic institutions are rooted prominantly among the Northwest Coast Indians, and vestiges thereof are discernible, for example, in the *noreshi* concept of the Yanomamö in the Amazon rain forest.

Several opinions varyingly uphold the primacy of totemism over shamanism; a few others maintain a contrary opinion. An attempt to forge a kinship bond with the animal world might have drawn sanctions

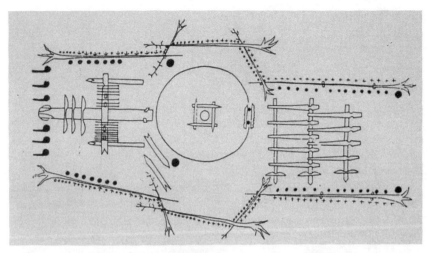

Figure 2.2 Floor plan of an Evenk shaman's tent. In the middle of the tent was placed a young larch to symbolize the shamanistic World-Tree. At the entrance stood two figures representing the shaman's guardian spirits. A figure of a pike, outside by the tent, protected it from evil spirits, while effigies of birds perched on sticks watched over the tent for any malintrusion from above, i.e., "from the air." (Source: A. F. Anisimov, (In): H. N. Michael (ed.), *Studies in Siberian Shamanism;* p. 95).

prohibiting the killing of members of the species from which a given hunting band claimed its ideological and existential descent. On the other hand, it is not altogether unrealistic to suggest that the totemic proscriptions against the slaughter of such creatures might have developed as the result of encounters with the animal spirits on soul-journeys during shamanic states of consciousness. The shaman's friendships and interactions with some of the animal spirits, pervading the realm of the Otherworld, afford a support base from which he can enlist the spirits' interventions as patrons, helpers, or familiars. Such relationships and bonds could promote the development of totemic systems, reckoned as being derived from the animals linked to the shaman. Consequently, not only the shaman, but the entire entourage of his kinsmen came possibly to be associated with the animal spirit, eventually formulating their descent from such a mythical ancestor.

Master of the Animals—The Lady of Wild Things

It is a very serious matter, and of far reaching consequence, that a shaman be able to forge links with Master of the Animals, if he himself is not

Figure 2.3 A shaman's mask, representing the spirit of the octopus. Northwest Coast (Kwakiutl?), before 1900. (Museum of the American Indian, Heye Foundation, New York).

one, and foster the latter's good will and positive sentiments by establishing viable channels of communication between two of them. To be successful in such a task, the Tukanoan shaman, in the Colombian northwest Amazon needs to enter a trance, with the aid of hallucinogenic substances, during which he can visit the hill or the water pool abode occupied by the Master. The encounter enables the shaman to communicate the purpose of his visit, and hopefully secure the permission from the Master to have the tribesmen hunt and fish all the creatures under the Master's dominion. However, such a transaction does not occur without a premium. The shaman must pay with human souls. "In fact, he must pledge himself to kill a certain number of people—of his or of a neighboring group—whose soul-stuff must then enter the Master's realm."[37] Although in another passage, the eminent anthropologist, Gérardo Reichel-Dolmatoff, chooses to interpret the killings allegorically,[38] there remains no doubt that here we have a reference to a practice from the olden days, when human victims were offered in sacrifice to propitiate Master of the Animals.

Among these people, the Master is considered to be "a phallic forest spirit," guarding the game animals against overkill. He is said to dwell in rocky outcrops, resembling the Mesas, which are believed to be hollow "like a huge womb-like longhouse." Within the context of shamanistic symbolism, and a mythological framework that equates women and animals, these transcendental dwellings serve as places where the ritual exchanges of women take place, in a strict adherence to the prescribed exogamous marriage rules.[39]

Similarly, the Gilyak people of the Amur River basin in eastern Siberia have had a Master of the Animals, who made his dwelling in the mountain, from where he controlled the movements of the animal spirits passing between this world and his domain. Curiously, when the Gilyaks had killed a bear and enacted the ritual of disposal properly, they afterwards "danced as bears."[40] Regretfully, I was unable to discover the actual meaning of this description. An identical phrase had been used for the female acolytes of Artemis, more than two thousand years ago, in the context of a bear cult that the goddess had in Attica. With the insular Ainus, on the other hand, the killing of the sacred bear points to shamanistic hunting magic; perhaps the last few centuries have also witnessed, among them, the relaxation of a taboo on a one-time totem animal.

There is sufficient evidence to acknowledge that the Cult of the Bear flourished in the Upper Palaeolithic, that is, a period spanning from 40/35,000 to 15/10,000 B.C. Some pundits have tried to suggest that the beginnings of the cult go back much further in time, and that, in fact, it was the Neanderthal man in the high Alps of Germany and

Switzerland, who had developed ritual practices around the cave-bear during the Middle, if not the Lower, Palaeolithic.⁴¹ In the vicinity of St. Gallen and Velden, in Germany, several caves were examined that disclosed some kind of an intentional arrangement of the unearthed bear skulls, which, thus, formed a purposeful configuration. Emil Bächler excavated, between 1903 and 1927, three caves in the Swiss high Alps, ranging in altitude from 7,000 to 8,000 feet. His discoveries included allegedly pre-Mousterian flint implements (from the Lower-Middle Palaeolithic), charcoal, flagstone floor, work tables and benches, skulls of the cave-bear, and, most interestingly, altars to attend the cultic rites of the bear—the earliest altars of any kind in the world. Two of the caves pointed definitely to a ceremonial practice, since they contained stone enclosures used as areas for the placement of the cave-bear skulls, either on slabs or within a circle of stones. Bächler claimed that the caves had to be occupied 75,000 years ago, at the very latest, since for the following 35,000-40,000 years, the caves would have been inaccessible due to the glaciers and the extended ice sheet.⁴² I guess he felt that the presence of pre-Mousterian (if this is what they were) flints precluded the furnishings and the altars from being of a later date, such as, perhaps, the Upper Palaeolithic, during which the Würm glaciation had its warmest interval and a final recession. There is no certainty that all the material found on each stratigraphic level in the German and the Swiss caves, did, unequivocally, belong to the same time phase, and that the possibility of later intrusions must be totally discounted. Therefore, it might be somewhat unfounded to group the flint tools and the altars in the same chronological spectrum. Irrespectively, however, these caves belong to the complex of the circumpolar Palaeolithic bear cult, known to have existed in the Arctic circle, stretching from the Hudson Bay, the Labrador Peninsula, Alaska, and northern Eurasia—including Siberia, Finland, and the higher Alpine ranges.

In the northern islands of Japan, the indigenous Ainus developed a special concept, shared by the Siberian Gilyaks, about the existence of animal spirits on earth. However, they regard such presence as an invitation to hunt, so that the killed animals can make room for the arriving, new souls. It is, you might say, transcendental resource management, maintaining the balance in an existential ecosystem. The Ainus, in their own right, present an enigma to the discriminating eyes of anthropologists. With their white skin and wavy hair, they are an anathema, on land and at sea, amidst vast Mongoloid populations. In physical stature, on the other hand, they can play passable doubles to any imperial subject of the rising sun. To create more colloidal matter in the suspension we call culture history, it has been suggested that the Ainus resemble the Russian stock of peasants and even some landed

Figure 2.4. An Ainu shaman-priest performing rites of the bear-cult. (American Museum of Natural History, New York, exhibit).

gentry, for example, the phenotype characterized by the soil-bound author of *Anna Karenina*.[43] But crowning the paradox is the Ainu language, which still remains unclassified. Nonetheless, there seem to exist elements, in the archaic infra-structure of Japanese, which suggest that both are derived from the same proto-language.[44] At the same time, some features in the Ainu religion and folk tradition exhibit similarities to Shinto.[45]

The important role of Master of the Animals is not only confined to the so-called primitive cultures. In the rural parts of Poland, we can find authentic survivals of the activities performed by Master of the Animals, even in this day. His practice is enveloped in mystery, perceived as bordering on the sinister, and regarded with an admixed confusion of fear and awe. My native informant recounted her personal experiences of the long winters during which the barns had been literally taken over by large rats in still larger numbers:

> The barn animals would starve, since all the food given to them would be instantly devoured by the blatantly emerging packs

of rats. Whenever any food for the animals was placed into the troughs, the rats would come forward and take over the troughs, and they would do so unafraid, right in front of us, as we came with the feed. It reached a point when the rats would even attack people as they entered the barn. One of the rats attacked me! I entered our barn, and all I suddenly saw were two glowing eyeballs. Before I knew it, he jumped on my head. The others followed him, jumping in all directions. It was horrible! There seemed to be no way of being rid of them, without first killing their leader, the king-rat. And that was not always possible to do. The rat packs invaded many households during that winter.

But there lived in the area an older man, who had only one eye. He was very strange, appeared to live all by himself, and no one knew much about him. People in the village knew that only he could help with this terrible problem, and so they charged him with this task. Once he had agreed to do so, he told everybody to remain inside their homes, while he, himself, entered the barn, being sure to shut its gate behind him. He had with him a wooden flute, or a similar wind instrument, on which he began to play a special tune, and after a short time, he exited the barn, and started walking in the direction of the fields. And all this time, he was playing his instrument. To the never-ending amazement of the villagers, peering behind the window glass, the rats were following him behind, not in a single file, but rather a scattered band attempting to consolidate behind its leader. The one-eyed man kept playing the wooden flute, taking along with him the coven of rats into the fields, far away from the village site, so they could not return. When this strange man died, so did his secret; he never shared it with anyone. I shall never forget this incident as long as I live.

For an epoch much more removed into the past than the above incident with the rats, but certainly more congruent in its geographic scope, George Dumézil contended that the Indo-European tribes in general, and the Celtic population in particular, had in common three categories of divinities, with each corresponding to a given social group. One of them was a fertility, or a regenerative deity, representing the agricultural unit in the social organization. Another divinity was of war and battle, linked with warlords and other knightly pursuits. The third one ruled over magic, and was, thus, associated with shamanism. The Welsh *Mabinogion* contains a black giant, who is Master of the Animals, including stags and serpents, and, like the Lapp shaman calling in the reindeer, he, too, can summon the animals at will. Deities showing indications of having been, at one time or another, Masters, Mistresses, or Lords of the Animals are likely to have shamanistic roots, suggesting that certain ones could have been actual shamans, who, in later periods, became deified. Thus, the Scandinavian god, Cernunnos, is depicted on the Gundestrupp cauldron of the second century B.C. as a horned divinity, seated in a lotus position, and surrounded by animals. In two places, at least, he is called Lord of the Animals, while the name Cernunnos means the Horned One.

Other ancient counterparts can be found in Greece and India. In the Aegean world, two clear exponents stand out immediately. The first is the horned Pan, an Arcadian divinity of small herd animals, who later came to be associated with Dionysos. The second is the mystic Orpheus of Thrace, who, apart of displaying preternatural powers over animals, introduced also elaborate catechisms and eschatology to the mystery religion of Dionysos. An exceedingly close version of the ancient Orphic tradition, and which resembles the Greek counterpart with an astonishing detail—all the way down to the flute pipes and decapitation—exists in northwest Amazon. It was recorded by Theodor Koch-Grünberg during his field researches among the Brazilian Indians, between 1903 and 1905.

The Hindu Shiva-Paśupati, also represented with horns, is likewise alluded to as Lord of the Animals. His horned images were discovered in the Indus Valley, going back to 1500 B.C., and showing him, like Cernunnos, seated in a lotus posture, flanked by all kinds of animals and snakes. In the Vedas, Paśupati is described as Lord of the Animals, both wild and domestic, who dwells in the mountains and the forests. Amidst the lush vegetation, according to Śaiva mythology, he roams divested of garments, filled with strong sexual energy, not unlike his counterpart Dionysos. Moreover, Paśupati imparts secret knowledge and wisdom through music, dance, and dramaturgy—techniques used in shamanistic performances. These arts he introduced to mankind, a deed also reminiscent of Dionysos. Paśupati bestows his secrets in an egalitarian fashion, without regard to a person's social rank or standing. In spite of the "democratic" appearance, it is of particular value to recognize that Shiva-Paśupati, the lord of the herd of living creatures, may be linked with the Brahmin-priestly caste in India.[46] Paśupati, as an aspect of Shiva, is also Lord of the Souls, intimating a correspondence with the shaman's function as a psychopomp, or a guide of the souls of the deceased. The shamanistic elements of the ancient figures are underscored by the presence of horns and serpents, as well as by the title Lord of the Animals.

Until now, almost nothing has been said about Mistress of the Animals, or the Lady of Wild Things, who seems to be a more ancient religious entity than her male counterparts. This title is ordinarily associated, in the Hellenic tradition, with the goddess Artemis. In her aspect as Brauronian Artemis, it is believed, she retained vestiges of the patroness of clan totems from earlier days. The bear cult of Artemis Brauronia, celebrated in her most sacred sanctuary on the eastern coast of Attica,[47] with little girls playing the part of bears, must have been a survival of very old totemic and shamanistic rituals. The name Artemis, as it has come down to us, does not yield a Greek etymology. However, Ar*k*temis or Ar*k*temisa, which, I believe, stand closer to the original, will render easily a linguistic affinity with the Hellenic tongue. *Arktos* means "a bear" and the topographical "north," or the Arctic, in both ancient and modern Greek. *Arkteia* was a festival, held every five years, in honor of Artemis at her temple in Brauron, at which the young girls of Athens, garbed in saffron dresses, "danced like bears" (*arktoi*). They played the bear, *arkteïein*, it was said of them, and perhaps the saffron hue was to recall the color of bears' fur.[48] Both the Greek *arktos* and Latin *ursus* stem from the same Indo-European root, as is demonstrated by their relationship to the Sanskrit *rksas*, which gave us the word Arctic, a region, or a habitat, of the bear. Near Cyzicus, in the Pontus ranges of Asia Minor, there was a place known as Arcton to the ancient geographers, meaning "Bear Mountain." It would hardly be disputed, today, that the arrival of Artemis into Greece took place from the north, where she could have been a totemic deity associated with the cult of the bear or even with some form of shamanism.

The lovely Arcadian nymph, Callisto, having been sworn to chastity as a dedicated companion of Artemis, had been nonetheless seduced by Zeus. The angered goddess destroyed Callisto by transforming her into a she-bear (*arktos*), and killed her in a hunt. In another version, Zeus intervened by coming to rescue Callisto, who, then, was turned into the northern constellation of *Ursa Major* (the Big [She]-Bear). Yet, because of this legend, it is significant to note that by an amazing coincidence— perhaps too amazing to be a coincidence—Calliste (the Fairest) was one of the titles used by Artemis.

Another and older appellation of Artemis was the Triple-Moon-Goddess, with her silver bow representing the new moon. At Ephesus, she was worshipped in another personification still, as the Nymph Artemis, a version of an orgiastic deity (Aphrodite) with a male lover, the date palm (a male fertilizing principle), the stag (the horns), and the bee (the Earth-Goddess).[49] The association she held with fertility is signified by a different name under which she was known there, too, as Artemis Polymastus (Many-Breasted). Plutarch[50] reports of Greek cultic rites practiced on Mount Lycaeum in Arcadia as late as the first century A.D., where a man dressed in a stag's skin and antlers was chased by the hounds of hell and killed. Numerous instances of similar ritualistic parallels exist in the Celtic tradition, as well.

The significance of the Celtic parallels becomes clearer with the implicit fact that in one of her aspects Artemis functioned as Mistress of the Horses, and, to this effect, was sometimes known as Eurippa, the Horse-Finder, not unlike a Lapp shaman who finds the reindeer. The Celts, a horse-loving people, were an offshoot of the horse-raising Indo-European tribes. Compare, for example, the Welsh *Epona*, the Irish *Macha*, and the British *Rhiannon*—different names for the same Mare-Goddess. This lends credence not only to the northern origins of Artemis, but makes it also plausible that, in one of her earlier phases, Artemis had been a European Horse-Goddess before joining the Hellenic pantheon. The connection between Eurippa and Europa (or Europe)—Land of the Horses—cannot be ignored.

Our Lady of the Nets and the Hunt might be the name of the dual goddess, Britomartis-Diktynna, a very old immortal from Crete, who displayed her acumen in temperance with nature. The primary motif in the Britomartis myth is the net, while Diktynna's sacred plants induce life-growth and self-healing.[51] In the fashion of a semi-divine shamaness, the Lady of the Nets and the Hunt wielded her powers by the specific manner in which she tempered with natural phenomena (e.g., rainfall, game animals, etc.) to achieve her desired effect in the process of nature. Perhaps, after all, her sacred plants did evolve into a corpus of magical substances, as encountered in shamanistic healing and trance, or even constructed a base for the Greek *materia medica*.

Mistress of the Animals, or a kindred title, was also given to the High Priestess on ancient Crete, and predated the patriarchal tradition arriving from the mainland. Ariadne the Holy Lady, daughter of King Minos and Pasiphaë, received the title of Mistress of the Animals and Wild Things when she succeeded to her mother's position as the High Priestess in the cult of Zagreus Taurogenes, that is Zagreus born of the bull. The cult of the enigmatic Zagreus had been strongly entrenched on Crete. Queen Pasiphaë, discharging her sacral duties, had mated ritually with Zagreus the bull-horned, giving birth to Zagreus the Minotaur, dweller of the Labyrinth—a structure representing the spiral of the infinite process, leading from this World to the Other.

The Spiral and the Labyrinth

In certain deeper stages of meditation, the spiral may appear as an involuntary mental image, as it also may to persons whose sleep has been induced with ether. It may do well to be reminded of the turning, spiral wheel used to bring on a hypnotic trance. The significance of this pattern will be examined more closely in another section of this book, under the discussion of phosphenes. It suffices to say, meanwhile, that this form bears the imprint of the cosmic paradigm, the transcendental cavity tunneling to the *axis mundi*, which joins the antipodal centers of this World and the Other. It demarcates an existential place or point, wherein the arcana of creation and entropy are but reflected images of each other—both, at once, self-generating and self-destructive. Accordingly, we can surmise readily the meaning behind the symbolism of the thirteenth-century spiral maze in the nave of Chartres Cathedral, and in a similarly carved design on a medieval buttress of Lucca Cathedral. Entrance to the Lowerworld is often depicted by concentric squares, as is well illustrated by the religious art of the Pueblo Indians in the Southwestern United States. The square in the middle is, of course, the center, or the Navel of the World. The mandalas on the Tibetan tankas seem to gain meditative effectiveness by traditionally combining into their designs concentric squares inside concentric circles. "The concentric circles of a mandala," Michael Harner writes, "often resemble the ribbed aspect that the Tunnel frequently presents, and meditation with the mandala can lead to an experience resembling the entrance into the Tunnel."[52]

The labyrinth, clearly related to the concentric patterns, is likewise symbolic of the antipodal Worlds, and represents a path to the center—signifying, in a mystical sense, the cave/womb—the objective in every shaman's journey. The shaman's conception of the labyrinth as comprising a uterine aspect has been demonstrated by anthropological field research.[53] We may find schematic representations of mazes in the numerous swastika signs encountered on both hemispheres. The labyrinthine theme is of great antiquity, occurring as an archetypal, transcultural metaphor not only within the ancient Aegean culture area, but elsewhere as well. Among many others, it appears in the rock art of the Bronze and Iron Ages in India, western Spain, England, Ireland, northen Italy, and Greece. In the Alpine regions of northern Italy, these designs appear ubiquitously in the Bronze and Iron Age rock art, especially in the Camonica Valley and the adjacent areas. However, in the burials of the second millennium B.C. in New Grange, Ireland, the spiral labyrinths proliferate, among others, on the massive stone blocks placed at the entrances. On the Maltese islands, too, there are beautiful renditions of spiral and labyrinthine patterns to be found in conjunction with ceremonial monuments. For a more contemporary setting, we can look to the Melanesian island of Malekula, where the entrance to the Lowerworld is guarded by a female spirit, who draws a labyrinth on the path of the approaching soul, carried across the waters of death, then only to erase half of the design before it is known to the deceased. The journeying soul must reconstruct the missing portion of the labyrinth, lest it be prevented from passing through the entrance of the Lowerworld, and thus become destined to eternal oblivion, by the ravishing teeth of the menacing female spirit-guardian. Thus, the secret of the labyrinth holds the secret to perpetual cosmic existence, and the female spirit is a surviving manifestation of the Mother-Goddess of birth, death, and rebirth. Furthermore, today, on the island of Malekula, marriageable and married women have their front teeth painfully knocked out with a stone and a stick, during special ceremonies pertaining to female rites of passage; probably as a covert and symbolic act to assuage the danger, particularly to men, represented by the female spirit residing in all women.

At the same time, one of the oldest of the more familiar themes is presented by the Labyrinth of Knossos, built by the legendary master-craftsman, Daedalus, to house the Minotaur—half man, half bull—a shamanistic creature in its own right. Chronologically, the Minoan labyrinth precedes that at Nestor's palace in Pylos, Greece, which dates from about the thirteenth century B.C. The tradition of the Labyrinth and the Minotaur was so deeply entrenched in the memory of the people, tantalizing their imagination, that the Greek coinage issued in Crete during the seventh and the sixth centuries B.C., a long time after the reign of King Minos, depicted labyrinths of circular and square formats on one side of the coin. A labyrinthine square pattern is also preserved, although in damaged condition, on the Athenian acropolis. The Etruscans, who readily borrowed many Greek traits, had their own local representations of the labyrinth, as exemplified by a late seventh-century B.C. vessel from a cemetery at Tagliatella in Italy. A curious, but admittedly a very late, example of a square labyrinth, in the style found on Cretan coins, comes from Pompeii and dates to the first century A.D. It is flanked by a Latin inscription: *LABYRINTHVS HIC HABITAT MINOTAVRVS.*

In a provocative and very stimulating article dealing with maze symbolism, Knight proposed that in ancient Crete and in Babylon, the labyrinth and the spiral were associated with human anatomical organs, as well as with the Underworld, and both categories interchanged as equivalent metaphors for each other. In order for the spirit to be reborn, a tomb (e.g., a tholos with its domed roof resembling a spiral) would be constructed "as much like the body of the mother as he [the tomb-builder] was able." On the other hand, the meaning of the elaborate spiral is conveyed through the significance placed on virginity and sexuality: The successful accomplishment of an ordeal, or an *agon*, terminates often, for the hero, in rewarding circumstances permitting cohabitation with a princess or a corollary.[54] If we allow for the almost certain probability that the spiral pattern is related to the labyrinth, or even an occasional schematic representation thereof, then little wonder that we see this symbol used, as well, to represent the unknown origin point to the Hereafter and to the womb (and the cave) of the Great Mother. The spiral cycle is a metaphor for the *infinite process*, and resonates the vibrations and rhythms of the universe.

In turn, the navel, or the center, is an alchemical concept that is incorporated into the symbolic language of Jungian psychology. The patients of the Swiss psychiatrist, Carl G. Jung, signaled their approach towards a successful completion of therapy by beginning to draw intuitively such motifs, in particular, those resembling the mandala. This apparent manifestation of recovery demonstrates, somehow, that the patients are nearing the "individuation" phase, that through the probing of the psyche they reach into the center. In certain respects, each person's existence is like a labyrinth, at the core of which the forces of destruction reside alongside the forces of creation; the individual's oblivion lurks in the center. The Self, once annihilated, is freed and liberated from all sorts of earthly constraints, and becomes transformed into a spiritual essence. It is a perplexing, lifelong enigma of the human condition to believe innately that the closer we approach the center, the freer we become.

Whether the spiral passage, which connects the antipods of this and the Otherworld, stands for the mystical return to the womb and its blissfully oblivious state, as some Jungian followers have chosen to interpret,[55] is a point to be seriously considered, but not resolved. The fear of the dark labyrinth, on the other hand, could be seen as the fear of the "mystical" return to the prenatal darkness sensed inside the womb—ultimately, that is, of a reversal to the state of non-being, or, again, to Martin Heidegger's elegant metaphysical concept of "concealment"—and consequently viewed as a condition of anxiety over dissolving the dimensions of one's consciousness, as well as over disintegration of the structure of one's individuality. This perspective must then be counteracted with an argument showing that the fear of the dark is not merely an ontogenetic trait, appearing in the development of the individual from an embryonic stage, but a phylogenetic characteristic shared by all the members of the species and other non-human primates, as well. This instinct has been genetically inherited by man, and most living primates, from our hominid ancestors during the ongoing process of biological evolution. Adapted to diurnal activities, our primate ancestors were most vulnerable to fall prey under the cover of night, and thus most endangered by the nocturnal predators. This fear is encoded, somewhere, in the genetic structure of the human DNA double-helix.

The analyses of dreams and myths serve as a potent tool in effective therapy. Myths, as Joseph Campbell observes perceptively, are the collective dreams of a culture; dreams the personal myths of an individual. Similarly, Franz Kafka offers profound intimations into the question of mythogenesis. Through his extraordinary faculties of introspection, Kafka's parables are infused with the archetypal vision of the unfathomable dilemma manifest in the cosmic parody of creation and destruction; of the Dionysiac paradox borne by the passionately exalted fusion of rapture and terror; of the ineffable center where life and death merge into an indistinguishable vortex, a point of both a beginning and an end. This deeply troubled individual manages to capture the hidden essence of metaphysical reality when he observes, with uncanny perception, that all myths originate in a place of truth, and terminate in a place of inexplicability. And for us, interested in the human condition and the psyche, it must become an intellectual dictum that if myths are metaphors, then, by the same reasoning, dreams must be too.

Shamanism and Ancient Egyptian Religion

The ancient Egyptians, Herodotus (ii.122) believed, had been the first to learn about the immortality of the human soul and its various stages of reincarnation. This dogma, according to him, was taken up by the Greeks, and, by the time of Plato (*Phaedo*, 70 c), it was established as "an ancient doctrine that the souls of men that come Here are from There and that they go There again and come to birth from the dead." While Empedocles, quoted by Diogenes Laertius (viii.77) proclaimed in verse: "Once on a time a youth was I, and I was a maiden,/ A bush, a bird, and a fish with scales that gleam in the ocean."

The idea of the surviving, or eternal, soul is fundamental to the tenets of shamanism. The crucial aspect of this notion can be clearly seen during the healing activities, which for the most part are undertaken in a shamanic state of consciousness (SSC), or a trance. Should the patient not survive, the shaman will then act as a psychopomp, or an escort to the Otherworld, for the soul of the deceased. Often, as it happens, the entranced shaman will describe aloud the adventures and perils of his soul-journey on which he confronts all kinds of dangerous spirits, and even, at times, the spirit of a malevolent shaman, expert in black magic. Flashes of such sojourns could be glimpsed from the ancient Egyptian cult surrounding the particularistic nature of Osiris. This deity made his descent, or rather a transcendental ascent, into the Underworld

Figure 2.5. The Egyptian god Osiris, in his black form, seated on a black throne as a ruler of the realm of the dead. This illustrates the strong preoccupation with fates of human souls in ancient Egypt. 19th Dynasty. (The Louvre, Paris).

domain of the gods, upon having been slain and dismembered by his pernicious adversary and brother, Set—the god of chaos. To ascertain a rebirth, his newcoming, Osiris had to rely on the support of the ancestral spirits, who would need to undergo physical ordeals on his behalf by self-inflicting wounds and pain to facilitate the resurrection of the god. "The souls of Buto dance for you; they smite their flesh for you; they beat their arms for you; they dishelve their hair for you; they smite their legs for you."[56]

The highly esteemed, Colombian authority on shamanism, Gérardo Reichel-Dolmatoff, who has studied intensively the Amazonian conceptions of the cosmos and the worldviews of the shamans, reports on frightening ordeals that the Underworld spirits of the Tukanoan Indians, who dwell in the Colombian Amazon, must undergo in order to effect spiritual rehabilitation and eternal existence in the Hereafter.[57] As mentioned earlier, the shaman may either consolidate the assistance of helpful spirits and familiars or transform himself into an animal spirit, instead, to enhance his skills for evading pitfalls and entrapments along the soul-journey. Similarly, in Mongolia, ancestral spirits are venerated because their help can be enlisted in times of natural peril. It becomes quite clear why the role played by shamanism in hunting societies has remained of such characteristic importance.

> The identification of man's nature with that of the animals, the interchangeability of the two forms of existence, is the characteristic phenomenon of the spiritualism of hunting cultures, and one to which the origin of shamanistic beliefs is attributed.[58]

In the metamorphoses of the Egyptian and the Greek divinities into the various animals or animal-headed gods, we are confronted with the remnants of an older, shamanistic past. The Egyptian pantheon, until the Old Kingdom period, represented female deities in human shapes, while the male gods were depicted in four progressively diverse forms as: (1) zoomorphic, either animals or birds; (2) zoomorphic, but with parts of the human body; (3) humans, with animal or bird heads; and (4) fully anthropomorphic. It can be argued readily that polytheism had its roots in totemism and shamanism. The symbolic contingencies leading to the transition from the totemic-shamanistic to the polytheistic system are attributed to the interplay of newly emerging phenomena; an increased preponderance for conceptual thinking effected a decline in the use of visual imagery in cognitive processes, in turn, leading to intensified reliance on metaphors and analogues in conceptualization. These phenomenological developments threw open the doors for speculative and abstract configurations in symbolic thought.

The Egyptians demonstrated their mystical bond with the animal world not merely through the transformation of their deities into zoomorphic beings, or the ceremonial use of animal masks by their priests, but, no less, with the use of shamanistic themes in art, such as those appearing in the wall painting (now in the Cairo Museum), from a Late Gerzean (about 3400 B.C.) tomb at Hierakonpolis in the upper reaches of the Nile. One important motif consists of a man, who may readily represent the Master of the Animals, flanked by an upright beast on each side. This group is reminiscent of the Gilgamesh epic and suggests a Mesopotamian influence. Another more significant scene on the same wall panel, and one that is encountered much later as characteristic with the Indians of the American Southwest, depicts a composition of the so-called medicine wheel (a solar symbol) encircled by five horned ungulates along the circumference, probably representing the cosmic spirits of the animals. The solar disc in the celestial firmament became the emblem of Osiris. ". . .The sun, not as rising and setting and so forth, but viewed as creative, fertilising, the source and the giver of life. Vegetation, its growth and decay come to some extent into the myth. But Osiris is neither the corn nor a sort, as he [Sir James Frazer] says, of corn-god."[59]

This generative and fertilizing power of the solar deity finds a corresponding existence as the Sun-Father among some Tukanoan shamans, who maintain that the earth was created out of a void when the Sun-Father utilized on the cosmos "the male fertilising principle."[60] Another version of such a "principle," with undeniably shamanistic roots, is the White Old Man (Tsaghan Ebügen) among the Mongols.[61] He wields a dragon-headed staff (Lamaist influence) in clear counterpart to the shaman's magical, horse-headed staff, used as a mount in the soul-journeys. Both staffs are known by the same name, *tayagh*.[62] The German historian of religions, Father Wilhelm Schmidt, was apparently the first to observe, in his monumental work on the origin of the idea of God, the recurrence of sky-gods in shamanistic religions, leading him to conclude that shamanism, like totemism, was based on a male tradition and thus was a precursor to the development of a monotheistic father godhead.[63] In regions as remote from each other as the Nile Valley, the Amazonian rain forest, and the wild steppes of Mongolia, the structural components in shamanistic religions seem to bear him out. As an exponent of the culture-historical school, he also argued that a major cultural shift of global dimensions, a historical cataclysm of sorts, had occurred in the past. The wide and rich gamut of myths, stemming from diverse and unrelated culture areas, yet containing related folklore-motifs, is a living memory of this event.

It is not surprising that the role of the Egyptian priest resembled, in many ways, the function of the shaman, with whom he shared more traits than either the Hebrew prophets or Christian priests. This contrast expresses theological differences. As a result, the priesthood in ancient Egypt comprised a class of ritual specialists and "technicians," whose purpose was to "maintain the universe in the form in which the gods have created it."[64] Rather than infer our contemporary meaning for it, Serge Sauneron rightly contends when he remarks, "We ought above all to guard ourselves, in using the term *priests*, against considering them as the guardians of a revelation which would make them a sect apart, living on the edge of society and only venturing to convert the crowds by impassioned sermons to a richer or more active moral life...."[65] Perhaps, he makes, nonetheless, the priests appear too secular in their functions, stripping them of the essential mystic qualities required for the operation of a well-oiled theocracy. He adds, furthermore, that they

> ...are men like any others, not profiting from any divine privilege, not having to win over crowds, nor to convert the gentiles....The personal religion of the people is not indebted to them, and the priests themselves can even be fertile thinkers or saintly men—but as a consequence of their individual tendencies, not as a necessary result of their professional activity.[66]

The above description can just as well apply to shamans, and like the shamans, the Egyptian priests ritually donned animal masks. Although it went unnoticed, for the most part, this practice had been remarked upon by some Egyptologists as early as 1899, when Gaston Maspero published a book review alluding to a wall scene in the Temple of Hatshepsut, depicting priests and priestesses wearing masks during a ceremony.[67] With the exception of Margaret Murray, who picked up Maspero's idea in 1934,[68] others who noted the use of animal masks in ancient Egypt failed to connect their function with ceremonial practices. Even much earlier, in 1873, Auguste Mariette had published *Dendera IV*, in which he provided graphic evidence of a masked priest in a context of a funeral scene. It took forty-six years before Mariette's item came to the attention of another Egyptologist:

> a priest [is] wearing a jackal mask as required for some ritual purposes, and his head is visible inside because the artist wished to show how the priest was placed in the mask and needed to be led. But it is a rare exception....Instead the priest playing the role of the god is always represented as if he really had an animal head.[69]

For a very long time, the Egyptologists have shown a considerable reluctance to see in the Egyptian religion anything but the structural components of a sophisticated religious ideology developed by an enlightened civilization. They enjoined from noticing anything that might be unseemly, suggestive of animism, "primitive" conceptions, and "backward" rituals. Thus, Sauneron, too, falls into the mainstream of convention when he remarks on the ostensible absence of priests officiating in religous ceremonies depicted on temple walls. His comment echoes the idea that all masked figures represented the deities, instead that, on occasion, certain ones might belong to priests in masks. Likewise, his explanation suffers from overrationalization when he states that the primacy of the king's role in discharging sacerdotal duties rendered the depiction of priests unnecessary.[70] It was not until the recent appearance of insightful observations on the subject of Egyptian masks[71] that a coherent perspective of their function has been gained, suggesting that it was not unusual for the priests to assume the guise of the gods whom they were representing.

Shamanistic Metaphors, Techniques, and Appurtenances

The ritual function of the mask dates back many thousands of years. We have evidence from the Palaeolithic caves of southwestern Europe which clearly shows that such practices had been in vogue for, at least, over 30,000 years. The shamanic custom of putting on animal and bird masks is, undoubtedly, a survival from the Upper Palaeolithic and into the Neolithic, at a time when human beings were keen on establishing bonds with the spirit of nature and creating interchangeability between animal and human forms. A total transformation requires also the transference of the spirit or soul, so the mask, becoming a metaphor, allowed the wearer, through *mimesis*, to take over the *animus*, as well as the *persona*, of the creature or being it represented. Conversely, the mask could also be worn, more infrequently, to prevent the onlookers from capturing the soul behind the face that it covered. All secret organizations, which prescribe the ceremonial use of masks, have been founded on myths relating to the origins of man and society. When a man puts on a mask, his symbolic position is enhanced, for he assumes the significance of something other than himself. The contrary was true for women in the time of the Great Mother, who, through her revealing nakedness alone, underscored the profound mystery of her magic. This potency would have been covered up, remaining without impact, had she been depicted otherwise. And so it is today for every Hindu woman, as she in the nude, becomes the incarnation of *prakrti*—the primordial matter, the womanly prototype, and nature itself.

The Neolithic cultures of Old Europe, that is, before the Indo-European invasion, had also adopted the practice of masking from the Palaeolithic inhabitants preceding them. These Old European peoples occupied the southeastern lands and shared a common stylistic phase which found expression in the schematic mode by which they depicted the masked faces of their ceremonial figurines. In the Central Balkans, during the fifth and the fourth millennia B.C., the Vinča culture was a remarkable producer of masked effigies, displaying the widest diversification of style and a lesser schematization. The wearing of masks by anthropomorphic and zoomorphic figurines implies specific "divine epiphanies," which, in turn, signify the presence of a cult and a ritual that have been generally interpreted as dealing with fertility.[72] A different position, on the other hand, is taken by the Rumanian archaeologist, Eugen Comsa, who sees in the early Neolithic (c. 7000-5500 B.C.) female figurines from the Rumanian territories (that is, the Danube plain between the Transylvanian Alps and the Balkan Mountains) a connection with hunting rites, rather than representations of fertility divinities and their death-rebirth cycles. He maintains that only later, with the intensification of plant cultivation, did the regenerative and agricultural aspects of the female deities develop.[73] Whether correct or not, it is in hunting societies that the strongest roots of shamanism are to be found. Masked animals, like the quadruped (a bull ?) with a human face, from Fafos in southern Yugoslavia, dating from the latter part of the fifth millennium B.C.,[74] may very well represent shamans transformed into animal spirits, or perhaps even Masters of the Animals. The belief in such transformations contributed, undoubtedly, to the creation of traditions, such as the Minotaur legend. Life-size, human masks from pre-Columbian Colima, western Mexico, are known to exist as separate artistic entities. However, the dog is the only non-human effigy wearing a human mask. The exact meaning of this iconography cannot be ascertained, but the various speculations regarding these occurrences have created a mill of ideas, some of them suggesting that the masked dog was intended to act as a psychopomp, or a companion, leading the deceased on the journeys to the Underworld, as well as guarding the realm of the dead. Irrespectively, the Colima dog effigy, with a human mask, shows parallel developments in the symbolic language of metaphor to those exhibited in the Vinča artistic mode. We must assume, at this point, that the dog is transformed by the mask into a man, since the general purpose of masks is to accomplish precisely that. Perhaps, we have here a case of the alter-ego, or the shaman's avatar: man $\geqq$ dog, man = shaman, shaman $\geqq$ dog.

It is interesting, for our discussion of shamanism, to note the existence of a Vinča vessel in the shape of a duck, with its head surmounted by two mushrooms. If these mushrooms, as Marija Gimbutas has speculated, were meant to represent the hallucinogenic variety—which, very plausibly, they do—then we can establish a probable case for the occurrence of an ecstatic technique, or shamanism, in the Vinča culture of the Central Balkans, between the fifth and the fourth millennium B.C. The connection between hallucinogens and shamanism and their impact on cultural development has been demonstrated, more than adequately, by many.[75] Eliade's belief that the use of psychotropic plants in shamanistic techniques represents a more recent, degenerated innovation,[76] is not supported by evidence from either the Old or the New World—just the opposite. Current studies point favorably to strong Upper Palaeolithic beginnings for the use of psychotropic flora. La Barre, while repeatedly stressing the shamanistic character of native religions in the Americas, notes that the ecstatic nature of shamanism is "culturally programmed for an interest in hallucinogens and other psychotropic drugs."[77]

The mask, the face, the horns, and the head have been varyingly important, but always significant,[78] for the magician of the hunt and for the shaman. The horns have continued to be associated with shamanism, in both hemispheres, since remote antiquity. They are believed to be the seat of shaman's power; particularly, the single horn in the center, still to be detected in the old European unicorn lore. It is interesting to note, in this connection, the horns of power attributed to Moses in some interpretations. By the same token, the horned helmet of the Anatolian Turks is residual from a shamanistic past, and its ontology preserved in many a folk account. The Christian devil, on the other hand, equipped with the stag's antlers (Celtic-Scandinavian influences) in his early history, particularly in northern and central Europe, reflects the degradation of the horned shamans and the deer cult at the hands of the priests who spread the new religion. Under the influence of elements borrowed from Byzantine Christianity and esoteric Gnosticism, the devil cast away his antlers in favor of the goat's horns (Greek Pan). In Gnostic iconography, for example, Pan and the devil coalesce very closely and can sometimes be differentiated only by virtue of a single detail or a minor attribute. Yet, sporadically, the devil persisted in his guise as a stag, and, even as late as the final stages of the fifteenth century, he appears in a painting motif from 1482 in the Abbey of Novacella.[79] The ancient deer cult, however, could be found in the Eastern Hemisphere as far as the remote regions of Russia, China, and Japan. The Shintoist priests in Nara still perform an annual ceremony in which they cut off the antlers of about one thousand sacred deer.[80]

Today, the shaman's headband is a replacement for his horns and, when worn around the forehead, especially during religious ceremonies, serves as a substitute for the shaman's "horns of power." Good practical examples, as pointed out by the anthropologist Peter Furst, can be witnessed among the Huichol Indians in Sierra Madre Occidental of western Mexico,[81] as well as by the many North American Indian tribes who wear headbands during rituals and ceremonial functions. But this custom is not limited by any measure to the Western Hemisphere; it is to be found just as much in Eurasia. One obvious example that comes to mind is Japan, where the ceremonial headband is perhaps more ubiquitous even in everyday life. One is prompted to ask whether the headband is not a social replacement, by a modern and westernizing nation, for the horns of the totemic clans of the not so ancient past.

Already in 1965, Peter Furst proposed in an article[82] that archaeologists, art historians, and others interested in ancient and comparative religions take another look at the pre-Columbian shaft-tomb figurines that had been discovered in western Mexico. He particularly stressed the Colima armed figurines, with a single horn, and the double-horned statuettes from Nayarit.[83] Both these groups had been previously labeled as "warriors" by experts. Since horns are emblems of supernatural, totemic, and, in particular, shamanistic attributes, Furst urged a reassessment of the symbolic meaning of these figural groups in terms of shamanistic categories. He based his hypothesis on the iconography of the figures, often termed as being in "warlike attitudes," and suggested that the "warlike" postures are far from being in conflict with the traits of shamans, since they are expected to combat supernatural evil and other malevolent shamans to protect the community's spiritual well-being from its enemies. An added feature to his interpretation was the fact that most of the horned figures face in the left direction—an orientation quite commonly associated with death, sorcery, and a host of other supernatural dangers. Furst also brought up the important notion that these shamanic figures, placed in tombs, were meant to represent psychopomps for the deceased; guardians of the dead and their souls.

He extended the argument by taking into consideration the originally sacred, rather than secular, nature of music. Consequently, the pre-Columbian whistle-figurines may bear a new scrutiny in the light of a shamanistic context. Whistling is a practice known to be commonly employed by the shamans to summon the ancestral spirits; it is also used in healing for the retrieval of strayed souls. Since the drum is universally of primary importance in shamanism, figures of "drummers" might therefore reasonably be interpreted as "shamans" or "shaman helpers"; while an effigy with a flute, an instrument connected with rituals pertaining to rain-making and fertility of the earth, could be seen in a corresponding light. Furst obtained a recording of Huichol music played on a real ancient flute, discovered in an archaeological site in Colima. The Indian player had no trouble recognizing the flute, which he "identified as a rain-making instrument because it was decorated with a modeled snake—symbol of the Huichol Rain Mothers."[84]

In Europe, at one time, the brain was attributed with several roles: encompassing the spiritual domain as the alleged seat of the soul, and the procreative area as the producer of seminal fluid, which was believed to have been channeled through the bone cavity—the plumbing system, as it were, of the body. The horns growing out of the head—the seat of the brain—were by extension construed to be ritually sacred, and presumed to ramify the areas where the flow of semen was especially intensified. As a consequence, they were considered vital to the enhancement of sexual activities.[85] One obvious example comes from ancient Crete, where the Minoan bull horns were all-pervasive in the religious cult, and the enormous ritual significance of the bull could only be compared to the importance of the *labrys*, or the double-axe. The shamans may or may not wear masks, but they are more likely to use horns. At the very least, a headband, ornamented with avian feathers, will be worn. The Russian folklore scholar, G. V. Ksenofontov—a true Siberian Yakut by birth—narrates a tradition from amongst his own people, heard from an old, native informant, Alexeyev Mikhail, who lived in the vicinity of the Lena River. In the days of yesteryear (i.e., around 1900), the entranced Yakut shamans would not only emit the sounds of bulls, but would grow, as well, bull horns on their heads—something old Alexeyev had witnessed once himself.[86]

However, without question, the most important attributes of the shaman, particularly in Mongolia, Siberia, and Lapland, are the drum and the drumstick. Animal hide, usually from a horse or a reindeer, provides the covering for the shaman's drum, which is always covered with a single skin membrane. It is considered the "most powerful of all the shaman's helpers," and is his mystical horse or a boat employed in the soul-journey. The Yuraks of the tundra refer to the drum that is used in trance-induction as the shaman's bow, which dispatches him into the Otherworld. The choice of wood for the drum is a very serious matter, and consequently cannot come from an ordinary tree species. Its source must be the World Tree, which several different tribes locate by means of an ecstatic trance. The predominant drum type, among the Sibero-Tungusic tribes in northeastern Siberia, consists of a round form with crossway wooden strips. Farther south, as we near Manchuria, a somewhat different variety of a drum can be found. It is distinguished, primarily, by the presence of a handle, inserted into an iron ring—occasionally of an oval shape—which is covered by a stretched goatskin.

Figure 2.6. The Karagass shaman Tulayev, Siberia. His vestments depict a rich lore of cosmological symbolism—moon, stars, animal helpers, etc. Astral designs are also featured on the long ribbon at the back of the shaman's cap, which symbolizes his spine. The drum is made of deerskin stretched over a wooden frame. Two metal pieces (*kulak*, ears) with iron rattles are attached to the upper part of the frame. They serve as "ears" with which the shaman hears the voices of the spirits. The drumstick is made of reindeer horn, covered with the skin taken from the same animal. It serves as a knout for guiding the spirit animals on which the shaman travels to the Otherworld. The coat was acquired by Professor Petri in Irkutsk, in 1927. The coat and the drum are in the collection of the Staatliches Museum für Völkerkunde, Munich (Mus. No. 27-48-1 a and e).

Figure 2.7. A detail from the costume of a Tungus shaman, showing an iron doll and two copper alloy masks. Since iron is the predominant metal used by Siberian shamans, the copper masks are somewhat unusual. The second half of 18th century. (Museum für Völkerkunde, Göttingen University).

The shapes of the handle, where there is one, may be represented in a slight variance from the simple perpendicular type, by having the base terminate in the figure of a cross or the symbol **Y** or **X**. In most cases, the skin membrane is ornamented with designs, among which the number nine, appearing sometimes in various aspects, has an obvious symbolic significance, possibly as a product of three threes. In the Mongol cosmography, the number nine, together with the planet Venus and the constellation of the Great Bear, particularly the star Polaris, occupy central positions.

The importance attributed to the drum and its keynote characteristics conjure shamanistic practices even in territories that are not believed to contain "pure" and "classic" forms of shamanism—as if "purity" and "objectivity" were quantifiable values, possessed of their own particularistic state of existence. Rather, these values express a psychocultural by-product of cognitive subjectivity, representing an interplay between conception and perception. An origin myth in Papua New Guinea (Irian) recounts the descent of some aboriginal clans from the iguana-woman (Kasip) and the crocodile-man (Wonggor). Nowadays, the clansmen stretch iguana skins over their drums, "So the drum became the voice of the primeval mother, their ancestor mother."[87] Here, therefore, we have clearly an indication of transformational continuance from the figure of a primordial mother to a shamanistic metaphor, underscored by tales of metamorphoses involving interchanges between animal and human forms.

The drumstick, of wood or horn, may be decorated with zoomorphic and anthropomorphic designs as well as rings which amplify the sound with their rattling. It is commonly referred to as the shaman's scepter, and terminates frequently in a horse's head, thus representing the animal onto which the shaman embarks for his soul-journey to the Otherworld during an ecstatic trance. This shamanic state of consciousness (SSC) is induced by dancing, pounding the drum, and consuming inebrients.[88] The importance of musical sound, as a transporting technique, is a fundamental phenomenon in every shamanistic culture. Music serves, more often, a sacred, ceremonial function rather than as plain entertainment. This transporting quality of music is even well illustrated in cultural contexts which are not ordinarily regarded as shamanistic. In the Dionysiac cults, where the ecstasy and terror of existence are so overwhelming precisely because they are infused with the awesomeness of finality and death, music and trance appear to come from the fathomless nadir of the life-death cycle. Here, through deeply rooted intuitions going back as far as human time, life is seen as a blissful *security* and death as the darkest *calamity*. As an inhabitant of the two abodes, of this World and the Other, the essence of Dionysos is revealed in his dual nature of antithesis and paradox. Thus, by decimating the conventional order of things, life turns simultaneously into rapture of spiritual numen and earthly terror. The French poet, Charles Baudelaire, whose spiritual and experiential sense of this dilemma was profound, observed allegorically, "Man has two constant aspirations: One to God, the other to Satan."

The late Hungarian scholar, Vilmos Diószegi, felt that the shaman was brought to a state of ecstasy by the sound of drumming, causing the spirits to enter either the drum or the shaman, or, alternately, send the shaman's soul off on a journey to the Otherworld.[89] In such situations, the drum becomes the shaman's mount and the drumstick his riding crop. The Buryat shaman may embark on a soul-journey by means of a staff terminating in "the figure of a horse's head." Among the reindeer-breeding Tungus, the shaman may go on his journey by means of a staff surmounted with a figure of a reindeer's head. He may dispense with the drumstick altogether and have his assistant beat a rhythm to the tempo of his dance, which is amplified by the sounds of a higher pitch produced by bells and other trinkets attached to the shaman's garb. So, the dance may be partly ancillary, or a means to satisfy the Tungus requirement for rhythmic sounds.[90] The importance of ritual music is underscored also by Eliade's remarks about certain linguistically related groups in Siberia:

> Among the Ugrians shamanic ecstasy is less a trance than a "state of inspiration"; the shaman sees and hears spirits; he is "carried out of himself" because he is journeying in ecstasy through distant regions, but he is not unconscious. He is a visionary and inspired. However, the basic experience is ecstatic, and the principal means of obtaining it is, as in other regions, magico-religious music.[91]

The shamanic soul-journey can lead upward to the heaven, even though it may occur at the bottom of a lake. When the journey is on a waterway, such as a river, the drum becomes his boat, and the drumstick the oar or the paddle. The Siberian shaman, who can frequently become transformed into an aquatic species, is able to remain in the lake and commune with some of the water creatures. However, it should be remembered that different cultures have devised or adapted different metaphors for analogous ritual idioms.

Reichel-Dolmatoff, reporting on the Eastern Tukano speakers in the northwestern parts of the Amazon, notes that a stick rattle—a hardwood rod over two meters long with a small rattle on one end—symbolizes for them the navel of the earth, or the *axis mundi*, and at the same time stands for strong phallicism, representing the sib's sperm being transmitted by its rattling sound.[92] In addition to the usual magical and ceremonial attributes, the shaman's equipment may also be vested with other characteristics, such as sexual and procreative symbolisms, which also proliferate among the Tukano speaking Indians.

The oropendola bird (Icteridea)—whose native name, *umu*, is closely linked with *ëmë*, "day" or "sun"—signifies the solar element in the tradition of the Desana Indians, a group of the Tukano linguistic family. The bird's yellow feathers decorate the shaman's rattle, a standing allegory not only for the fertilizing aspect of the sun, but also for the masculine component. Apparently, there is no consistent adherence to a uniform scheme of color classification, which seems to vary according to a specific conceptual mode. Yellow in the *umu* bird's feathers is solar and male; yellow in the metaphoric threads, running the length of the psychotropic *yajé* vine (*Banisteriopsis* spp.), is female, while, again, white is solar energy. The structural content of the Desana world thus manifests the principle of duality, although not in the strictest sense of the term. The shaman's rattle stands for the universal antipodes, the cosmic archetype of the dimorphic principles encapsulated in the dipoles of the masculine and the feminine elements. The gourd of the rattle represents the womb. Its handle, inserted completely through the hollowness of the chamber, is compared to the phallus. The shaking of the rattle inseminates the womb-gourd by the penis-handle, resulting in an act of creation. The rattle contains small particles of quartz crystals, which, when shaken against the interior walls of the gourd, become energized and ignite its soft inner lining, producing smoke and even sparks, to be seen escaping from the slits and holes in the rattle. This practice is not exclusive to the Desana shamans; it was reputedly first observed by the UCLA anthropologist, Johannes Wilbert, among the Warao Indians of Venezuela.[93] The igniting sparks are assigned an expanded meaning during a healing seance, when the rattle assumes a broader aspect and becomes a curing wand. The sparks become a metaphor for procreation *in utero*—a new, life-engendering process, symbol of transformation in a new passage.

> It is important to keep in mind that all *sacra* that are used during these various shamanic ceremonies have mainly sexual and fertility associations: the stick rattle is a phallus and so is the bone flute; seed rattles are testes, the mouthpiece of the *yuruparí* trumpet is a vagina, the vessel in which narcotic potions are prepared is a womb, and the rock crystal symbolizes semen.[94]

The shaman conveys metaphors addressed to the spirit world through drumming, chants, dance, myths, drama, or more appropriately, psychodrama. These contain "obligatory" allusions and formulas. As a rule, the shamanic drama occurs after the hours of daylight and is set around the fire inside the tent. When spectators are present, which is more often than not, the shaman attempts to create the appropriate mood. Among the Rufaim, also known as the Howling Dervishes, chanting is practiced as a main technique for approaching *melboos,* a mystical state or ecstasy. Rhythmically timed, they chant, "Al-lah," until each of the participants begins to incant the name of *Allah* in a mad, ecstatic frenzy. What follows turns into a frantic dance, during which they wave hot implements in their hands, howling in a wild unison rhythm, a "frenzied chant, savage, exultant, ecstatic."[95] Afterwards, they pierce their bodies with the sharp utensils. Eliade termed such displays as "fakiristic phenomena." But fakiristic or not, I observed how they can precipitate states of trance-like ecstasy.

Sheila Ostrander and Lynn Schroeder, who had travelled to the Soviet Union in 1968 to report on the First Annual Parapsychology Conference in Moscow, interviewed and talked to many specialists and others with kindred interests. Their account of fairly recent occurrences in Russia forms an interesting and a colorful piece of journalistic reporting:

> *Shamans* took drugs and flung themselves into sacred dances to catapult into the psychic. The fire blazed, the drum beat, the *shaman* danced faster and faster until he collapsed in a trance. Singing and drum brought him round and again the *shaman* danced, leaping, stamping, a fury of motion until his body fell to the ground and he, hopefully, shot out into the world of the unseen. Dancing into psychic powers has sprung up elsewhere in Russia. Country witches often do a slow dance to help secure their spells. Rasputin, a hybrid of *shamanism* and Christian mysticism, was famous for frenzied all-night dancing that seemed to leave him buoyant and his onlookers exhausted.[96]

The use of dance to glide into a trance is a very important technique. It is not an exclusive feature of shamanism; different sects and individuals have used it, too: the Whirling Dervishes, from Turkey to Iran; the Rufaim, or the mystic self-mutilators and snake handlers, whose feats I witnessed in Egypt; Gurdjieff; Nijinsky—the list has not even begun. Nijinsky's biographer, Nandor Fodor—an experienced reporter in his own right, and a psychiatrist with very strong interests in psychic research (and reportedly in his subject's wife)— observed in *Between Two Worlds,* his book on the life of the great Russian dancer, that the audiences in Paris had seemed captivated by an incredible peculiarity: it was not so much the height of Nijinsky's leaps as the slow speed of his descent. In a conversation with Nijinsky's wife, Romola, who was also Fodor's friend, the biographer was informed of Nijinsky's inability to comprehend why other dancers could not control the rate at which they came down in their leaps, and Romola added, too, that when she had once told her husband how unfortunate it was that he could not observe himself dance, his reply had been, "I do! Always. I am outside. I make myself dance from the outside." Today, this method may be termed "creative visualization." However, how far removed, indeed, is visualization from one of the techniques employed by a shaman or by a disciple of Zen?

The Whirling (*Mevlevi*) Dervishes have chosen the rhythm of dance for their technique to the ecstatic state. The participants perform the final phases of the ritual in a spinning momentum, with revolutions per minute varying from thirty to sixty-five and above. With rigid bodies, and tranquil faces, the men whirl and whirl until they enter *hal*, a state of trance by which they achieve fusion with "the divine harmony." This specific path consists of three stages: (1) Negative Unity—where the soul, exalted, is rid of its identity and emptied of all substance; yet, harmonized through simple bliss with all creation. (2) Power—not achievable by all; it requires purposive manipulations of consciousness and will, at a time when the soul is divested of ordinary desires. All so-called paranormal activities, which are associated with shamanistic flights of ecstasy, are manifest in this stage, including the understanding of other people's thoughts, and the awareness of events occurring in other places (a phenomenon which occurs also in a trance induced by hallucinogenic substances, such as *yajé*). These mysterious powers are explained by analogy with western technology, such as radio waves, where, by tuning to a certain (invisible) frequency, one becomes aware of happenings elesewhere. (3) Positive Unity—a mystical state in which the soul is infused with "emotional beautitude" and abilities to form "conscious visions of beauty and glory," while being, at the same time, cognizant of its higher state of consciousness (SSC). From this point onward begins the transcendental locus of the ultimate mystery, an awesome power, capable of both good and evil.

The Sufi philosophy, nevertheless, recognizes that such doctrines, if taken in lieu of experience, account for very little, and constitute hollow shells. The real meaning must be placed into them by each individual. God is neither a judge nor an admonishing parental moralizer, but Life itself. A Sufi mystic seeks unity with all life, through the profundity of ecstatic and visionary experiences.

As an adjunct in the induction of trance, controlled breathing is practiced seriously in many different areas. Mircea Eliade, who spent a considerable time among the yogins of India, has conjectured that the breathing technique encountered in yogic disciplines had been received from Indo-European shamanism, with which he has, in particular, connected the breathing method. However, breath-control, as a technique in the attainment of mystical states, is found to be distributed the world over and is not the exclusive domain of Indo-European shamans and their direct successors. The Jewish Kabbalists have practiced a technique of shallow, but rapid breathing in their meditative trances to attain the feeling of God's spirit within, described by the Greek word *entheoi*, and comparable to the ascending soul-journey of the shaman.

The Chinese Taoists have been known to utilize a similar method, in addition to a technique of ecstatic dance. Both procedures in this mystical system were inspired by certain animals, which, to this day, have remained significant components in the ancient niche of Chinese shamanistic memory. A great ruler should possess the abilities of a magician. Ecstasy is one of his main attributes—bestowing sovereignty, or authority, over men and the natural world (as witnessed, too, among the Celtic kings). A dance is one of the ancient techniques that can bring on the ecstatic experience. The Sinologist, Marcel Granet, remarks that the dance step of a certain great king, Yü, "does not differ from the dances that induce trance in the sorcerers *(t'iao-shen)*. . . . The ecstatic dance forms part of the procedures for acquiring a power of command over men and nature. We know that this regulating power, in the so-called Taoist as in the so-called Confucian texts, is called Tao."[97] In order to incarnate the spirits that possessed her, a sorceress in a ceremonial garb, and cleansed with scented water, "with a flower in her hand, she mimed her journey [in quest of a mystical experience] by a dance accompanied by music and songs, to the sound of drums and flutes, until she fell exhausted. This was the moment of the presence of the god [the numen] who answered through her mouth."[98]

In his monumental work on the religions of China, Jan de Groot, most unsympathetic to supernatural phenomena, informs us of the whirling dances performed by the female *wu*, of their becoming mouth-pieces for the spirits and the souls of the deceased, and of telekinetics involving all kinds of rising objects moving through the air.[99] These practices, which Eliade calls fakiristic phenomena, have survived until this day among Chinese magicians and spirit-handlers. Magic was rooted deeply in the ancient tradition of China and the Far East. Among the many categories included were "magical flights" or ecstatic journeys and, among the better-informed Chinese folk in antiquity, the word "flight" became a euphemism for "ecstasy."

A stone carving from the Han Dynasty depicts two horned and winged shamans kneeling with the celestial *Ling-chih* mushroom (of Emperor Wu's famous odes) visible behind one of them, while a raven—an avian creature abounding in shamanistic power—hovers above. There is little doubt that the horned individuals with wings indeed represent shamans. Magical flights, as noted above, have shamanistic origins in China. An ascent-journey of transformation and immortality is accomplished by means of wings (translated as "feathers"), according to Taoist doctrines,[100] which abound in the descriptions of ascending flights and other preternatural happenings. The feather is a common symbol of shamanistic flights, and it is quite likely, as Eliade conjectures,[101] that the Taoists, devising more systematic techniques, expanded the shamanistic practices of prehistoric and protohistoric China.

As seemingly indicated by his actions, Emperor Wu (of the beloved fungus) appears to be a shaman-king. Unquestionably, it is noteworthy that in China *wu* was a general term for a shaman. Certainly not shamans in the true meaning of the word, but rather more like shaman-priests, the *wu* priests and *wu*-ism—(as de Groot refers to it) dominated the religious scene in China during the first century before the present era. Thus, prior to the spread of Confucianism and the state religion, these hierophants performed the roles of healers, exorcists, intermediaries between men and the spirits, and reincarnators of souls of the dead.[102] The designation of the *wu*, however, had been initially reserved for any of the female-shamans, or so-called sorceresses, and was still in use in its original sense during the fifth century B.C. The female *wu* had been most likely preceded by the "dancing shaman," vested in bearskin and reverberating the religious male ideology surrounding the magic of the hunt. These ancient, bearskin-covered shamans were identified possibly among the inscriptions coming from the Shang (?1766–?1122 B.C.) and the early Chou (c. 1127/22–770 B.C.) periods.[103] Two dancing figures wearing antlers, depicted on a bronze vessel from a late Chou period, are recognized unilaterally as representing shamans.[104] The Chinese record for the archaic period offers also sufficient documentation on the shamans and their costumes.[105]

With the birth of the religion of the Mother-Goddess and the re-emergence of women-oriented cults in the Mesolithic and the Neolithic, there was not much to preclude, in later China, the coexistence of the male shamans with the female *wu* and her magico-religious beliefs, leading to the eventual predominance of the latter. The erotic and "wanton" elements surfaced in *wu* rituals, as well. Thus, the female *wu* grew to astonishing numbers, even in the midst of the fifth and the first century B.C., at a time when both men and women were embracing this religious belief.[106] In the course of time, the phenomenon of possession, strongly associated with *wu*-ism as a whole, came to resemble shamanism encountered among Manchu, Tungus, and the Siberian folk—and the ranks of women as ritual practitioners were drastically reduced.

Mongolian Shamanism

A great deal that can be learned about the nature of Siberian and Mongolian shamanism comes from centuries-old oral traditions in the form of hymns, prayers, and chants. It was in the Altaic region that the shamanistic religion, with the worship of ancestral spirits as its corner-stone, had reached its classic expression before later infusions from external sources, particularly Lamaist Buddhism, produced a more recent hybrid. The spirits could "offer help against the threat to life posed by the powers of evil, forces of nature conceived of in personified form . . . [and] the protection of man and of his property against all dangers and afflictions from illness or other catastrophe brought about by the powers of evil appears to be the primary function of shamanism."[107]

However, the impressions forged by visiting European clerics were not indicative of such an understanding. One of the first European descriptions of a shamanistic ceremony anywhere is to be found in the report by a Franciscan monk, Vilhelms av Ruysbroeck, who was sent to Mongolia, from 1253 to 1255, by King Louis IX of France. Though he perceived the hand of the devil, as was the custom of the day, in all religious rites that were considered heathen by the church , his account proves to be invaluable, for it demonstrates that the shamanistic ritual of the Mongols has stayed, in principle, very much the same for many centuries.

> Some of them appeal to devils and gather together by night those seeking an oracular answer from an evil spirit at their home, where they place boiled meat in the middle of the house. The oracle (*cham*) intending to invoke the spirits begins his sorcery and frenziedly beats the ground with drum. At last he begins to get wild and lets himself be bound. Then the evil spirit comes in the dark, he gives it meat to eat, and it utters the oracular answer.[108]

The shaman's practice was not always confined to matters con-cerning spirits and the supernatural. What held true for certain parts of Siberia could also be encountered in Mongolia, where the shamans exerted, at times, so strong an influence in the cultural and political spheres of the society that it created powerful undercurrents, if not outright visible impacts, in the course of history and development of their people.

The mighty Chingis Khan was a very strong believer in shamanistic powers, and genuinely concerned with the will of the Heavenly Being, called the Everlasting Blue Sky, and of his own guardian spirits. To this effect, he very frequently sought the counsel of the shamans, who could also augur the future. One of his spiritual advisors was Kokchu, later to be known as Teb-Tngri, who belonged to a family somewhat related to that of the great Khan. Kokchu, the shaman, possessed high aspirations towards political leadership and a talent for Machiavellian machinations. He conspired against Chingis Khan by plotting to implicate falsely the latter's brother, Qasar. Teb-Tngri informed the Khan that the guardian spirits had appeared with a warning against Qasar, pointing him as a dangerous element to the cause of the Mongol leader, and consequently the shaman urged strongly that Qasar be eliminated.

For quite some time, the family of Chingis Khan, especially his brothers, endured indignations from the offices of shaman Teb-Tngri, while the latter took advantage of the Khan's respect and awe for shamanistic practices. Nevertheless, this situation could not continue indefinitely, for the authority of Chingis Khan was being indirectly challenged. Therefore, when the shaman arrogantly spread a new slander against the Khan's youngest brother, Chingis this time issued instructions that his brother deal with Teb-Tngri in any way he saw fit. The shaman died from a broken spine, and his death marked the demise of the last considerable opposition to the confederated authority of Chingis Khan.

A special tradition had developed, and then assembled, known as *The Secret History of the Mongols*. It is the oldest Mongol historical source and resembles secret shamanic lore, of which it is probably a by-product. Hence, when a religious cult was established around the apotheosis of the historical Chingis Khan it was nothing else than the application of an old, basic tenet of shamanism known so well to the Mongols.

The origin of Mongolian shamanism is rendered by a traditional account from the Chahar region, undoubtedly of an aetiological nature—that is, an old myth attempting to explain the existence of a still older ritual behavior—which underscores the importance of the ancestor cult and the shaman's relevance as a socio-religious mediator.

At a time when the Mongols still lived in their ancestral home in northern Khangai there was an old man who already had access to certain magical practices. When he felt his death approaching, he told his son that he would continue to protect him after his death into his later life, if he would bury him with all honour and make offerings to him at later times as well. The son did this after his father's death and buried him on a high place, the Red Rock. Burial on a high place is a trait which can be followed through the entire history of the Mongols. The example of Ulanhad or Hungshan, a hill near the town of Lin-hsi in south-western Manchuria, shows that high-lying places were especially sought after as burial sites. Here various Stone-Age burial sites were found of a mixed population of Tungus and Mongols, which shows into what distant times the memory of Mongolian tradition reaches back. The legend reports further that the son made regular offerings to the dead man of tea, water and milk and spirits at his father's grave on the first, seventh and ninth day of each new moon. At this time the father's spirit became friendly with the Lords of the Earth, the local spirits, and became ever more powerful. Thus he became able to make lightning and hail fall and to cause misfortune. In this manner he placed himself under Ataγa Tngri, one of the oldest and most widely known shamanist deities, who is often thought of as being personally identical with the all-ruling Eternal Sky. When his mother died, the son buried her too in a similar manner in a high place and sacrificed to her too. She also associated as a spirit with the other ancestral spirits and so acquired the power of flying, of controlling clouds, thunder and lightning and also commanding rain and hail. Besides this she could cause misfortune to men and cattle and poison their health and blood. She began to be worshipped as Emegelji Eji, "the very old grandmother". The population, which in this way began to feel the might of these two powerful spirits, discussed what they could do to propitiate and pacify them. The spirits were requested through the offerings to be merciful. Thereupon the spirit of the dead father entered a man, who began to tremble. From then on he was worshipped as the black protective spirit (Qara Sakiγulsun). The spirit of the dead mother did the same, entering a girl who also began to tremble convulsively. This spirit was from then on worshipped as Emegelji Eji. These two were now able to fly while they were possessed by their protective spirits. Once, when they were in ecstasy and possessed by the spirits, they flew to the burial place of the two ancestors. There they found drums with wooden supports and also head-ornaments made of the feathers of a yellow bird. Both were handed on to them by the protective spirits. When they struck their drums, they flew back and stepped on one tent after another. Striking their drums they sang as they went, "To help all living beings we bear the golden drums. We have descended from Ataγa Tngri to protect all living beings on this earth." The people that heard them said that they must indeed be very mighty protective gods. Thereupon the two requested them to be pious and to offer the libations of tea, milk, spirits and water, so that they could protect them from all evil. Thereupon the people called them shaman *(böge)* and shamaness *(niduγan)* and made offerings to them as they requested. Later they made images of them, making the body from the skin of a year-old lamb and its eyes from black berries. They called these images by their names and referred to them as Ongghon.[109]

Thus, shamanism was born in Mongolia—at least, according to a native legend—through the will of ancestral spirits, ecstatic seizures, and flying mounts (the shamans' drums). Mountain tops have been the dwelling places of deities and spirits. However, in the face of the awesomeness exuded by the high sanctity of such places, coming from the numen of the residing supernatural beings, it is forbidden to utter the name of such a sacred mountain. The shamanistic attributes, if not origins, of the cult of the mountain gods can be observed unequivocally in the northwest corner of Mongolia, near the lake of Khobso Gol, where the shamans and other religious suppliants have venerated the mountain god, Khan Boγda Dayan Degereki Khayirkhan, in the form of the holy mountain. The designation *khayirkhan*, meaning "the loved, the beautiful," is a euphemistic allusion to this sacred topographic outcrop. Perhaps Dayan Degereki is to be equated with Odin, the Great Shaman of the Norsemen, also a healer and a master of metals.

Khan, Black Tngri [a sometime epithet of Dayan Degereki]
With medicine in your thumb,
With magical healing-power in your index-finger,
With a breast of mineral bronze,
With a hindpart of iron ore. . . .[110]

The Celtic Religion

"The Chosen Ones" among the Irish Celts were able to reside at the bottom of the water, transformed into fish, only to emerge later as deified personages or heavenly beings. The source of all life was the principal goddess, with whom the prospective king entered into a sexual union. All too frequently, she was a water deity, as well. In the Irish *Lebhar na Huidre*, we have a story of the rape of the female guardian of a magic spring in Ulster. As a result of this assault, the water in the spring rises, innundating the land and effecting disaster. The king loses his life; however, his daughter, Libane, changed into a salmon, manages to survive for one year at the bottom of Lough Neagh. After three hundred years, she returns as the Great Goddess Morrigan.[111] The French scholar, Jean Markale, offers the following comment in his *Celtic Civilization*:

> The overflowing spring is obviously a sexual symbol of fertility. The woman guarding it is identified with the spring, just as the vagina is symbolized by the well. The fact that once raped she becomes fertile is sufficient an argument to suggest that the myth of the flood is not always a myth of punishment and destruction.[112]

In contrast to the flood, Markale elaborates with an additional remark, "The Hebraic tradition, in which woman's status was diminished and god became a solitary male warrior or shepherd, and the Islamic religion which it inspired, were both conceived by nomads used to the dryness of the desert."[113] Therefore, the Celtic goddess is linked to floodwaters, wetness, and fertility, while the solitary sky-god is associated with heat (fire), dryness, and dessication. Since water is the medium for the goddess's power, it becomes evident that the water theme is associated, here, with death and rebirth. But we also have a description of a shamanic journey into the Lowerworld. After an ordeal, which distinctly qualifies as an inner personal crisis, the shamaness (perhaps still an initiate) embarks on her soul-journey to the bottom of a lake, which, as an archetypal symbol, corresponds to the labyrinthine maze. At the bottom of the lake co-exist, as a part of the same continuum, forces of creation and destruction—life and death, wisdom and eternity. After a long and patient journey to the Otherworld, she returns revitalized, transformed, and transcended—even immortal.

In the late autumnal ritual, known as *Samain*, one of the principal Celtic rites centered around the selection and installation of a new chieftain, or a king, the chief acquired his validated sovereignty, that is, the authority to rule, through a sexual union with the goddess of the land (the Earth-Goddess). The latter endowed her mate with the gift of clear intelligence and ability to experience visions and dreams.[114] ". . .The power of sovereignty bestows upon its holder the gift of wisdom and vision, in actuality an ability to dream dreams."[115] At the same time, the connection between shamanistic techniques of visionary experiences and the use of psychotropic substances is clearly evidenced in the following content: "One of the personifications of the goddess of sovereignty to whom the king is wed is Flaith. The Irish word *flaith* translates as sovereignty but also has association in myth with strong drink or intoxication."[116] There is reason to believe that "sovereignty is a bride, the server of a powerful drink, and the drink itself."[117] Thus, the meaning can be further distilled to yield ". . . an identity between woman/goddess, beer/intoxication, and wisdom/vision,"[118] a notion likewise reinforced by the second meaning of the name Medb, used by the goddess of the land as her other personifications. Medb, according to the Rees brothers, translates as intoxication, and its Welsh and English cognates are, respectively, *meddw* (drink) and *mead* (the fermented beer/wine).

The Celts constituted an integral part of the Indo-European tribal populations, among whom hunting, cattle raiding, and bride stealing were traditional activities with very strong roots in the cultural history. Two of the practices, perhaps even all three, fit into analogous structural patterns, demonstrating similarities at the mythopoeic level. All of them serve as reflections of the *imago mundi*, or the archetypal paradigm of the universe and its re-creation. The archetypal, or Otherworldly connections between the shaman, the smith, hunting magic, and hallucinogens are loomed in many a folk tale, such as of Niall and his half-brothers. A smith furnishes them with implements forged specially for the hunt, and thus, duly equipped, they venture into a forest wherein they lose their way (inner personal crisis, or IPC). The brothers take turns in their efforts to deal with a black hag (symbol of oblivion and death) guarding a watersource. Finally, it is Niall who consents to kiss and embrace her (IPC of a high degree) in exchange for water. On account of his willingness to mate with her (i.e., death), the hag transforms herself into an exceptional beauty, whom Niall finds laying beside him upon opening his eyes. At this point, the woman discloses her identity as Flaith, sovereignty incarnate, and foretells Niall his fate as a future king[119] and the founder of a ruling dynasty.

Structurally, this tale exhibits a transcultural theme, which fits into the seasonal cycles of regeneration associated with the Earth-Goddess, whom the king or a would-be king must annually wed and fertilize in order to promote bounty of the hunt and fecundity of the earth. Niall's willingness to become the consort of the black hag (the dying year) qualifies him for the candidacy of a kingship. Willingness is the will to transcend, to assent to a sacrifice—and the gods and goddesses are pleased by a willing offering. In exchange, as a reward, Flaith will infuse him with wisdom by drugging or intoxicating Niall during their union. To reach the source of wisdom, therefore, the prospective king must cohabit with the goddess. It is through his dying (IPC) and being reborn (initiation) that he will obtain the gift of vision, and through this union, which is a form of sacrifice, nature will be revitalized and reborn, too. The king, as the cosmic fertilizer—producer of the archetypal sperm—stands for both entities at the same time: the essential substance and its symbol. When he, in due time, grows old, a younger seed will replace his; unlike the eternal goddess who merely transits through the phases of lunar cycles—new, full, and waning—yet, always combining into a single whole. The processes of death and rebirth make up the formative strata of the cyclical (repetitive) traditions and do not contribute as much to the historical (linear) traditions, where the events become fixed in space and time, as witnessed by the theologies and sacred histories of the so-called revealed religions. Here, we thus possess an interesting phase of syncretism, involving the Mother-Goddess—her tradition of eternal return and "the ritual of returned blood"—as she becomes assimilated with some of the transculturally recurrent themes of shamanism, including the use of hallucinogenic substances.

It is distinctly possible, although not proven, that, in addition to a strong goddess cult, shamanistic practices were deeply entrenched among the Celts, and women played a crucial role in them. W.J. Brenneman, Jr. astutely observes that "Feminine power, for the most part, lay in the background, or more precisely underground in what was termed the Otherworld,"[120] a place to which, he should have been aware, the shamans travel to gain knowledge and insight, and encounter their helping spirits and familiars. Thus, however perceptive his observation might be, I believe that he did not realize the full import of his remark.

The Role of the Shaman

The institution of shamanism, in its general form, gave rise to a number of particular functions, one of them being that of a ritual specialist, in the sense of a religious leader, or a priest. Consequently, a shaman can be described as a man, or less frequently a woman (shamaness), whose roles in the community, in addition to the obvious religious one, entail several of secular nature. His rank affords him social status, economic considerations, and political influence, if not outright authority. It was noted that as early as the seventeenth century, the Buryat Mongols had been fighting under the leaderships of their shamans in wars against the Russians. Among some clans of the Tungus, as with the Vadeyev Samoyed of northern Siberia, the shamans were, on occasions, the actual chiefs.

At the same time, rivaling shamans of the Evenks led combat groups, on the opposite sides of the Yenisei River, against one another.

By the same token it should not be surprising, Harner tells us,[121] that among the Jívaro, who believe intensely in shamanistic powers to cause ailments and fatalities; who maintain strife over women, and a state of requiting, tribal, feuding warfare; who lack "any formal political organization" and a unilineal kinship structure; we find their chiefs to be "outstanding killers and shamans." Such positions of leadership, however informal, are earned and valued within the social group. Shamans (*uwišin*) are in preponderance to "outstanding killers" (*kakaram*). The former adhere to their tasks, openly motivated by the principal goal of acquiring material rewards—a situation that tends to make them the most affluent members in their community. Combined with the fact that they almost never participate in the customary gift exchange—a very strong, traditional, native practice—and instead always receive without reciprocating, the shamans are the only ones capable of accumulating large quantities of material wealth.

Similarly, the roles of the Cubeo shamans, in the Northwest Amazon, include many of the general functions encountered in other shamanistic cultures: from weather control to the supernatural combat between shamans. The latter activity is, of course, important in the demonstration of the jaguar-shaman's power. As a result, the *yavi* (jaguar-shaman) is feared for his brutal destructiveness to the extent that even his benevolent deeds, such as curing and other ecologically important tasks, do not assuage his awesome fame as a "killer."[122]

As a consequence of his "calling," the shaman is, generally, prevented from subsistence activities, such as hunting and fishing. In northern Siberia, the reindeer-breeding Evenks were obligated to combine their efforts in sustaining the shamans with regular contributions of supplies by the clan members and annual gifts of animals from each family.[123] The Eskimo shaman (*angakok*, pl. *angákut*) engages in healing, ecstatic trances, underwater descent-journeys to the Mother of Animals (cf., for example, Mistress of the Animals in the ancient Aegean and Asia Minor) for abundant game and fish, as well as, for cures of female sterility. Like the Mongol counterpart, his social rank is intermixed with political authority, adding to his influence in the community. The Eskimo terms for the shaman, *angakok*, and for the "leader," *angajkok*, share the same root. The Lapp shamans, *noiaidi*, can summon herds of wild reindeer, by possessing the ability to communicate with wild animals, as well as being able to transform themselves into animal forms, as, for example, a wolf, a bear, a reindeer, or a fish.

As a point of related interest, we may note that the belief in a human's ability to change into an animal form also flourished in Europe and other parts of the world. In Renaissance Italy, where the growth and development of the arts and the sciences were looked upon as the beacons of the civilizing influence of the new age of scientific materialism, and which produced such giants as Leonardo da Vinci, many learned and respected books were published on the metamorphosis of people into animals. Among such authors was a friend and a colleague of Galileo, Giovanni Batista Porta, who published on this topic in the book, *Naturall Magick*, describing the process of metamorphosis by the use of psychotropic substances. In a preface to the 1658 edition of this work, Giovanni Porta wrote: "I pass over other men. . . who affirm that I am a Witch and a Conjurer, whereas I never writ here nor elsewhere, what is not contain'd within the bounds of Nature." Perhaps the stories of the werewolf are, indeed, relics of a shamanic lore, and the tales about Dracula bite back further than Vlad the Impaler of Rumania.

Hence, in the person of a shaman is embodied, all at once, the community's healer, the mystic, and the intellectual. Among the North American Indians, leadership does not depend solely on bravery, intelligence, and individual ability, but also on the power of the chief's medicine. One of the basic functions within the chief's scope is the comprehension of processes and situations, both natural and supernatural, and the possession of a store of knowledge pertaining to all things necessary in human existence. Thus, he acts as a seer, or a clairvoyant, auguring natural and man-made events, such as cataclysms or warfare, and it may be expected of him to seek intervention with the spirits—at least, explanations for such happenings—and to abort their future recurrences. He will deal with matters pertaining to the community as a social unit, or apply his skills to individual cases. As a custodian of the sacred myths and traditions, the shaman is the "memory of his people," a mythologue and a genealogist. As an epic singer, he is the chanter of tribal lore. Along with being a ritual practitioner, his complementary function consists of keeping the calendar for all the important phases that define the lives of his people. After his death, a powerful shaman may become the helping spirit of living shamans. On rare occasions, after years of repeated propitiations and calls for assistance, the spirit of a great shaman, dwelling in the Otherworld, may come gradually to be identified with a deity. Such happenings define the transcendental process of apotheosis, whereby one is transformed from mortal status and attains a divine one.

The shaman's participation is required at the rites of passage, the vital points in one's life, such as birth, marriage, and death. His involvement does not include the deliveries of newborn, a task left to the midwives still from the days of the Great Mother and her followers. He acts, however, as a spiritual figure and a mediator between the spirit world and this one during the marriage ritual, and as the soul-guide, or a psychopomp, for the deceased on their journeys to the Otherworld. The shamans of the Tukanoan Indians in the Amazon rain forest, for example, are entrusted with overseeing the community's welfare, caring both for the individual and the group. However, their primary function, which takes precedent over everything else—reports Gérardo Reichel-Dolmatoff, the prominent authority on Amazonian religious concepts—consists of maintaining a balance within the society and nature.

Based upon a vast store of empirical knowledge (ethnoscience) and a probing insight into human behavior, the shaman performs the function of an important psychological and cultural *adaptive mechanism*. When the physical and spiritual conditions are not in equilibrium, resulting in illness, natural calamity or other disaster, a Navajo *hatali*, or medicine man, is expected to bring back *hozho*—harmony, balance, and beauty. He may do so with the aid of a ceremonial sand painting. Thus, he is not merely a healer of diseases, but also a restorer of balance to social dysfunctions, where "a syndrome of maladaptive behavior" may exist. The sociocultural importance of his role as an agent in transcendental and metaphysical realities is, as a result, de-emphasized by those who tend to view the shaman's role more in ecological terms.[124] As such, his intellectual abilities, especially those concerned with issues related to the culture-environment system, are held to be immensely critical, surpassing all others in importance.[125]

The mental and physical processes involved in shamanistic states of consciousness are not necessarily regarded by the practitioners as phenomenonologically extra-ordinary, mysterious, or arcane. Neither is the coexistence of other realities viewed in a dualistic perspective, nor as a dichotomy, but rather it is perceived in a holistic sense, as a part of a larger monistic system. Humans devise subjective categories, analytic constructs, by which they slice and interpret the world. However, to ensure survival on all levels cognitive meanings must be acquired; these can readily be found in the parallel extensions comprising the Other-worlds, and accessible via the mechanisms embodied in the techniques employed by the shamans. Through the rituals, the shaman structures the perennial quest for purpose and metaphor. He formulates meanings, relevant on both the individual and the social levels, which afford ideological worth and ecological possibility to human existence. As a result, the social status of shamans, as leaders in the community, commands respect, and these individuals tend to comprise the "intellectuals" of the social unit.[126] It has been suggested that observing a ceremony directed by a shaman may help illuminate the developmental process by which the shaman was gradually transformed into a priest.[127]

The methods by which the Mongol shaman is able to perform his shamanizing[128] activities involve "the seeing of things," or visions, and the helpful participation of well-disposed spirits. Two journalists, a Canadian and an American, offered the following description upon their return from the Soviet Union, where they had pursued information on psychic phenomena:

> The *shamans*, the holy men or "witch doctors" of Siberia, could supposedly communicate telepathically, see clairvoyantly, travel out of their bodies, predict the future, and heal the sick. They did not use psychic talent for its own sake. *Shamans* were the mainstays, the social pivots of their peoples. As their talent could mean life or death to the tribe, it was not a position lightly come by. If you felt the calling, your retired to the woods to learn. Periodically the apprentice underwent extreme examinations.[129]

It has been reported that a potential shaman exhibits a psychological predisposition to "the calling," which eliminates his choice, and assumes a compulsory guise. "Had I not become a shaman, I would have died," was a statement confided by a Gilyak shaman from southeastern Siberia. The various psychological and neurophysiological factors that enter into play in determining or indicating the future shaman, often manifest themselves as a so-called shamanic illness, and in the far north such a condition may occur at the time of the Arctic sickness. This condition may be the possible result of physiochemical changes in the individual's nervous system, and is particularly apt to occur in the Arctic environment. Whatever the case may be, it is clear that in the majority of instances, the shamans undergo incredible initiatory experiences and agons.

A true shaman-neophyte can refine his shamanizing skills by serving as an apprentice to a master shaman, but, unlike a medicine man or a sorceror, he must acquire these abilities by intuition, as it were, which is enhanced in the course of his initiatory experiences—that is, through the teachings of the spirits—and not by learning a specific body of doctrines. The prominent scholar of shamanism, Vilmos Diószegi, rightly stressed an important distinction with his remark:

> Phenomena similar to some of the traits of shamanism may be found among primitive peoples everywhere in the world. Such detached traits, however, are not necessarily shamanistic. The central personalities in such systems—sorcerers, medicine men, and the like—may communicate with the other world through ecstasy, but, unlike the shaman, they have attained their

position through deliberate study and the application of rational knowledge. Although they perform ceremonies as priests, hold positions of authority, and possess magical abilities, the structure and quality of their transcendental activities are entirely different from that of the shaman.[130]

To classify a native culture qualitatively as not shamanistic does not imply a derision of its spiritual depth, ritual prowess, healing knowledge, or, for that matter, the transformative impact of its religious ecstasy. There are many paths that can be followed to achieve these manifestations, and some of them are, indeed, akin to those taken up by the shamans. Shamanism is not an end unto itself; it constitutes a specialized body of acquired techniques, leading to altered states of consciousness to facilitate ecstatic transformations, with the purpose of attaining mystical or spiritual experiences. The meaning of these experiences is derived from the glimpses into a corresponding reality, which we call the Otherworld. So, it is not the goal that separates shamanism from the other forms, it is its method. Consequently, those who perceive shamanistic beliefs in every old religion are prompted to exercise caution. It is easy to confuse folk beliefs and spirit possession with shamanism.[131] Thus, the following passage could appear as a description of the latter—and yet!

Old Russia, [write Sheila Ostrander and Lynn Schroeder, without a dispassionate tone but not without an ethnocentric bias] wasn't just a hotbed of superstition; she was a six-thousand-mile botanical garden of superstition. Almost every grotesque known to the world and some not known elsewhere sucked up nourishment in Russia. . . . Superstition in old Russia was as concrete and pernicious as the lice infesting most of the populace. Magic spells, amulets, potions, powders, and counter-hexes were widely considered to be necessities of life. . . .

Generally, however, there was more of Caliban than Ariel in the omnipresent unseen. Judging from accounts, there were traffic jams of unclean spirits to get in and out of benighted Russians. Doctors' records of the late nineteenth century speak of women in a part of northern Russia who were all periodically possessed by screaming demons who drove them to beat everyone in sight, break dishes, froth, dance, and curse until they keeled over and the demons fled. The society expected this possession and, probably as a result of this, it occurred more or less annually.[132]

The role played by an indigenous society in creating and in acknowledging shamans is expressed through the cultural dynamics affecting the designation, rather than the definition, of what constitutes mental and physical anomalies. Extraordinary behavior, or various forms of so-called mental disorders, may help in recognizing or designating a future shaman; so may certain physical abnormalities, such as an extra finger or a toe, special birth markings, or even an extra tooth. Whether we deal with individuals whose mental states can be assessed, by Western criteria, as being on a fringe of sanity or schizophrenia, is hardly an appropriate issue. The Western cultures do not possess equivalent metaphors (existential wisdom, as opposed to didactic knowledge) to pass value or diagnostic judgments on phenomena that have definitely proven to be functionally adaptive within their respective cultural contexts, and which are neither fully understood nor adequately experienced in the West. Shamanism, if I may adapt an idea I expressed long ago, is an idiomatic expression of culture, and not merely a behavioral response—the relationship of a single individual (the shaman) to his biocultural environment:

> It concerns a social community, often a cultural unit, which accepted a mode of behavior suited for a homeostatic relationship with the prevailing conditions. This mode, if socially approved, becomes the preferred, even the ideal, form of responses to a prescribed situation. Thus, possessing an adaptive feature, as far as function is concerned... [shamanism] constitutes a broader dimension... by which the relationship of human society to its milieu is reflected not through the instrumentality of technology, but through the system of [metaphors and] social organization.[133]

3

Subtance and Function
of Shamanism

Definitions and Problems

THE TERM "SHAMAN"¹ is derived from the Tungus-Mongol, or the
Tungus-Manchu, noun-word, *šaman*, which is constructed from the Indo-
European verb-root, *ša-*, meaning "to know." Thus, the French *savoir* and
the Spanish *saber*, "to know," produce also linguistic relationships with
such words as "witch" or "wizard" from the Indo-European root "to see"
or "to know," as in the French *voir* and Latin *videre*, "to see," and the
German *wissen*, "to know." Hence, the cognate *šaman* conveys the literal
meaning of "he who knows." It is very possible that the Tungus-Mongol
šaman possesses a cognate in the Sanskrit *sramana*, meaning "an
ascetic." While in Pali, *samana*, "a beggar monk," may represent a true,
but a later, cognate of the Altaic *šaman*.

The spiritual character of shamanism is defined, not by a codified
body of dogmas, but rather by a particularistic quality of its belief system,
typified, no less, by the structural elements in representing its Otherworldly reality. How are we, otherwise, to interpret the religious beliefs
of the Palaeolithic inhabitants of the painted caves? Or, for that matter,
what can be said about the religion of the Uralic tribes in Siberia, the
Amazonian Indians, or the dreamtime of the Australian aborigines?
These peoples have not devised elaborate pantheons. Nor do they worship

69

a single supreme demiurge or possess codified scriptures. Have they a religion?

Any genuine, mystical experience of the preternatural (be it highly personal or structured by codices) must be recognized as part of a religious phenomenology. The impact of shamanism as a proto-religious and religious idiom on the dynamics of the historico- and the psychocultural processes the world over, has been felt, very likely, for the last 100,000 years or so. In his erudite study on the development of religion, Weston La Barre writes: ". . . the ancestor of the god is the shaman himself, both historically and psychologically. There were shamans before there were gods. The very earliest religious data we know from archaeology show dancing masked sorcerors or shamans of Lascaux, Trois Frères, and other Old Stone Age caves."[2]

Despite the fact that Eliade considered shamanism to be a religious complex, he did, at one point, suggest that perhaps this phenomenon might more appropriately belong "among the mysticisms than with what is commonly called a religion."[3] The data generated by current research in this field do not support such a narrow view without major qualifications. This contention, however, did find a reverberation in Åke Hultkrantz, who prefers to regard shamanism as "a religious configuration" (a mythico-ritual system, a religious metaphor), instead of a true religion.[4] Moreover, states Hultkrantz elsewhere, "The religious pattern," in North and South America, is "somewhat inappropriately called shamanism," owing to the crucial role played by the medicine man, or shaman, in the spiritual and ceremonial life of the indigenous community. Yet, not all medicine men in the New World are shamans in a strict adherence to this concept, which presupposes ecstasy to be the main technique in achieving communication with the spirit world. Therefore, he feels that this term should be used to signify the shaman's worldviews and ritual performances instead of denoting "an entire religious pattern."[5]

Though many cultures exhibit traits which, on the surface, may appear to be shamanistic, such features may create a misleading perspective of "detached traits," if viewed outside their ritual context and not as traits that are in adhesion with the entire cultural complex. Therefore, it is essential to differentiate between true shamanistic ideology and practice, and a religious complex where shamanistic phenomena form marginal and isolated traits. The late specialist on shamanistic religion Vilmos Diószegi was among the first to make a distinction between shamans, on one hand, and, on the other, ordinary medicine men, sorcerors, the Middle American *curanderos*, the prosaic Vodoun priests, and other mediators of the preternatural.[6]

Figure 3.1. Curandero's *botanicas* and power objects, displayed for sale in the town of Minatitlan, Veracruz, Mexico. (Photograph by the author).

Of course, it must be understood that religious syncretisms have inadvertently occurred between shamanistic complexes and other belief systems composing the framework of world religions. However, an important question still remains: What are the psychocultural processes leading a person toward the path of shamanism?

"Answering the Call," Initiation, and Shamanic Enlightenment

Irrespective of space and time, whether in the tropical forest of the Amazon, in the ice-cold of the Arctic, or in the steppes and the highlands of Central Asia; in the present or in the ancient past, those with the need to respond to the call of becoming shamans have done so in very similar ways, undergoing analogous ordeals, which indicate to us the transcultural nature of the phenomenology of shamanistic experience. A prospective shaman is chosen by the spirits, and he discovers his calling through an inner personal crisis (IPC). He may find out that his selection has been underscored by some physical or mental anomaly, like an extra digit on his hand or foot or an extra tooth; he may be prone to spells of possession or fainting. The Finnish counterpart of a shaman, *tietäjä*, can also be identified by a physical abnormality. The patronage and good will of the spirits elevate the shaman's rank in his society. Personal ethos and worldview are a product of the individual's mental state and physiological condition, and the balance between the last two influences his internal harmony and the level of stress or anxiety. Hence, the often-quoted statement of a Gilyak from southeast Siberia: "Had I not become a shaman, I would have died," rings true for many of the candidates, revealing, at the same time, a great deal about the personal characteristics of the acolytes and the nature of this religion.

Neither do the Mehinaku Indians of the Upper Xingu River in central Brazil select purposively the shamanic vocation of *yetamá*; this choice is owed to an inner personal crisis manifest as encounters with spirits, such as monkey demons, impelling the persons in question to become *yetamá*. After such a dream, or a sequence thereof, follows shamanic illness, bringing in the local *yetamá* shaman, who arranges for proper tutorials in shamanism and smoking. The candidate receives initiatory cleansing and is subjected to prolonged sessions of tobacco (cigar) smoking. This marks the beginning of an isolation period lasting three months, during which the novice adheres strictly to the proscribed restrictions, furthered by endeavors, dietary and otherwise, to facilitate the novice's communication with the spirit world. After several months, the tutors visit the initiate, declaring him a *yetamá*, and each offers him a long cigar.[7] Now, he is ready to perform.

> He sat down by the fire, lit a long cigar, and began to smoke furiously. After several long drags on his cigar, apparently swallowing the smoke in great gulps, he gasped and rolled his eyes so that only the whites were visible. He slowly leaned further and further forward until his head was on the ground while his father, blowing smoke over his body, summoned his son's "pet," Walama, the Anaconda spirit. . . . And then suddenly, the uncanny clicking noise of the jaws of the Anaconda were heard. Walama . . . lodged himself in the back of the *yakapa* between his shoulder blades. Teme, the Mehinaku, no longer existed. His eyes were eyes of the Anaconda and his body was the body of the Anaconda.[8]

Teme, the *yakapa*[9] shaman, "began to move slowly, shouting in pain at his transformation into a spirit."[10] Unfortunately, a society wherein shamans proliferate tends to create not only diverse specializations among them, but a competitive environment that may lead to trickery and dramaturgy. As a result, many gifted individuals with desirable predispositions and true precognitive abilities, may become submerged by opportunists and others of questionable competence. In the eyes of a capable ethnographer, such as Thomas Gregor, who witnessed the session described above, such manifestations are imbued with elements of psychological and social significance. However, his assessment of their preternatural character does not rise beyond mere scepticism:

> The shaman may remove an intrusive object from the patient's body by sleight of hand, he may go on a trip with the aid of hallucinogenic drugs to retrieve the victim's soul which has been stolen by spirits, or he may do battle with spirits on behalf of his client. Although the shaman may sincerely believe he can cure disease, he often resorts to tricks and other staged effects to convince his patients. Among the Mehinaku, where the theatrical side to the shaman's role is unusually developed, and where the successful shaman is above all a good performer, the dramaturgical approach to the art seems particularly appropriate.[11]

Admittedly, some Amazonian Indians, such as the Jívaro of Ecuador, the Urubu of Brazil, and the Cubeo of Colombia elect to learn the craft of shamanism by making pre-arranged payments in goods to their selected tutors. It is my contention that, among these peoples, shamanism, as a truly coherent aspect of religious ideology, is rather poorly developed. Instead, a much greater emphasis is placed on black magic and sorcery, which, among the Cubeo, are considered the most perilous aspects of life. This situation is clearly reflected in their attitudes towards the supernatural world. "The Cubeo have no great interest in speculating about the life of the spirits of the dead, [and] except for the Ancients, they have no formal relationship with them."[12] Moreover, it is claimed that the Cubeo shamans do not exhibit psychopathological symptoms, such as those found in Siberian and North American shamanism, since there exists "neither trance nor other form of hysterical behavior." It is very unfortunate that, by equating trance with emotional instability, Goldman demonstrates such a poor grasp of native shamanism in his otherwise commendable ethnography. His limited interest in the subject, furthermore, is foisted with his very brief gloss over the Cubeo use of the narcotic snuff, *kúria*, prepared from the bark of the *kuriákü* tree, from which is made also a narcotic drink known by the same name as the snuff. ". . . Shaman and novice sit side by side and under the influence of *kúria* sing and shake the rattle from dawn to sunset."[13] Does not this narcotized condition induce a trancelike state?

A more elaborate and meaningful example of an inner personal crisis may be drawn from the description provided by the Iglulik (Caribou) Eskimo shaman named Aua, native of the chilly Hudson Bay, who, while acting as an informant to the renowned Danish scholar-explorer Knud Rasmussen, provided an account of his own experiences. The Eskimo had been thoroughly committed to the notion of becoming a shaman but, unfortunately, he had been constantly refused by all whom he had approached as prospective teachers. Eventually, Aua had decided to venture alone into the desolate Arctic expanse, intent on either finding an answer or not to return. The solitary bleakness, the constant wind, and the howling of the wolves created alternating moods of dismal depression and manic ebullience. Overwhelmed by the imposing snowscape, he experienced the *genius loci*, the spirit of the place—what Freud referred to as the "oceanic feeling."

> In the midst of such a fit of mysterious and overwhelming delight I became a shaman, not knowing myself how it came about. . . . I could see and hear in a totally different way. I had gained my *quamanEq*, my enlightenment, the shaman-light of brain and body, and this in such a manner that it was not only I who could see through the darkness of life, but the same bright light also shone out from me, imperceptible to human beings but visible to all the spirits of earth and sky and sea, and these now came to me and became my helping spirits.[14]

A characteristic element in the shamanic crisis is formed by spontaneous rapture, resembling a neurophysiological disorder, which consists of visions of dismemberment, journeys in the Otherworld among the various spirits, and reparations of the status quo by the process of initiatory rebirth. The true shaman must attain his knowledge and position through trance, vision, and soul-journey to the Otherworld. All these states of enlightenment are reached through an IPC condition, during a shamanic state of consciousness (SSC), and not by purposive study and application of a corpus of systematic knowledge. Hence, only after the shamanic ancestors of the Tungus, Semyonov Semyon, had initiated him into the path of the shaman, and after subjecting him to terrible ordeals, such as cutting up his body, consuming his raw flesh, and separating his bones, could Semyon begin to practice. In a statement heavily steeped in existential mysticism, not infrequently encountered among the shamans, Igjugarjuk, yet another Iglulik Eskimo shaman, told Rasmussen: "The only true wisdom lives far from mankind, out in the great loneliness, and it can be reached only through suffering. Privation and suffering alone can open the mind of man to all that is hidden to others."[15] In one sense, Hermann Hesse reverberated this realization in *Siddhartha*, when he said with a profound insight: "Wisdom is not communicable. . . . Knowledge can be communicated, but not wisdom. One can find it, live it, be fortified by it, do wonders through it, but one cannot communicate and teach it."[16]

In choosing the shamanic calling, erotic and sexual elements may, at times, enter into play and, on occasion, even culminate in rapture. Whether voluntary or forced, the ongoing relationship that ensues between the candidate and the tutelary spirit will be ramified, in such instances, by a sexual bond shared between the two. In his interesting treatment of the growth of religion, Weston La Barre remarked that "The shamanistic dream-vision. . . often proposes sexuality with a succubus animal, a spirit marriage, or some other 'forced' choice, which if disobeyed will drive the initiate mad."[17] A refusal may even terminate in death.

The Goldi of the Amur region in Siberia characterize in strong sexual terms the emerging liaison between the shaman and his *ayami*—the tutelary spirit that evokes the shamanic calling in the individual and assigns the helping spirits (*syvén*). Leo Sternberg offers an interesting recount of a Goldi shaman's own personal story.[18] The man, who happened to be Sternberg's informant, had fallen ill and was asleep, when a graceful and alluring woman-spirit approached his bedside. She was dressed in a native fashion. The spirit told the ailing man that she had been the *ayami* of his shamanic ancestors. She had taught them how to shamanize, and now she would likewise do the same for him. With declarations of her love for him, she further informed the bedridden man that he was to become her husband, and she a wife unto him. All was going to work out just fine: Her intentions were to provide him with the helping spirits whose assistance he would require in healing the people. The community would, naturally, provide for them. She concluded, with a foreboding note, that should he choose not to heed her instructions, she would have him killed.

The shaman continued with his story: The female spirit had been visiting him since, and he had had relations with her, the same as with his own wife. The *ayami* dwelled alone on a mountain, frequently changing her habitat, as well as the aspects of her appearance. At times, she was an old hag (cf. supra for the role of the hag among the Celts), at others a wolf, while still another time, a flying tiger, which the Goldi shaman mounted to be carried on his ecstatic journeys all over the world. Eventually, the *ayami* reduced the number of her nuptial visits, no longer sharing her nights with him so frequently as during the period in which she had been instructing him to shamanize. She did, nevertheless, grant him three helping animal spirits: *jarga* (the panther), *doonto* (the bear), and *amba* (the tiger). These spirits would come to him in dreams, or whenever he called them during a shamanic ceremony. Now, whenever he shamanizes, the spirits penetrate his body, taking possession of it, and whenever his *ayami* is within him, it is she who speaks through him and performs all the tasks.

Thus, we see that among the Siberian Goldi, despite the obvious erotic components in some of their visionary contents, the shamanic instructions and enlightenment are not the instant results of a libidinal fulfillment, but take place over a longer period of time. In contrast to the Siberian folk, the Celtic goddess/consort or the hag/mistress of the Otherworld bestowed the secret knowldge and the ecstatic journey by commencing sexual relations with the candidate.[19] The Yakut shamans and shamanesses also enter into sexual unions with the spirit masters and mistresses (*abbasy*) of the Upper and the Lowerworld, but after their implicit initiations attained through the ecstatic visions of these spirits, Sternberg was told by another native informant.[20] The soul of a Buryat novice travels to the center of the world, where it meets, in an amorous enounter, the nine wives of Tekha—the god of wealth, fertility, and dance. Eventually, the soul meets there his future celestial spouse. However, another two or three years must pass before the candidate actually goes through initiation, which includes an ascent-journey to the sky, followed by an earthly repast and celebration of sensual pleasures. The shamanic initiation constitutes, as well, a marriage to the celestial bride.[21]

Even here, the choice of the shaman, Eliade affirms, includes the primary ecstatic experience involving deprivation, torture, dismemberment, and symbolic death and rebirth. "*It is only this initiatory death and resurrection that consecrates a shaman*" [author's italics]. ". . .The role of the celestial bride appears to be secondary."[22] In fact, the choice of the shaman and the actual shamanic initiation do involve ecstatic experiences induced by one or more of the ritualized techniques. Reichel-Dolmatoff convincingly shows in his ethnographic material that the Desana initiation consists of progressive hallucinogenic trances, signifying "a slow rebirth" of the neophyte, "who first must suffer a symbolic death, after months of severe deprivations and the frequent ingestion of highly toxic drugs. He then must be reborn from the bones, from a skeletonized state." The whole process must be viewed as "an ecstatic metamorphosis."[23] Such terrifying visions of skeletons, dismembered bodies, blood, and the like, are most significant features in shamanistic initiations the world over, including such disparate cultures as those of Siberia, the Amazon forest, and of the Matlatzinca Indians, who inhabit a pine-forest valley near the Toluca volcano, southwest of Mexico City.

The Siberian and the Arctic shamans receive the protection of their *ayami*, their tutelary spirit, no doubt a relic from a matriarchal era of long ago, as manifested by the Great Mother of the Animals, with whom both maintain the best of relationships. Just as the Great Mother of the Animals (it is Master of the Animals in hunting societies, such as the Tukanoan) bestows on men, particularly the shamans, the rights of the hunt, the female tutelary spirits grant the shaman his indispensable entourage of spirit helpers,[24] so critical to ecstasy, healing, and soul-journey.

The sexual theme is not confined to these instances alone; it has a much wider cross-cultural distribution. As a result, Sternberg believed that the sexual element was the primary factor—the impetus—in the origins and the development of shamanism, and that such concepts as the spirit ancestors belong to a secondary or a more elaborated later phase. He based his argument not only on his own field work, but relied, as well, on the data collected by other observers. For one, Sergei Shirokogoroff, the eminent Russian scholar of Siberian cultures, had witnessed a shamaness becoming highly aroused sexually during initiatory ordeals.[25] Yet, sexual performance alone does not a shaman make. Potentially, anyone can have sexual intercourse with the spirits of the opposite gender, without realizing the attainment of shamanic prowess, as is quite common among the aforementioned Yakuts. When, in the course of human evolution, libidinal energy became repressed and sublimated is very difficult to pronounce. Perhaps the astute Sternberg overstressed the *singular* role that eroticism and sexuality had played at the roots of shamanistic origins? Perhaps, again, the propensities and personality traits for becoming a shaman do entail a specific class of libidinal impulse, but also much more than Sternberg's assessment would allow? Unless, of course, he subscribed to the view that the sexual element is the underlying cause for all symptoms that display, according to our own sociocultural norms, psycho- and neuro-pathological characteristics. This is neither an attack on Freud's ground-breaking and illuminating ideas nor an attempt to diminish the apparent significance of sexual energy, and the part it has had, in shamanic practices and in the religious impulse as a whole. Indeed, sex and religion have always been interwoven and inseparable components since men's primordial existence.

Whatever secondary and other minor contingencies may enter into the selection of a shaman among the Tukanoan Indians, the primary conditions are always based on mental and emotional propensities, which will enable the candidate to unveil recondite matters—those which are hidden—to the common folk, foster a vital relationship with Master of the Animals, incant spells, and heal. The shamans, in turn, depend on hallucinogenic substances obtained from the regional psychotropic biota to embark on trance-journeys to the Otherworld, in search of esoteric wisdom and experience. It is believed that the narcotic substances serve as the primary mechanism of communication between the shaman and his Other Reality. Called *payés*, the shamans represent civil and spiritual authorities in the tribe. Today, many of them are aware of the environmental problems confronting the Amazonian Indians, and act skillfully in sanctioning control over the natural resources. The preoccupation with the maintenance of stable natural conditions permeates into other aspects of daily existence, influencing community life. As a result, birth and all the activities surrounding the procreative process with its elaborating rituals fall today within the domain of the shaman's regulatory authority.[26]

The features described above are not indicative of the entire, vast, geographical and cultural area delineated by the Amazon basin. In contrast to the Tukanoan, some other Amazonian tribe places different social meanings on the institution of shamanism. The Jívaro Indians of Ecuador, researched by Harner,[27] may rightly boast of having one-fourth of their male population consist of shamans. The prospect of acquiring political status and wealth acts as a major factor in electing to pursue this calling, while the relative ease with which the *natem*ä drink (a preparation made from an admixture of the narcotic vine species of *Banisteriopsis*) is available, enables almost anyone to enter into trance. The shamans admit quite freely that their primary interest in curing the sick lies in the material rewards to be gained from this activity. By offering a gift of an appropriate value to an established shaman, a business-like agreement is reached, for the right price. The prospective man or woman candidate will be administered the *natem*ä to induce trance and visions, given some of the shaman's spirit helpers (*tsentsak*), and be on the way to a profitable apprenticeship in a new career. Of course, the candidate's success will be determined eventually by his or her ability to manipulate, for good or for evil, the supernatural world by means of the spirit helpers. In turn, this will influence the degree of respect and fear commanded by such an individual.

Although social prominence characterizes the shaman's status among the Urubu Indians of Brazil, on the Gurupí river in the Amazon forest, "true shamans" (*payé-té*) have disappeared long since, owing to historical factors. Due to pressures generated by culture contacts, the tribe had broken up, and when a handful survivors attempted to restore the old tradition, there was no shaman to be found with the knowledge of the secret techniques (so the local story recounts). To countermand this cultural lacuna, the Urubu seek shamanistic apprenticeship among the Tembé Indians at Jararaca, down south the Gurupí, in exchange for appropriate payments in goods. The latter appear to rely on the inhalation of tobacco smoke for the induction of shamanistic trance. The skills that the Urubu develop are limited primarily to curing practices. Still, many members of their community are content with the absence of true shamans, for they dread the malevolent potential of shamanistic powers.

The Urubu aetiology (probably recent) explains that there had been, in fact, only two shamans, born at the beginning of the world, who escaped into the sky to avoid the all-engulfing fire. With the shamans departed their special knowledge. They left no successors behind, owing to physical anomalies—tiny penises—which prevented successful cohabitations with women[28] (cf. supra, for physical abnormalities as the mark of a shaman).

The demise of certain altruistic values ascribed to shamanism in various regions of Siberia is, likewise, reflected in the heavy political overtones—and nepotism, one might add—attached to this calling among the Uralic populations. Unlike the Tukanoans, the Tungus people have required a descent line to pass on the secrets of the trade. It was believed that the gift to shamanize, along with the appropriate traditions, was inherited by each successive generation belonging to the prescribed lineage. "A person cannot become a shaman if there have been no shamans in his sib," so was informed the diligent student of Siberian folklore, G. V. Ksenofontov, in 1925 by the Tungus shaman, Semyonov Semyon, at the latter's place of residence on the Lower Tunguska River. "Only those possessing shamanic ancestors in their background can receive the shamanistic gift, for the gift comes down from generation to generation."[29]

The intrinsic experience undergone by the shaman, effecting in his acquisition of the power, and the formats of the rituals connected with this technique are best illustrated by the words of the same Tungus shaman:

> When I shamanize, the spirit of my dead brother, Ilya, enters and speaks through my mouth. My shamanic ancestors compelled me to walk the course of the shaman's way. Prior to becoming a shaman and beginning to shamanize, I was laid out by sickness for an entire year, and became a shaman at fifteen years of age. The malady, which took hold of me and forced me towards this path, showed itself through my bodily swellings and fainting spells. This condition would vanish, generally, when I would start singing [shamanistically].
>
> Thereafter, my ancestors started shamanizing with me. They set me up like a block of wood, and shot at me from their bows until I was no longer conscious. Then, they sliced me up, removed the bones to be counted, and partook of my raw flesh. They found that I had one bone too many; if there had been

too few, I could not become a shaman. All this time, while the ancestors were busy with this rite, I had nothing to eat or drink for the entire summer. Towards the end, the shamanic spirits had some reindeer blood to drink, and let me some of it, too. The shaman has less blood, and looks pale, after such occurrences.

Every Tungus shaman undergoes this experience. He can begin to practice, but not before his shamanic ancestors sectioned his body, in this fashion, and took a count of his bones.[30]

From a quite different part of the world, the account of the initiatory ordeal of an Iglulik (Caribou) Eskimo shaman, a native of much harsher environs around Baker Lake, is recorded by Knud Rasmussen, who mentions this individual in numerous entries. The shaman's name was Igjugarjuk, and he had been experiencing intense dreams, the meaning of which he had not been able to grasp. In *Across Arctic America*, the great explorer writes:

Strange unknown beings came and spoke to him, and when he awoke, he saw all the visions of his dream so distinctly that he could tell his fellows all about them. Soon it became evident to all that he was destined to become an *angakoq* [a shaman] and an old man named Perqanaoq was appointed his instructor. . . . [After taken to a special site, Igjugarjuk] was not allowed to set foot on the snow, but was lifted from the sledge and carried into the hut, where a piece of skin just large enough for him to sit on served as a carpet. Not food or drink was given him; he was exhorted to think only of the Great Spirit and of the helping spirit that should presently appear—and so he was left to himself and his meditations.

After five days had elapsed, the instructor brought him a drink of lukewarm water, and with similar exhortations, left him as before. He fasted for fifteen days, when he was given another drink of water and a very small piece of meat, which had to last him a further ten days. At the end of this period, his instructor came for him and fetched him home. Igjugarjuk declared that the strain of those thirty days of cold and fasting was so severe that he 'sometimes died a little.' During all that time he thought only of the Great Spirit, and endeavored to keep his mind free from all memory of human beings and everyday things. Toward the end of the thirty days there came to him a helping spirit in the shape of a woman. She came while he was asleep and seemed to hover in the air above him. After that he dreamed no more of her, but she became his helping spirit. For five months following this period of trial, he was kept on the strictest diet, and required to abstain from all intercourse with women. The fasting was then repeated; for such fasts at frequent intervals are the best means of attaining. . . knowledge of hidden things. As a matter of fact, there is no limit to the period of study; it depends on how much one is willing to suffer and anxious to learn.[31]

The Caribou Eskimo women can also become shamans or shamanesses. Rasmussen relates of "a young woman, very intelligent, kind hearted, clean and good looking." Her name was Kinalik, and she was able to communicate to him her views and experiences openly and without reservations. Kinalik's instructor, or mentor, was Igjugarjuk, who also happened to be her brother-in-law. Perhaps for reasons of jealousy, Rasmussen does not tell us, she was required to undergo extreme forms of initiation—*agons* and ordeals, in the true sense of the word. "She was hung up to some tent poles planted in the snow and left there for five days. It was midwinter, with intense cold and frequent blizzards, but she did not feel the cold, for the spirit protected her." At the end of the five-day ordeal, Kinalik was brought down and removed into the house. It was then decided that "in order that she might attain to intimacy with the supernatural by visions of death," Igjugarjuk was to shoot her with a gun loaded with real powder, but a stone instead of a lead bullet. He fired at her, in the presence of the gathering, and she fell unconscious. The next morning, Kinalik rose on her own, just before Igjugarjuk was making ready to bring her back to life. He claimed, afterwards, that the stone had penetrated her heart, but it became her old mother's keepsake after he had removed it.[32]

Prior to 1870, the Wintu Indians of northern California organized elaborate ceremonies, during which the community's shamans were selected and put through the first stage of their initiation. They all began, naked, in the fading light of the evening hour. The master-shamans and their candidates, dancing around the fire of burning manzanita wood, invoked with their songs spirits, who, as yet, had not selected their favorites. Soon, however, the spirits would make their choices known to all present by entering the bodies of the selected candidates. These, in turn, would become frenetic, overcome with frenzy and fits of convulsions, with saliva drooling, and even blood secreting from the mouth and nostrils. The Wintu understood that a strong tie had been forged between the shaman and his guiding spirits—the spirits who enter his body to inform. Like his counterpart in the Amazon, the Wintu shaman does not find, solely on his own, special answers during the ecstatic soul-journeys.

Nowadays, more specifically in the mid-1970's, only a memory lingers on, and only one recognized, true shaman has remained.[33] Her Wintu name means "Eastern Flower Woman," but to the white people she is Flora Jones, an Indian medicine-woman who conducts shamanistic "seances." Her methods represent syncretism between the ancient, traditional techniques and the ethos resulting from the cataclysmic changes wrought in modern times by exogenous pressures. Eastern Flower Woman has no one from her tribe to follow in her foorsteps and continue the shamanistic heritage. Thus, it appears that Flora might very well end up being the last ritual practitioner of her people.

We have seen a number of situations dealing with shamanistic initiations, and, even though there exist variances as far as specific details are concerned, nevertheless, it is quite apparent that the over-all nature of the primary structural components remains consistent throughout the culturally diverse episodes. Let us briefly examine the principal elements comprising these initiations:

First, there is the physical *ordeal of a death-rebirth type*, constituting the traditional pattern of initiation and comprised of regional variations. At times, such an ordeal may have only a symbolic form. Generally speaking, however, it consists of an isolation in a forest or a cave, accompanied by deprivations, resulting in mental and physical exhaustion. The subject may have to undergo beatings, burning, laceration, exposure to the coldness of snow—naked, without nourishment or drink—and even hanging upside down for days on end. If the end result terminates in a successful emergence from these trials and tribulations, then the person will have become reborn and gained "shamanic enlightenment," henceforth enabling this individual to become a practicing shaman. Odin of the Norsemen, anxious to quench a thirst of quite a different kind than for water or other type of refreshing liquid, offered his eye for a sip from Mimir's well of knowledge. His honorific title was the Great Shaman. Likewise, in the Garden of Eden, the taste of the fruit from the Tree of Knowledge was bound with the loss of immortality. One has to die in order to be transcended onto another plane. The mortality of the physical body is necessary for the soul's transcendence onto a more spiritual level of consciousness or awareness. Different systems of metaphysics essentially encapsulate this conception by submitting that upon dying, or leaving the body, one can transcend and become reborn—that the energy which we call the soul is transmitted to a different plane of existence in its eternal process of transition.

So, meanwhile, the neophyte must die, too! This involved process is accomplished under the guidance of an older, experienced shaman, who acts as a mentor during the initiate's prolonged seclusion. Among the Desana Indians of the Vaupés territory in the equatorial rain forest, Colombian northwest Amazon, the initiate and the master-shamans recede into a remote area, where no one else is allowed, especially women. The first stage of initiation is marked by the neophyte's symbolic death, signified by his trance-journey to the other plane of existence. The second stage designates his transformation and rebirth at the source of a symbolic river, and consists of a galaxy of metaphors forming the cosmic models that reflect both realities.[34] The initiatory death of a Desana neophyte may occur after several months of deprivations and can take place around a river course, in an area which can be said to demarcate a hexagon. His spirit, proceeding to the river outlet, "penetrated the fiery *tabu* door and submerged himself into the primeval waters of the Lake of Milk (*ahpikon dia*)." Finally, he attains new life as a shaman, and rising anew from a skeletal form, is being reborn through the phases of transformation as he completes his passage by entering the secured "flaming" portals of "the hexagon of the headwater."

Therefore, behind the gate of fire lies the passage of water. A specific depth of the lake marks the door through which the shaman passes into another plane of existence. Both entrances are demarcated by vivid colors of the rainbow.[35] It is quite obvious that we are confronted, here, with the recapitulation of the ontogenetic process of human transformation and development from the very onset of a zygote formation. The initiate retraces his footsteps to the locked, "flaming" portals of the labias, the cosmic source of life, beneath the waters of fecundity and rejuvenation that make up the Lake of Milk. He dies in transit, along the way, of his individual journey, having reached a penetrating depth to enter the vortex behind the forbidden fiery porte, which leads to the infinite chasm where death and life co-exist. As the novice emerges, once again, on the other side of the fiery portals, he has already been transformed in death, and, like the eternal phoenix rising whole from its own ashes, he emerges reborn.

The Desana shamanistic initiation encapsulates several overlapping models. The primary one, as mentioned priorly, represents the cycle of human development from the pre-natal stage of insemination. This cycle is recapitulated by another model, evident in the ritual of pottery making—a metaphor for "a process of life's transformation"—where mixing of the raw materials represents insemination, consolidating the built-up clay is equivalent to pregnancy, and the final phase of firing signifies rebirth. Consequently, the pottery vessel stands as a metaphor for a woman, or her womb (the Great Mother), and the food prepared in it by cooking is the emerging child. The lip of the cooking pot delineates metaphorically the vaginal orifice, and may feature a **Y**-shaped design, symbolic of the clitoris; the latter rendered with an "elastic stick from a *tooka* plant," representing a strong phallic component. In the Desana metaphysical worldview, the clitoris plays a role in the bone-soul concept pertaining to rejuvenation and rebirth.[36]

Ma'mari is a Desana verb of many diverse, but related meanings, among which the following denotations apply: "to adorn oneself," "to make oneself look younger by applying body paint, aromatic herbs, and by wearing adornments." It also signifies "to become worthy of something"; but it means also "rejuvenation" and being "reborn in a spiritual sense."[37] The importance of the concept of rebirth can hardly be overemphasized. It would appear that by applying body paint, the keynote objective is to look younger, rejuvenated, and not just merely prettier. The acolyte, thus, manifests his or her signs of rejuvenation as exponents of a symbolic rebirth. At the same time, as a sign of rebirth in other cultures, the initiate may be prompted to take up a new name; or, even, as found more rarely in several other places, such as the Arctic Siberia, he may desire to undergo a sex "change," and become transexual, assuming feminine behavior and dress. In southern Borneo, the Ngadju-Dayak have a special category of hermaphrodite-shamans, whom they call *basir*, meaning "unable to reproduce." These individuals vest themselves in women's attire and emulate, likewise, feminine demeanor. As a consequence of their biological (hermaphroditic) and personality (bisexual) characteristics, these shamans represent the union of the opposites—a complementarity of polar biunity—of the feminine (earth) and masculine (heaven) principles. Henceforth, they are viewed as the intermediaries between the worldly and heavenly realms.

Apparently, the transexuality and impotence of the *basir* arise as important issues because, as Eliade believes, these priest-shamans are regarded as the mediators and significators of the union of two cosmic planes, and because of the psychological need to fuse polarities.[38] Joan Halifax adds interesting insight to this subject matter:

> The dissolution of the contraries—life and death, light and dark, male and female—and reconstitution of the fractured forms is one of the most consistent impulses in the initiation and transformation process as experienced by the shaman. To bring back to an original state that which was in primordial times whole and is now broken and dismembered is not only an act of unification but also a divine remembrance of a time when a complete reality existed. . . .The occasional androgyny of the shaman is one inflection of paradise, where the two become one. The death of separation dissolves all worldly distinctions, and balance is attained. . . .The shaman thus becomes a double

being that like the philosopher's stone, the Rebis, has the potential of transmutation as an intrinsic condition.[39]

The second phase in the initiations often involves the *administration of hallucinogenic preparations* by the master-shaman to the neophyte. Its purpose is to induce trance in order to dispatch the initiate on the profound soul-journey to the Otherworld. In the Desana initiation ceremonies, narcotic preparations are taken to induce trance in a particular sequence, which corresponds to stages of rebirth. Yet, in contrast to the Uralo-Altaic shamans, their ecstatic transformations are not ascent- or descent-journeys into the world of spirits, but consist of raptures of colors and forms. The trance is meant to be a gateway to an introspective experience, aimed at helping the novice gain awareness of his own existence, to meditate, and observe his own reactions to the psychotropic drugs. An echo of a strong sexual tenor permeates all the aspects of the trance. In turn, the preparation of *ayahuasca*—or *yajé*, as it is called in different parts of the Amazon—is laden, too, with an array of sexual symbolisms, and the actual process of mixing the psychotropic ingredients is connotative of an intercourse between the *yajé* vessel, a metaphor for the female body, and the mixing rod, a metaphor for the male principle.[40] Insemination is a transformative process, leading to birth or a symbolic rebirth. The allusions, in the drug ceremonial, invoke sexual intercourse as a process in transformative rebirth, and not as a mere representation of the physical act.

The psychotropic plants employed for the induction of trance for shamanic journeys are numerous and used frequently in combinations. In the Western Hemisphere, the main varieties include the psilocybe, peyote, datura, coca (a stimulant only), and yajé (also yagé; or *ayahuasca*, a Quechua term meaning "the vine of the souls" or "the vine of the dead")—a tree-climbing vine of paramount importance in the Amazon rain forest. In the Old World, we have the fly-agaric, psilocybe, datura, opium, ergot, and, of course, hemp (a stimulant). The drinking mead, in use among the Norsemen and the Celts, was probably different in substance from what we know it to be today. The existence of the all-important bee-goddess cult in Neolithic Greece, which persisted into later times, may point to the mead as being a significant hallucinatory drink, if not even the divine nectar.[41] Curiously enough, the secret knowledge of mead was stolen from the abode of the Norse gods by Odin, almost in the same manner of betrayal and cunning as Ixion's theft of the nectar from the Olympians.

The third main element in the initiation must allude to *the ecstatic soul-journey*, induced by entering the shamanic state of consciousness (SSC), a phrase aptly introduced by Michael Harner. During this transcendental voyage, the new shaman will hopefully meet his or her "power animals," frequently of the opposite gender, who are likely to remain his lifelong assistants. One of them may even become the shaman's spiritual spouse. Occasionally, the shaman may transform himself into an animal "spirit-helper," or, as the case stands in the northwest Amazon, he may be fortunate enough to meet his own avatars,[42] such as the jaguar, the anaconda, or the harpy eagle.

Clearly, the shaman's technique of ecstasy is the main component in the shamanic state of consciousness. I speak of *the* shamanic state because, I believe, there is only one *quantitative* shamanic state of consciousness, as opposed to such forms as spirit possession, for example. SSC may be experienced in varying degrees of amplification (power), intensity (depth), and wave-frequency (level), but there still is only one. An experienced shaman may enter into a very deep ecstatic trance, which may effect the superficial appearance of induced death. Nevertheless, even in such a state, it is very uncommon for the shaman to lose control over his or her personality. The individual retains cognizance or apprehension of purpose and becomes actively involved in the encounters with the spirit-beings of the Otherworld. The shaman does not dissociate, in the clinical definition of this term (according to Carl Jung, neurosis is defined as a dissociated personality). The old-fashioned view, which considered shamans to be suffering from psychopathological conditions, is being justifiably abandoned in favor of a more objective assessment (cf. the section "Shamanism and Psychopathology," in this chapter). This outmoded idea was advocated by those (including Eliade) who refused to recognize the significant role played by hallucinogens in the history and process of shamanism.

In spite of all that has been mentioned above, the techniques of ecstasy and rapture may be absent among certain peoples. As a result, we consider such groups to be practicing marginal, or fringe, shamanism. The Chukchees, in northeast Siberia, exhibit all the cultural characteristics associated with a true shamanistic religion, yet it has been reported that genuine ecstatic trances play no part in their techniques. Another group, discussed below, is composed of the Seri Indians, who have been reported not to attain states of ecstasy, or rapture. Diószegi observes perceptively that the *focus* of a shamanistic religion is not on the mere experience of ecstasy, but rather on the goals to be derived from it. Since ecstasy, as a psychosomatic phenomenon, may be entered at will, it is not its own teleological end, but the means, a mechanism of conveyance, to a special goal. Therefore, he implies, as long as these goals are met and satisfied, then rapture can attain secondary importance.

The fourth component marks a second stage in the *initiation-training* process, which, according to Eliade, underscores the "traditional" system. The neophyte is now a *bona fide* shaman, but his learning and enlightenment do not stop here! The mentor instructs him in the shamanistic lore, techniques, and the oral traditions and myths of their people. He also introduces the new shaman to the knowledge of healing and magical plants, teaching him, at the same time, the methods employed in their preparations. The shaman continues to acquire knowledge from instructions and wisdom through rapture and trance.

The revelation and awareness of one's own inclination to become a shaman may be the cause of much anxiety, effecting in physical and mental imbalance, or in the so-called "shamanic illness," sometimes accompanied by loss of consciousness or a temporary comatose state. Apparently, the bodily torment and the mental anguish deliver the individual to the breaking point of endurance, and the illness may continue unless the sick person accepts the "call" and sheds all resistance. Most shamans believe that the only reprieve from this torturous condition is to answer the "call," for otherwise one is exposed to great jeopardy. The tenor of this peril can be heard in the, by now, familiar confession of a Siberian shaman, "Had I not become a shaman, I would have died." Once the "chosen" individual surrenders to his vocation, he wanders off, usually to some remote parts in the wilderness, where he spends the time in complete solitude, living off whatever he can find, experiencing hunger, thirst, and privation. The prolonged indigence and physical deprivation are followed by hallucinatory experiences of dreams and trance. He has become an ascetic.

The genuine importance of the first, main component, involving death-rebirth transformation and enlightenment, can be appreciated better if we remember that the founders of, what are commonly known as, the great religions had achieved deep states of meditation in caves. Muhammed, for one, used to isolate himself in a mountain cave, and as a result of the enlightenment he attained—which undoubtedly was that of an "inspired" person, and could be compared to a shamanistic experience—the Quran was born, setting down the tenets of Islam. We know for a historical fact that Muhammed had been a member of the influential Quraish tribe, and a camel caravaneer in the district of Mekka in Arabia. A colossal dispute with his kinsmen resulted in altercations and outright warfare. His recurrent seizures, of the epilelptic type, gained for Muhammed a reputation as a special individual, which we may compare to that of a prospective shaman born with an anomaly, pre-selecting him culturally for the spiritual vocation. The "possessions" continued to earn him the mark of a holy man, chosen by heaven, while he would find spiritual reprieve and transformation in a cave, where he spent long periods in isolation, in a deep state of meditation and seizure-like trances, resembling the "shamanic illness." One day, during a state of enlightened revelation, the holy writ of the Muslims was given a creation. It has been remarked, on several occasions, that the difference between a shamanic trance and an epileptic seizure lies only in the fact that an epileptic cannot enter the trance at will. It is, thus, not so far-fetched to presuppose that Muhammed's alleged epileptic fits were, in fact, trance-induced raptures and soul-journeys of shamanic states of consciousness. An elaboration of the shamanistic aspect[43] is, among others, to be found behind the apocryphal story of his ascent-journey to heaven, a few days following his death, from the Rock of the Moriah in Jerusalem—a sacred place to the Jews, Christians, and Muslims, alike, on which stands today the magnificent Dome of the Rock, a wonderful achievement of architectural genius and a cathedral of the Islamic faith. According to a still more ancient tradition, this had also been the place where the patriarch Abraham had prepared to sacrifice his beloved son, Isaac.

The experience of an epileptic fit may, in fact, approach that of a serene mystical state, ecstatic rapture, or even of the *entheoi*. In a letter written by Dostoyevsky to Nikolai Strakhov, the luminous Russian writer tells, with profound insight, of his own sensations immediately preceding the onset of an epileptic seizure, to which he was a frequent subject. "For a few moments before the fit, I experience a feeling of happiness such as it is quite impossible to imagine in a normal state and which other people have no idea of. I feel entirely in harmony with myself and the whole world. . . ."[44] Uncanny, realistic descriptions crept into the pages of one of his remarkable books, *The Idiot*, whose protagonist is modeled after Dostoyevsky, himself, making the hero thunder with true to life realism, which is steeped in psychologically torturous feelings which "other people have no idea of."

Not only pathological disorders, but dreams may also possibly invoke endogenous experiences that can occasion states of rapture or spiritual ecstasy in the subject.[45] The renowned case of St. Teresa of Avila comes readily to mind. Born in Spain to a devout family, she entered the convent life very early. Recognized for extreme piety throughout her existence, she became the founder of the stern order of barefoot Carmelites. At the apogee of her spiritual growth, she dreamt of a rapturous encounter with an angel. This she recounted vividly in her autobiography:

> In his hands I saw a long golden spear and at the end of the iron tip I seemed to see a point of fire. With this he seemed to pierce my heart repeatedly so that it penetrated to my entrails. When he drew it out I thought he was drawing them [the entrails] out with it and he left me completely afire with a great love of God.

The pain was so great that I screamed aloud, but simultaneously felt such an infinite sweetness that I wished the pain would last eternally.[46]

Was the dream merely a case of subconscious libidinal sublimation? Perhaps, but it seems extremely unlikely that the dream content embodied an *affective* recall of some actual sexual antic in her past. Rather it can be likened to shamanistic experiences of dismemberment. The Cambridge University experimental psychologist Nicholas Humphrey believes that St. Teresa's psychic reaction to the events in her dream yields the former conjecture.

Not in every case do the shamanic "call" and initiation go hand-in-hand with profound ordeals of the IPC type. At the other, more extreme end of the spectrum, there are the Seri Indians[47] of Sonora, who have inhabited the Tiburon Island in the Gulf of California. As of this writing, they all may already be extinct. The Seri ritual life and mythology were pulverized by strong pressures from the Christianizing agencies, yet, shamanism was the only aspect of their belief world that held on firmly. The shaman, called *kô'tê*, becomes initiated by entering into a mountain cave (again!), which, according to the local belief, consists of a "solid rock." However, the initiate manages to create an opening by painting a recondite symbol on the rock's surface. At this point, the helping spirits and familiars may choose to assist the new shaman by entering his body. The entire ceremony is rather barren and uneventful, showing apparent lack of ecstatic techniques, raptures, and visions.

As a result of communication with the spirits inside him, the Seri shaman is able to effect cures and see the cause of illness within the patient. But even the healing method seems clearly unvaried and simplistic: the shaman encircles his hands over the patient's afflicted area, and, putting his mouth to them, utters "cho, cho, cho." No sucking out of an antigen-object takes place. Rain-making, a true shamanistic function, is not even delegated to the repertory of shamanistic techniques, but merely entrusted to amulets.

It appears that most of the old Seri men lay claim to some kind of "shamanistic power," which is indicative, in its own right, of a degenerated religious institution, characterizing a dying sociocultural vestige. Henceforth, we can attempt to guess the reasons for the low grade of spirituality among the Seri, and their impoverished ritual form, with its unspecialized techniques. Perhaps these occurrences are due to the powerful influences acting on the Indians from outside, and exhorting the people to give up their tribal spirits, traditions, and visions, leaving them with mundane emptiness instead. The well-known American anthropologist, Alfred Kroeber, was prompted to observe in 1930 that the Seri ". . . seem remarkably religionless. I do not know of a native people that appear so free from superstition and so unspiritual in its attitudes."[48] Seri shamanism is atypical, reflecting a waning culture, and probably should not be used as an illustration in the discussion of the general ritual complex. It does, however, show us the minimalism of structural and functional traits, which still, somehow when added up, fall under a broader definition of shamanistic practices.

Similarly, the Garifuna[49] in Belize practice the propitiatory and healing *dugu*[50] ritual, which otherwise (like the Polynesian ecstatic religions) may be classified mundanely as spirit possession, and which rests on a shamanistic substructure. Undoubtedly, spirit possession forms a major part in the Garifuna belief system, encompassing possession-sickness, or ailments believed to be caused by an ancestral spirit taking over a person's body, while inducing trance (*gubida*). This dissociation from ordinary state of consciousness (OSC) is a condition found mostly among women and is described as "being unable to find themselves" (*madairitiya hungua*).[51] To treat this condition, the medium (*buyai*) becomes possessed by his spirit helpers (*hiuruha*), who guide him in *arairaguni*, or the diagnostic procedure under a trance. The medium is, thus, allowed to avert the malevolent state of the afflicted individual by enacting the proper cure through the performance of the dugu.

Quite evidently, the substructure of the Garifuna ecstatic ritual comprises at least seven fundamental shamanistic elements: (1) The drum, or rather a set of three drums, is an integral part of the ceremony, with the focal instrument—*lanigi garaun*, which Foster appropriately calls the "heart drum" in a book by the same title—symbolizing the heartbeat, as well as a conveyor that brings the ancestral spirits into the ceremonial arena. (2) The gourd rattle[52] is equally important in this ritual, and complements the "heart drum" in accomplishing its objective. (3) The rhythm of music generates energy that impels the spirits to enter and take over the bodies of those involved in the performance of (4) the ritual dance. (5) The enlistment of spirit helpers to act as intermediaries between the medium and the ancestral spirits, whose good will is supplicated in the procurement of welfare on behalf of the ill. (6) The occurrence of possession, trance, and related conditions of altered states of consciousness, and, finally, (7) the shamanic illness and calling.

The contents of visions and dreams exhibit a characteristic trans-cultural unity in thematic form and substance, wherein the horrors of the experience that the neophyte undergoes consist of his death and dismemberment. He may be flayed or skinned, cut up into segments, and his flesh, stripped off the bone, eaten raw or cooked. Finally, the shaman is reconsituted, and, in some parts of Australia and tropical South America, his intestines are replaced with those made of quartz crystals, the strongest shamanistic power objects, which Eliade calls "solid light"—the inner light of vision.

When viewed as "solidified light," such crystals are connected with shamanic enlightenment and the spiritual ability to see through matter. Yet, when Eliade suggests that "they feel a relation between the condition of a supernatural being and a superabundance of light,"[53] he also engages, consciously or not, a relationship between the supernatural, or a visionary experience, and the production of phosphenes, a neurophysiological state. Furthermore, shamans are often perceived as individuals who emanate auras from their heads. Among the Jívaro Indians, such a vivid light radiates during a shamanic state of consciousness, induced by ingesting yajé (*ayahuasca*), and can be witnessed by another shaman in an equivalent state of consciousness.[54] Quartz crystal is considered a "living" object, and its use goes back many millennia. In California, for example, archaeological sites yielded quartz crystals, with other objects of material culture, which can be dated to 6000 B.C.

The ritual themes of cooking and consuming the flesh and of rebirth appear in the contexts of other ancient religious sects, for instance, in the Egyptian cult of Osiris and the Greek Orphic Mysteries, where both Osiris and Dionysos undergo very similar fates. This relationship in episodes may point to a significant link between early shamanism and its role and influence in the development of certain religious traditions. Hence, very likely the ancient worship of Osiris and Dionysos may stem from roots implanted in a still more ancient shamanistic soil. The significance of this death-rebirth process of initiation lies in the knowledge that it represents a form of sacrifice, such as encountered in the corresponding rites of the Mother-Earth, to maintain the cosmic homeostasis by supplicating the animal spirits in the universe, lest mankind should incur their wrath.

Although it remains beyond a doubt that shamanistic rituals have called, at times, for sacrifices, nowhere have they ever reached proportions of the intense blood-letting, associated with the fertility deities of the death-rebirth cycles, as found among the enormous numbers of human victims sacrificed to propitiate the bottomless thirst for blood of the gods of the pre-Columbian civilizations. However, the shamans of the Ugrian Ostyaks in northern Siberia may determine the number of reindeer for an effective sacrifice; while some Altaic shamans will sacrifice a horse before an ascent-journey.[55] The horse, it should be remembered, was an ancient solar symbol and the life-force incarnate for the neighboring Indo-European tribes.

The tradition of sacrificing horses has not been confined only to Asiatic cultures where shamanism has played an active role. In certain areas in medieval Europe, the inauguration of a new king also called for such a ritual. According to the account of Gerald of Wales, the crowning of a new monarch in the town of Kenelcunnil in Ulster, during the thirteenth century, required copulation with a mare before it was offered in a blood sacrifice. The divine names Epona, Macha, or Rhiannon were but different appelations for the Celtic mare-goddess, one of their chief deities. There is also evidence that in ancient India a similar ritual had been practiced by the queen, although in later times it was reduced to a simulated act.

At the completion of the sacrifice, the horse changes into a spirit, or a heavenly mount, to convey the shaman on his soul-journey. According to the Mongols this mount transports him to the side of the celestial seat of Bai Uelgaen. The animal's hide provides the covering for the Altaic shaman's drum, considered to be "the most powerful of all shaman's helpers" and referred to as his horse or a boat for the soul-journey. The tundra-dwelling Yuraks allude to the drum, used in trance-induction, as the shaman's bow, dispatching him into the Otherworld. Certain Siberian tribes choose the tree (the World Tree) for the wood of the drum by a non-conscious technique while remaining in the SSC condition. The drumstick is the shaman's whip or a paddle.

The Shamanistic Experience

An essential feature, characteristic of shamanism as a trans-cultural, magico-religious manifestation, consists of the "shaman's journey." This notion, stemming likely from the psychedelic trips, expresses the belief that, while engaged in the procurement of remedies, the shaman undertakes a dangerous voyage to the world of the spirits. It is a fundamental tenet, found throughout the world, be it in Central and South America or in Mongolia, where it independently evolved complex regional variances. Each person's life mirrors the labyrinth of existence. It is the destiny of a true shaman to realize that the closer he moves toward the center of existence, the more transcendent and freer his essence becomes. Intuitively, he is aware that at the core of the maze dwell the forces of life alongside the forces of death. The shaman's soul, once annihilated, is freed and liberated from all sorts of earthly constraints and becomes transformed into a divine spirit. Death is no longer an evil to be apprehended, but a path to blessedness and purification.

The nucleus of such quintessential dualism is to be found in the spirit of nature's paradox, carrying an imprint of the cosmic paradigm. Here the arcana of creation and entropy are but reflected images of one another—both, at once, self-generating and self-destructive. To promulgate live matter, to transmute the innate into the living, the earthly into the spiritual, the profane into the sacred, the shaman-alchemist must plunge his soul into the primeval abyss to penetrate and revet its secrets, for the primeval contains forces vital to existence. The chasm of life, at the bottom of which stills death, forms the mainstay of heavenly rapture and harmony. Both of these transform the reality in which death, through the habits of long ago is regarded as the darkest scourge, and life is an assurance. For the shaman, fortunate to experience the heavenly music and rapture, life attains the heights of ecstasy, of purification, of catharsis. . . and sometimes even destruction. The structure of the ordinary world must be demolished so that the shaman can make room for the preternatural one. Ecstasy and frenzy, rapture and terror become awe-inspiring experiences, precisely because they are permeated with a sense of death.

The title of W. Somerset Maugham's book, *The Razor's Edge*, was drawn from the Hindu *Katha Upanishad*. In this story, the author alludes to the shamanistic ordeals of the spiritual experience inferred from the Eskimo shaman's crossing of the abyss of the life-death continuum, on a bridge no wider than a knife's edge, to re-establish the natural balance in the universe by making the proper sacrificial restitutions. In the Arthurian cycle, as retold by Chretien de Troyes, Sir Lancelot rides out in quest of the abducted Guinevere (identified here with the dual *imago* of the Mother/Madonna), who is being kept hidden on the other end of a sword-bridge, guarded by two ferocious lions. On the way to this spirit place, Sir Lancelot loses his sense of being alive, as if he has died (initiatory death). He performs his agon of crossing the terrible sword-bridge with an intense emotional pain and by sustaining many physical injuries to his body; yet with a deep detachment, as if he were actually outside himself, so characteristic of a shamanic state of consciousness. Only afterwards does he realize that this occurrence existed in another, distorted reality of a trance, for some of the things he thought he perceived were comprised of visionary experiences.

The significance of the sword is consistently evidenced throughout the diverse facets of the Arthurian epic, and in such accounts as of the magical sword Excalibur and the Lady of the Lake. Oftentime, such swords became the objects of worship and were identified with the war deity Mars or his local counterpart. The sacred element associated with swords, from Mongolia to Gaul, is attested by the fact that people swore solemn oaths on them. The Huns were believed to hold a certain sword sacred. Ancient sources report that this particular sword was held sacred and honored among the Scythian [related to the Huns] kings, dedicated to the overseer of wars (Mars). It had vanished in ancient times.[56]

In India, where the heirloom of its shamanistic tradition richly embroiders the garb of its subsequent beliefs, the great Kali—who is none other than the Mother-Creatrix and a blood-thirsty mistress—is also the goddess of the Life-Death continuum in her aspect as the incarnation of the time force. The Hindu *Mahābhārata* alludes to her thus: "I bow to you, leader of the Realized, noble goddess who dwells in heaven. O tenebrous maiden garlanded with skulls, tawny, bronze-dark, I bow to you who are the auspicious Power of Time, the Transcendent-Power-of-Time." One is, of course, much tempted to draw a comparison between the skulls of Kali and those worn on the shaman's vestments. In *The Religion of India*, Max Weber educed that the Brahmins had once been an elite group of magicians, like the magi (or shamans?), who in time became high-ranking ritual practitioners and gurus. During a sacrificial offering, the Brahmin, just as his shamanistic counterpart, ascends symbolically to heaven on a ladder. The Judaeo-Christian counterpart of this motif is contained in the Old Testament version of Jacob's dream, in which he, too, climbs a ladder reaching all the way to heaven.

The shaman's descent-journey, on the other hand, may symbolize *regresso in utero*, since the Lowerworld is considered to be the realm of the female. Likewise, the symbolism of the shamanic travel to the bottom of the lake or on the river carries a complexity of meanings for the individual involved. Reichel-Dolmatoff reports that among the Tukanoan Indians a river journey may allude to the ontogenetic development of the person—that is, the person's life—or it may connote, instead, his pre-natal growth *in utero* or the flourishing of the biota or even a hallucinogenic trance. For a neophyte of the Desana Indians, who inhabit the same general region as the rest of the Tukanoan speakers, the second stage of shamanic initiation consists of an abstract experience at the source of a symbolic river. Immersion forms an important part in the whole ritual and may be likened to baptism. In each case, the sojourner undergoes a cathartic transformation and comes forth cleansed in a new, reborn phase.[57]

Sir James G. Frazer suggested that to create an actual boundary between the world of the living and the realm of the souls, or the Underworld, was the reason for the initial purification ceremonies by water and fire, "and that the conceptions of pollution and purification are merely the fictions of a later age invented to explain the purpose of a ceremony of which the original intention was forgotten."[58] The existence of such a separation in early times would indubitably point to a shamanistic conception implicit in the early theory of the soul, according to which the soul must traverse the existential space dividing this World from the Other.

This form of a journey, to be undertaken by the deceased, resembles very much the situation among certain contemporary tribal societies, where the shaman, in his role as a psychopomp, guides the souls across the transcendental space into the antipodal World.[59] The Tukanoan Indian shaman helps the dead with their encounter of the frightful, black, women ancestors, through whom the souls will be reborn.[60] In a similar fashion, the ancient Greeks, who retained many shamanistic characteristics in their pantheistic religion, had the black female spirits, or furies, as fright-inspiring entities, capable of terrifying a person into a maddening frenzy. Pausanias (viii, 34. 3) provides us with a comment regarding his visit to the sanctuary of the avenging Eumenides: "They say that when these goddesses would drive Orestes mad they appeared to him black, but that after he had bitten off his finger they seemed to him white. . . ." It seems that after the spirits (furies) were propitiated with the blood, flesh, and bone of his finger, the mad Orestes was allowed to pass through the danger zone of his ecstatic journey.

It is very much the shaman's concern that the human soul finds reprieve from potential danger awaiting it on its course to the Otherworld. In contemporary societies, the Greek Orthodox Church still manifests this shamanistic function of the psychopomp. The soul remains undetached from the body until the Greek priest arranges for its release through a ritual contained in the funeral mass. In the northwest Amazon and southeast Siberia, the soul, thus freed, pauses briefly on earth, and moves on to the Beyond and Nothingness to make room for the newcomers. The Beyond consists of complete nothingness, a transcendental space totally devoid of all Kantian forms of sensibilities and things abstract and material—a complete void, analogous to Sartre's existential dialectic in *Being and Nothingness*, and to the main philosophical questions raised by Camus. Thus, by seeking the path of return, one will find the only true reality in death, at which point the full potential of the person is revealed. However, the individuals who elevated themselves to higher planes of learning through the observance of rituals and mores, as well as by espousing the traditional values, will act as guiding torches only for the living, casting light on the dark pitfalls of earthly existence.

Yet, the journey to be undertaken by the soul is very perilous, with monstrous creatures lurking along the way. The shaman, as a psychopomp, enters into a trance by taking hallucinatory substances in order to guide the soul and abet in its confrontations with the harmful elements. Among the Nambas on Malekula island in the New Hebrides, it is a menacing female spirit who meets the transcended voyager at the portals to the Otherworld. In the case of the Tukanoans, the soul is encountered by the spirits of the female ancestors, "the black women," who are instrumental in arranging for the soul's rebirth once it enters the realm of the Beyond.

The shaman's guidance is not only restricted to the Hereafter. He also assists his people on their brief journey of life—pointing the way and treading before them on the uncertain path. However, life in this world is treated as an earthly illusion. Through transformation, alone, the essence of substances can be uncovered (an alchemical concept), and behind this notion we find the reason for the shaman's all-important quest for the Other (transformed) Realities. This is where the *truth* is to be found. Like the Jívaro Indian, who conceives this World to be an illusion and does not recognize a reality separate from the Otherworld, the Tukanoan is transformed during a hallucinogenic trance to another reality of a shamanic state of consciousness, "whence he returns to ordinary reality on this earth with the firm conviction of having had a glimpse of Paradise. And then he will know that it is Paradise which is reality and that life is but an illusion."[61] Irrespective of the fact that the image of the Otherworld encountered on his trance-journey may appear to him as a distorted reflection of this one, the "Tukanoan thought operates on the principle of analogy: man is central and nature is an analogy of man."[62] Here, the macrocosm is a projected image of the microcosm; not the other way around. As mentioned before, in the constant effort to absorb spiritual knowledge, the shamans almost everywhere seek to comprehend the enigmas of creation through shamanistic transformations, which provide the individual with the experience of understanding, knowing, and of creating a valid worldview. This they accomplish by means of visions, which make such transformations possible.

Trance, which consists of "what might be called a state of suspended animation for its duration,"[63] is regarded by many specialists as a prerequisite for any kind of true shamanism. The basic difference between shamanistic ecstasy and ecstasy of the mystery cults lies in the experience of the *entheoi* (the experience of god within), which is available to all participants initiated into the mystery religion. The ecstasy of the shaman is restricted to those who embark actively on soul-journeys by trance-inducing techniques, through which they attain the ecstatic state. The mystery cults, therefore, foster a commonality of experience, providing more generalized forms of ecstasy to a larger number of participants. Shamanism, on the other hand, offers more individualized, spiritual experience to a select few. The former falls within a public domain, the other is a personal passage. However, it must be clearly understood, as Mircea Eliade has intimated and Åke Hultkrantz pointed out, that not all shamanic trances consist of the same degree of intensity, and, consequently, not all shamanistic experiences can be regarded as equivalent. These span from the very light, for the North American Indians, to the very intense, for the Lapps, while covering a wide range of degrees in Siberia. In the eye witness report of the thirteenth century, *Historia Norwegiae*, written by a Norwegian Lapp, we are told of a shaman, who was earnestly described as fallen dead, while his spirit was believed to roam at large. Henceforth, "Pronouncements to the effect that the shamanic trance is invariably of the same depth are therefore misleading."[64]

Yet, the difficulty in using the word "trance" is reflected in the general impression that a state of trance is a state of unconsciousness, or nonconsciousness, while ". . .what we are really trying to establish," as Johan Reinhard notes properly in his contribution to Nepalese shamanism, "is that the shaman is in a nonordinary psychic state which in some cases means not a loss of consciousness but rather an altered state of consciousness."[65]

Nevertheless, there seem to be substantive, if not structural, regularities in the psychotropically induced visions among the divergent populations ingesting a kindred drug substance.[66] The ayahuasca-induced visions quite often bring on recurrent themes of large serpents seen in vivid colors, jaguars and ocelots, spirits and demons in the form of animal-headed people, views of distant places and people, forests and thickly-wooded gardens covered with fruit, and, last but not least, divinatory experiences of clairvoyance and astral projection, that is, the separation of the soul from the physical body.

The altered, or shamanic, state of consciousness induced by the hallucinogenic ayahuasca potion is reported by the anthropologist Kenneth Kensinger, who studied and lived with the Cashinahua Indians of Peru for a number of years. His account forms an interesting description of an ayahuasca-induced shamanic journey undertaken by several indigenous people. This account demonstrates the attainment of a state of consciousness that clearly promotes the ability to "see" into other temporal and spatial dimensions while under the influence of this hallucinogenic substance.

> Several informants who have never been to or seen pictures of Pucallpa, the large town on the Ucayali River terminus of the Central Highway, have described their visits under the influence of ayahuasca to the town with sufficient detail for me to be able to recognize specific shops and sights. On the day following one ayahuasca party, six of the nine men informed me of seeing the death of my *chai*, "my mother's father." This occurred two days before I was informed by radio of his death.[67]

Figure 3.2. Sculpture of a stone mushroom with a toad on top. The objects signifies, most probably, not only the close folk association between the two, but also the hallucinogenic properties of the sacred mushroom and the Bufo toad, as well as their roles in shamanistic-priestly rituals. Allegedly from Uxmal in Yucatan, Mexico. (Author's archives).

One may wish to speculate, in view of the above, about the stimuli behind the widespread cults of the jaguar and the feather-serpent as having a possible, if only partial, basis in the ancient pharmacological preparations made with the *Banisteriopsis* species (ayahuasca, yajé, etc.). Such concoctions are known to be responsible for extremely terrifying hallucinatory visions of jaguars, birds, and serpents (bird + serpent = feather-serpent). By the same token, the psychoactive ingredients of another hallucinogen employed in Mexico may throw some light on the position of the enigmatic Olmec dwarf figurines, which, in reality, might have portrayed the material representations of their preternatural counterparts, as seen during the drug-induced trances. Another example is afforded by the mushroom *Psilocybe mexicana*, known to the Aztecs as *teonanacatl* ("flesh of the gods"), and used far more extensively than is suggested by the comparatively limited distribution of the mushroom, or toadstool, stones. The use of *P. mexicana* in Mesoamerica has been uninterrupted for at least three thousand years. Michael Coe even goes so far as to suggest that the use of these mushrooms by the Maya ritual specialists might have played a considerable role in the design of such ceremonial centers as Palenque.

Now, I must ask: To what extent might certain old, but widely distributed beliefs have arisen from noncultural, or biochemical stimuli, operating at the very formative levels, and rendering constant reinforcements? The transcultural recurrence of the central themes in the visions leans towards the consideration of certain shamanistic worldviews as manifestations of mankind's syncretic experiences rather than the experience of a cognitive system depicting particularistic traits of a local tradition.[68] Drug-induced visual experience, structured through a learning input, is a key in the process of culture change. Such experience contributes, through the cognitive system, to the organization of the output fed via the perceptual sensations—namely, it contributes to the demarcation of social roles, the reinforcement of cultural proscriptions, and perhaps, in some instances, to the development of language. The chemical properties of the psilocybin mushroom seem to activate centers of the brain connected with language and speaking.[69]

The Jívaro perceive the ordinary world not as real, but a distortion. They believe that the only reality is to be found in the preternatural experience.[70] "Consensual validation," according to Carlos Castaneda, is the mode by which one learns to separate culturally approved forms from the incorrect ones. "The shaman has a conception of *poesis* in its original sense," writes Henry Munn in his deeply sensitive and illuminating essay entitled "The Mushrooms of Language." Here he describes some of the psilocybin-related factors that enter into the structure and formation of personal cognition. "To enunciate and give

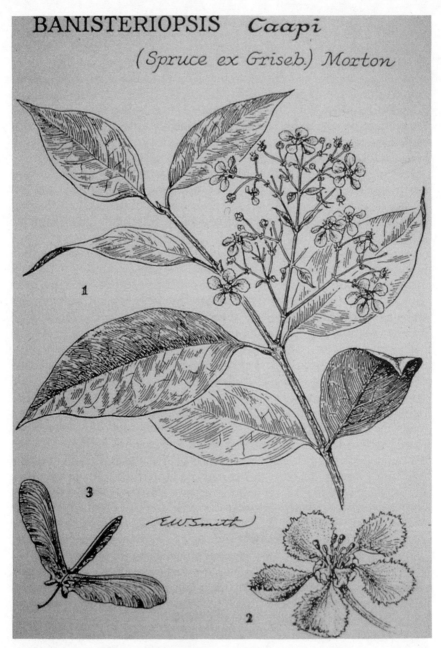

Figure 3.3. An old botanical illustration of the powerful plant hallucinogen, *Banisteriopsis caapi*, known as yajé in the Amazon.

meaning to the events and situations of existence is life giving in itself,"[71] he states in the same passage.

> The vivid dreams of the psychedelic experience suggested hallucinations: such imaginations do occur in these visionary conditions, but they are marginal, not essential phenomena of a general liberation of the spontaneous, ecstatic, creative activity of conscious existence. Hallucinations predominated in the experiences of the investigators because they were passive experimenters of the transformative effect of the mushrooms. . . . The shamanistic condition provoked by the mushrooms is intuitionary, not hallucinatory. What one envisions has an ethical relation to reality, is indeed often the path to be followed. To see is to realize, to understand. . . . The phenomenon most distinctive of the mushrooms' effect is the inspired capacity to speak. . . . The shaman, chanting in a melodic singsong, saying *says* at the end of each phrase of saying, is in communication with the origins of creation, the sources of the voice, and the fountains of the word, related to reality from the heart of his existential ecstasy by the active mediation of language: the articulation of meaning and experience. To call such transcendental experiences of light, vision, and speech hallucinatory is to deny that they are revelatory of reality."[72]

Shamanism and Psychopathology

If glimpses of another reality were awarded to a select few and recounted to others who, locked into Platonic and Aristotelean ideas of fixed images, possessed accordingly a conception of their worldview as a system of shadows cast on the walls of a cave, the latter would undoubtedly regard the descriptions of alternate states of consciousness as fables fabricated by sheer lunatics. The Scientific Revolution, ushered in by the Ages of Reason and Enlightenment, brought with it the tenets of scientific materialism. Anton Mesmer had been ridiculed and called a charlatan by the medical and scientific professions of his day for introducing hypnotism to eighteenth century western Europe. It took about one hundred years for a few pioneering spirits to break the barrier of the stigma and give this conjecture a serious evaluation, with startling implications for medicine and psychiatry. The renowned Charcot, in Paris; the young Freud, who had studied with him in France and afterwards practiced in Vienna; and Braid in Manchester were those few willing to stake their reputations to investigate objectively Mesmer's postulates of animal magnetism. The eventual application of hypnosis as a viable tool in certain areas of mental dysfunctions proved to be a landmark achievement, especially in cases suffering from symptoms which were, then, perhaps too broadly classified as hysteria. As a result, medical literature has been enriched by such classics as *Studies in Hysteria*, the product of a collaboration between by Breuer and Freud.

In the introduction to Géza Róheim's *Children of the Desert*, Werner Muensterberger states, perhaps only too galantly and too hopefully: "Empathy with solitary imagination and, by implication, with the sublimities of dreams, hopes, despair—in other words, that voyage from the mundane to the spiritual—is the clinician's concern." How much more aptly, in fact, does the last sentence describe a shaman? I do not know, for one, of any clinical psychotherapist who would venture to take the great leap, along with his client, onto the spiritual plane. Yet, every single shaman worthy of his drum would do precisely that. He participates by becoming actively involved in finding and administering the curative treatment—unlike the psychotherapist, who passively assists the patient in finding his or her own solution, and, at the very best, functions as an uninvolved catalytic agent. "The psychoanalyst listens, whereas the shaman speaks," surmised Claude Lévi-Strauss. The latter affords his client a *language* that provides an instant outlet for mental and psychic states that otherwise could remain buried within or incapable of finding expression. As a result, and at the same time, a cognitive format is created by which the client can undergo and internalize a genuine experience in an organized fashion. Otherwise, lacking a channel and the metaphors of language to express, by verb or action, a traumatic psychic condition could easily precipitate repressed and chaotic situations, possibly leading to acute states of mental disorder.[73] After all, the contemporary grandchild of a shamanistic technique is, quite clearly, as much an integral part of our modern society as shamanism and hunting magic were in the past. Freud might have founded psychoanalysis, but he did so, consciously or not, on much older foundations laid by practicing shamans throughout the world and over the millennia.

This widespread occurrence of mental crises associated with the shamanic "calling" is a transcultural phenomenon to be witnessed wherever shamanism has been practiced. The resulting powerful crisis may have the outward appearance of a mental imbalance or a nervous breakdown. In no way, however, must it be designated lightly as such. It does not constitute, in itself, a pathological indication, but manifests its own particularistic and phenomenological occurrence, which is confined exclusively within the perimeters of what is designated as normal for the exceptional individuals within their own respective cultural frameworks. Mental disorders fall, very much, under the society's designation of what constitutes mentally deviant or extraordinary behavior, and the selection of a prospective candidate for a shaman is also marked by the cultural ethos. It is true that the person in the midst of a shamanistic experience may stay on the fringe of all social interactions and become totally aloof and isolated. He may remain so for a long period of time, until the deep personal crisis passes, leaving him reconstituted, reborn, and preternaturally transformed. His society recognizes that the person "answering the call" is merely responding to the approaching mystical states connected with IPC, or the states of awareness. The inside and the outside frontiers of being lend to this worldly existence a sacred character, not discernible by the ordinary, the matter-of-fact person, but only by the inordinary individual. Other endogenous factors, such as a predisposition to epilepsy, have also been implicated in shamanism. Epileptoid characteristics, exhibited by seizures of convulsions, can be found in widely divergent cultures. The Wintu Indians of northern California are but one good example.

As mentioned in the preceding chapter, no lesser a scholar of religious history and ideas than Mircea Eliade failed to recognize the critical role of hallucinogens in shamanistic techniques. Instead, following the earlier speculations of Åke Ohlmarks about Arctic shamanism, as well as of others who had preceded him, Eliade assented to the idea that the compulsary nature of "the call," the "shamanic illness," and the "trance" are only products of a psychopathological mode, whether cured or still symptomatic, of the reintegrated personality of the ritual practitioner. In fact, this state of mental disorder, or the so-called Arctic sickness—and even named Arctic hysteria by some—may result from a number of neurobiochemical factors responsible for changes in the neural functions, such as those produced by the lack of certain vitamins and minerals, as well as by the acute psychological stress created by the harsh Arctic environment. The shaman manifests the symptoms of a mental disorder precisely because he functions on a borderline territory, infiltrated with all kinds of hazards emanating from the antipodal worlds constituting his realities. Accordingly, Eliade felt that the visionary experience ought to be classified, most frequently, as abnormal.[74] Even the good Joseph Campbell could not free himself from the ethnocentric burden inflicted by others in his attempt to conceive of shamanism as a controlled schizophrenic condition. How different an outlook, indeed, we encounter here from that presented, only a few paragraphs above by the poignant soul-searching in "The Mushrooms of Language"! And how do we account for similar phenomenological occurrences, in function and substance, prevailing in parts of the world where the environmental conditions present drastic contrasts to the Arctic habitat?

Carl Jung defines neurosis as a dissociated personality. Yet, it is most important to realize that, unlike neurosis, which disables the particular sufferer by exerting disruptive influence on life and living, the "shamanic crisis" may enhance the intelligence, sensitivity, and vitality of the person. Consequently, the latter condition must not be perceived as a deepening chasm between an estranged and shattered human spirit, on one hand, and the antagonistic world-at-large, on the other. Just the opposite appears to be true. It is the signification of awareness of the profound intensity permeating matter and the spirit—an awareness which, as Joseph Campbell keenly observed, escapes the greater majority, being reserved only for the exceptional few.[75] Thus, the shamanic inner personal crisis (IPC) is, in actuality, no less than a major rite of passage. The initiate's successful transition through this crisis elevates the individual beyond sheer tribal perspective into a level of cosmic perception. This offers a more effective vantage point for observing the emergence of a broader personality structure and validates also the universal format of shamanism by endowing it with many transcultural characteristcs.

Let us draw a basic distinction between a schizophrenic, or a psychopathological, personality and that of a true shaman: A schizophrenic personality perceives the environment as disparate and fragmented, lacking structural unity; the structural elements of this mental condition display idiosyncratic patterns. The world of such a mentally dysfunctional individual is disintegrated. On the other hand, just the opposite may be said about a shaman. First, his worldview is characterized by an intrinsic unity, with all the components fitted and integrated, yielding a cohesive world structure. Second, a shamanic state of consciousness is not a condition limited exclusively to the idiosyncratic experience of a single person, instead the structural elements of shamanism manifest recurrent themes across transcultural boundaries.

Of vital importance, moreover, to the shamanic trance and visionary experience is the ritual drug complex, or the so-called drug ceremonial. Mentioned only briefly until now, its functional and substantive considerations warrant that it be given a more extensive treatment elsewhere in this book.

4

The Psychotropic Universe: Cosmology of the Spirit World

Cosmic Transformations

THE GREAT HUMAN DREAM is that of transformation: from man to god. The divine plants opened up a way to god and the heavenly abode. Those vested with the secret knowledge of these plants were the chosen ones, and such unique individuals learned the secrets of the universe not piecemeal, but by sudden visions from within. The changes in seasonal cycles, the structure and behavior of matter, were all nature's mysteries. The early arts of healing, religion, agriculture, and finally metallurgy/alchemy were, essentially, inseparable.

In the course of its long existence as a cultural feature of mankind, shamanism endeavored to unravel the universal enigmas: the origins of the cosmos, the earth, humans, animals, and plants. It ventured to illuminate the proverbial, existential quest for the meaning and sense of life and death. Shamanism molded the qualitative aspect of religious phenomenology in human societies by bestowing the knowledge of the supernatural order as perceived by means of the psychodynamic processes entailed in the techniques of ecstasy, which have been frequently induced by the use of hallucinogenic plants. The supernatural experience of the cosmic order is only a reflection of the sociocultural system known at a particular phase of cultural development, while the secular knowledge of the supernatural is the shaman's version of his visionary experience. In the process, the physico-biotic environment was observed, and the ways of plants and animals were studied, as were the movements of the celestial bodies and the properties of metals. The healing potencies of the divine plants came to be understood, and meanings were given to dreams and visionary experiences; thus, the beginnings of rationalistic epistemology. The signification of a need in a particular society to relate causality (input) to the shaman's worldview and to offer a response through the mode of a visionary context (output) are both the cause and effect, interacting as a complex system, in a dynamic process that we perceive as culture change. This change is in itself only an abstract modality—a culturally accepted product, among others, of anteceding, yet extensive, experimentations with the ethnoflora.

Consequently, one must not underestimate the effect of shamanistic beliefs—hence, the role played by hallucinogenic agents—in man's attempts to interpret the universe into a meaningful order. Under the influence of the psychoactive alkaloid harmaline, for example, the different religio-philosophical attitudes strove to unravel the cosmic arcana, to bring structure and organizational sense into the frustrated intellect. They attempted to do this by constructing the *imago mundi*— the archetypal image—in accordance with a cosmic blueprint manifest in the transcultural acceptance of the divine paradigm, and along the recognizable guidelines of psychotropic experiences. Through the understanding of the cognitive experiences, interrelating the various facets of supernatural reality with their ordinary counterparts, a much fuller insight can be gained into the causalities underlying the origins and the development of a culture trait. In other words, one should consider the extent to which the shaman's techniques have depended on hallucinogenic agents in his formulation of supernatural and physical worldviews. Only through such an understanding, can we develop a more profound appreciation of the interconnecting dynamic processes weaving a cultural experience. A good illustration is offered by the nexus formed between the ritual drug complex and the beginnings of agriculture, and even metallurgy—of gold, in particular—and alchemy.[1]

That metal working has been considered to be an activity imbued with cosmological significance can be easily recognized, not only in ancient societies, but in numerous contemporary settings recounting their metallurgical traditions, and to be found in diverse cultural complexes, as those, for instance, of the Desana Indians inhabiting the Amazonian equatorial rain forest. The cosmological allusions contained in their sexual symbolism are expressed by the idiomatic meanings attached to certain objects of adornment and social performance. For the Indians of northern Colombia, gold, silver, and copper articles have been fashioned and worn as things replete with shamanistic meanings.[2] Prehispanic gold artifacts, especially from Panama and Colombia, offer a wide array of intriguing specimens to this effect.[3] Europe and Asia, in their own right, possessed rich lores and wide ranges of symbolism associated with precious metals and gemstones, inferring tightly woven relationships with such cosmic phenomena as magic, astrology, and astronomy.

In the study of the shamanistic phenomenon, some pundits have cautioned[4] that the mere features characteristic of the spirit world should not constitute the primary focus. Instead, it is the cosmological configuration, the structure, that is important for the understanding of the existing nexus between the shaman and his spirit realm. By the same token, those students of cultures and ethnohistory who have been steeped in the dialectic of cultural materialism[5] have leaned towards "functional" and "ecological" interpretations of the ideological worldviews and cosmological concepts encountered in the various indigenous societies. They regard such ideas as expressions of the human awareness and responses to the social, material, and other environmental conditions, while at the same time, they are compelled to acknowledge, the impact of a prevailing conception on the perception of all the concepts that preceded it. So, at least in the case of the pragmatic functionalists, it is a positive sign of recognition of the inescapable universal principle inherent in all observations: the manner in which we see things is conditioned by the ideas that we already possess about them. However, it leaves doubts as to whether our understanding of shamanism, and the indigenous cosmological concepts, for that matter, is to be enhanced by demystifying the phenomena, and by avoiding symbolic contents and religious metaphors. All constituents, living and inanimate—beings, objects, and places—of shamanistic traditions, are metaphors for abstract constructs and symbolic thoughts, delineating the essential parameters of the shamanistic worldview.

A genuinely mystical occurrence belongs to a variety of true religious experiences. Religion, in turn, is a transformational process; a profound religious transformation becomes a cosmic process. Finally, death marks the threshold of a great personal transformation. However, not every culture, or an individual, perceives this event in a similar light. Death, for the Druzes, creates an impact on the existence of the soul by causing it to flee and transfer its essence into a newborn Druze baby. This type of reincarnation has very little to do with the notion of karma, for the body that the soul occupies anew need not constitute an improvement of the soul's physical lot.[6] The Druze religious doctrine maintains that the number of Druze souls remains fixed. With every death, there must inadvertently occur a birth;[7] thus, the overall balance of souls is maintained in the universe.

Much respected in the Middle Eastern societies is the power of religious practitioners, spiritualists, and even tricksters, who can manipulate invisible forces. The mental and physical conditions of a person, according to the Druzes, can definitely be impaired by the possession of an evil spirit or demon. Such grievous times require that the inflicted man or a woman be chained by an iron collar; the assumption being that a confined body makes for an uncomfortable habitat.[8]

The reality of spirits is as much a matter of course for the Mehinaku of the Upper Xingu River as that of trees, flowers, and rocks. However, the spirits can only be perceived in altered states of consciousness—trance, dreams, or at the very moment of death—and since the spirits can be dangerous and destructive, special considerations are warranted on their behalf. As a result of a non-existent linguistic differentiation between the natural and the supernatural, a competent shaman is very helpful in guiding across the "razor-edged" bridge spanning the gap. The occurrence of death and sickness is primarily effected with the theft of a soul by a supernatural being, or, as among the Cubeo, by an object imbued with evil magic penetrating a person's body. The origin of demons has no particular explanation in the cosmogony of the Mehinaku, who credit the shamans with such discoveries, since primeval times, and with the contriving of rituals for the spirits' sustenance and propitiation. As a matter of fact, if not for the shamans, the Mehinaku would still be unaware of the existence of spirits and demons and of the appropriate rituals surrounding them. It is believed that other forms of spirits exist, not as yet discovered or identified by the shamans, leaving the Mehinaku spiritual world not explored quite fully.[9]

Dreams, the Cubeo Indians believe, are caused by the soul's wanderings and excursions away from the physical body. In contrast to the Yąnomamö's concern for the soul aspect of the *noreshi*, the Cubeo are never fearful that the ethereal essence may fail to return. Upon death, the soul, *umé*, travels to the spirit world at a nearby river, and it assumes a human form that can be heard and seen by the shaman. Individuals guilty of violating cultural proscriptions and social bonds, such as incest, ritual friendship, and adultery, will have their souls in animal forms: "Since they did not care for people . . . they cannot live among the souls of people after death." However, unlike the afterlife of the Yąnomamö, whose construct mirrors earthly existence, it appears that the Cubeo "have visualized an afterlife that is lacking in the essences of life . . . the ingredients that the Cubeo associate with vital intensity. . . . Literally, then, the Cubeo visualize a shadow existence after death."[10]

The Cubeo concept of power, like many others in the Amazon rain forest, does not recognize a distinction between natural and supernatural categories: the cognate *parié* expresses a state—a manifestation—of "being able." It may apply to shamanistic powers or simply to the prowess of a warrior. Their supernatural beings bestow non-personal, more generalized attention on the people, something that is easier to deal with and to combat than a human evil force, which tends to be evermore so perilous and formidable. Sorcery is the most dreaded aspect of Cubeo life. Indisputedly, it is the shaman, known as either *pariékokü* ("man of power") or as *yaví* ("jaguar"), who is the main possessor of power; the former denoting power in its neutral, benign aspect, while "jaguar" carries frightening and awesome implications. Shamanistic power, *parúkü*, is designated by a cognate word implying a substance, that enables the shaman to perform his tasks. Definitely not commonplace, a *yaví* is extremely powerful—a great shaman, who can transform into a jaguar or have his soul enter the animal, maintain intimate relations with it, and have it for a spiritual familiar and as a pet (usually a dog). In short, the jaguar is yaví's avatar, and the shaman's soul becomes a jaguar upon death. Accordingly, the Cubeo's fear of the jaguar is based on the realization that it is not a mere jungle beast, but an aggressive manifestation with human origins.[11] We can witness, here, just another expression of the ancient culture myth, found in Middle and South America, which has to do with the were-jaguar. Incidently, in contrast to the Western Hemisphere, the tiger is the avatar of the Malay shaman, who can not only transform himself into this creature, but has tigers for his closest animal familiars.

Within each person is contained a *noreshi*, claim the Yąnomamö. This concept can be translated as the alter-ego, the anima/animus, the spiritual were-beast, or the animal aspect of the soul. It vaguely resembles totemism, for the *noreshi* animal is inherited from a relative of the same gender, except that, unlike a totem, it shows no connection to any marriage rules or lineage exogamy. The *noreshi* is an actual animal of the jungle, and its behavior corresponds to that of the person containing its spirit. A happy individual will have a content *noreshi* roaming the forest; a *noreshi* of a journeying person will travel, too, and so forth. Nevertheless, the ego and the alter-ego must never meet, for such an incident will bring about their mutual deaths. Yet, the soul aspect of the *noreshi* may wander off at will, resulting in the person's sickness attributed to soul-loss, and unless it returns or is brought promptly back, death will follow. The *noreshi* makes an easy target for witchcraft and black magic, and, like the supernatural beings (*hekura*), it can be approached by means of a narcotic trance. All such affairs are the obvious business of the shaman (*shabori*),[12] as are the transformations of men into deer, attained during a trance induced by a hallucinogenic snuff, which seem to form the basis for the Yạnomamö origin myths. It may be added that, traditionally, these natives did not employ medicinal plants for healing, but mostly relied on shamanistic curative techniques.

The shadows of totemism and were-animals are clearly visible in the complex of Siberian shamanism. A strong totemic-shamanistic theme is to be found among the Evenks, where several variants of folklore motifs exist recounting their ethnogenesis from a bear, who sacrificed himself on behalf of his people.[13] The most important aspect of the Evenk shaman's soul—his animal-double (*khargi*)—is promulgated in the Lowerworld, the dwelling place of his ancestral spirits. Certain among these possess dual nature, allowing their transformation into "the animal-double of the shaman," that is, his avatar. The *khargi* return to the World Tree, along with the shaman, in their changed, alternate aspect as the animal. In the native lore, the birth of the shaman's animal-double represents an act that transforms man into animal and animal into man, and takes place at the matrilocal area of the shaman's and his clan's births. It is to this location that the human counterpart of the shaman's soul ventures, to be transformed by the "mother-animal" into an animal creature, which then returns to this World (i.e., the Middle) as a shaman-man. The importance—cognitive, at least—of the clan and the covert totemic implications, are evidenced also in the notion of the shamanistic clan-river, guarded by the spirit elk-deer and used for travel to the Otherworlds by the Evenk shaman and his spirit helpers.[14]

The domain formed by the shamanistic clan-river marks the topographic *axis mundi* of the three worlds comprising the universe. This in itself constitutes an important aspect of the shamanistic cosmography, but particularly in view of the shaman's transport, along this river, of the soul of the deceased on a raft. The soul will be judged by the old woman, the mistress of the dead, who decides whether it is suitable for admission to the Netherworld. Nor surprisingly, she also plays a part in the shamanistic rite *anan*—a funeral repast. Among still different Siberian tribes, such as the Nivkhs, the deceased is met on the road by such an old woman,[15] a belief somewhat reminiscent of the Tukanoan soul's encounter on its last earthly journey, as it is guided by the shaman to the world Hereafter.

In the Celtic cosmology, like in the extant Siberian counterpart, entrances to the Otherworlds were associated with cosmic trees and sources of water, such as lakes, wells, and streams. Its ancient tradition is replete with myths associating water, the Otherworld, and transformation. In one of the early Irish myths, relating to Angus, the son of the benign deity, In Dagda, the youth becomes enamoured with a maiden whom he sees in his dream. As matters usually turn out in such cases, the sentiment turns into passion, and passion into obsession. Resigned to find her at all costs, Angus discovers her existence in this worldly reality as the daughter of a well known personage in Connaught. After spying upon her by a lake, the youth applies to the girl's father for her hand in marriage. No and nay, the father asserts; the girl is under a spell! One year she must spend as a maiden fair, the alternate one she is to become a swan. To bring even more consternation to this hexed situation, young Angus must, if compulsion takes him, cohabit with the maiden in her avian incarnation, while he, too, becomes a swan. It should be remembered that such aquatic birds form, transculturally, recurrent motifs with strong shamanistic associations. Thus, once more we encounter in the Celtic lore, if not a shamanistic tradition that is substantively obvious, at least a spirit world that represents unquestionably a cultural memory of such a past.

As ought to be apparent by now, "All shamans are transformers," states Reichel-Dolmatoff. They are capable of achieving metamorphosis by assuming the shapes of jaguars, giant serpents, and other terrifying lifeforms. However, it must be understood, he warns, that all shamanic allusions to transformations into and communications with animals are meant to be metaphoric. Likewise, all other manifestations of the Tukanoan religion, including the concept of Master of the Animals,

> . . . are nothing but metaphors that stand for abstract concepts, for vital energies, that underlie biological evolution, fertility, circadian rhythms or ecological balance, as these processes are understood by shamans. . . .There is then no dogma and no church, no cult and no divine personification. . . .And there is no religion in terms of prayers or sacrifice."[16]

This valuable piece of ethnographic insight, from a cultural complex in the northwest Amazon, sheds some light on the Upper Palaeolithic and Mesolithic horizons of the archaeological present. It affords us glimpses into the female principle—the feminine power—that has survived there as an archetypal reality in the form of a gigantic womb, being the repository of a cosmic force and intelligence that are masculine in principle. The boundaries of the whole universe are confined within this cosmic womb, its physical configuration reflecting the shape of the all-important hexagonal rock crystals, and being propagated by the masculine force residing within it.[17] "An impossible, unthinkable cosmic potency"—symbolized by the esoteric Protogonos: the mystic, androgynous syncretism of Eros and Aphrodite—was the way Jane Harrison described its analogue among the ancient Greeks. This Amazonian universe has a tripartite structure: upper, middle, and lower. The upper, celestial, is represented by the Milky Way, which, according to a native shamanistic cosmography, serves as an axis mundi—the transcendental center—interfacing the antipodal worlds: the abstract (male) and the material (female), or the spiritual and the earthly.

The two antipods designate parallel world realities within a single universe, coexisting on each side of the axis mundi which is metaphorized by the imposing stick rattle of the shaman. Cultural metaphors are drawn, to represent processes and events of the ordinary reality, from the shamanistic drug ceremonial, which inadvertently opens up a path to the Otherworld. This differs from the spiritual grammar of traditional Western cultures, where the dialectic of conventions utilizes symbols and metaphors as representations of mystical or divine aspects. In contrast, for the Barasana Indians of the Pira-paraña river, certain acts involving the ritual preparation of the hallucinogenic potion, made from *Banisteriopsis* spp., symbolize important events in the cycle of human life, such as those associated with the processes of birth and rebirth. Consequently, some of the metaphors expressed in the Amazonian ceremonial art may signify interfaces between boundaries of consciousness; others may represent a cosmic model, with a transformational vortex, or a center, between the Upper and the Lower Worlds. This zone of transformation creates a nexus, like the ritual itself, of concepts pertaining to birth, rebirth, female fertility, labyrinths, and whirlpools or spirals. For example, the **U**-shaped design, found commonly on the foot of a ritual hallucinogenic vessel, symbolizes "the portal"—in all its affective connotations—through which the participant must enter to undergo the transformation of rebirth.[18] The whirlpool and the labyrinth allude to a path, the spiral of the infinite process, leading from this World to the Other beneath.

Corresponding Realities and Otherworlds

The center, the sacred and secular domains, the spiral (rather than a circular) process of eternal return, all are elements in the structure of the shaman's universe. The spiral is both a passageway to the Lowerworld and annihilation, as well as to re-emergence and rebirth. Entropy precedes revival. This principle of eternal return appears to be basic in the religious lives of ancient and aboriginal societies, and its surviving forms still thrive, nowadays, among many so-called modern peoples. To cite one example, seemingly allegorical and perhaps from the far end of the spectrum, but, yet, forming an integral part in the beliefs of a creatively resourceful individual: What if one dreamed about picking exotic flowers in heaven, "and what if when you awoke you had the flower in your hand? Ah, what then?" Thus mused very earnestly, the opium-habituated, visionary poet, Samuel Taylor Coleridge, about the ambiguities of reality, noting over and over that certain human experiences do not conform to our established concepts of space, time, and matter. Space, on the other hand, physical or existential, is the abstract vessel into which humans organize their universe. They have devised realms that accommodate their spiritual and ordinary requirements: the former under the sole authority and possession of a deity or a spirit; the latter inhabited by humans and overtly subjected to their manipulations as prescribed by the norms of ritualized forms of behavior. Sacred space does not necessarily imply an upper realm, as envisaged in our idea of the heaven, but refers to an existential concept of inordinary dimension, as opposed to a mere physical or material realm.

The notion of the Center is, however, fundamental to shamanistic, cosmological symbolism, for it converges onto the two previous ideas. It is an axis, the navel joining the Earth, the Upperworld, and the Lowerworld—or the earth, heaven, and hell of the Western tradition. Claudio Naranjo, the Chilean psychiatrist who experimented medically with harmaline-containing substances—such as, *yajé*, or *ayahuasca*—used by South American shamans to induce trance, offers a valuable and illuminating perspective, gained from clinical experience, on the "shamanistic center."

> The "center" can appear in the different visions as a source of motion or the region to which motion flows [eternal return], a source of light or a perceiving eye, a geometric region such as a circular pond in the middle of Heaven or Hell [navel of the earth], a being at the center of the earth, of the universe, the skull or inside of the subject's body. . . . From the subject's experiences and associations, as from the context in which these images appear, I definitely believe that this contraposition of center and periphery, the core and the surface [sacred and secular], the immobile and the incessant turning, the source, beginning and end [rebirth and death], and the everchanging flow, is that of the deepest self and the multiplicity of experience, and it encompasses but transcends the duality of mind and body. More precisely, it is that of being and becoming, and it matches the traditional Hindu symbol for *samsāra* and *nirvāna:* the wheel of incessant death and rebirth, and its hub. Or, according to. . .the *tao-tê-ching*, the practical materiality of a jar and the enclosed void that constitutes its essence.[19]

The sacred aspect of the existential *center* has obvious counterparts among the so-called revealed religions. The Judaeo-Christian tradition abounds with numerous examples, spanning across many centuries. For the faithful Muslims, it is a credo that Muhammed's soul, after his burial in the city of Medina, had journeyed on a white steed to Jerusalem, ascending to the Upperworld from the Rock of the Moriah, the site of the Dome of the Rock, and considered to be—just like the dome— symbolic of the Cosmic Mountain (following), thus, closest to heaven. In a transcendental sense, it is the highest place on earth. With respect to the dome and the sphere, the religious and intellectual significance[20] of these topological forms was a phenomenon well-recognized through- out the ancient world. The actual spatial relationship, symbolic and architectonic, between a dome and the sacred area that it encapsulates, is well exemplified, incidently, by the two most famous domes in Jerusalem. One is over the alleged tomb of Jesus at the Church of the Holy Sepulcher and the other is over the aforementioned sacred rock; their interior geometries and basic architecture are essentially the same, but not their features of adornment.

The Center of the World is also represented by the image of the Cosmic Mountain, seen also as a connecting axis between the earth and the Upperworld. Often conceived of as ziggurat-shaped, the Cosmic Mountain is believed to consist of either three to four tiers (e.g., for the Mongols and the Kalmucks) or seven (for the Siberian Tatars and the Yakuts), with its peak reaching the polar star. Mount Meru, in Indian mythology, emerges from the Center of the World, right beneath the radiating Polaris. The significant roles of Mounts Zion and Sinai as the Cosmic Mountains are featured prominantly in the Old Testament tradition. The name of Mount Tabor in the Holy Land, just like Delphi, may signify omphalos, the navel. The Biblical progenitor, Adam, had been created and buried on a Cosmic Mountain, while Jesus, too, was allegorically crucified on the same mountain, with Adam's skull soaking the blood of the new Messiah at the base of the cross. All the peoples of the ancient Near East had developed concepts of the Cosmic Center or Mountain.[21] Even the ancient Egyptians, for whom mountainous topography played such a small part in actual life, had their "primal" mountain, or hill, where creation had taken place. To ascend the Cosmic Mountain is equivalent to climbing the shamanistic World Tree, or the cosmic pillar (see infra, this section).

The pivotal significance of the Cosmic Center is well evidenced in the remote and different culture of the Kogi Indians, where the notion of the sacred mountain functions as a nucleus around which is construed a rich body of cosmological concepts, steeped in elaborate religious imagery and rich metaphor.[22] The Kogi, who inhabit the massif of the isolated Sierra Nevada de Santa Marta adjoining the Caribbean coast in northern Colombia, still bear witness, today, to the much cherished and persistent tradition stemming from the period before the European conquest. To them, the sacred mountain not only represents the Center of the World, but is the center of their entire existence—their universe.

The Kogi religion and worldview are as complex as any exemplified by the known traditions of the more "sophisticated" cultures of Middle or South America. Their belief system focuses around the "catechisms" of the Great Mother Goddess, who is the beginning and the end of Life. She exhorts a transpersonal and, at the same time, an orderly attitude towards existence on earth, wherein happenings are seen as reflections and cosmic models mirroring the behavior of celestial bodies and the occurrences of all sorts of astral phenomena. Life's end completes the earthly cycle by redirecting the individual to the Cosmic Center. In the shamanistic worldview of the Hereafter, the dead ascend the snow-covered, sacred apex of the Sierra Nevada.[23]

In western Mexico, the Sierra Madre Occidental forms the habitat of the only major Indian group in Mesoamerica that has managed to preserve much of its indigenous religion and ethos. In a distant place, located in the desert of San Luis Potosi, the Huichols have their Cosmic Center—*Wirikúta*, the land of the divine ancestors, the sacred peyote country—to which a person must journey at least five times before he can become a shaman, or a *mara'akáme*. The many ritual appurtenances, such as divine plants, rock crystals, horns, and skeletons, play as important roles in the Huichol shamanistic complex as they do in the great Amazon basin or Siberia. The significance of such objects is often expressed in the ceremonial art idiom, *nearika* (meaning "face," "aspect," "design"), exclusive to the Huichol Indians and represented by a form of vibrantly colored yarn painting set into beeswax admixed with resin. One talented exponent of this indigenous colored-yarn medium was Ramón Medina Silva, later to become a full mara'akáme, and through whom Peter Furst and his associates obtained much of their valuable information, insight, and experience in the areas of Huichol ritual life and metaphor.[24]

In a series of remarkable nearikas,[25] appropriately called "The Adventures of a Huichol Soul," housed in the collection of the UCLA Museum of Cultural History, Ramón depicts the journey begun, at death, by human souls to the Hereafter, a Lowerworld aspect of the Cosmic Center. Transgressors of sexual norms (i.e., violators of the incest taboo and those who had sexual relations with non-Indians) proceed along the road forking to the left, while the right is for the righteous. The condemned soul, depicted as a skeleton (equivalent to a shamanistic initiation), undergoes an interim "sentence" of a type recalling a

Figure 4.1. An ancient Mexican clay figurine with a shamanistic theme, showing a body with its soul or a spirit counterpart. (Municipal Museum of Benalmadena, Spain).

Christian purgatory, since there exists no concept of eternal punishment among the Huichols.

The journey to the Netherworld takes five (apparently a number of cosmological significance, also witnessed in a different Otherworldly context) days, and all this time the souls carry along with them the evidence of their sexual adventures on earth. At times, they diverge themselves with repasts of drinking maize beer (*náwa*), consuming the sacred peyote, and dancing around the fire with other deceased. However, before the final act of departure can take place, the soul must be retrieved by the shaman so that its relatives may offer it the proper farewell and feast. With these ceremonies duly enacted, the shaman, then in his capacity as a psychopomp, escorts the soul part of the way to a transcended center of existence—to the Otherworld.

From a considerably different part of the world, delineated by the greater Pacific basin, we can just as readily draw another example of the Cosmic Center, as perceived in terms of an axis mundi connecting, or interfacing, different transcendental planes and realms. The Biak shamans[26] from the Sorong area, in the Raja-Empat region of western New Guinea, believe that the axis mundi bisects the universe into the mystical and ethereal (ephemeral) sphere, called "the world of the wind" (*dunia wam*), and the ordinary sphere of physical matter, known as "the world of the body" (*dunia baken*). This idea reflects, quite aptly, the principle of dualism imbedded in their cosmological concepts. Thus, the two domains of the universe are intersected by four cosmic planes: (1) The Sky (*Nangi*), where Manseren Nangi, or the high-god Sky, has his adobe, surrounded by the heavenly canopy of stars. The souls of those whose heads were decapitated find, eventually, their resting place in the Milky Way. (2) The Domain of the Clouds (*Mandep*) has the cardinal axis of the four winds and the chiefs (*Korano*) of the corresponding four quarters. The chiefs of the northern and the eastern winds are benign, while the lords of the southern and the western winds represent malignant forces. Travel on the east-west axis may, sometimes, mean life's journey. (3) The World of Man (*dunia snonkaku*) is the earthly domain, where the souls of the inhabitants are threatened by the evil spirits from the realm of the clouds. (4) The Lowerworld (*jenaibu*) is the dwelling place of the ancestors and the dead, with locations in the earth (and on the mountaintops among the Birds Head tribes) and at the bottom of the sea, with insular grottos and caverns as possible entrances. All animal and plant life is engendered from inside the earth, as well. The earth, holding eternity within it (the center), is the ultimate life source.[27]

As among the Biak of western New Guinea, the cosmology of the Yanomamö in the Brazilian rain forest subsumes four overlaying planes. The first and the highest one (*duku kä misi*, meaning "tender layer"), was once the source of the universe. However, it has been emptied of the essential substance, and, as a result, it is presently a void (broke). This primordial plane, this "tender layer," corresponds to the zenith and nadir of very existence, where all things had their beginnings and an end (void). It is reachable only by a powerful shaman. The second plane (hedu kä misi, "sky layer") comprises the realm of the spirits—the Otherworld—and serves as the cosmic paradigm; however, no longer primordial. As an existential region, it becomes the destination of the human soul after a person's death, where it travels to continue its existence in an ethereal form and to perform the very tasks that one finds as ready counterparts on this earth. What distinguishes the Yąnomamö of today from the first beings—the original Yąnomamö—is that the latter were, in part, human and spirit (yai), who, upon death became all yai. Apparently, however, not all souls are destined for "the sky" (hedu), for there exists a place, in Yąnomamö eschatology, where men's souls are punished by burning for lack of generosity during their lifetime. It is difficult, though, to assess the role of the missionaries and contacts with Christianizing elements in the formulation of this particular belief. Fire, nevertheless, is the great releaser of souls, and the Yąnomamǫ cremate their dead. In function and structure, therefore, hedu resembles this World, being a complete reflection of life on earth, except that its inhabitants are spirits. The underlayer of hedu constitutes the visible aspect of the sky, to which are affixed the heavenly beings as they move across it in an astral procession.

When a fragment of hedu had separated, dropping off to a lower plane, it created "this layer" (hei kä misi), which came to be inhabited by men, and the jungle terrain spotted with Yąnomamö villages. All people, including foreigners, originally derive from Yąnomamö, and thus, are either Yąnomamö proper or degenerate entities thereof. The fourth plane (the Lowerworld), which is extremely barren, was formed last by another chunk of hedu colliding with the earth, and falling through it at a locus occupied by the Amahiri-teri, who inhabited "this layer" (this World) during the time of the first beings. Only the Amahiri-teri, with their garden homes, were ejected unto the new plane below. Since neither tribal domain nor hunting territory was transposed along with the rest of them, to hunt and eat they dispatch their spirits to capture the souls of living children on earth. Consequently, owing to the relentless strife between spiritual forces, the evil spirits of the earthly shamans are engaged in combat with the evil spirits of the Amahiri-teri shamans.[28] Once again, the cosmic equilibrium is maintained.

The separation of sky and earth can also be a personal and temporal occurrence in the individual eschatology of the Urubu Indians of Brazil. The sky, which is hard in substance, meets the earth at the ends of the flat world, at a place known as *iwi pita*—a domain of the macaw-owner (Master of the Animals, of sorts). From here the soul of the dead ascends to the sky, which opens up momentarily to receive it, thus, making a transcendental reunion between the loved ones an existential possibility. On its east-west journey across the sky, the sun must travel through the Lowerworld. As a result the three worlds, with their distinct inhabitants comprise the entire universe.[29]

Neither last nor least, another group of Indians, in the equatorial rain forest, for whom there exist reliable field data, make a vitally enriching contribution to the diversified imagery of the Amazonian cosmos. The Desana shaman's ecstatic journey may take him skyward to the clouds, the Milky Way, or even beyond to the edge of the universe. By shaking their rattles, they are able to remain suspended amidst the white clouds. In the endemic shamanistic worldview, the white clouds constitute the generative essence of the harpy eagle—"a state of insem-ination, of impregnating whiteness"—which the initiate must absorb in order to acquire the "generative energies,"[30] needed for successful shamanizing.

Among many peoples of the North, the universe is conceived as a living organism. In Siberian cosmology, it is sometimes associated with animal concepts, as well, such as the elk for the Middleworld, and the bear for Master of the Animals or for the ethnogenic father of the Evenks. For them, just like in the transcendental reality of the Urubu Indians in the tropics, the universe has a tripartite structure, consisting of the Upper, Middle, and Lower worlds, with each one representing, essentially, an imago mundi (a replica) of the other two. The cosmological tradition of the Samoyed actually held the polar star to be not merely an astral body, but also the "Sky Nail" from which the heavenly drapery, suspended at the apex, hung like a Siberian yurt from the top of a pole. The Mongols, for whom the constellation of the Great Bear and the planet Venus are infused with important shamanistic meanings, refer to the polar star as the "Golden Nail," and feature Venus on the cosmic diagrams depicted on many a drum of the Altaic shaman. At the same time, they believe that the earth is imbued with forces of good and evil.

The Upperworld of the Evenk shaman is inhabited by powerful supreme spirits, reigning over natural events, the taiga (the vast Siberian forest), animals, and men. The blue sky is the taiga counterpart of the Upperworld, and the constellation of the Great Bear is represented by the cosmic elk, Kheglen. The concept of a deity (as opposed to a spirit) is rather vague, as can be witnessed by the personification of the solar deity, Dylacha, mirroring in the Upperworld the toil and labor known to men on this one. Other deities play minor roles and, as abtract notions, are poorly developed, too. Where there exists a Mistress of the Universe, she is, then, also the mother of people and animals, as well as the important Mistress of the Animals.

The Middleworld is divided into human and animal groups. Thus, the Master of the Animals, Eksheri, rules also over the taiga, while Amaka's domain consists of everything involving people. The shamanistic Lowerworld is often comprised of mirror and converse images of this one, depicted so vividly in Celtic mythology. The rivers may flow to their sources rather than from them, day corresponds to a night, and human beings in the realm beneath may fall prey to the creatures that they hunted in this World. In comparison, the Evenks uphold, all living things exist as non-living, substances "flowing" from the Lowerworld to the Middle are changed in essence by becoming invisible, etc. And, just like the Upperworld, the Lower one contains seven planes, or levels.[31]

A sacred pole, a symbol of the cosmic pillar, or the World Tree, is the celestial ladder that the shaman ascends[32] into the company of the spirits, to reach another cosmic plane, or a star, a river, a bridge, or a "razor's edge." The Finnish hero, Vainamoinen, and his shamanic companions must cross a bridge contructed of piercing knife points and swords to get to the Otherworld, Tuonela. Similar themes are to be found in Celtic folklore, too. We have already mentioned Sir Lancelot's deathlike trance and visionary experiences, during which he struggled across the mortifying sword-bridge. These motifs are commonly encountered on a spiritual voyage and in shamanistic cosmography, in general.

The soul-journeys to the spiritual abodes of the Yakut and the Dolgan shamans, by the progressive ascents of several celestial poles, attest to the general importance of the World Tree ideology and to its specific importance in maintaining shamanistic contact with the spirit world. Of particular significance is the notion that the Siberian shaman's drum is made from the wood of the World Tree. The cosmological symbolism depicted on the drumskin, in conjunction with the whole drum, stands for the entire universe.[33] The Tungus and the Lapp shamanistic drums represent all of their cosmic worlds and the gods and the spirits.[34] In some shamanistic ideologies, the World Tree is connected into the World River, which, in the Buryat religious metaphor, functions as a linkage with all the three worlds and must be traversed by the shaman to reach any part of the Otherworld.[35] Clearly, these types of symbolic devices are constructed to facilitate communication with all the three worlds, internalized by the shaman as his personal metaphors.

Numerical Potencies

At this point, a few words should be mentioned about the function of mystical numbers. "Things are numbers," stated a Babylonian principle, undoubtedly a precursor to Pythagorean philosophy, and numbers stand for order. The Bible speaks of God ordering things according to number, weight, and measure. The importance of observing the movements of the celestial bodies—thus, it follows, of astronomy—is obvious, and so is the connection between astronomy, mathematics, and related endeavors. The Pythagoreans ascribed sexual qualities to numerical values: odd numbers were masculine, phallic, because of a generative middle digit; even numbers had female characteristics, owing to "a certain receptive opening and a space within," underscored by the fact that when even numbers were divided into two equal parts, there was no remainder left. In contrast, an odd number thus divided left an appendage behind to reckon with and, consequently, manifested its male characteristics and strength by not making it possible to become entirely annihilated.

The sixteenth-century German philosopher, Cornelius Agrippa, using Pythagorean doctrines, developed an intricate schema involving numbers, harmony, and the proportions in the human form. Numbers were thought to be not only metaphors for divine paradigms, but to contain the actual essence of the cosmos. Hence, the magic of numbers. The numbers three, seven, and nine (9 being the number 3 multiplied by itself)[36] appear to predominate in the cosmological numerology of Eurasia, though others—12, 16, 17, 33, etc.—representing the different celestial levels, occur also in a widespread mode. The number six (also a multiple of 3), encountered more infrequently in the West,[37] plays a vital role in the shamanistic cosmological concepts of many indigenous groups in South America, particularly Colombia, for whom it forms a topological schema reflecting the hexagonal character of universal order (see Rock Crystals and the Hexagonal Universe, below). On the other hand, the number five seems to carry analogous significance for the Huichol Indians in western Mexico.[38] Nevertheless, a real correlation between the number of deities and that of the heavenly levels seems to be lacking, on the whole. Although in northern Eurasia we sometimes encounter nine heavens, with nine gods, and nine branches of the Cosmic Tree (9 = 3 × 3). The number three symbolizes, of course, the three cosmic worlds.

The Earth-Spirit of the Yurak-Samoyed has seven sons; the *sjaadai* (idols), associated with sacred trees, either have seven faces or seven lacerations on each face. The novice remains unconscious for seven days and nights, while the spirits dismember him and then reassemble him. Later on, he may wear a glove with seven fingers.[39] The Ugrian shaman has seven helping spirits, and the seven bells adorning his vestments signify the voices of the seven heavenly maidens.[40] On the Yenisei river, a prospective Ostyak shaman aportions a cooked flying squirrel into eight sections, eating only seven, and discarding the eighth. He returns after seven days to receive the determining sign of his new profession.[41] In time, as a full shaman, he will select "magic" mushrooms with seven spots (Amanita spp.) for eating, to induce an ecstatic journey. Similarly, the Lapp shamans not only consume mushrooms with seven spots, but offer them, as well, to neophytes during their initiation.[42]

In some cosmologies, there exist Cosmic Trees with seven arms, identified with seven planetary heavens. The Evenks in Siberia count seven cosmic planes. The Altaic shaman ascends a tree or a post with seven or nine wedged notches (tapty), representing the seven or nine celestial levels, which he must overcome. A tree with nine notches is set up by a shaman to sanctify a blood offering made by a Yakut, and the officiating shaman must climb it while carrying the offerings intended for the supernatural being, Ai Toyon.[43] The Jewish menorah[44] is a seven-branched Tree of Light, equivalent to the Tree of Life with just as many boughs. The menorah on the emblem of the State of Israel has nine branches, after the festival of Hanukkah lights. Here, the symbol of a historico-political event, representing an ancient fight for freedom and independence, took precedent over ritual considerations alone.

It is quite possible that the apparent predominance of the numbers seven and nine is merely a function of a long cultural predisposition to observe natural phenomena, and then to select and focus on certain quantitative values in the belief that they are intrinsically imbued with mystical attributes. For instance, the recurrence of number seven is based, in part, on the traditional measure of time, such as the lunar month, consisting of four phases that last seven days each, which, in turn, make up a seven-day week. There were alleged to be seven colors in the chromatic spectrum, seven notes comprising the musical scale (and musical notes, to retain their substantial essence, must be played in an orderly sequence), seven bodies in the planetary system, made to correspond to seven metals, and even to the seven vowels of the Greek alphabet. Seven prominently features also in the Bible. In the Old Testament, there are, of course, the seven days of creation (actually, six plus a day of rest); Joshua marched his armies around the walls of Jericho for seven days, in the company of seven priests, carrying seven trumpets. In the New Testament, St. John of Patmos inundates the Book of Revelations with the occurrences of the number seven; for example, the seven epistles addressed to the seven original Christian churches. Yet, irrespective of all epistemological and didactic considerations, the mystical associations of the number seven do enter, unquestionably, into play in shamanistic cosmology, initiation, and ecstasy. Unfortunately, however, our understanding of the significance of these values does not extend much beyond the descriptive delineations, failing to grasp the full esoteric and arcane meanings of the mystical powers behind them, as envisioned by those whose transforming experience carried them into the ecstatic dimension.

Rock Crystals and the Hexagonal Universe

Rock crystals are shamanistic, transformational, power objects and spirit helpers, valued most highly for their potency and regarded as vitally essential among peoples throughout the globe, ranging from the rain forests of South America[45] to the arid regions of Australia. Their use goes back many millennia, and quartz crystals from archaeological sites in California date back 8,000 years. The prominent role and cosmological significance of crystals and gemstones can be also noticed in what we construe as non-shamanistic contexts. In fact, the celestial domains of all religious traditions abound in precious and semi-precious stones. In Ezekiel's Otherworld—Eden, the garden of God—"Every precious stone was thy covering. . . thou has walked up and down in the midst of the stones of fire." Likewise, the Otherworld of the Buddhists is adorned with luminous, brilliant "stones of fire," possessed of "preternatural significance." "The material objects which most nearly resemble these sources of visionary illumination are gem stones,"[46] which contain crystal planes. Yet, there are some, admittedly, who feel that it is neither the brilliance nor luminosity, but only crystal geometry that endows these objects with shamanistic attributes, at least among certain native peoples.[47] However, it ought to be remembered that "Light, color and significance do not exist in isolation. They modify, or are manifested by, objects." Be that as it may, Huxley would undoubtedly agree with the Desana shamans, who envision the structure of the universe in the hexagons of crystals. For, as he justifiably notes, "to acquire such a stone is to acquire something whose preciousness is guaranteed by the fact that it exists in the Other World."[48]

> The typical mescalin or lysergic-acid experience begins with perceptions of colored, moving, living geometrical forms. In time, pure geometry becomes concrete, and the visionary perceives not patterns, but patterned things. . . . Every mescalin experience, every vision arising under hypnosis, is unique; but all recognizably belong to the same species. The landscapes, the architectures, the clustering gems, the brilliant and intricate

patterns—these, in their atmosphere of preternatural light, preternatural color and preternatural significance, are the stuff of which the mind's antipodes are made. . . . Heroic figures, of the kind that Blake called "The Seraphim," may make their appearance, alone or in multitudes. Fabulous animals move across the scene.[49]

In many cultures, including the California Yuman Indians, as well as the Australian aborigines, the quartz crystal is considered "living," or a "live rock," and, like the Jívaro, who feed tobacco water to their spirit helpers, the Yuman shamans sustain with nourishment their quartz crystals.[50] In societies that view it as "solidified light," the quartz crystal is connected with shamanistic enlightenment and the spiritual ability to see through matter. When a shaman is treated with quartz crystals (i.e., rubbed, exposed to, or inserted metaphorically), he develops heightened senses of perception and his powers become more extraordinary.[51] The insertion of quartz crystals into the stomach of a Cubeo about to become a shaman is one of the crucial processes in the transformational passage from a layman to a shaman. Later on, these crystals will be used by him as shamanistic weapons.[52] Due to its unique properties, the quartz crystal appears in an unchanged form and substance to a Jívaro shaman, whether he is in an ordinary or shamanistic state of consciousness.[53] Its physical qualities merge with its ephemeral essence to produce a oneness, which cannot be treated as separate aspects of a single whole. Quartz is the essence of souls.

This concept is clearly expressed in the context of another culture by specific idioms incorporated into the designs of certain nearikas, folk art yarn paintings, executed by the Huichol artist Ramón. In one particular theme honoring the deified Sun, the shaman (*mara'akáme*) must triumph over the Sun's burning rays and "fiery sparks," as he ascends into the celestial sphere in quest for the rock crystals, believed to be the crystallized souls of dead shamans, who now can furnish the seeker with guardian power. The subject of a complementary nearika deals also with the shaman's journey to the spirit world, but contains a more narrative theme. It takes five years (repeated significance of this number) for the soul of a shaman, or a sage, to become transformed into a rock crystal. At the end of this period, the present mara'akáme embarks on an ascent-journey to the domain of the Sun to bring the crystallized soul to earth, so it can dwell among its kin as a guardian spirit. It does not present to be an easy task, for the shaman must pass through the consuming fiery rays, an ordeal that can be accomplished only with the assistance of the spirit helpers. In order to emphasize his own shamanic powers, the mara'akáme Ramón depicted himself with horns of the Sacred Deer.[54]

To the shaman, the most important aspect of the rock crystal is encapsulated by its hexagonal structure, which allows the patterns and processes of nature, and the shape of the universe, to be translated into a crystal model (imago mundi). As a matter of fact, the keynote concern with the hexagonal pattern seems to overshadow all other considerations in a crystal for the Indians. As a result, only the crystals whose lattice points form such a plane structure—which is to be found in quartz crystal, tourmaline, and emerald—are much desired and valued by the Indians. The recurrent structural pattern of rock crystals serves as a model and a symbol for the processes of nature's continuity and cosmic stability. It is this form which manifests potent procreative forces that can be witnessed in such displays of nature as the common land tortoise in the rain forest. This creature's carapace possesses several hexagonal plates, which the Desana shaman interprets as "power" and "force" quantities related to those in rock crystals. Moreover, he believes that the plates of the tortoise shell mimic the information code on the origins of the universe and the Desana social order. Thus, by extension, the tortoise also represents stability, regenerative potential, and so forth.[55] Through such cosmological analogies, the shamanistic mind has displayed a precognitive awareness, as it were, anticipating the existence of Fibonacci numerical sequence and, the much more recent, development of fractal mathematics.

In the Desana shamanistic thought, the sun is a rock crystal; thus, conversely, a rock crystal is a scaled-down sun, replete with "vital energies." In one shamanistic metaphor, rock crystals are made of solidified, concentrated semen (generative power), which, in turn, is believed to contain solar energy (cosmic generative power). The Desana lexicography, incorporated into the larger Tukanoan linguistic group, contains broad allusions to rock crystals as condensed solar enegy or "condensed objects," created by the sun, of masculine gender and transforming potency. Understandably, these are thought to contain "heat energy." This belief parallels very closely the Huichol tradition, which maintains that such crystals are to be found in the realm of the sun deity. To integrate the essential cosmic properties, recognized by the Desana, with their solar religion, the quartz crystal becomes the penis of the Sun Father, or the crystallized semen. At the same time, the quartz crystal cylinder, worn by the shaman around his neck, is called *abé yeeru*, the "sun-penis."[56]

Yet, the vitality and balance of nature do not operate on a unisex principle. In Desana shamanism, the crystal can be androgynous, or bisexual, and consist also of the female aspect, in which case it is alluded to as a womb or a clitoris. The Desana explain this in terms of their topological concepts, namely, that the hexagon is constructed by two superimposed triangles—a veritable union between an upward pointing one (male) and a downward pointing one (female). The male and female principles are also perceived in the different energies of the colors of the spectrum reflected in a crystal (a rather modern scientific notion) and are vital to life. These energies have to be balanced by various manipulations to assure constant and consistent fecundity for all aspects of life on earth. Since color energies are intrinsic to all life forms, any changes manifest, with the aid of the crystal as a diagnostic implement, are linked to functional changes in the homeostasis of the organism. Such dysfunctions can be remedied by reconstituting the energy balance in the ailing individual.[57]

The Kogi Indians of northern Colombia perceive their habitat as a reflection of the hexagonal cosmic model—a vast rock crystal faceted into six domains, each functioning to satisfy the conditions of specific social sanctions and ritual behavior. In their linguistic category, *téishua* is the cognate for "six," but it carries with it a wide range of fertility-related connotations, as well as implying "male ancestor, ancient, seminal, primordial," and also implying the original Tairona language (pronounced, *teiyúna*), an offshoot of which is spoken today by the Kogi Indians.[58] However, the far-reaching significance and sacred attributes of the number six are to be found, as mentioned earlier, in the belief that the hexagonal configuration of rock crystals mirrors universal design and process—a cosmic paradigm, a hexagonal imago mundi.

Hexagons, therefore, define existential spaces of transformation and points of origin from which people and sacred ritual objects emerge. They do not necessarily have to represent true spatial areas and volumes, in the sense of solid geometry. River sources and estuaries are deemed by the Desana to be points of origin, and, as such, are considered hexagonal areas. During gestation period, the womb is conceived of as "a hexagonal crystal," where the developing embryo is placed on "a hexagonal shield." In the actual childbirth, the newborn baby is thought to be coming through a passage formed by "adjoining" crystal planes. A difficult labor, therefore, is attributed to the baby's inability to part the two crystal walls. The Desana also prepare separate hexagonal enclosures for initiatory transformations of the Desana girls who arrive at their menstrual rites of passage.[59]

In addition, the Desana shamans exhibit great interest in flames and the thermodynamic interactions regulating the flame's properties. They developed explanations for the different thermal zones, based on their own theories of heat and color, distinguishing between energy levels visible in the open flame. These zones correspond to the phases of initiation (transformations) through which the neophyte must pass. The door of flames (or the door of water, for that matter) is a portal to the Otherworld. This point was rather vividly described by a Desana shaman:

> The master shaman and the initiate had established themselves in a small hexagonal area lying between the large hexagon of the river-mouth and the somewhat smaller one of the head-waters, but not on the river itself, rather at some small affluent of the middle course. There the initiate had "died"; but his spirit-essence had gone to the rivermouth where he penetrated the fiery *tabú* door and submerged himself into the primeval waters of the Lake of Milk (*ahpikon dia*). Passing through the *marari-nomeri/doberi-dari* stages of transformation, he had penetrated through a flaming, vaulted *tabú* door into the hexagon of the headwaters. This marked his rebirth into a new life, that of the shaman he was going to be, and from there he returned to his local group, to his own people. His initiation had ended in rebirth from himself.[60]

Consequently, it becomes quite evident that the number six forms a schema combining the hexagonal order with the cosmic energy of creation, yielding to man a definite place in the design of the cosmos. However, the real sociocultural significance of the hexagonal paragon is in its underlying function as a model for social organization and ideologies that give meaning to human interactions. Hexagon is, for some people, the principle of order.

Reason and Order

Thus, with the rise and development of shamanistic practices, we cross the threshold marking the beginnings of systematization of the preternatural world. The shamanistic systems, largely arising from the male-oriented tradition of the Palaeolithic hunters, lie near the center of Wilhelm Schmidt's thesis expressed in his monumental work on *The Origins of the Idea of God*, specifically as these pertain to the contingent tenet of the "sky god." This patriarchal theme of the sky god is recurrent not only as a transcultural phenomenon in the cosmogonies of diverse shamanistic and archaic contexts, but is also formulated by Father Wilhelm as evolving into the single Judaeo-Christian godhead.

Cosmic balance, harmony, and social order are universal phenomena that are not functions of chance. Only chaos and disorder can prevail through the latter. Even the "black color" of human tragedy and death is considered, by some, as part of the total scheme of colors making up the harmony in cosmic beauty. As the religious patriarch of the mystic Whirling Dervishes, Sheikh Shefieh el Melewi explained with poetic stoicism: "As it unfolds. . .the unwitting evil he [the man responsible for the death of the Sheikh's daughter] wrought here was but one dark thread woven into a tapestry of many colors which made a design of harmonious beauty at the last."[61] Consequently, the universal order must be the visible effect of an intelligent force, such as the Craftsman God, the Demiurge, or *The Great Spirit*.

Man's activities, however, purloin the earth's bounty, causing imbalance both in vegetative nature and among the souls of the animal world. To prevent catastrophic results, sacrificial offerings must be provided to propitiate the spirits so they may be willing to restore the world to its proper balance. In the perceptive words of the Eskimo shaman to the Danish explorer, Knud Rasmussen: "The greatest peril of life lies in the fact that human food consists entirely of souls. All the creatures we have to kill and eat, all those we have to strike down and destroy to make clothes for ourselves, have souls, as we have."[62]

The abstract and nebulous aspect of The Great Spirit gave way, among others, to the more regular supplications and appeals to deities, whose nature and specialized functions allowed them to be defined in more concrete terms, satisfying the people's need to have tangible spiritual forces to which they could resort in their daily affairs. Thus, as the Altaic Bai Uelgaen displaced evidently the older Tngri Khayirkhan, so did Zeus triumph over the Titan Cronus, who, in turn, had also replaced his own father, Uranus (meaning, literally, the "heaven"), by castrating him with a sickle. The severed organ, falling into the sea, gave birth to Aphrodite, sometimes called also Urania, whose real name, *Aphrogeneia*, means the "Foam-born." It is rightly contended that Zeus, himself, was about to cede to the first, true panhellenic god, Apollo, whose divinity came to be regarded as corresponding to the intellectual and rational principles of the cosmos. The existence of shamanistic fonts at the roots of Greek intellectual thought, although poorly understood as a phenomenon, is not a matter of historical contention. In a shamanistic cosmography, for example, the boundary between this World and the Other is quite often demarcated by a river, along which one encounters strange and horrifying creatures. A shaman's embarkation upon his soul-journey, with the aid of a drum and a drumstick which correspond metaphorically to a boat and a paddle, finds a reflection among the ancient Greeks in the deceased's soul journeying to the Otherworld and having to negotiate the River Styx, but only through the offices of the old boatman-guide, Charon, who is accompanied by the fierce, three-headed dog, Kerberos. (Savage dogs, by the way, are also encountered along rivercourses in Altaic shamanism). Charon's function here is clearly residual of a shaman in his role as a psychopomp. Undoubtedly, the Styx boatman personifies a much older version of a shaman, whose real character and existence had been suppressed by the Olympian state religion and forgotten long ago.

It is, therefore, not surprising to notice the survival of some of the archaic shamanistic elements in the eloquent Greek cosmology and philosophy, both of the Pythagoreans and the Socrats alike. The enigmatic figure of Pythagoras, himself, is believed by some to bear vestments of strong shamanistic attributes. With inference to Apollonian rationalism, the term, *cosmos*, is derived from the Greek root meaning "to order," and refers to any orderly system, including social. Alternately, however, it also means "adornment", an orderly arrangement of traits, wherefore order implies beauty. Since cosmic order was interchangeable with social order, both were regarded, by analogy, as organic systems. Such was, too, the intellectual and moral climate among the Greek thinkers of the Ionian school, in particular, and from Miletus, especially. The entire Hellenic world felt its impact. The philosophers elaborated upon the doctrines of the cosmos, proceeded to adorn their credos with the highest, positive attributes of their natural world, and extended these concepts to sociopolitical and ethical questions by making analogies between natural and social harmonies. Furthermore, to confirm the transcendental position of man amidst the cosmic scheme, they sought authority for their dogmas in celestial paradigms, through the formulation of such concepts as sacred space, the cosmic center, and, down the line, to Plato's theory of the World-soul. Observable constants in natural laws offered credence to those paradigms, and what seemed to work for the natural system had to work for the social one, as well. Thus, attempts were made to formulate common denominators from syllogistic analogies between universal constants and patterns in social organization.

Plato proceeded to draw numerous comparisons between the world of nature, *cosmos*, and the community of men, *polis*. In spite of his anthropocentric ideas of the universe, Plato maintained a rather sophisticated and modern notion that the frame of reference for man's conception of the cosmos is derived from the manner in which man perceives himself as a microcosm. Once again, Plato managed to fuse the elements of religion, physics, music, and psychology in developing his concepts of the World-soul; whereas, he considered time and its measure, to be aspects of the cosmic order. Eventually, the term *cosmos* degenerated from its original, lofty ideal of a harmonious arrangement (cosmic) to a more secular, make-up adornment (cosmetic). Hence, the syllogistic relationships between harmony, beauty, and finery.

The philosophical and ethical doctrines gave a definite moral shape to the Greek worldview, becoming deeply imbedded into the existential *moira*, which provided the individual with a sense of being a part of the cosmic design. Since moira called for the individual to make an acceptable choice among the opportunities availed by one's destiny, it served also as a course of reconciliation with one's own fate. It may be viewed as a sort of harmonious balance affording a choice of purpose: an ultimate, voluntary interplay between humans and their universe. A person's willingness to accept his or her destiny, and act upon it, was a mark of a special character, which transcended the individual unto a cosmic plane, placing him or her amidst the company of gods.

5

The Ritual Drug Complex: Ethnobiology of Heaven and Hell

The Drug Ceremonial

AN ABSOLUTELY VITAL DISTINCTION must be drawn between the uses of hallucinogenic plants in an aboriginal society within the context of a religious-ritualistic experience, and their recreational use in the West. The traditional uses in a native culture are not intended to provide, as Peter Furst points out, "a temporary means of escape from it," but, to the contrary, they validate instead the culturally prescribed norms of behavior, social values, and beliefs. One partakes of the magic plants to become aware of things, such as the tribal cosmology and origin myths, which will, in turn, help the person learn how to become whatever it is that he or she *is*. Thus, the hallucinatory experience in some cultures permeates not only the spiritual domain, but may extend into other fundamental facets of the cultural milieu. "Everything we would designate as art," writes Reichel-Dolmatoff, "is inspired and based upon the hallucinatory experience" among the Tukanoan Indians.[1]

Hence, it becomes sadly apparent how inadequate certain portrayals are of aboriginal cultures where the ritual drug complex has assumed a leading social function, yet, only to be allotted desultory remarks by the people who studied them. Michael Harner offers a sensible explanation for the causes responsible for the underestimation, on the part of many scholars, of the extremely important role played by hallucinogenic substances in spiritual experiences throughout history. He rightly assesses that only very few of them have ever taken an active part in such rituals.[2] All the others have managed, rather than to write accurate accounts of first-hand experiences, to report about their own preconceptions on the subject or to filter down stories recounted to them by informants—stories which, more often than not, sounded too fantastic to be believed. And such biased preconceptions led, among hosts of others, to this hapless and unfounded assertion by an eminent historian of religions that the use of hallucinogens in shamanistic practices was "a vulgar substitute for 'pure' trance," merely a degenerated version to be "called on to provide an *imitation* of a state that the shaman is no longer capable of attaining otherwise."[3]

Let us examine the cultural elements that play roles in the activities connected with the ritual drug use. For one, the mythic tradition serves as an umbilical line between the past and the present, and between the sociocultural unit and its physico-biotic environment. The myths describe the formulation, in a mythical past, of the sanctions and prescriptions governing the drug ceremonial. They also infer guidelines for the processes relating to the training of shamanistic initiates, which may involve many months or even years of disciplined apprenticeship in the care of an experienced shaman. The neophyte learns vital knowledge of his people, including that of the flora and the fauna, origin myths and traditions, genealogies, drug use, and the appropriate rituals; not to mention gaining skills with hallucinogenic drugs, which are considered the essential channels of communication with the Otherworld. The myths discuss also the fundamental laws promoting the sociobiological survival and welfare of the group and the rules of interactions that allow cooperation with other groups by means of clearly articulated kinship mechanics and marriage laws.[4] And it is to such mythic times that the origins of shamanism are assigned by the Tukanoan Indians.[5]

Besides aetiological reasoning, we encounter constructs of religious philosophy and metaphoric syllogism attached to the purpose of the ritual. Its intent, according to shamanistic notions, is to effect transitions—alchemical transmutations, of sorts—during the times of critical events, such as the rites of passage surrounding birth, death, puberty, etc. Even certain sequences in the ritual preparation of the hallucinogenic potion from the vine *Banisteriopsis* spp. signify major occurrences in the lives of the Barasana Indians of Pira-paraña river. The sifting of crushed stem fiber, with its psychoactive alkaloid content, through a rattan sieve symbolizes the process of birth among these tribesmen. The foot of the vessel containing the ritual hallucinogen is often decorated with the **U**-sign, which stands for the tunnel, or the vaginal passage through which the participants in the shamanic trance proceed toward "the body of the vessel in order to be reborn." Similarly, such metaphoric constructs are familiar to the Tukanoan Indian, who dies symbolically when he drinks the narcotic preparation, and is thus "returned to the womb, that is, to the vessel containing the drink." By re-enacting the transformations that the participants are compelled to experience, the ritual provides the facilities to precipitate such transitions by abetting the acolyte in the confrontation and passage through the individual crisis (IPC). For ". . . life is livable only when its threatening annihilation is mediated by ritual."[6]

The spiritual and metaphysical contingencies of the energies and the forces of life may be tapped, the Jívaro believe, by means of hallucinogens. The spiritual realm, this antipodal World, thus entered, is where the knowledge of the great cosmic causality can be apprehended. All the events, that occur inside the Otherworld are manifestations of the "true" reality and exert and impact on the daily, physical aspect of existence. Consequently, the everyday, non-visionary life is considered "fake" and "false." Within the last few days of its awaited birth, a baby may be given (through the mother) hallucinogens so it can encounter the features of the true reality and hopefully establish contacts with the entities of the "ancient specter," which may be willing to assist the infant in coping with the immediate hazards of this ordinary life, and prepare it better to avoid the pitfalls scattered along its path. Even older children are not exempt from a similar treatment at the hands of their parents, who may feel the need to re-substantiate, by "consensual validation," their own authority and values, as well as those of the community. By experiencing visions of the "true" reality, the child can perceive glimpses of the root-matrix of his traditional (and the only valid) culture and be helped to come to terms with the essence of what it is to be a Jívaro. So important is to them the encounter with the spiritual dimension that, sometimes, they offer a special hallucinogenic admixture to the hunting dogs, so the animals, too, may validate their souls by confronting the realities from another plane of existence.[7]

By far, the two people for whom hallucinogens have most important meaning are the shaman (*uwišin*) and "the outstanding killer" (*kakaram*), both of whom must locate and use the souls and the spirits in the Otherworld. Of the three kinds of souls recognized by the Jívaro, the *arutam wakaní* is of the greatest importance. It must be acquired, for no one possesses it at birth. Obtaining the arutam soul is so vital to one's well-being that a boy is not expected to survive past puberty without its protection. When he becomes about six years of age, a boy embarks upon the quest of this soul.[8]

It is the initial search for the arutam that represents the first real encounter with a drug ceremonial. The boy and his father leave home for their sacred waterfall, which constitutes a meeting place for these supernatural entities. The father and son stride about the waterfall, with the aid of a ceremonial staff made of balsa wood for this purpose. The thundering sounds of the cascading waters bounce off the syllables of their persistent chant: *tau, tau, tau.* With the coming of nightfall, they prepare to sleep near the waterfall and to await the arutam. But first, they must fast and drink the tobacco water (a cold decoction of green tobacco leaves). The two may repeat, up to five nights, their immersions in the watery mists, fasting, and partaking of the tobacco water. Should they fail in the encounter with the soul during those five days, they must return home unsuccessful. A repeated attempt is permitted after a given interval. However, they may chance upon *maikua*, probably *Datura arborea*, and drink raw the hallucinogenic juice contained in its stem, thus, propelling their quest of the arutam. They recognize six types of *maikua*, or species of *Datura*, and consider them to be the most potent and dangerous of all substances in their psychotropic pharmacopoeia. Due to the extremely dangerous, psychoactive properties of *Datura* the seeker of visions must not consume *maikua* without the presence of a supervising adult, who is in a position to offer psychological encouragement and, if necessary, physical restraint. Especially in the initial phase of the drug intoxication, a likely delirium of the initiate may result in a fatal fall from a precipice, or a physical injury.[9]

Owing to the illusory nature of the daily, waking condition of life, and to the true aspect comprising the preternatural world, the role of a ritual specialist, the shaman, becomes essential in safeguarding the transitions from one reality to another and in handling the confluences encountered on such trance-journeys. For this purpose, shamans rely on the use of hallucinogenic plants. In South America, however, they generally prefer (as in the case of the Jívaro in Ecuador, who favor *natemä* to *maikua*)[10] to use preparations from the vine *Banisteriopsis* rather than *Datura*, due to the latter's dangerous high potency, which may stymie the shamans' enactments of full ritual performances, as well as due to the intrinsic perils of insanity effected by the repeated uses of *Datura*.

The Desana shamans perceive, in the preparation of the narcotic *yajé* (*Banisteriopsis* spp.), explicit allusions to the sexual act, not in the sense of plain mechanical eroticism, but linked to the process of creation. When the desired variety of *Banisteriopsis* spp. is used to prepare the hallucinogenic potion, it is done so by a judicious selection of different parts of the vine, varying with the age of the plant, because each differentiated section is responsible for visions involving specific dominant colors, which coincide with different dimensions of the visionary experience. Thus, red is the carrier of male fertility, yellow of female, and white is the generalized, all-encompassing solar energy. The container, or vessel, in which the plant is processed is analogous with the vagina and the uterus; the stirring rod signifies the penis. The notion underscored behind these concepts is, at least partly, derived from the fact that pottery making is viewed as a transformational process, modelled on the transitions in life. Therefore, in this world of allusions and metaphors, the finished clay vessel is a woman, decorated with motifs extracted from the varied repertory of Desana shamanistic symbolism which, in instances like this one, offers the **Y**-shaped ideogram to signify the clitoris (and probably the labias, or the portals of the vaginal opening). This symbol, like the **U**-sign, has a metaphoric relationship to the bone-soul concept entailed in the rebirth and resurrection cycle of the Desana. The **Y**-shaped design is painted, likewise, in a string-like fashion, by the women as ornamental body motifs around their waists. The association between the Desana women and the symbolic design becomes quite obvious. To underscore further the close link between sexuality and the spiritual realm, the term for "shaman" (and "jaguar") is represented by the cognate *yee* (plural, *yeea*), which is related to *yeeri*, a word meaning "to copulate."[11] We can sense a resonance of these practices and abstract constructs in the more esoteric Tantric mysticism, where the transcendent qualities of sexual energy play a vital role in opening the doors of perception, and becoming a transporting vehicle to another dimension of awareness.

This hallucinogenic potion is known by different names in the native pharmacopoeias of South America and in the shamanistic rituals of the Amazonian tribes. In Colombia, and in anthropological literature, it is known as *yajé*, or *yagé*, made famous by Gérardo Reichel-Dolmatoff's brilliant studies of the cosmology and the religious beliefs among the aboriginal cultures in northwest Amazon. Another common ethnic name, *ayahuasca*, comes from Peru and Ecuador.[12] As noted before, it is a Quechua term, denoting "vine of the dead" or "vine of the souls."[13] The Jívaro Indians call this substance *natemä*, while in Brazil, it is *caapi*, and *camalampi* in Campa.

Another important form of a potent narcotic is a snuff prepared from the inner bark of the *Virola* tree, a member of the family Myristicacea, which includes three varieties of species in the Vaupés territory of the equatorial rain forest of the northwest Amazon: *Virola calophylla*, *V. calophylloidea*, and *V. theidora*. The resulting snuff, used by the Tukano-speaking Desana, is a function of the diverse admixtures, which are varied in accordance with the desired effect to be produced for a specific ceremonial purpose. The final composition may, thus, consist of the *Virola* inner bark, as a base, powdered tobacco, powdered coca leaves, the ashes of *Cecropia* leaves, or dehydrated stem fiber of the yajé plant. In more special circumstances, such as shamanistic initiations, tiny segments scraped off small stalactites are pulverized into fine powder, which is then added to the snuff. The stalactite (about 12 cm. in height) is referred to by the Desana as "sun-penis" (*abé yeru*), while the hallucinogenic snuff is thought to be a divine generative exudence, or semen. The snuff is taken internally by blowing through a bone of the powerful harpy eagle (*Harpia harpyja*), a highly shamanistic bird in its own right, and a shaman's avatar. Since the bone has the function of conveying a passage for the "seminal" substance—a notion not entirely foreign to early European thought, and discussed elsewhere in this book—it is also a phallic metaphor, while the off-white, down feathers (*vihto*) of the harpy eagle represent further associations with the semen by evoking notions of fertility in shamanistic rituals. In fact, swallowing the soft, downy feathers during initiation ceremonies symbolizes impregnation.[14]

The North American Indians have, likewise, been alert to the dangers confronting the frequent user of *Datura*. In southern California, the cult of *Datura* has been an important focus of solemn religious activities, practically among all the Indian tribes. *D. meteloides* is the only psychotomimetic plant employed by the Coahuilla Indians (in the proximity of Palm Springs) to produce a state of narcosis. Its native name is *kiksawva'al*, and it consists of a small variety, with broad leaves and a large burr for fruit. The Indians are fully aware of the toxic properties and unpredictability encountered in this plant, cautioning against uninformed use, and admit that its occasional use was known at times "to produce death." Towards the end of the nineteenth century, Valery Havard had noted that the tribes of the Colorado River and the Payute Indians smoked *Datura*, in addition to mixing it with other inebriants.[15] As a hallucinogenic concoction, the plant was macerated and mixed with water. The amount of water, essentially, distinguished the drinking potion from a medicinal salve, which was used, among many other applications, as the most drastic remedy in very severe cases of saddle-gall. Under such circumstances, the whole plant was crushed between two flat stones, mixed with some water, and rubbed into the horse's wound.[16]

All parts of the *Datura* plant contain psychoactive compounds, and different sections are utilized depending upon the desired effect. Roots are most commonly used in the ritual drink (*toloache*), while the leaves are generally smoked. The entire plant is crushed to make a therapeutic salve. Called the dream weed, Coahuilla shamans have used *Datura*, in conservative doses, to prognosticate illness and devise proper remedies.

This plant has also been crucial in the shaman's performance of his essential functions, including the magical flights enacted on his soul-journeys to the Otherworlds in quest of guardian spirits (*nukatem*), to transform into an eagle or a cougar, or bring back lost souls to their proper owners.[17] Its ritual use has been stressed particularly during puberty ceremonies, called *manet*, primarily representing boys' initiation rites, and has focused around drinking toloache (*Datura* concoction). The word *manet* signifies, probably, "the grass (weed) which talks"; however, it can only be heard by the shamans (*pualem*; sing. *puul*). All the chants performed during this ritual were offered to the Great Shaman and other supernatural beings of the Lowerworld. Each song constituted, in fact, a prayer in the "ocean language," and was not in the language of the Coahuilla (*iviat*). The "ocean language" is intelligible to the shamans only, and *Datura* is a great "human" shaman with whom the Coahuilla Indians can communicate.[18] During the enactment of these vital rites, the Coahuilla reality and cosmology received confirmations in the minds of the neophytes, who experienced all the significant aspects in their visions, and thus, ultimately, could "objectively" and "empirically" assess the validity of their people's tradition. Once the re-confirmation was established through the visions, the initiates were locked into the old belief system.

Similarly, as noted in a previous chapter, the Luiseño have held sacred ceremonies, resembling death-rebirth and puberty rites, during which they administered to the young initiates very powerful doses of preparation made with the dried roots of *D. inoxia*, crushed into powder and mixed with hot water. A deep state of narcosis is followed by experiences of trance, which, as Kroeber reported,[19] remain the most sacred experiences to the participants throughout their lives. Most often, the vision is of an animal, which instructs the novice in a sacred mythic chant that becomes specifically his own. The youth will not hunt or kill any animal of the species encountered in the vision, and a permanent, spiritual bond is forever established. In about two months time, they return to perform the second and last phase of the ritual, which is more profoundly shamanistic in character. At the completion of this rite of passage, the participants leave their childhood days behind, and will never again drink toloache, the powerful and sacred *Datura*. The injunction against partaking of *Datura* more than once in a lifetime is, undoubtedly, related to the common knowldge among the North American Indians, regarding the highly dangerous and unpredictable character exhibited by this plant.

Based on his field observations, the Colombian anthropologist Gérardo Reichel-Dolmatoff offers a poignant summary involving the ritual use of hallucinogens among an Eastern Tukanoan tribe of Colombia Northwest Amazon:

> The entire ceremonial is highly structured in that the participants are exposed, in the course of twelve hours, to an escalated sequence of different sensorial stimuli. For several days preceding the ceremony the participants have observed certain dietary restrictions, sexual abstinences and other deprivations, so that on the eve of the ceremony, they are in a mood of expectancy and euphoria. . . . It is clear that the entire ceremony and its individual ritual aspects consist of sensorially acted-out components and aim at the control of sensory manifestations.
>
> The active guidance of the shamans is of the essence. They constantly encourage and admonish the audience, answer anxious questions about individual hallucinations, and orchestrate music, dance, recitals, the taking of drugs and short periods of rest in such a manner that the ceremony produces a strong impact upon all its participants. Hallucination is to be enjoyed intellectually and imaginatively but above all it constitutes the principal expression of Tukanoan religion.[20]

In 1955, Wasson and his companion, Alan Richardson, were the first outsiders to actually participate in a Mazatec sacred mushroom healing ceremonial. Wasson's profound experience during this soul-moving, bemushroomed, transcended state is best captured by his own words:

> It permits you to see, more clearly than our perishing mortal eye can see, vistas beyond the horizons of this life, to travel backward and forward in time, to enter other planes of existence even (as the Indians say) to know God. . . . All that you see during this night has a pristine quality: the landscape, the edifices, the carvings, the animals—they look as though they had come straight from the Maker's workshop.[21]

His immense insights, gained during the ecstatic transformation of the soul-self, peeled some of the perplexing covers veiling the nature of mystical states and of uncommonly intense spurts of creative energy, leading Wasson to comment elsewhere: "I do not suggest that St. John of Patmos ate mushrooms in order to write the Book of Revelation. Yet the succession of images in his vision, so clearly seen and yet such a phantasmagoria, means for me that he was in the same state as one bemushroomed."[22]

In a pine-forest valley, overlooked by the high-rising Toluca volcano, situated about one hundred miles southwest of Mexico City, the Matlatzinca Indians consume *ne-to-chu-táta*, the sacred mushroom *Psilocybe muliercula*, which flourishes along riverbanks. The native name denotes "divine ancient beings," "dear little sacred lords," etc., or they are alluded to by the Spanish *santitos*, meaning "saints." These "sacred beings" can communicate with an ailing part of the body, determine its dysfunction, and prescribe the right remedy. They can also grant the Matlatzincas magnificent visions of flowers, gardens, and stars; as much as terrifying ones, of great shamanic import, containing skeletons, out-pouring blood, and serpents. Whenever the divine mushrooms are gathered by the Indians, they must be replaced with offerings of wild flowers.[23]

Such drug ceremonials may richly portray a syncretism between the old indigenous ways and newer Christian beliefs. According to a tradition held by one Indian group in Mexico, the sacred mushrooms grow only where the spittle from Christ's mouth had fallen unto the earth, and consequently it is *Jesucristo* who speaks and acts via the divine mushrooms. This local tradition, as Furst brings rightly to our attention, dates back to the shamanistic practices of aboriginal Mexico. The spittle is considered to be, not only in the New World, the seat of the shaman's preternatural power and is often regarded as a liquified rock crystal, which, in turn is thought, almost transculturally, to comprise the crystallized form of the spirits. In Siberian shamanism, as only one example, we can find a causative relationship, too, between a divine spittle and the sacred fly-agaric.[24] The Goths shared with many the belief that the rings of mushrooms growing under the canopy of trees arose from the spittle of the mischievous forest elves.

It is is not surprising that, today, the Huichol Indians of western Mexico possess a developed concept of transubstantiation, a syncretic product based on the ancient pre-Columbian tradition, fused with quantitative traits ensuing from the Catholic dogma. All these elements, integrated neatly into a mesh, form a native religious cult based on peyote.[25] The plant, transformed into a metaphor, corresponds in substance to what Peter Furst termed, "the divine deer or supernatural Master of the Deer Species,"[26] or, more simply, to the Master of the Animals, encountered in so many cultures.

In a mythological time sequence of the Huichol, the Great Shaman, Grandfather Fire, had led ancestral beings on the first peyote expedition. The ancestors, suffering from discomforts and various ailing symptoms, had besieged the Great Shaman for assistance. He diagnosed their illness as caused by the lack of contact with the revitalizing divine Deer (Peyote), since they were "deprived of the healing powers of its miraculous flesh," not having had hunted the divine entity. So, the ancestors resolved to follow the Great Shaman in quest of the Deer-Peyote.

Sometime in the month of October, the Huichol launch an expedition into the desert region of San Luis Potosi (Real Catorce) in pursuit of the sacred peyote. Such a venture represents the hunting of the divine deer, in which the cactus plant, identified as Deer-Peyote, is "tracked" and slain with a cermonial bow and arrow. After some involved mythico-religious juxtaposition, the peyote-seekers achieve the status of divine beings. The pilgrimage to seek the peyote becomes, in turn, a metaphor for the mystical return to "the place of origin," where "the primordial hunt for the Deer-Peyote" takes place. On the eve of the departure, the pilgrims and their spouses bathe and spend the night in the temple. They all receive new names (rites of rebirth) and perform prayers around the fire (the Great Shaman), sacrificing tortillas to it. They will not wash again until the arrival date of the peyote ceremony, around January.[27] All participants have been ritually cleansed earlier by the shaman and prepared to transcend onto a spiritual plane during the sacred "hunt." This fulfills the partial requirement, which enables the individual to pass through the peril-laden portals of "Clashing Clouds" that separate the ordinary reality of this world from the inordinary, or shamanic, reality of the other. (Note the similarity in theme with other traditions, both ancient and contemporary.)

Before this spiritual task can be accomplished successfully, the participants must consume the cactus plant. This is implemented in two ways, each conveying a different symbolic meaning. The first manner consists of ingesting the fresh cactus, either whole or cut to pieces, in which case the fleshy aspect of the plant becomes consecrated metaphorically as the flesh of the sacred deer. The second method is to eat the peyote chopped up or ground, mixed with water, where its metaphoric significance changes from a mystical dimension to the symbolic and cosmic aspects of natural existence. Thus, the act stands for the seasonal cycles of dry and wet seasons (principle of parallels, or duality), hunting and agriculture (another aspect of the seasonality of nature), and the parallel principle of masculine and feminine (male = peyote cactus, deer; female = water).[28]

Until very recently, the important role of tobacco in shamanistic rituals, in pre-Hispanic and later times, was not appreciated fully. This long-neglected aspect of New World shamanism has been aptly broached by the anthropologist, Johannes Wilbert, in his excellent and authoritative study on *Tobacco and Shamanism in South America* (1987). While an ambitious effort to dwell on the functions of tobacco among the ancient Maya is provided by Robicsek's *The Smoking Gods: Tobacco in Maya Art, History, and Religion* (1978). In spite of the fact that, generally, tobacco is not considered to be a member of the hallucinogenic flora, its active chemicals, especially the alkaloid nicotine, can produce very dramatic psychodynamic effects, if the smoke is inhaled in profuse amounts. This native New World plant, *Nicotiana* spp., has been known to be a very strong psychoactive substance—ingested not only as smoke, but also taken as enema—in the induction of shamanistic trance by the ancient and contemporary Indian cultures. The ritual offering of this plant to the indigenous gods was a fact that had amazed the early Spaniards, especially when they had witnessed the intoxicating effects of this weed on the native users. In the present day, the ceremonial use of tobacco is a well-documented phenomenon, particularly, among many South American Indians (the Warao, Tembé, Urubu, Mehinaku, to mention but a few).

Through biophysical and psychological dependence on this plant, the South American tobacco shaman has developed a specialty technique, setting him apart from the shamans using other psychotropic substances. The tobacco, indeed, is a very special kind of food to him—food which not only men crave, but one on which a host of supernatural beings depend for survival. The latter, through reciprocity of action, bestow upon humanity rains, crops, health, and other conditions that render life an ecological possibility. Consequently, nicotine dependence in the shaman—and in men, in general—is explained, by transference, from the shaman's tobacco habit to the specific requisites ensuing from the spirit world. Thus, some technique modes connected with tobacco shamanism become illuminated in the light of our developing awareness regarding the effects of peripheral smoking.[29]

Among numerous South American tribes, curing ceremonies involve tobacco. The Mehinaku, in central Brazil, summon the tobacco shaman, *yetamá*, whenever there is any occurrence of illness. Tobacco, like in other ritual settings, is considered the food of the supernatural beings, and, as such, when the shaman blows it at the ailing individual, it is believed to permeate through the patient's skin, reaching the obtrusive object, *kaukí*, inside the body. So strong are the associations between curing and smoking that one researcher attributed to them the reasons for the application of the same word, *yetamá*, to denote a "shaman" and a "smoker."[30] Indeed, this close relationship in meanings must signify a historical aspect, linking shamanism with tobacco smoke. As an interesting bynote raised by the Soviet scholar of shamanism V. N. Basilov,[31] it may be observed that by the nineteenth century, when tobacco had reached the vast expanses of northern Asia, it gained a preferential status, such as it had possessed in the Western Hemisphere for millennia, in the ritual drug complex of several Siberian cultures.

Here it replaced, for some shamans, the traditional fly-agaric mushroom as an agent in the induction of ecstatic trance.

Psychoactivity and Mechanisms of Hallucinations

The psychodynamic chemistry of hallucinogenic plants does not provide the only means of attaining a shamanic state of consciousness. Other techniques have been known and used, as well. These include fasting, self-immolation, physical and mental deprivations, torture, lack of sleep and other exhaustions, ceaseless dancing, and rhythmic activities, such as drumming and chanting.

Nevertheless, psychoactive substances began to draw scholarly attention towards the end of the nineteenth century, as a result of scientific inquiries into the phenomena of hallucination and mystical experiences by leading figures such as Francis Galton, J.M. Charcot, Sigmund Freud, and William James. While the American psychologist Hevelock Ellis studied the subjective effects of peyote, then called anhalonium, its principal alkaloid was isolated in 1896, and, by 1919, mescaline was shown to resemble the molecular structure of the hormone epinephrine, produced by the adrenal gland. Although all hallucinogenic compounds are, by definition, psychoactive (i.e., acting on psychological process), not every psychoactive alkaloid is hallucinogenic. The more familiar ones consist of the ergot derivative, lysergic acid diethylamide (LSD); 2,5-dimethoxy-4-methylamphetamine (DOM); mescaline in the peyote cactus, *Lophophora williamsii*; psilocin and, to a lesser extent, psilocybin in the *Psilocybe* mushroom; N,N-dimethyltryptamine (DMT); and other closely related members. LSD has a molecular structure resembling serotonin; DOM and mescaline are phenylethylamines; DMT and psilocin belong to the indoleamine group. Curiously, the stereoisomer of lysergic acid diethylamide (l-LSD), in which the positions of the ethyl chains are transposed from the left side to the right without altering the chemical composition of the molecule itself, produces neither psychoactive effects nor serotonin antagonism.

The Western Hemisphere outnumbers, by far, its eastern counterpart in the richness and diversity of psychotropic flora.[32] One of the most potent hallucinogens in South America, as noted above, consists of a preparation derived by boiling the stalks of the lianas of the *Banisteriopsis* spp., frequently mixed with the leaves of a member of the *Psychotria* spp. or *Prestonia* spp. A generic member of the family Malpighiaceae, *Banisteriopsis* is a tree-climbing, leafy, forest vine, with four known species comprising its genus: *B. rusbyana, B. inebrians, B.*

caapi, and *B. quitensis*. The psychoactive chemistry of the concoction is similar in composition, but not identical, to LSD, to psilocybin in the hallucinogenic mushroom, and to mescaline in peyote. Ingested cool, it contains powerful, psychoactive chemical compounds: harmaline, harmine, d-tetrahydroharmine, and N,N-dimethyltryptamine.[33] The first two are members of the four harmala alkaloids, which, together with harmalol and harman, belong to the group of *beta*-carbolines. The content of *beta*-carboline derivatives, or harmala alkaloids, is a function of the *Banisteriopsis* species that are used in the final admixture. To release the psychoactive harmala alkaloids in *B. caapi* and *B. inebrians*, the hallucinogenic compounds must be acted upon by tryptamines, which are contained in the leaves of *B. rusbyana*,[34] *Psychotria viridis*, and probably in *Prestonia* spp. (also known as *Haemadictyon*). The Cofan Indians of eastern Ecuador and Peru are known to add the tryptamine-rich leaves of *Psychotria* to the stalks of *Banisteriopsis*. The Tukanoan Indians of Colombian Amazon use *B. rusbyana*, for its tryptamine action as monoamine oxidase inhibitor, to release the harmala alkaloids present in *B. caapi* and *B. inebrians*.

Claudio Naranjo, the Chilean-born psychiatrist, performed highly illuminating experiments with the harmaline alkaloid, on volunteer subjects in the the University of Chile's Center for the Study in Medical Anthropology. His findings show harmaline to be most relevant to the understanding of the psycho-chemistry of the human brain and that this chemical agent may play a pertinent biochemical role in the formation of a repertoire of, so-called, Jungian archetypes. Consequently, it is a major factor in structuring the phenomena of transcultural experiences. We can easily recognize, among the motif-symbols of harmaline-induced visions, universally recurrent themes from shamanic states of consciousness (SSC). Most frequent mind-manifest scenarios, enumerated by the experimental subjects, included all sorts of felines (particularly, tigers) and other four-legged animals, proverbial serpents, birds and flights, ascent-descent journeys, solar patterns and circles (implying the notion of a source, center, the *axis mundi*, or a coordinate), life-threatening passage, and death-rebirth symbolism. Thus, the special value of harmaline, to the study of the psycho-neurochemical functions of the brain, lies in

> . . . its close resemblence to substances derived from the pineal gland of mammals. In particular, 10-methoxy-harmaline, which may be obtained in vitro from the incubation of serotonin in pineal tissue, resembles harmaline in its subjective effects and is of greater activity than the latter. This suggests that harmaline (differing from 10-methoxy-harmaline only in the position

of the methoxy group) may derive its activity from the mimicry of a metabolite normally involved in the control of states of consciousness.[35]

The potential transformation of serotonin into a harmaline-type compound, in the pineal gland of the brain, perhaps indicates that one of the functions of serotonin may consist of elevating a person's "inner" consciousness. It does this by secreting into the bloodstream a metabolite capable of interfacing with the ordinary-kind stimuli, which, upon reaching the sensory part of the brain, would interfere with the activities vital to alternate states of consciousness. Serotonin is a neurotransmitter, essential in the functions of brain cells, where it is released from an axon of one neuron to be transmitted across a synaptic gap to the receptor of another. It occurs naturally in the human brain and in that of other mammals, and, curiously, in the venomous and psychoactive secretions of the *Bufo* toads. Its direct involvement in the mind-manifest, or psychedelic, experience cannot be precluded. In view of the above, it should not be surprising to learn that schizophrenics exhibit, ordinarily, the highest concentration of serotonin in the brain. At the same time, the pineal gland seems to be implicated in the activities controlling the various states of consciousness, although its function still remains obscure. It is attached to the central, posterior part of the brain, behind and above the third ventricle, slightly higher than the pituitary gland. In size, it is not larger than an average medicinal capsule, but was believed, in the past, to form the seat where the soul resided.

It was believed that LSD, as a serotonin agitator, seemed either to inhibit or facilitate some neurohumoral (substance which chemically transmits impulses between two nerve cells) activity of serotonin. Insufficient levels of this chemical in certain specific regions of the brain result in catatonic and depressive states, while excessive levels cause hallucination and excitability.[36] New research has indicated, however, that hallucinogens do not seem to exert their primary effect on serotonin neurons, but instead act directly on the specific receptor sites of the neuron that is to receive serotonin, thus, initiating a chain of chemical events in the various complex neural systems of the brain. The insignificant roles of mescaline and DOM as serotonin inhibitors lend support to this concept. The important studies of Jacobs, as well as of others, offer evidence that hallucinogens, such as LSD, do not exert primary effects on serotonin neurons (brain cells), but instead form a critical bond at the 5-HT_2 receptor sites of this neurotransmitter, where effectively they block the action of serotonin. Among others, neurons (brain cells) are inhibited in their utilization of serotonin, the absence of which at the receptor points reduces interference with the chemical activities of the hallucinogens. The common change effected by LSD-type hallu-cinogens in serotonin is exhibited in its synthesis, receptor action, release, and catabolism.[37] It would appear, therefore, that serotonin displays a double factor in the mechanism of hallucination. The more obvious one can be seen in its inhibited efficiency to bond itself to the receptor neurons, particularly at the 5-HT$_2$ sites. The second one, and perhaps much more significant, consists of the biochemical transforma-tion of serotonin in the pineal gland into 10-methoxy-harmaline. This compound seems to be naturally involved in consciousness-altering functions.

The potency of *Datura* and other members of the Solanaceae, as hallucinogenic drugs, is well known throughout the world. Its psycho-dynamic biochemistry results, primarily, from the high concentration of the alkaloids hyoscyamine, scopolamine, and norhyoscyamine—all members of the tropane series. Environment and phytogenetics appear to be determinant factors in the alkaloid content of the *Datura* plant, which consists of four sub-genera and over fifteen species. When administered in large dosage, *Datura* preparations tend to produce excitation, hallucination, delirium, and thereafter a state of narcosis.[38] The extremely crucial role played by *Datura* in European witchcraft has been recently demonstrated quite conclusively.[39]

Richard Schultes referred to the peyote cactus as "a veritable factory of alkaloids."[40] From a biochemical standpoint, he was more than justified. The best known substance contained in a peyote cactus is mescaline, but it is only one of more than thirty alkaloids, also amine derivatives, which have, until now, been isolated from a mature plant (*Lophophora williamsii*); there appear to be more. The majority of the chemical compounds belong to the phenylethylamine and the simpler isoquinoline groups, and they all seem to induce some psychodynamic effects, with mescaline, needless to say, being the primary hallucinogenic constituent. Nevertheless, the actions of these alkaloids on the central nervous system can be grouped into two distinct categories: On one end of the spectrum, there is mescaline, which crystallizes only in the presence of atmospheric carbon dioxide and acts on the brain to evoke the most predominant morphine-like effects of the entire chemical group; on the other end is lophophorine, a non-narcotic, oily, colorless liquid, yet the most toxic amidst the company, causing the most strychnine-like actions (i.e., heightened reflex agitations, resulting possibly in tetanus), which affect the spinal cord and its elongations. The various biochemical interactions of the naturally produced alkaloids in the phytochemically complex peyote, have caused Schultes to express serious doubts about simple, off-hand comparisons between visionary experi-ences based on synthetic mescaline and those experienced by the Indians, as a result of ingesting parts of the actual peyote cactus. The plant is also an effective stimulant and contains a large number of chemical compounds of great pharmacological value, many of which have yet to be exploited.

In 1937, Albert Hofmann of Sandoz, a Swiss pharmaceutical firm, was the first to succeed in the synthesis of an ergot alkaloid—more specifically, ergonovine—from lysergic acid and propanolamine, obtaining a chemical structure of d-lysergic acid, L-2-propanolamide. This achievement opened up the way to wider, commercial, therapeutic uses of this substance in a maleate form. In 1977 and 1978, Hofmann reported that ergonovine maleate possessed entheogenic properties, a fact that should not be too surprising, since ergot had been an important contingency to the experience of divine epiphanies in sacred religious mysteries, as those of Demeter and Dionysos. While in Greece working on sections of this book, I had the opportunity to duplicate Hofmann's experiment with ergonovine maleate, in a controlled environment. The objective was to find out the entheogenic characteristics of this alkaloid. Each one of us ingested 6.0 mg. of the substance dissolved in a little water, three times the dosage taken by Hofmann and his colleagues. We experienced low intensity perceptual alterations, if one might call it so, of the surroundings, both natural and man-made, characterized by a sense of spiritual profoundness imbedded in outdoor nature. There was a mild awareness of inner personal spirituality and insight (*entheoi*), without hallucination or euphoria. The somatic effects consisted primarily of mild leg cramps. As an entheogen, on the whole, ergonovine maleate did not prove so impressive as, for instance, LSD or psilocybin. This may be ascribed to the fact that ergonovine is only one of the psychoactive alkaloids present in ergot. In antiquity, the entire mass of the ergot was used in the preparation of the hallucinogenic potion, in which the combined actions of ergonovine and ergine could enhance the potency of each other and produce a considerably more powerful effect.

The biochemistry of *Psilocybe* mushroom became better understood with the publication of Albert Hofmann's laboratory results in 1964.[41] He isolated the main psychodynamic chemical agents, which he named psilocybin and psilocin. The first alkaloid, psilocybin, is a phosphoric acid ester of 4-hydroxydimethyltryptamine, with a chemical structure resembling that of serotonin, a substance with an important role in the chemical function of mammalian brain; the other, psilocin, is an unstable compound. The psychoactive ingredients comprise about 0.03% of the total weight of the mushroom. This structural relationship of the chemical compounds is responsible for the mystical effects caused by the excitation of the sympathetic nervous system. Visual and auditory senses become considerably heightened, resulting in visionary experiences, and the person's memory bank often becomes unlocked to release events of a far removed and forgotten past. Dramatic transformations of consciousness, with changes in allopsychic orientations and perceptual alterations of one's own psychic and physical states, can be brought about in human beings with doses ranging from 6.0 to 20.0 milligrams, without any physical side-effects.

It seems, almost, to be the fate of Swiss scientists to decode the enigmas of mycological perplexities. Conrad H. Eugster, a chemist, and Peter G. Waser, a pharmacologist, both professors at the University of Zurich, provided the world with clues to the nature of the fly-agaric, *Amanita muscaria*.[42] For a long time, it was believed that muscarine played an important role in the psychodynamic chemistry of this mushroom. Although, in fact, muscarine is present, it has but a minor position in its chemical structure. Instead, two other substances contribute, mainly, to the neurochemical activities: muscimole and ibotenic acid, both isoxazoles, with others still to be examined in closer detail. Muscimole is formed by unsaturated cyclic hydroxamic acid, and, essentially, manages to retain in the kidneys its unchanged characteristics; it, therefore, constitutes the pharmacological keynote to the urine phenomenon (discussed in the previous chapter), a unique property of the fly-agaric. Wasson, who was not a stranger to the effects of *A. muscaria* commented: "A peculiar feature of the fly-agaric is that its hallucinogenic properties pass into the urine, and another may drink this urine to enjoy the same effect."[43] Muscarine, on the other hand, believed to cause heavy sweating and twitching, seems to be filtered out by the kidneys, and is absent in the urine.

At the same time, the ibotenic acid tends to convert naturally to the more stable muscimole, producing more of the active ingredient for progressively induced neurophysiological processes.

Ibotenic acid is present in the fresh fly-agaric in widely varying amounts, ranging from 0.03% to 0.1%. When the fly-agaric dries, the ibotenic acid steadily disintegrates and disappears. Thus we have the unique situation where a psychotomimetic agent converts itself through simple drying into another active agent that is more potent and far more stable. In *Soma* I [Wasson writes] give *in extenso* (and in summary on pp. 153 ff.) the almost unanimous testimony, extending over two centuries and throughout almost the whole of the northern tier of tribes from the valley of the Ob to the Chukotka, that the fly-agaric must *not* be eaten fresh: it should be dried, preferably sun-dried. The empirical knowledge of the Siberian natives is now confirmed by [Conrad] Eugster.[44]

Lest I be charged with a major omission, a comment ought to be made about the psychoactive qualities of tobacco, especially the constituent alkaloid nicotine. Wilbert, who directs the Latin American Center at UCLA, observes that the revered use of tobacco throughout the ancient Western Hemisphere is shown to be conditioned by the psycho-physiological effects tying its use, even today, to the "basic tenets of shamanistic ideology."[45] The various phenomena associated with tobacco shamanism, such as night vision[46] and shamanic voices, must be regarded as functions of the rate of nicotine absorption by the human body, and of the biophysical conditions under which the particular variety of *Nicotiana* spp. is flourishing. The exceedingly widespread popularity of this weed can be understood better in light of the instant rapidity of its biochemical action—within seven seconds from the onset of smoking—that is induced by nicotine on the central and peripheral nervous systems, by which it reaches the brain, the adrenal medulla, and the sympathetic ganglia.[47]

Phosphenes

Somewhere in the neural network of the brain and the retina is spurred a phenomenon that actuates inner sight, or luminous visions, and which may constitute the basis for an objective, physical framework for the visions encountered among religious adepts, such as shamans and mystics. This process is neurochemical in origin and evokes subjective light patterns, such as stars, within the brain and the eye, induced by agents other than outside sources of illumination. Called phosphenes (from the Greek *phos* = "light", *phainein* = "to show"), these patterns can be generated during the subject's condition of half-sleep, closed-eye meditation, a state pre-emptied of external stimuli, or by electrical, mechanical (e.g., a physical trauma to the eye), or chemical (alcohol, psychotropic substances, etc.) means. Certain ophthalmological and brain disorders may be responsible, as well, for the induction of phosphenes. Hallucinogenic drugs, such as mescaline, psilocybin, and LSD bring about such abstract patterns, and, in the case of the last substance, its phosphene effect may recur long after the other symptoms have vanished. Darkness is not essential for the creation of phosphenes, which can also occur spontaneously, especially following prolonged visual deprivation.[48]

While in Paris, Benjamin Franklin had participated in phosphene demonstrations with the aid of an electrostatic generator; Alessandro Volta had spent time researching their occurrences; but it was the physiologist Johannes Purkinje, who published in 1819 the most comprehensive treatment on phosphenes known to that date. The late Max Knoll and his associates, at the *Technische Hochschule* in Munich, were responsible for the most extensive experiments with phosphenes induced by electrical methods. In the course of their studies, with more than one thousand subjects, it was discovered that electrical pulses in the same frequency range as brain waves were most apt to create phosphenes, and that their design patterns were a direct function of this frequency pulse. In addition to the technique based on electrical impulses, the researchers were able to generate phosphenes chemically by administering mescaline, psilocybin, and LSD to different subjects. Despite his subsequent work on the neural system, Max Knoll is better known for his earlier accomplishment as the builder, with E.A.F. Ruska, of the first electron microscope in 1932.

Since the phenomenon is generated by a biochemically induced response, the sensation of these light patterns constitutes the realm of common experience to all, which might have supplied an innate source for the artistic inspiration in early cultures.[49] Phosphenes are typical of the early phases of all hallucinogenic trances, and the experience thereof is followed by the perception of symbolic images, which seem to be culturally-bound and a function of the individual's cognitive system, if not, even his or her subconscious processes. As noted above, these luminous sensations can be triggered by exogenous stimuli, and the *marari* and *nomeri*—Desana native terms for phosphene images—which are claimed to be perceived by the Indians also during sexual intercourse, compare sexual activity to a hallucinogenic experience. Thus, Reichel-Dolmatoff surmises that "The entire transformative sequence [in Desana shamanistic initiation] is also comparable to the succession of neurological sensations perceived during an advancing state of drug-induced trance, and many of all these states and conditions have a strong sexual resonance." The psychic journey of the initiate "is described as an ecstatic metamorphosis, a dream world of colors and shapes, projected by an intoxicated mind."[50]

As observed earlier, the shamanistic experience forms the basis for the Tukanoan aesthetic expression, with phosphene designs acting as a storeroom, which provides the source for almost all of their art motifs. "What we are inclined to call art and enjoy as an aesthetic impression, to the Indians is a more sober means of communication in which each shape, each colour, each sound, each combination or sequence expresses a deeply felt truth which must be perpetuated and propagated."[51] And since the Tukanoan art has a biochemical basis, it is possible to look for similar foundations beneath the universality of certain basic art motifs and patterns as a functional expression of corresponding biochemical and neurophysiological process. Carl G. Jung, observing the transcultural character of the neurally stimulated phosphene shapes, pioneered the idea that certain archetypal symbols might originate in the personal experience of such luminous designs. This idea seems to be borne out by the Indians of Colombian Amazon, who readily acknowledge that their source for generating the designs comes from perceiving the images during a hallucinogenic experience. Genuine archetypes do not possess physical configurations, but are only abstractions to be found within the person. Henceforth, the neurophysiological and biochemical impetus behind the origins of art must be recognized as antecedent to the sociocultural foundations of aesthetic expressions.[52]

Limited in the varieties of patterns into which they are manifest, phosphene images do not form a random assortment, but fall into at least fifteen categories, (and may even be classified into as many as thirty), which were "isolated" by Knoll on a statistical basis, derived from the census of over a thousand volunteers. However, there is a definite correspondence established between phosphene shapes and the underlying artistic designs found in different culture areas, including certain subcultures within the United States.[53] The almost visionary, later paintings, executed in an asylum, by Vincent van Gogh, exhibit phosphene patterns, as do many unskilled crayon drawings of youngsters between the ages of two and four years. As can be also expected, a large number of designs encountered in ancient and aboriginal cultures display phosphene-like characters. The Tukano Indians, for instance, derive their fundamental artistic elements from phosphenes, which they induce hallucinogenically; however, they interpret the basic designs according to their own cultural metaphors.[54] If we, in another case, recognize the spiral to be an archetypal pattern and its schematic representations as the labyrinth, then this conception may help elucidate our understanding of why this motif has been used to symbolize the unknown origin-point leading to the Hereafter, the cave, the tomb, and the womb of the Great Mother. The tomb, as has been noted, was constructed in resemblance of the body of the Great Mother, whose energy and procreative sexuality are conveyed by the element of the spiral.

There exists particularly strong evidence indicating that sound resonance of certain frequencies stimulates the vision of colors among human beings. The known philosopher of science, Guy Murchie, writes that phosphenes are far from consisting of haphazard shapes, but may, in fact, represent an undecoded grammar of a hidden universal dimension, or manifest the characters of universal psychic units (constants).[55] Perhaps it might be more accurate to describe phosphenes as the "archetypes" of the collective neural system. In either case, it would prove of unquestionable value to understand the role played by phosphenes in precognitive functions, as well as to grasp their impact on the development of symbolic thought.

6

The Botanic Experience: Hallucinogens in Archaeology and Ethnohistory

IT IS NOT INTENDED HERE, by any means, to present a complete exposition of the historical continuity accounting for the familiarity of psychotropic flora throughout the world. The purpose, instead, is to provide a rather broad archaeological and ethnohistorical framework against which to sight our discussion of a characteristic religious phenomenon. As a belief system, shamanism bridges the gap between symbolic experience and culture change. The striking similarities, in a transcultural experience, between the basic precepts and structural motifs of shamanism, as a universal *Ur*-religion, go back far into the Palaeolithic. Recent studies offer substantial support favoring strong Palaeolithic and Mesolithic roots for the use of psychotropic plants among the Old World and New World shamans. This is not only witnessed in the ethnographic present, but, indeed, the aboriginal religions in the Western Hemisphere can be viewed as the archaeological present of the Mesolithic horizon. We hear a great deal nowadays about drug use in our own society. Unfortunately, little time has been allotted to ethno-archaeological studies of the dynamic contributions to the cultural process made by ritual drug use in the past.[1] As a matter of fact, most of whatever little archaeological information we have comes to us by analogous inference from the corpus of ethnographic observations.

Figure 6.1. Rock painting of an enigmatic personage, Aouanrhet, from whose body mushrooms appear to emerge. This may refer to the ceremonial importance of hallucinogenic mushrooms in the remote anitquity of North Africa. Tassili n'Ajjer, Algeria; Late Roundhead period, before sixth millennium B.C. (Author's archives).

The Old World

The oldest documented use of hallucinogenic mushrooms (not implied to mean the earliest use of psychotropic plants) in the world does not come from Asia or the Americas, as might be expected, but is shown in the prehistoric rock art of central Sahara, especially in the Tassili n'Ajjer massif of southern Algeria. It offers sufficient archaeological evidence for a developed, ethno-mycological ritual complex, already in existence during the African Later Stone Age, characterized by rainy interludes, a phase known as the "Round Head" period, around 9000–6000 years ago.[2] In the rock art, one encounters mushroom-men, with heads resembling fungi. Each individual holds a mushroom in the hand, while interrupted lines indicate a connection, a route, between the head of the man and the mushroom that he is holding. Another drawing, which depicts a person grasping a bunch of mushrooms, also shows mushrooms growing from his skin—or, rather, the skin (flesh) being formed into mushroom shapes, as if meant to represent "the flesh of the god." Although it is very difficult to identify the mycoflora categories shown in the rock drawings, Giorgio Samorini[3] noted the striking similarities between their forms and those of the two widespread hallucinogenic genera: the *Psilocybe* species and a variety of *Amanita* spp.

Another example of a similar genre, presumably involving hallucinogenic non-fungal flora, consists of a dance scene depicting plant foliage and three figures with upraised arms in attitudes of worship (?). This rock art is from Tadrart Acacus in Libya, and on stylistic grounds it fits into the aforementioned "Round Head" period, belonging to the pre-Neolithic cultures of North Africa. According to Emmanuel Anati's classification, the "Round Head" phase in rock art corresponds to the Epi-Palaeolithic horizons of the "Early Gatherers," with evidence for this cognitive category to be found in the Sahara, Tanzania, Baja California, and Texas.[4] The major contention forwarded by Anati, and generally accepted by specialists in this field, advocates a meaningful correlation between the overall theme and style of a particular rock art tradition and the socioeconomic patterns of the population that produced it. More specifically, this applies to the Early Hunters, Early Gatherers, Late Hunters, pastoral nomads, and societies with mixed or complex economies.

A rock painting from Pla de Petracos in Alicante, Spain, dated to the fifth millennium B.C., belongs to an anthropomorphic group of diverse forms.[5] It had been most probably executed either under the influence of hallucinogens or intended to depict a psychedelic state, if not both. The renowned authority on prehistoric art, Antonio Beltrán, commented that the artist responsible for this piece must have been undergoing a hallucinogenic experience.[6] Another example from the same place, quite possibly a companion piece in the same genre, is described as a geometric meander ending in fingers and small circles, or orbits.[7] Although omitted in Beltrán's comments, in essence it belongs to the same anthropomorphic type described above. The possibility has already been considered that the Vinča culture, in central Balkans, was acquainted with the use of hallucinogens between the fifth and fourth millennium B.C.

The Alpine environment of the Camonica Valley in northern Italy has offered a suitable habitat, both in the palaeo and the present times, for the proliferation of the mycoflora (i.e., the mushroom family of plants), to which belong several varieties containing strong psychoactive chemical compositions. The presence of mushroom species belonging to the genus *Psilocybe*, for example, can be traced back to the Great Glacial phase of the Pleistocene in the Würmian period, during which the range in soil acidity of 5.2–6.3 pH was characteristically appropriate; in simple chronology this means about 12,000–10,000 years ago. The predominant mushroom among all the varieties growing in the higher altitudes of the Camonica Valley, and not limited only to the psychotropic kind, is the *Psilocybe semilanceata*. To this day as well, this species is the most characteristic of the Italian psychotropic mycoflora, particularly flourishing in the territories surrounding Brescia in northern Italy.[8]

In the region of Monte Bego in the Franco-Italian Alps, we find a rock carving depicting an individual, or some other effigy, together with an identifiable representation of the *Amanita muscaria*. Unfortunately, all that we can say, for the moment, about the rock art in this area is that it points to a familiarity with the *Amanita* spp. since Indo-European contacts. In Monte Bego, the *A. muscaria* is depicted in a naturalistic form, in contrast to Valcamonica (Camonica Valley), where, until now, the mushroom is found to be represented "symbolically," so to speak. The inhabitants of Valcamonica possessed a practical knowledge of the psychoactive effects induced by the use of certain native mushrooms belonging to the genera *Psilocybe, Panaeolus,* and *Amanita*. A ritual drug complex, focusing on ecstatic and visionary experiences produced by the use of hallucinogenic plants, came into existence in the Camonica Valley before the onset of the Indo-European phase, that is, prior to the termination of the proto-Camunian Period II-B, which ended about 3000 B.C. It may be safely hypothesized that the techniques employed in such experiences were closely akin to those found in use among the shamans in other cultures. Some have compared the iconographic content and style of Monte Bego rock art with the "Indo-European" motifs to be found at the base of Vedic mythology, while others have attempted to define the occurrence of *Amanita muscaria* in the rock carvings of Monte Bego as an Indo-European phenomenon, wherein the mushroom (*A. muscaria*) corresponds to the Vedic god, Soma.[9]

Giorgio Samorini, with the Camunian Center of Prehistoric Studies in Capo di Ponte, as of this writing, is responsible for invaluable, and virtually pioneering, contributions to the study of the psychotropic ethnoflora in this geographical area.[10] The psychotropic plants in Valcamonica, both of fungal and non-fungal varieties, are listed below:

Psychotropic Mushrooms in Valcamonica

Psilocybe semilanceata	*Panaeolus ater*
Psilocybe callosa	*Panaeolus subbalteatus*
Amanita muscaria	*Panaeolus retirugis*
Amanita pantherina	*Panaeolus foenisecii*
	Panaeolus sphinctrinus
	Panaeolus campanulatus

Psychotropic Plants (non-fungal) in Valcamonica

Datura stramonium	*Atropa belladonna*
Datura metel	*Hyoscyamus niger*

All four species in the table above are members of the family Solanaceae, and, thus, are known as solanaceous plants. It is extremely difficult, if not outright impossible, to find archaeological evidence in the Old World indicating the use of psychotropic plants in the solanaceous category. Their use, on the other hand, among the numberless witches and sorcerors, is well documented for the Middle Ages and the subsequent periods, contributing to the rich and mysterious witchcraft lore of ecstatic flights and in-gatherings. However, the extensive knowledge involved in effective use of psychotropic plants remained, for obvious reasons, limited to narrow circles, failing to assume the proportions of a widespread social phenomenon. It should be pointed out, nevertheless, that the *metel* species of *Datura* is definitely a recent arrival in the Alpine valleys.[11]

In the vicinity of the charming Capo di Ponte in Valcamonica, situated between Foppe di Nadro and Zurla, the site of Naquane contains a rich heritage of prehistoric rock art. From its southern area, we have two classic representations of shamans performing ritual dances around or over a small tree (the shamanistic tree-to-the-heaven?). The head of one of the shamans is hidden completely inside a mask, and he wears a costume—which, among the Altaic shamans of later date, appears to be a fitted, animal skin dress—embellished with short "ribbons" on his

Figure 6.2. The author examines an ancient rock carving of a horned shamanic figure in Valcamonica, Italy, 1989. (Author's archives).

torso. As he prances in the dance, bent over at the hips, imitating some quadruped creature, the hanging "ribbons" may, at a first glance, suggest rain from the sky. In reality, however, this paraphernalia of the shaman's attire alludes to his animal and spiritual familiars and very likely represents the long hair and, or, teats at an animal's underside. The figure's entire posture suggests an animal—an animal of the hunt.

The other figure, conversely, is in an upright stance, also wearing a helmet-type mask. His left hand is holding the proverbial drum, and the right one brandishes a drumstick—both, as has been seen, universal appurtenances of the shaman. Emanuele Süss, who described both figures, states that they are executed on the same plane and that their style and technique recall those appearing on certain Gaelic coins of the sixth century B.C., as apparently suggested by L. Langyel in *L'art gaulois dans le medailles*. Süss, who seems inclined toward pragmatic materialism and, thus, de-emphasizes the role of the symbolic in a cultural process, identifies the first figure, incorrectly, as a rain-god *("dio della pioggia"*) and the other, much too broadly to be effective, as a dancer-musician *("danzatore-musico")*.[12] It should be pointed out that, in addition to all the shamanistic attributes already mentioned as belonging to the engraved figures, no god dances for himself, or in his own honor, to influence an action or an event which is engendered by his very own nature. In other words, a rain-god does not dance to produce rain; a shaman or a rain-priest does. We may also be prone to ask to what an extent was it necessary in the damp climate of an Alpine region, 3000 or 4000 years ago, to promote agricultural fertility by depending on a ritual complex designed to bring rainfall

From the Iron Age (first millennium B.C.), we have the well-known engraving, on Rock 35 in Naquane, of the so-called running priest (!) who, in fact, does not seem to be running at all, but dancing. The right hand placed on the hip and the left arm extended outward can hardly be described as a posture one assumes in running. The figure's headgear, consisting of a helmet or a cap, is crowned with feathers or stalks of vegetation. A photograph,[13] which in rock art may actually reveal more detail—for I have examined the original engraving, as well—suggests vaguely that the "priest" might be holding something next to his right hip. The dancing individual may be a hunter or a warrior engaged in a ceremonial dance before a hunt or a battle; yet, there are no weapons discernibly associated with this figure, who appears to be the sole performer. Therefore, it is very likely that the characteristics of this personage represent the attributes of a shaman, and not those of a hunter, a warrior, or a running priest.

In all likelihood, the Late Bronze and the Iron Age cultures of the Alpine north Italy, especially those around the Camonica Valley, had provided an impetus to the growth of a proto-Etruscan culture complex, with some of its basic characteristics leading to the development of a core that formed modal elements in the newly emerging civilization. The Villanovan tribal culture, with its elaborate hunting magic, constituted one of the bases from which arose Etruscan urban centers, and these, in turn, adapted the tribal hunting rituals into their own rich lore of magical practices, which included divining from animal livers. In some ways, the Valcamonica engraved figures bring to mind Etruscan bronze sculpture. In fact, the crudeness and the size of the hands are suggestive of not only Etruscan features, but even of the earlier Sardinian bronze warriors. And the similarity does not end here: The representation of the human body follows that style, too. Of particular interest to our subject is a known Etruscan bronze mirror, showing the Thessalian hero, Ixion, an uncle of the widely reputed Greek healer, Asklepios. Here, Ixion, spread-eagled on a fire-wheel for breaching the confidence of the gods, is shown with a hallucinogenic mushroom under his feet, which Robert Graves believes to be *Amanita muscaria*.

The heralded name of Mycenae (*Mykines* in Greek, which became almost synonymous with the Helladic civilization of the Bronze Age, as well as being the fortified site of the city of Agamemnon, the king

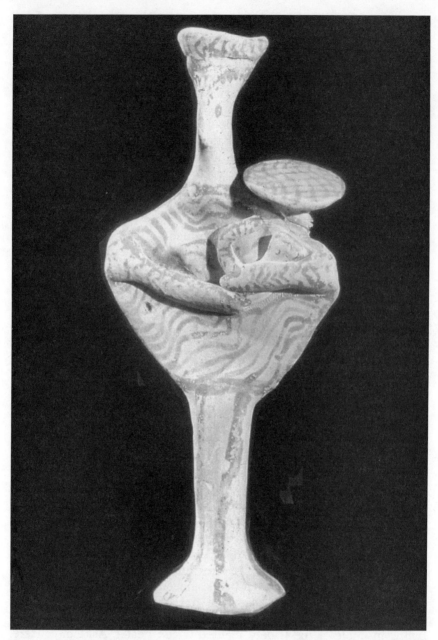

Figure 6.3. Ancient Greek ceramic figurine, known as *kourotrophos* ("a milk nurse"). The nurse and the infant have mushroom forms, intimating the ritual importance of this plant in Bronze Age Greece. 13th century B.C. (National Archaeological Museum, Athens).

who had led the confederated armies against Troy) derives its origins from the Greek cognate *mykes*,[14] meaning mushroom (ancient μύχης; modern μύχης). One is prompted to ask what kind of a mushroom would be identified with an existential dwelling of the gods, a sacred place, an axis mundi, demarcated by the boundary of a city? Curiously enough, the Greek word for a poppy pod or poppy juice is *mekon* (ancient μήχων; modern μήχων). The poet Hesiod (c. 800 B.C.) is credited with leaving the first written mention of the (opium) poppy with his reference to Mekone, city of the poppy, supposedly near Corinth in the Peloponese.[15] However, I believe that the ancient sources might have confused the town Mykines (city of the mushroom) with the Cycladic island of Mykonos, which abounds in poppies. At the same time, it certainly falls within the realm of possibility that some of the sacred emblems used on Minoan Crete[16] (approximately 1500 B.C.) could depict stylized hallucinogenic mushrooms, as well as poppy or opium pods.

The opium plant is only a variety of the poppy. Minoan and Mycenaean goddesses from the thirteenth century B.C. are shown in ritualized postures, with naturalistic poppy pods on their heads. An effigy wearing a headdress adorned with poppy pods was found at Gazi in Crete; while in Palaiokastro, also on Crete, near the alleged birthplace of Zeus in the Diktaean Cave, a mold was discovered for making clay figurines, showing a goddess (?) holding poppies. From the acropolis at Mycenae—that is, its fortified walls on the mountain promontories—comes a gold ring depicting Demeter handing to Perseus (the mythical founder of Mycenae) three poppy heads. While on a Boeotian plate[17] we again see the great Corn Goddess, Demeter, enthroned, draped, with a high polos on her head. She is holding two ears of cereal, two poppy pods, and a torch (for the descent-journey?). Behind the goddess, a black bird, possibly representing a soul, is ascending in flight. The well-known Cypriot Bronze Age ceramic vessel, now in the Archaeological Museum of Cyprus in Nicossia, shows a bull feeding happily in the field of poppy flowers. This iconographic motif persisted well into the later epochs, where it continued to be depicted in bronze during the Geometric Period (c. 700 B.C.). It was the poppy, Ovid tells us, that Persephone was picking when her uncle, Hades, kidnapped her into his realm in the Underworld. Today in the center of Athens, one can still see the triglyph in Pentelic marble belonging to an ancient temple, possibly constructed for the sacred precinct, *temelos*, of the Athenian Eleusinion, with beautifully carved opium pods in bas relief representing sacred emblems in the mystery cult of the Earth-Goddess Demeter.

The semi-annual descent and ascent of Persephone, to the land of the spirits and back to earth, represent the ascent and descent of a shamanic soul-journey. Rituals commemorating her ascent were re-

Figure 6.4. The Little Metropolitan Church, one of the oldest in Athens. Built partly with marble stones taken from pre-Christian buildings. Pods of poppies or opium are clearly depicted on this ancient protome of Pentelic marble, which most likely came from the Athenian Eleusinion, sacred to Demeter. (Photograph by the author).

created at the sanctuary of Eleusis, for about 1,500 years without interruption, during the solemn observance of this ancient Greek mystery cult.[18] These rites were accompanied by heavy doses of libation (*kykeon*), the secret ingredients of which were never fully disclosed. We can be certain today, however, that the active chemical constituents came from the hallucinogenic, water-soluble, ergot alkaloids—the ergonovine and the ergine—which are chemically very close to LSD-25 and found on the barley cultivated in the sacred precinct of Eleusis, where ecstasy and the flight of the soul were understood to mean the same thing.[19] Ergot is a fungal parasite, growing as sclerotium of *Claviceps purpurea* and *C. paspali*, and can infest rye, barley, and other cereal. Near Eleusis is located the sacred Rharian field, where, according to Pausanias, the first planting of cereal had occurred, thus, constituting the birthplace of grain agriculture in Greece, and, at the same time, of Demeter's epiphany. It was on this field that the priests of Demeter grew the sacred barley for the secret *kykeon* drink. It was also there that Triptolemus, an Eleusinian divinity, had a threshing floor, most likely to process the ingredient for the sacred potion. How probable is it that the sanctified Rharian field was, in fact, celebrated for its ergot-infested barley? To experience the sacred epiphany at Eleusis was a cultural aspiration and a personal ambition of a Greek adult. This experience reconfirmed, year after year, the validity of a belief system. And by allowing the laymen to witness the divine instance of Persephone's sojourn between this World and the Underworld, the sociocultural values and ethos became strengthened by consistent affirmations.

Evidence for the use of the sacred mushrooms (*A. muscaria?*) has been noted in conjunction with the solar cult in Scandinavia during the Bronze Age Periods IV and V, about 1100–700 B.C. The sacred mushroom emblems, shown as part of boat designs, occur on bronze razors from Denmark and on two rock carvings from Åby in Bohuslën, Sweden.[20] Even though there are no obvious indications linking such representations with shamanistic practices, we can justifiably expect these occurrences to exist.

In Finland, on the other hand, we can observe rock art iconography of what, undoubtedly, are meant to be representations of shamans. Found at Ristiina Astuvansalmi, near Helsinki, they have been dated to around 3000 B.C. by shore displacement chronology. Two arrowheads discovered at this location confirm the occupation of the archaeological horizons. One of the implements dates from the end of the Comb Ceramic Period, *c.* 2200–1800 B.C., while the other is of Bronze Age manufacture, *c.* 1300–500 B.C.[21]

The prehistoric ethnomycological motif, suggesting the use of psychoactive agents, that we encounter in the Vinča culture in a biomorphic vessel as early as the fifth or the fourth millennium B.C., has persisted for additional thousands of years in this and the surrounding habitats. As late as the fifth century of the present era, the Huns had produced bronze cauldrons depicting prominent mushrooms cast in full relief around the sections of the handles. At least five such metal cauldrons and seven fragments, with mycological ornamental themes, were found in Rumania, Hungary, Czechoslovakia, and different parts of the Soviet Union. The finds were uncovered near or, as a few cases inform us, in rivercourses and lakes.[22] Soviet scholars have inferred that the transhumant nomads in Kirghizia and Kazakhstan were bound by ritual to perform some kind of ceremonies at certain watercourses in the springtime of every year, where they would leave their heavy bronze cauldrons behind and re-use them upon their cyclical return from the quest for summer verdure in higher altitudes.[23] Other established authorities—such as Otto Maenchen-Helfen, who had been Privatdozent at the University of Berlin and later Professor of Art at the University of California, Berkeley—seem to concur with this notion, feeling that the associations of several cauldrons with other ritual objects lend support to such a contention. There are those who further think that, owing to the fact that several handle-fragments depicting mushrooms were discovered buried separately, the most sacred aspect of the Hunnic vessels was formed precisely by the mushroom-decorated handles, which consequently needed to be protected from becoming profaned.[24]

However, the idea that the mushrooms might have, possibly, signified the ritual use of a hallucinogenic substance was not seriously considered by any of them, with the probable exception of László. In 1955, he contended that the mushrooms on the handles of the Hunnic bronze cauldrons represented "shaman crowns,"[25] thus, drawing a connection between mushroom iconography and ecstatic religion among these people. Inasmuch as the environmental conditions prevailing on the plains of Hungary and Rumania precluded subsistance based on pastoral mountain nomadism (transhumance), as the situation existed on the plateaus of Central Asia, the Huns retained, undoubtedly, their old mode of behavior, consisting of depositing cauldrons near the water source, and which Maenchen-Helfen sought to explain in terms of ceremonialism. Whether or not the mushroom-design possessed a religious connotation for the Huns constitutes an issue which does not, necessarily, have to bear directly on the reasons motivating these nomadic tribesmen to leave their cauldrons behind. A different perspective on this matter may offer a simpler and more pragmatic answer; mainly, that the bronze cauldrons were very heavy and, since cooking in them required large quantities of water, it made common sense to situate the vessels within close proximity to a water source.

Nevertheless, the use of hallucinogenic mushrooms in Siberia, Mongolia, and the adjoining steppe regions is well-documented, and is definitely several millennia older than the bronze cauldrons of Attila and his Huns, who probably learned the production of these vessels in the borderlands of northern China. We have no certain evidence indicating the specific function and use of the mushrooms among the warlike Huns. To augur was a common practice with the Huns, and the fearsome Attila was described as "a man who sought counsel of omens in all warfare. . . [and] decided to inquire into the future through haruspices,"[26] or scapulimancy—that is, "reading" animal bones and the entrails to cast prognostications. Since most of the epigraphic reports on the custom of divination were written by Christian priests and theologians of the day, set on denouncing the practice as ungodly and heathen, it is more than likely that they did not grasp—or even care to—without prejudice the full dimension and meaning of what they were describing. However, "that the Huns had shamans is certain. *Kam* in the names Atakam and Eskam is *qam*, the common Turkish word for shamans. To judge from the two names of high-ranking Huns, the shamans seem to have belonged to the upper stratum of Hun society."[27]

The earliest known eye-witness account on the consumption of the mushroom fly-agaric among the Siberian folk dates back to 1658 and comes to us in the form of an entry made by a Polish war prisoner, Adam Kamieński Dłużyk, on the customs of the Ostyak tribes in the Irtysh-Ob river valleys in western Siberia. "They eat certain fungi in the shape of fly-agarics, and thus get drunk worse than on vodka, and for them that's the very best banquet."[28] Unfortunately, having no proper frame of reference, very few of the early travelers were in a position to recognize the difference betwen intoxication and hallucination or a visionary experience, and consequently many of the early narratives, informing on the use of hallucinogens, describe this practice in a rather degenerate light.

The Ostyaks, living in the valleys formed by the two rivers—the Irtysh being a tributary of the Ob—are an Ugrian people in the Finno-Ugric linguistic family. Currently, it is common knowledge that, within the Siberian Culture Area, other groups—mainly, the Samoyeds, the Voguls, and the Kets of the Yenisei river (which together with the Irtysh-Ob forms one of the major areas of shamanism in the world)—make up the Ob-Ugrians, who, together with the Finno-Ugrians, consitute the major Uralic group. Many different groups, unrelated to the latter, have also been avid users of the fly-agaric. Among them, we can readily mention the Evenks, then the Palaeo-Siberian Kamchadels, the Chukchees, and the Koryaks on the northeastern coast of the Pacific. It has been reported that a Koryak tribesman would eagerly exchange a reindeer for a single fly-agaric. The Yukaghirs, dwelling in settlements by the harsh Arctic Ocean—which neighbor the Chukchees and the Lamuts—and the Inari Lapps in Finland have kept alive the memory of fly-agaric use in the current oral traditions. It is also probable that, due to the frowning by the authorities, both the Lapps and the Yukaghirs would not acknowledge openly the present-day function of the hallucinogen, but prefer to relegate its use to the past only.

Based on ethnological and linguistic evidence, the Finno-Ugrian tribes (of the Uralic family of languages), which include the Hungarians, used the hallucinogenic mushroom, fly-agaric, already in protohistoric times,[29] although some of them might have guarded the practice with profound secrecy.[30] The appearance in 1907 of B. Munkácsi's *Collection of Vogul Heroic Songs*, and its subsequent publication in 1910, brought to light definite allusions to the state of "ecstasy caused by seven one-footed, notch-edged, fly-agarics" and to "the ecstasy caused by seven fly-agarics with spotted heads." János Balázs, in his contribution on Hungarian shamanism, refers to the use of the fly-agaric by the Siberian and the Ugrian shamans as forming part in the repertory of the techniques to achieve ecstasy.[31]

In his pioneering work, *Soma: Divine Mushroom of Immortality*, R. Gordon Wasson aptly demonstrated the widespread use of the hallucinogenic *Amanita muscaria* in Europe and Asia, pointing to its connection with shamanism. "The original 'toadstool' was the fly-agaric." In some French conservative dialects and parts of the Basque country, the fly-agaric still is called by an equivalent cognate—"toad"—*crapaudin* and *amoroto*, respectively.[32] In *Mushrooms, Russia and History*, the Wassons amassed intriguing evidence on the enigmatic character and status of the fly-agaric in European countries, especially in the north, where a folk "scare" and mystery surrounds the mushroom, even to this day.[33] It is very likely that this attitude of perplexed apprehension resulted from a very ancient taboo or fear of a sacrilege.

R.G. Wasson also identified successfully the divine Soma, glorified in the *Rigveda*, with the fly-agaric. Sometime in the second millennium B.C., the "original" Aryans had marched into India from the northwest, sweeping across the land in their great military and cultural conquest, bringing with them new customs and sacred traditions, some of which have survived to this day in the Vedic texts, such as the *Rigveda*. It is distinctly possible that the ancestors of the Ob-Ugrian Ostyaks and Voguls, who still today imbibe the amanita drink on the banks of the Yenisei, had passed the secrets of the Soma to the Indo-Iranians, who apparently developed improved methods for the ritual preparation of this substance by removing successfully the toxic ingredients, and thus by-passing the occasional need to rely on the urine of those with apparent immunity. In this "recycled" state, Soma loses its toxicity without forfeiting its effect.[34] Apparently, so it would appear, the imminent familiarization with Soma, and its intensive use by the Indo-Iranians sometime during the course of their history, caused Eliade to issue this spurious and unfounded pronouncement: ". . . the magico-religious value of intoxication for achieving ecstasy [psychotropically-induced trance] is of Iranian origin," and it represents a later, degenerated change in the techniques of ecstasy. "Narcotics are only a vulgar substitute for 'pure' trance. . . .The use of intoxicants. . .is a recent innovation and points to a decadence in shamanic technique. Narcotic intoxication is called on to provide an *imitation* of a state that the shaman is no longer capable of attaining otherwise."[35] However, as mentioned earlier, recent studies tend to describe a different situation.

The *Rigveda* mentions a non-flowering, non-leafy, fruitless, and rootless plant, growing in the high mountains, which can be no other than the Hindu Kush and the Himalayas, since the plant can only be found between the birch and the conifer. In India, and south of the Oxus, this fact means 8,000 to 16,000 feet in elevation. It suitably corresponds to the preferred Alpine altitudes for this species, at which *Amanita muscaria* not only thrives, but is believed to be a motif in the "Indo-European" iconography of Monte Bego (France[36]) rock art, which, according to the same source, shows a relationship with certain aspects of Vedic mythology.[37] The texts make also frequent allusions to the plant's stem and cap, as well as to its ability to produce visions resulting in mental and physical enhancements. These Indo-Aryan people (of the Vedas) were the first, as far as we know, to deify a plant, and make it into a god—Soma. The existing 1,082 Vedic hymns, of which 120 are totally devoted to this deity-plant, exalt Soma the god, praising his sensuality, luminous appearance, and comparing him to "the back of the sky," "navel of the way," "the Immortal Principle," "the Sacred Element," to name but several epithets only. *Amanita muscaria*, the fly-agaric, or *mukhomor*, as it is called in several Slavic languages, is the "Sacred Element" in the shamanistic religion of the north Siberian folk, especially those enclaved in the river valleys of the Yenisei and the Irtysh-Ob, as well as the tribes to be found in the farthest reaches of northeast Siberia.[38] Soma can impart to humans the same characteristics as those that can be witnessed in the attributes of the gods.

The paeans to Soma, which we encounter in the *Rigveda*, may just as easily apply to another Indo-European deity, perhaps not altogether unrelated in the mystical content, particularly if we consider a possible route for his diffusion, although, this time, not believed to be of Indo-Aryan origins.[39] These Vedic paeans use epithets which are very similar—if not identical, at times—to those describing the god Dionysos in the numerous Greek epigraphic sources. In fact, if we remove the word Soma and, in its stead, insert "Dionysos," I doubt if any, without a careful scrutiny, will think twice about the accuracy, or even the authenticity of some of the verses. "He [Soma] bellows, terrifying bull, sharpening [hari] horns, gazing afar. The Soma rests in his well-appointed birthplace. The hide is of bull, the dress of sheep."[40] The skin, or the hide, of the bull is red (as mentioned in a passage of the *Rigveda* 9.97.13), the dress is like wool puffs of a white sheep. In fact, as the fly-agaric matures, it produces a white, cotton-like ball, which inflates rather quickly, blowing up into white fragments. These adhere to the vivid red skin beneath, looking like marshmallow fluffs. With time, the rains may wash off the last remaining white patch on the red cap, and the mushroom will, then, thrive in its unblemished hue.

By comparison to the *Rigveda*, the *Avesta*—which consists of the sacred writings of the Zoroastrians—makes a comment about Haoma, a psychoactive plant venerated by the believers, and which Wasson established to be the same as Soma.[41] It is not surprising that in both cases the same variety of plants is indicated, since both sacred texts are related. It is exceedingly strange, however—especially in view of the hallucinogenic properties of these substances, known to induce mystical states—that a specialist in Zoroastrian religion could claim so ethnocentrically and unfoundedly that mysticism has had no part in the *Avesta*. "Zoroastrianism, the one major religion that never developed mysticism of any kind. . . ."[42] Can a religion, that had a likely role in affecting other mystical movements, such as Sufism, be non-transcendent; can any religion be so mundanely sterile?

In indication of the Vedic hymns celebrating Soma, the Chinese Emperor Wu composed an ode—a paean—to a mushroom, praising it as "the mysterious breath. . .this miracle." This enigmatic fungus was the *Ling-chih*, an antler-like form of "nine-bifurcate lobes," thriving in the inner quarters of the emperor's newly redone palace, who interpreted its presence as a divine omen of grace, for the mushroom was thought to augur good fortune and longevity. In fact, so taken was the emperor with his beloved mushroom—*"this miracle"*—that his poetic composition was incorporated into a corpus of ritual odes, totaling nineteen altogether, to be vocally performed on important religious and state occasions. As a sign of good luck and felicitation, its design proliferated later among the decorative motifs on Chinese ceramics and textiles.

Ling-chih (*Ganoderma lucidum*) is a large, woody fungus, usually with a dark, twisted stem, ranging from mahogany to ebony in color. Its characteristic peculiarity is exhibited in the structural dimorphism, with the initial form of overlapping caps, shaped like oyster shells, transforming into a second morphological phase ensuing in a bifurcated, antler-like shape. According to a Chinese tradition of the first century B.C., a raven carried this mushroom to resurrect a man who had been dead for three days. This familiar theme of resurrection from the sepulcher, involving the mystical number 3 (after three days), is to be found among many religious sects of that day. As for this sacred mushroom and its connection with the shamans, it is obvious that it played a role in the shamanistic flights of ecstasy.

The New World

The list of hallucinogenic plants in the New World is very extensive, and it is almost impossible to enumerate all the floristic varieties which exist in the northern and southern parts of the Western Hemisphere. It is very unlikely that there has been a true new discovery of unknown species added to the indigenous pharmacopeia since the time of the

Hispanic conquests of the Americas. There are, nevertheless, a number of important plants, which we know were used in ancient times by the aboriginal populations in connection with religious ceremonies involving ecstatic flights, as an inherent part of traditional shamanistic techniques. These drug ceremonials were initially known to us from the "histories," or codices, principally compiled for or by the Spanish friars, who had accompanied the armies in their pillage and conquests. Later on, archaeological and ethnohistorical fieldwork not only corroborated the "histories," but widened our perspectives by adding cultural and temporal depths to the local ethnopharmacological practices.

In the transitional phases occurring between the fifteenth and the sixteenth centuries, the European invaders stumbled upon a large assortment of psychotropic substances in use among the local Indian populations. These included different varieties of sacred mushrooms, peyote, datura, a type of potent tobacco known as *picietl*, and a certain kind of morning glory. The seeds of the latter were considered to contain divine essence by the central Mesoamerican peoples, including the Aztecs. The psychoactive chemical properties of the seeds are closely related to the powerful synthetic, ergot-derivative, LSD-25. Among the invaluable sources containing precious information on the taxonomic and ethnobotanical knowledge, as well as those describing the medicinal properties of many sacred hallucinogens, we must specifically include the fascinating works of Fray Bernardino de Sahagún, known collectively today as the *Florentine Codex*, the equally informative writings of Fray Diego Durán, whose original manuscript in the National Library in Madrid is labeled as the *Codex Durán*, the writings of the physician Francisco Hernández, and the elucidatingly illustrated Aztec herbal from the middle of the sixteenth century, referred to as the *Codex Badianus*.

During the early colonial period in the seventeenth century, Jacinto de la Serna and Ruiz de Alarcón compiled reports on the traditional hallucinogens in use among the natives, which essentially listed the same categories of plants as have been mentioned above. Our store of knowledge was slightly enhanced in 1851, when Richard Spruce, the English ethnobotanist from Yorkshire, collected and assigned scientific nomenclature to the first specimens of *Banisteriopsis caapi*, which he had noted as the plant substance used for the preparation of the hallucinogenic potion among the Indians of tropical South America. However, it was not until the prolific and endeavored researches of Richard E. Schultes of Harvard University, in the field of New World psychotropic biota, that our knowledge of the subject has truly become enriched, opening up our "doors of perception." We owe him a great debt, directly and indirectly, for practically all that we know today about these plants.

Some of the oldest and persisting archaeological evidence that we possess for the earliest hallucinogen in the New World pertains to the so-called "mescal bean," which consists of a red seed resembling a bean, from a leguminous shrub *Sophora secundiflora*, indigenous to northern Mexico and Texas. The chemical composition of the *Sophora* seed is partly made up of cytisine—a quinolizidine alkaloid—which can produce convulsive fits, hallucinations, and, if used imprudently, even fatal respiratory failure.[43] Based on the radiocarbon dates supplied by the archaeometric laboratory of the Smithsonian Institution, it is apparent that the Palaeo-Indian hunters had been familiar with and used the red bean 10,000–11,000 years ago.[44] The *Sophora* seeds were found at several sites in northern Mexico and Texas, together with artifacts and shamanistic rock paintings, and not infrequently with other psychotropic varieties of flora. Excavations at the Bonfire Shelter in Texas yielded radiocarbon dates of 8440–8120 B.C. for the earliest level of human occupation of this site and unearthed the narcotic *Sophora* seeds together with Folsom points and Plainview-type projectiles, as well as the fossil remains of an extinct, large, Pleistocene bison, *Bison antiquus*. Such an occurrence should be of very little surprise to us, since this early stratum corresponds to the Late Pleistocene period of large mammal hunting.

The evidence for the use of *Sophora* spp. at other prehistoric sites has demonstrated its continued prevalence from the earliest archaeological substrata in which this plant was found, that is, about 9000 years ago, until *circa* A.D. 1000. Thus, for example, studies conducted of the Fate Bell Shelter in the Amistad Reservoir area of Trans-Pecos Texas, revealed the seeds of the hallucinogens *S. secundiflora* and *Ungnadia speciosa* in every stratigraphic level spanning the range from 7000 B.C. to A.D. 1000. The absence of the psychotropic species in the subsequent archaeological strata coincides with the drastic cultural and economic changes imparted by the transition from the ancient Desert Culture to a culture based on the cultivation of maize. We have, therefore, unequivocal indications that the red seed of the *Sophora* plant was utilized for the uninterrupted, and well-documented, time period of about 10,000 years—that is, until the nineteenth century, which marked a major demise in the aboriginal Indian culture centered around ecstatic-visionary experiences. Hence, it becomes quite clear that an ecstatic cult of a shamanistic type, focused on healing, proliferated around the hallucinogenic red bean, and which, in the southern Plains area by the end of the last century, was replaced entirely by the less harmful peyote cactus, *Lophophora williamsii*.

According to the archaeological evidence being presently unearthed in Mesoamerica, peyote is represented in tombs dating back over 2000 years. The archaeological culture known as Colima, in western Mexico, has been established by calibrated radiocarbon chronology to have flourished between 200 B.C. and A.D. 500. A figural vessel from Colima of a male holding a peyote cactus in each hand, easily identifiable as the psychotropic *L. williamsii*, attests to the use of this plant; as does the lovely Colima redware pot, ornamented with four naturalistic peyote motifs in raised relief. During that period, the peyote had been used in rituals by being, plausibly, ingested in a liquid form, a practice which can be witnessed today among the Huichol of the Sierra Madre Occidental, in the same part of Mexico.[45] The preponderance of the peyote motif in Colima art is a very significant index to the ritual behavior of the ancient inhabitants of that region. There remains little doubt, as Peter Furst has pointed out in his interesting book,[46] that future work will pronounce the ritual significance of this psychotropic cactus to be of much greater antiquity than mere two millennia.

It is clearly evident that the western part of Mexico abounds in psychotropic flora. One extremely important genus is represented by *Datura* spp., which plays a crucial role in the religious life not only among the Indians of western Mexico, but in the American Southwest, as well. Small, pre-Columbian Colima sculptures, depicting ceremonial scenes of men and mushrooms, point inadvertently to an ancient hallucinogenic ritual cult in West Mexico, comparable to the one we find in Oaxaca today. However, it is very likely that the Colima spheroid vessels in the shape of spiny seedpots represent the particularly dangerous hallucinogen, *Datura meteloides*, just like their analogues that depict peyote and the sacred mushroom. In fact, a more recent Pueblo Indian jar from the Southwest is shown with spiny "growth," and resembles these Colima pots. The differences in form are probably functional and can be attributed to the different purposes for which the vessels were intended.[47] The Aztecs knew *Datura stramonium* as *tlapatl*, to which they also gave the names of *toloache* or *toloaxihuitl*. When *tlapatl* was mixed with *mixitl* (unidentified), or the two names uttered together, the resulting effect was linked with "insanity."[48]

The Huichol, on the other hand, personify this hallucinogen as Kieri Tewíyari, meaning Kieri Person, who as a black sorceror may effect irrevocable damage in terms of mental disorder or death. Thus, people under the spell of Kieri may, for example, believe in their abilities to fly like the birds and consequently plunge from a precipice to an abysmal death. The shamans invoke Kieri tales during the peyote ceremonies, however, admonishing all present not to partake of the Kieri plant without the proper guidance from a shaman, who is the only one qualified to penetrate its secrets. It appears that, in time, the much older ritual use of *Datura*, in western Mexico, was replaced by the peyote cult, which became the dominant aspect in the native religious life;[49] just as this cactus replaced the red bean cult of the leguminous *Sophora* plant in the southern Plains area. In the world of western science, the plant form of Kieri was, for some time, known as *D. inoxia* (later as *D. meteloides*), and in common usage referred to as Jimson weed, a corruption of the eponym for Jamestown weed, or as Thorn-Apple, which also included the species of *D. stramonium*, and which the nineteenth-century Shakers bottled as a medicinal preparation under the name of "Extract of Thorn-Apple." As Thorn-Apple, *D. meteloides* is held sacred among the Zuñi Indians, especially by the members of the Zuñi Rain Priest lodge, who continue to induce spiritual visions by knowledgeable use and administration of this plant.

The perceptive and stimulating paper, delivered by Furst to the symposium on Middle American sculpture at the Metropolitan Museum of Art in 1970, made for a welcome breakthrough by another pioneering spirit who has worked to open up the field of ancient New World iconography to new and different interpretations. ". . . No primitive artist ever drew a meaningless symbol," argued Furst, bearing in mind Carl Lumholtz's foreboding remark. With a profound insight for the times, Lumholtz observed that "It should always be remembered that in interpreting primitive symbols and designs it is never the first and most obvious explanation which is true."[50]

Spherical objects are "balls," hence a figurine holding a "ball" must be a ballplayer—even if it happens to portray a seated, bare-breasted female. Because of some fancied resemblance to European court jesters, effigies of a certain Colima type are arbitrarily labeled "clowns." Joined pairs are "wedding couples," hunchbacks with enormously enlarged phalluses are "erotic." Distortions of the human form are portrayals of pathology. Any figurine holding a staff or club or some other weaponry is a "warrior." And so on, ad infinitum.

It could be said that such interpretations are at least comforting. [But] they neither tax our powers of analysis and imagination, nor do they require familiarity with the wide range of cultural facts, which, when used with care, might offer alternative interpretations of a more complex nature. . . .

This is not to say that no ballplayers, warriors, dancers, married couples, or other so-called secular subjects were portrayed. On the contrary, many sculptures at least seem to depict everyday life rather than recognizable ritual or religious activities or supernatural beings. . . .

[However], . . . a great many Colima figurines, as we know, have horns growing from their foreheads. By what criteria is this

Figure 6.5. Diagrams of the Maya and Navajo cosmos. In both cases, very pronounced shamanistic motifs are depicted. The Maya cosmos is shown resting on a multi-leveled pyramid, which is placed atop a cosmic monster amidst a primordial sea. Each quadrant is associated with a specific color. The center represents a fifth direction. Four supernatural beings uphold the celestial dome, represented by a two-headed dragon. Other astral entities consist of a sky band with celestial symbols, the moon goddess, the sun god, the planet Venus in a skeletonized form, and the Pleiades stars as the tail of a rattlesnake.

The Navajo cosmos is depicted as a sacred sand painting that is central to the family hogan. The point of emergence of ancestors marks the place where the first hogan was built. The ancestors journeyed through three past worlds prior to their arrival on this one through a hollow reed. The rainbow god watches over the sky, which is luminous with constellations and the Milky Way, here represented by a series of crosses. The blue sun and the white moon are carried by young warriors. Each earth quadrant is attributed with a specific color, a sacred mountain, time of day, and a sage. Big Wind and Big Thunder rule over land that lies beyond the sky. (Copyright National Geographic Society, Washington, D.C., used with permission).

an "everyday activity"? Or the wearing of human masks by dogs? Are hallucinogenic plants, known historically and ethnographically as sacred or even divine all over Mesoamerica, "secular" subjects?[51]

The highland Mayas regarded certain hallucinogenic mushrooms as sacred, and such mycoflora played an extremely important role in the

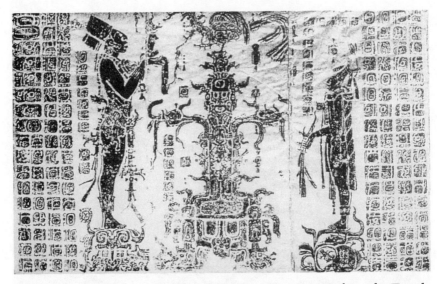

Figure 6.6. A Maya shamanistic World-Tree as a cosmic axis from the Temple of the Foliated Cross at Palenque, Mexico. The tree (the sacred giant ceiba?) stands in the center of the earth. Its roots reach the Underworld, and its branches and the trunk touch the various levels of the Upperworld. A rubbing after the original bas-relief.

indigenious religious system. In fact, the association of mushrooms with their gods and the Underworld induced the Mayas to produce diverse and numerous effigies of this plant. This ceremonial practice endured for about 2000 years, until the end of the Classic Maya period, around A.D. 900. The discovery of nine tiny stone mushroom figurines, along with nine equally small metates (to grind the mushrooms?), in a Kaminaljúyu grave site about 2200 years old in the vicinity of Guatemala City, suggested a correlation with the nine Lords of Xibalbá, or the nine rulers of the Maya Underworld,[52] for whose use the nine mushrooms, and the complementary stones for grinding them, might have been offered. The majority of similar mushroom stones has been found in Guatemala, but others have also come up from all over Mexico and Central America. However, already in 1957, Wasson and collaborators proposed a connection between the ancient stone mushroom sculptures and the ritual use of sacred hallucinogenic mushrooms.[53] In a late seventeenth-century manuscript, dating from around 1690, entitled *Vocabulario de la lengua Cakchiquel*, now in the library collection of the American Philosophical Society in Philadelphia, its author, Fray Tomás Coto, mentions a Cakchiquel-Maya name for a hallucinogenic mushroom, *xibalbaj okox* (*xibalbá* = the "Underworld"; *okox* = "mushroom"). Coto asserts that this mushroom was also known as *k'aizalah okox*, meaning a mushroom which causes one to lose judgment.

In connection with a project involving the establishment of the Central American Institute of Prehistoric and Traditional Cultures at Belize, I have had a recent opportunity to examine Uxbenka, a Maya ceremonial center outside the village of Santa Cruz in the Toledo District. The characteristic features of this site[54] resemble Classic and Late Classic aspects encountered in the relatively nearby Tikal, across the border in Guatemala. At the foot of the natural temple mound, on the northernly slope, where the architectural stones form the exterior base, my wife triumphantly discovered a small, red fly-agaric (*Amanita* spp.) thriving under a tree, amidst the moss-covered soil. She duly collected this specimen, for a later examination in the United States, and placed it for safekeeping inside the only thing which she had on hand—namely, an empty cardboard film box, which had already been slightly crushed. Unfortunately, this decision proved to be an imprudent one, for the crumbled box was mistaken later for empty, and thoughtlessly discarded without having its content checked. Notwithstanding, we can assert reasonably that the tropical jungle environment, in this part of Belize, has not changed very drastically since the construction of this site, and consequently, mushroom species of *Amanita* were indeed accessible to the ancient Mayas.

Many ceramic mushroom figurines were also discovered throughout Mexico and South America. Several terracotta mushroom representations were identified among the contents of a 2000-year-old burial site in western Mexico,[55] and it is obvious that psilocybin mushrooms are depicted in the art of this region.[56] R. Gordon Wasson, the re-discoverer of the paramount role played by the sacred mushrooms in rituals, had in his private collection a pre-Columbian clay figurine labeled a "mushroom priestess," which was modelled in the style known as Classic Veracruz, dating from about A.D. 500.

In the National Museum of Anthropology in Mexico City, there is a large, splendid, stone sculpture of the Aztec deity, Xochipilli, the so-called God of Flowers. R. Gordon Wasson and Richard Schultes were able to identify on the left leg of this fifteenth-century stone effigy three hallucinogenic plants, the first two of extremely important nature: a stylized representation of the sacred mushroom, *Psilocybe aztecorum*; an almost naturalistic rendition of the divine morning glory flowers, *Rivea corymbosa*; and the flowers of a sacred auditory hallucinogen, known as *sinucuichi*, *Heimia salicifolia*. In addition, they noticed the flowers of a ceremonial tobacco plant, *Nicotiana tabacum*. For reasons elucidated quite adequately in his article, Wasson submits a well-conceived and valid argument, in my opinion, that the Aztec cognate for "flower," *xochitl,* was employed in the ancient Valley of Mexico as a metaphor for divine hallucinogens.[57] The Aztec word for a hallucinogenic experience (*temixoch*) translates as a "flowery dream." The name for their sacred psilocybin mushroom, *teonanacatl* means "flesh of the gods" or "divine food"; but another name for a sacred mushroom was *xochinanacatl,* which can be translated as either "flowery food" or "flowery flesh." However, Doris Heyden of the National Institute of Anthropology and History in Mexico City, and an authority on the religious symbolism of plants in pre-Columbian Mexico, believes that *xochinanacatl* means "flowery mushroom," in reference to *Amanita muscaria.*[58] In either case, the generic word for "flower" is involved in hallucinogens.

Therefore, Wasson makes a strong case for the god Xochipilli not merely being a deity of spring, flowers, and rapture (the Aztec equivalent of the Greek Dionysos), but a god of the divine hallucinogens and the "flowery dreams." This assertion is lent further credibility by the fact that the Nahua-speaking Huichol Indians of western Mexico, as Peter Furst informs us, allude to the sacred peyote cactus by its delicate metaphor: "the flower."[59] The Nahua language is closely related to Nahuatl, spoken by the Aztecs.

Relevant graphic documentations, which bear importantly upon our present concern, can be found illustrated in the various codices. One particularly interesting scene, which has not been described in the context of our discussion, is contained in the *Codex Borbonicus.* Around the months of July and August, which fell in the middle of their year, the Aztecs celebrated *Tlaxochimaco,* a ceremony of the Offering of Flowers. The *Codex Borbonicus* records this event, with the depiction of three deities, who perhaps, originally, had been representations of the three aspects of the same divinity. Each one faces an arc, or a semicircle, comprised of a single row of alternating mushrooms, near-naturalistic representations of *A. muscaria,* and stylized flowers, which appear to be the sacred hallucinogen of the Aztecs, either the powerful *ololiuhqui* (*R. corymbosa*) or the auditory psychotrope *sinucuichi* (*H. salicifolia*); or perhaps an artistic syncretism of both.

Shamanism, as a phenomenology, must be credited with sinking the principal roots of the sacred mushroom complex in the New World. The formative clues to this phenomenon will be found in the corresponding Epi-Palaeolithic horizons rather than in the maritime diffusion of isolated culture traits from the Old World. This, in no way, is intended to cast doubt on the valuable contributions generated by comparative research in enthnohistory and ethnology. The tradition of the sacred mushrooms, developed among the Palaeo-Siberian hunters, had probably

Figure 6.7. An illustration from the Aztec *Codex Borbonicus*, depicting supernatural beings with the hallucinogenic mushrooms, *Amanita muscaria*.

established a transcultural basis for all the hallucinogenic ritual drug complexes in both the Eastern and the Western Hemispheres,[60] before the opening of a gap in the narrow Bering land strip, about 12,000 years ago, which had connected two large land masses across the north Pacific Ocean. This land bridge had served as a corridor for the transmission of the antecedents of the Proto-Uralic population into Alaska, together with their symbolic and material baggage. With time, however, this fortuitous passage became submerged beneath 200 to 300 feet of rising thalassic waters.

The Mochica of ancient Peru employed two representational modes in their ceramic wares intended to depict various personages. The first was to make the vessel into an actual portrait of the individual, effecting a realistic style which adhered to certain social conventions of perspective and fashion. The second mode consisted of painted figures rendered in a stylized manner, by a schematic technique using most identifiable elements—an artistic convention not unlike that to be found in the art of ancient Egypt. However, it is the second version that offers most interesting insights into Mochica religious symbolism. For instance, a stirrup-spouted vessel from the developed Period V (A.D. 550–700) shows a warrior-bird (hawk) gathering the psychotropic fruit of the *ullucho* tree, a native plant to the highland regions. In contrast, an earlier modeled version of a hawk-warrior with two mushroom-like elements on his headdress, from Period IV (A.D. 200–550),[61] forcefully conveys realism of form.

It is very frustrating, to say the very least, to notice how our ethnocentric perspectives influence the way in which we conceive and interpret symbols encountered in different cultures. In the American Museum of Natural History, there is a fine Mochica ceramic pot with fineline drawings depicting a rather peculiar scene. Its motifs, strangely enough, have been thought by some to form a sociopolitical message involving such themes as the loss of individual dignity.[62] Yet, in the excellent rolled-out reproduction of the scene, the outweighing elements more suitably pertain either to a mythological subject or the depiction of the Otherworld. It shows horrifying monsters, partaking of some mysterious substance, followed by depictions of fits, seizures, hallucinations, and terror. Then, we see an individual being carried in a litter, accompanied by some animal-spirits towards what appears to be a heavenly abode, where a seated personage is raising a goblet. In the distance, there is another structure, with its roof gables adorned with, what I believe to be, stylized mushrooms, although conventionally interpretted as war clubs. Within its walls there is a person drinking a concoction from his goblet. The overall impression of the scene leaves little doubt that we are dealing with themes relating to psychotropically-induced visions, with all the imparted terror, frenzy, and rapture.

By no means am I implying that ancient art does not treat socio-political issues, or that loss of dignity was not a worrisome concern for the Mochica of Peru. The ornaments on the gabled roofs may, justifiably, evoke the appearance of ancient Peruvian war clubs, inasmuch as they may also, if not even more, depict a mycoflora. After all, is it not more probable that they are representations of a degenerated form of what once used to depict the sacred mushroom, especially in the houses that were vested with ritual function, rather than with a purely social or political purpose? The sacerdotal character of the houses is often indicated by situating them on platforms in the shape of a stepped-pyramid,[63] symbolic of the transcended axis mundi. Perhaps the designs of the ceremonial "war" clubs, like those of certain kinds of ear ornaments, were inspired by the sacred mushroom or even by the San Pedro cactus, the Peruvian equivalent of the Mexican peyote.

Thus, in the Linden-Museum of Stuttgart, we encounter again another uncommon specimens of a decorated pot, modeled to show two adjoining houses of different heights, standing on a stepped platform. Three large ornaments protrude from the ridge of the roof belonging to the smaller house. Even though these fixtures have been described as "war clubs,"[64] I believe that we have here, instead, iconographically stylized representations of sacred mushrooms *Psilocybe* spp. or *Panaeolus* spp. It is only reasonable to assume, considering the undoubtedly religious character of this building, that it depicts the "house" of a priest or a shaman, where one could experience visions.

Judging from the abundant evidence in pottery, "two stimulants were used by the Mochica"—coca leaves, from which commercial cocaine is produced nowadays, and *chicha*, a fermented drink made from maize (corn). However, neither one is a hallucinogen, even though both have long associations with religious rites and sacrifices. Coca has mythopoeic origins in a legend coming from the Cordillera of the Andes. The chewing—or more properly, sucking—of its leaves[65] could have started in the region of Machu Yunga, in the highlands of what used to be Peru, but is now Bolivia. The Chibchas spread this custom to the Arawaks, diffusing it among the Aymaras and the Quechua. An Inca by the name of Mayta-Capac (A.D. 1230) and his successor Rocca (d. A.D. 1315) were heavily involved in the widespread dissemination of the coca sucking habit. We know for a fact that, by the end of the fifteenth century, this practice was deeply rooted among the Incas.

It is important to consider the iconographic attitudes of certain human figures shown with shut eyes, as in the fine example from Stuttgart's Linden-Museum. As Elizabeth Benson pointed out, such artistic schema might have intended to depict individuals in a state of trance.[66] She goes on to ask a fundamentally crucial question regarding the elaborately decorated Mochica vessels, with scenes of mythico-religious and cosmologico-ritual themes:

> All of these fantastic pots raise questions of meaning or, at least, of the reasons for their production. One possible answer is that they represent a psychedelic experience on the part of the priest or shaman. One pot with animated objects shows a human figure in a little house who might well be a shaman "experiencing" such a vision. Present-day Indian shamans in the Amazon area use *Piptadenia* snuff and drinks made from *Banisteriopsis, Datura,* and other plants to achieve hallucinogenic religious experiences. A snuffing-tube was found in the Chicama Valley at the pre-ceramic site of Huaca Prieta. In one scene, the Mochica radiant god has an object that looks like a snuffing-tube, although it seems to be held more to the mouth than to the nose.... A hallucinogenic cactus does grow, however, on the north coast.[67]

The Mexican sacred cactus of the Sierra Madre Occidental may have its archaeobotanical continuum in the hallucinogenic San Pedro cactus, used by the north Peruvian shamans and folk healers of present-day to achieve ecstatic flights. Its Spanish name is enigmatic and hard to explain. Perhaps, like the keys of St. Peter, the cactus opens the heavenly gates for those who place their faith in its spiritual nature? And not only the cactus!

There is ample evidence, albeit inadequately described, in Mochica art for hallucinogenic mushrooms and other psychotropic flora. Hallucinogenic snuff had been used in the Americas by at least the second millennium B.C.[68] Paraphernalia attesting to this practice are of particular importance, since they give witness to shamanism in the American tropics through the various motifs incorporated into the iconography; to wit, the jaguar, the harpy eagle, the condor, etc., which are the shamans' avatars. By now, it is totally apparent that such transculturally recurrent themes as the jaguar-shaman transformations are linked to trances induced by active hallucinogenic snuffs made from the shrub *Anadenanthera,* member of the pea-family, or from the Virola tree, of the nutmeg-family; or by drinking very potent hallucinogenic concoctions prepared from the psychoactive stalks of the lianas, *Banisteriopsis caapi, B. rusbyana,* or *B. inebriens.* This genus of the liana is a tree-climbing, leafy, forest vine, which—a very important thing to keep in mind—is considered the shaman's ladder to the Otherworld.

Peter Furst identified the psychotropic *Anadenanthera colubrina* as the tree with which the deer is frequently connected in the art of Mochica pottery, and which is not uncommonly shown as part of religious scenes on stirrup-spouted vessels. The seeds of *A. colubrina* and *A. peregrina* are used, throughout the wide Adean region, to make a highly valued, psychotomimetic snuff known as *huilca*, or *Wilka*; sometimes the seeds are mixed with *chicha*, the regional alcoholic inebriant.[69] The powerful alkaloid bufotenine (5-hydroxy-N,N-dimethyl-tryptamine) occurs in considerable quantities in both species of the leguminous tree *Anadenanthera*, and it is also the main active ingredient in a variety of toxic and psychotropic toads of the *Bufo* spp. Another popular snuff comes from the Virola tree, which, like *Anadenanthera*, contains tryptamines as the principal hallucinogenic alkaloids.

The snuff notwithstanding, many varieties of ceramic vessels show human figures adorned with sacred mushrooms of not only different species, but even different genera. One such vessel, also in the Linden-Museum, consists of a kneeling warrior, with a devotional expression adorning his face, while his headdress is surmounted by two mushrooms separated by an object resembling a Minoan *labrys*, or rather one half of the double-axe. This crescent-like form might have been intended to represent colorful plumage, of the kind that we know not only from the New World, but from the Greek and Roman helmets, too. An even more outstanding example of Mochica iconography is provided by a painted stirrup-spouted pot, in the collection of the Peabody Museum of Harvard University,[70] in the shape of a man's head with "log" earrings. His headdress, exhibiting delicate curvilinear waves transforming into bird-head motifs, is surmounted on the top of the forehead by a prominent naturalistic mushroom, which beyond doubt is in the likeness of the hallucinogenic *Amanita muscaria*.

An interesting ceramic vessel at the Art Institute of Chicago was described by Benson as a deity "apparently wounded in one of the combats with a sea monster," supported by "two anthropomorphic cormorants, one on each side...."[71] On closer scrutiny, however, we can see that there is nothing to intimate that the personage is connected with the sun, as Benson suggested in another passage; just the contrary. The fancy hat, in a semi-circular form, is decorated with dots and an arc-line. The large earrings that he is wearing are clearly the fly-agaric mushroom, *A. muscaria*, while the rest of his body and the belt—also dotted—reinforce the mushroom analogue. His closed eyes and facial expression suggest a state of trance. Could he *be* the divine mushroom-incarnate, brought up to earth from the dark abyss of the Underworld by the deep-diving cormorant birds? There exist numerous parallel myths, in the Old World, to tell us so.

Figure 6.8. A Mochica stirrup spout vessel in the form of a human head with the hallucinogenic mushroom *Amanita muscaria*. Peru, probably circa A.D. 500. (The Peabody Museum, Harvard University).

Two other figural pots in the Linden-Museum also involve scenes with the prominence of mushrooms.[72] One depicts a wrinkled-faced man, elaborately attired, who could be a shamanic figure playing the flute. His peculiar headdress includes a large mushroom, while for earrings he has two large discs resembling stylized *Amanita* spp. One cannot be absolutely certain about the mycological iconography of the earrings, but there remains little doubt as to the mushroom on top of his headgear. He makes one think of the one-eyed flute player in Poland who saved the barns from the rats. The second pot is of a person kneeling on one leg, with two large protruding mushroom-like forms "growing" from his forehead. His semi-circular headdress is of the type described above as crescent-shaped, which could have intended to signify plumage. The decorations on the "mushroom" caps seem to be inlaid, resembling Maltese-cross, which might be—one is tempted to speculate—a stylized manner to represent *Amanita* spp. The shape of these two objects can hardly invoke anything other than mushrooms, and possibly, as actual ornaments in real life, these were enhanced with precious multi-colored bird feathers. Of course, there always exists the potential danger of seeing everywhere the things close to our heart's desire. Admittedly, as mentioned earlier, there is some peril of this situation existing in the cases of the flat disc-earrings and the Maltese-cross design; otherwise, the evidence speaks for itself. Still, many have declared the roof gables to be war clubs; yet, both the context of these ornaments and their forms beg a different interpretation.

For a long time now, different types of pre-Columbian gold pectorals have been known to the contemporary world. A particular category of pectorals—deriving from an area roughly demarcated by the Darién Province of Panama in the north, and by the Quimbaya region of Colombia to the south—remained in a classificatory limbo. Although the dates for their manufacture can be placed, at the very earliest, around A.D. 500 until about 1500, their iconographic significance presented a unique puzzle. These ornaments could be described as stylized or schematic, anthropomorphic in shape, with a pair of domes superimposed on top, and, when viewed from the rear, are suggestive of the ancient "mushroom-men" in the rock art of central Sahara. In addition, two spiral-like "wings" are always manifest, as well as a toad sitting on the "chest." What the dome-shaped decorations were meant to depict may be best educed from the opinions of various well-informed sources. José Pérez de Barradas, in 1954, was apparently first to advance this perceptive and significant hypothesis:

.... The semi-spherical buttons. . . that remind one of the bells of old fashioned telephones or of a pair of mushrooms. . . . It would not be strange to reconsider with great reserve this casual attribution. It should be noted that these semi-spherical buttons are not fixed directly to the head but are attached by means of filaments soldered to the back of the piece. . . . .We know nothing about the ritual use of mushrooms amongst the Indians of Darién at the time of the discovery [of the gold pectorals]. . . . The secrecy with which these Indians guard their knowledge of the properties of plants and their shamanistic ceremonies could have hidden a possible use of hallucinogenic mushrooms— a use which might be very ancient and which possibly existed in distinct forms. The bridge between Guatemala and Darién is difficult to establish but easy to suspect. Our suggestion that these buttons represent mushrooms is accepted by Emmerich.[73]

André Emmerich, known in the field of pre-Columbian art, came forth subsequently with a statement of his own, having had benefited from the "original insight" of Mrs. Mary U. Light. Thus, in 1965, he wrote:

It appears likely that the puzzling, hitherto unidentified hemi-spherical headdress ornaments in fact represent a pair of mushrooms, probably of hallucinogenic properties. It is significant that such mushrooms are to this day traditionally counted, ceremonially used and consumed in pairs. . . .[74]

Although the important observation about paired mushrooms was derived from the comments appearing in *Mushrooms, Russia and History* by R. Gordon Wasson and his wife Valentina, who had collaborated together on this ground-breaking book,[75] it succeeded in drawing the attention of several better qualified specialists. In a long and important book article, Peter Furst, known for his contributions to the cultural role of hallucinogens, addressed himself to the above idea:

André Emmerich developed the interesting theory that the pairs of telephone bell-like, semi-spherical, hollow-stemmed ornaments surmounting the headdress of a certain class of conventionalized anthropomorphic gold pectorals in the Darién style from Colombia ("telephone gods") are in fact mushrooms. Emmerich demonstrated convincingly that, over time, these ornaments gradually changed position as the effigies themselves became more and more stylized. On the early, more realistic pieces, the mushroom form is unmistakable, the semi-spherical caps being separated from the headdress by stems or stipes attached to the top of the head. Subsequently, the stipes became shorter and the caps were slightly inclined forward. Eventually, the stipes, though still present beneath the cap, disappeared altogether from view and the two caps faced forward like a pair of female breasts. By this time the human characters had also been stylized to the point of abstraction.[76]

In spite of the previous testimonies, it is most rewarding to have the observations of one of the most prominent and leading figures in the field of hallucinogenic flora. Professor Richard Schultes published, in several places, the results of his findings and those of his collaborators. The following quotations aptly summarize his views on this subject matter:

Our own studies of the many gold pectorals in the Museo del Oro [in Bogotá, Colombia] and our familiarity with the complexities of magico-religious, shamanic or ceremonial use of hallucinogenic plants, together with consideration of the natural range of psilocybine-containing genera of mushrooms in the New World, lead us to the belief that this identification of the dome-shaped headdress ornaments is indeed correct and that, further, they strongly suggest the religious use in prehispanic Colombia of intoxicating mushrooms. This interpretation of the gold pectorals has already twice been supported.

[And further:] Our studies of the Darién and Darién-related gold pectorals of Colombia have strengthened our belief that mushrooms perhaps enjoyed a widespread magico-religious place in aboriginal cultures from Mexico, through Central America and in the Andes south to Peru.[77]

In order to avoid the pitfalls of omission, the following must be noted. The highly important role of tobacco, *Nicotiana* spp., in the ritual life of New World aborigines, in prehispanic and later times, was discussed briefly in the previous chapters. Once again, a detailed treatment of this subject, in the framework of indigenous cultural contexts, is to be found in Wilbert's excellent study, *Tobacco and Shamanism in South America* (1987). An ambitious effort to dwell on the functions of tobacco among the ancient Maya is provided by Robicsek's *The Smoking Gods: Tobacco in Maya Art, History, and Religion* (1978).

The Quest for Magical Plants and the Origins of Cultivation

"And the Lord God planted a garden eastward in Eden," the Scriptures inform. "He causeth herbs to grow for the service of man."[78] The garden's splendor can be perceived with the inner eye of the visionary looking within "the Other World of the mind's antipodes," Aldous Huxley tells us, whose first-hand knowledge of mescaline was quite considerable. Hence, the offering of flowers and fruits as sacrificial gifts held the essential significance of returning what was initially the creation of the gods, and thus belonging to the preternatural world. The bearer of the offerings considered it essential to help maintain a balanced state of affairs between heaven and earth.[79] We can view from an enhanced perspective the significance of the actions on the part of the early hunters and gatherers, when, aiming to appease the Mother-Earth, they returned to her parts of the beneficial plants.

An explanation for agricultural beginnings can no longer be sought in a single cause. The underlying sources are manifold, and one of them discloses to the world a deeply hidden psychological fact, to be understood, however, by the initiated alone: "God first planted a garden." This indicates to us that, at least psychologically, the origins of agriculture might have been religious. In those aboriginal cultures that lack ". . . knowledge of precious stones or of glass, heaven is adorned not with minerals, but flowers. Preternaturally brilliant flowers bloom in most of the Other Worlds described by primitive eschatologists. . . ."[80] The wonderful visions of flowers, gardens, and stars that the Matlatzinca Indians of Mexico experience with the sacred *Psilocybe* mushroom have undoubtedly contributed to the formations of their ideas of the Upperworld; inasmuch as the frightening scenes of serpents, dismemberment, skeletons, and blood helped form the conception of the Lowerworld, or Hell.

The signs of recognition and interest in nature's own vibrant fecundity stem from the vague similitudes of experience encountered through the inner visions. To what extent, we may want to ask, had the recurrent visions of trees and flowers acted as an impetus for the pre-agricultural man to manipulate experimentally the botanic environment? With the gradual loss of body hair covering, the Cro Magnon individuals had entered more directly, if not also more intensely, into contact with the botanic world; the bare bodies experiencing the effects of both pleasant and adverse reactions caused by skin interface with the flora. Truly, our ancestors stood naked amidst their environment—experiencing. Their initial interactions with the "magical" plants assumed the role of an active agency in the process of natural selection of these species.

Natural food resources comprise merely abstract constructs, which are best recognized as "cultural appraisals." What counts is not what can be *potentially* exploited, but the recognition of such a potential, coupled with the appropriate technology for such exploitation. In the wild state, wheat and barley are just grasses, useful neither to the dietary demands of humans nor to the everyday economy. It appears unlikely that the pre-Neolithic hunters and gatherers could anticipate the benefits locked in the genetic potential of these floristic taxa—benefits which could only, at first, be released through non-directed manipulation ongoing for several generations, and most likely not to be witnessed by the initial contributors to the impetus of domestication. Otherwise, it must be inferred that, despite the lack of any foreknowledge regarding the impact of human agency on certain varieties of plants, such biological transformations, that enter into the domestication phenomenon could be prognosticated on an *a priori* basis.[81] But where is the archaeological evidence to this effect?

Consequently, it may prove more rewarding to entertain the possibility that it was not a variety of grain or some other economically valuable plant species, but rather a plant with pharmacological properties, that had been among the first floristic species subjected to an effective manipulative agency of humans. Recent studies with the chimpanzees, conducted by Richard Wrangham of Harvard University in Tanzania's Gombe Stream National Park, seem to point out that the antecedents of ethnopharmacological phenomenology may date back to the hominid (prehuman) stages of our ancestors' history. For instance, the ailing chimpanzees' determined search for the young leaves of the aspilia plant, which is otherwise ignored by healthy apes, has been linked to the natural presence of an important chemical compound, thiarubrine-A, which contains powerful antibiotic and antiparasitic properties. The medicinal explanation for the consumption of aspilia by the chimpanzees found strong and independent confirmation when it was learned that a local group, the Tongwe, also uses different species of aspilia as native medication in their treatment of certain illnesses. Further observation revealed that the chimpanzees' "know-how" is not limited to the aspilia only, but they recognize quite readily the values of other medicinal plants, which they ingest in variance with their condition.

Accordingly, it seems only reasonable to conjecture that man's acquired experience with drug plants was later transferred to subsistence crops. Henceforth, the domestication of cereal was, most likely, an ancillary outcome—a by-product—of horticulture of the ergot-infested grass, which had been gathered and tended to on account of the sclerotium of its fungal parasite, *Claviceps purpurea* and *C. paspali*. Both species of this genus contain very small quantities of the active hallucinogenic alkaloids, ergonovine and ergine, and, hence, are much desired for their psychotropic properties, which proved to be of great value as entheogenic agents in the mystery religions in various parts of the world. Thus, the psychoactive effects of the water-soluble alkaloids in the ergot of *Claviceps* spp. were recognized and exploited for many centuries before the present era, as, for example, the principal ingredient in the secret formula for the vision-inducing, divine potion (*kykeon*) at Eleusis; so was their therapeutic value in obstetrics, in the treatment of female disorders, as a uterotonic remedy in childbirth (post-partum hemorrhage) and other conditions of abnormal bleeding.[82] Since rye and barley stalks appear to be more susceptible to ergot infection than wheat, one is prone to speculate about the former two as being the first of the three to undergo cultivation.

The drug plants with their powers to transport, heal, or kill became the subject of observation by the early medicine men, or shamans, and later by the priests. The shamans employed to treat the sick were often the same individuals involved in ceremonies aimed at promoting agricultural fecundity. Such experiential knowledge was transmitted with guarded jealousy within the specialists' circles. Inevitably, it was the shaman-priest who imparted some portion of his horticultural knowledge to the Neolithic cultivators, enhancing at the same time the complexity of ritual life. Here seems to lie a partial explanation for the rise of early theocratic communities, in which the success of agricultural yield was believed to have been under the influence of the shaman-priest. Indeed, the ancient shamans, or ritual specialists, were eventually transformed into the divine kings of Egypt, the rain kings of the Sudan, and the semi-divine weather controllers of South America.

7

The Power of Metaphors: Phenomenology of Symbolic Forms

Language, Perception, and Reality

> What if you slept, and what if in your sleep you dreamed, and what if in your dream you went to heaven and there plucked a strange and beautiful flower, and what if when you awoke you had the flower in your hand? Ah, what then?

THUS MUSED THE VISIONARY English poet, Samuel Taylor Coleridge, about the paradox of reality, inferring, as has been noted elsewhere in this book, that sometimes human experiences do not coincide with the conventional ideas of space, time, and matter. This brings us face to face with three very important questions: (1) By what conceptual device do we seek to understand a shamanistic or any transcendent experience, particularly, when viewed in the bleary and distorting light cast by the mores of our respective cultures? (2) How do we account for the built-in limitations of the physical mechanisms— including those of the intellect—used to differentiate between the various forms of human experience? (3) What constitutes the elements of experience and the nature of the transformative process that integrates an experience into the personality of the individual?

As has been shown only in the latter part of this century, the phenomenon of experience is rendered as a "highly inferential" matter, due to the very nature of the mechanism governing the perceptual functions of the senses. In the early years of his philosophical endeavors, Immanuel Kant espoused the development of natural philosophy based on the empirical processes to receive and give meaning to stimuli and experiences originating in the outside world. He was probably the first influential Western philosopher who sternly subscribed to the notion that human conceptions of the world are conditioned by the modalities of our perceptions. This profoundly critical idea has found its way into modern scientific thought, including theoretical physics, as exemplified by Werner Heisenberg. And since in perceiving the world we depend on our senses; therefore, it is axiomatic that form and substance are interconnected and cannot be isolated into completely separate entities. The sense of sight conditions very many intellectual activities, especially those involving empirical observations, and undeniably was an important biological trait in primate evolution, as can be discerned from the size of the visual cortex in the brain. Naturally, this process depended on human consciousness, which, to Kant, was a mode of analysis applicable to objects and actions. Such conscious activity played a principal role in the creation of knowledge, both in its form and substantive content. This state of things placed man in an awkward position, since he was both the theme of language, and the speaker of language; hence, the object of the symbolism, as well as the originator of symbols. Thus, the paradox of symbolic forms.

Already in classical antiquity, art had been construed to represent a phase in a "waking dream,"[1] and this state of dreaming, "whether the man is asleep or awake," is brought about by confusing the separate realities comprising this World and the Other. Plato's reality has a hierarchical structure,[2] not unlike that encountered in shamanistic cosmologies, with the empirical world only approximating the real.[3] Consequently, all "our thoughts and arguments are imitation of reality,"[4] as is art, for it is fashioned only after a model of reality,[5] and does not constitute a pure, a priori, primary creation in the divine and metaphysical sense. In Plato's doctrine of mimesis, artistic "imitation" constitutes an interpretation, a shadow of reality, by depicting a debased resemblance and a degraded manifestation of the ideal form. Therefore, art represents, with everything else fashioned by humans, the lowest plane of reality, which is removed "two grades" from the ideal, or the "essential nature of things."[6] On the other hand, real art, unlike its removed cousin, imitative art, is a pure, a priori creation, comprising ideal forms, and intent on transcending the material world. The intrinsic limitations of art, however, constrain it to a lower grade of reality than the subject of its theme, since no person's genius can even approach the divine in the primary creation of the ideal forms. The essential nature of art, and the very means in its employ, prevent it from reaching higher levels. Henceforth, the cosmogonic universe is the only true, divine work of art, being itself an ideal form.[7] Thus, real, "autonomous" art is the exclusive prerogative of divine intelligence.

Curiously enough, for all his concern with *images*, Plato seems to disregard entirely the value of symbols and metaphors. What in Platonic syllogism is designated as an imposture, in transcendental thought constitutes a positive quality. Hence, Bronowski's view (not shared by all), in spite of its obvious Neoplatonic, but especially Kantian, influences, emphasizes man's imaginative faculty as being one of the keynote factors on which human consciousness is dependent. If left to rely on the sense of sight, alone, as a doorway to experience of the outer and the inner worlds, a person would never attain a fresh perspective of things, since the scanning mechanism for differentiating the parameters and shapes in nature is already built into the eye. This pre-fabricated component of the organ sets limits on what the eye can or cannot do, and thus establishes the boundaries of our visual experience.[8] The visual image we, thus, receive is not an exact copy or an actual impression of what we are observing, but is comprised of "indirect inferences" created by the eye and the brain, in the same way that a computer processes data for the output of sophisticated imaging—still, not the actual impression of reality. Consequently, different species may perceive objects quite differently, depending on their respective visual mechanisms. To what a degree variances in human individual mechanisms are responsible for different perspectives of the world remains yet to be determined. However, it is beyond any question that such mechanisms play vital roles in structuring what we term as shamanistic realities, both individual and transcultural, across the globe.

Nonetheless, uniformities of forms do *appear* to exist in our empirical universe which transgress the quanta of the human mind— neither originating nor formulating within the creative process, but falling into the domain of Jungian "collective unconsciousness." For instance, Leonardo Fibonacci of Pisa rediscovered, in 1202, a logarithmic series through which he was able to demonstrate the occurrence of many analogous spiral forms in nature, all definable by a mathematical progression: 1, 1, 2, 3, 5, 8, 13, 21, 34, 55, 89, etc. This series underlies, today, the basic concepts in fractal mathematics, which allows the sophisticated computer imaging of our natural world. Examples of Fibonacci shapes can be found in the Whirlpool Galaxy, the spin of a hurricane, in the chambers of a nautilus shell, the double helix of the

DNA molecule, in the helical bacillus of syphilis, which, by the way, was responsible for the deaths of Baudelaire, de Maupassant, Manet, and Gaugin.

Again, according to Kant, reality manifests itself in the "context of experience," since it represents the substance of "empirical intuition" that recurs with certain probability, or is subject to some governing laws. However, Cassirer states, "mythic ideation and primitive verbal conception recognize no such 'context of experience.'" Language and myth are functions of symbolic reasoning and metaphorical thought.[9] The symbolic nature of language is based on *internalization* and *reconstitution*. Human language functions as a creative vehicle for organizing and giving meaningful shape to human experience. As a matter of fact, Bronowski asserts that cognitive knowledge should not be viewed as a cluster of analytic constructs within a specific discipline of study, but instead as an idiom of the human mind, which, through this action, gives meaning unto itself. Science and art, knowledge and imagination, form two facets of the same intellectual experience. They are the two creative activities, which are parts of the same continuum, not subject to an analytical or other empirical separation.[10]

Inasmuch as the essential character of all artistic creations must, by necessity, remain allegorical and metaphorical—art always appears to be striving to become or convey something other that what it actually is—the corollaries between the artistic and the non-artistic phenomena tend to escape an empirical analysis.[11] The only notable difference between an artistic and a scientific metaphor consists in the fact that the latter has a calculable value and is called an algorithm in the scientific parlance. Thus, the murky idea becomes gradually clearer that truth in art and science, alike, cannot be solely defined, or confined, by the internal consistency of substance; its very essence infers a reference to something other than itself. The Cartesian dichotomy of mind and matter, which was regarded as the "official theory" in western philosophy has finally been challenged by some contemporary thinkers.[12]

The unifying principle forming the coherent basis for all that constitutes art is to be found in the use of recognizable symbols. As such, we may hope to arrive, one day, at a general theory that will define and explain the universal structure of art, if such a phenomenon exists, in fact. But it will have to be sought in the philosophical framework and analytic concepts found in theoretical and particle physics—as, for example, in Neils Bohr's Principle of Complementarity, or Correspondence, and in Werner Heisenberg's Principle of Uncertainty. By invoking modern physics, we can say, together with many a shaman, that all of reality is only a continuum of the same spectrum. Put otherwise, reality is always in a state of Being or Existing, as if in a constant flux. There are only different levels of perceptions, which, in the philosophical discourses of the past, were conceived of as the hierarchal structure of reality.

Yet, what were the forms through which perception and conception came to be manifested? How did an early man or woman communicate with his or her own self at a time when mental verbalization was not possible, and before the development of a cognitive language? Was he or she capable of internalizing information before developing the ability to form words in his or her mind? Early humans visualized images— images with which they became familiar in the course of their life experience. This process enabled humans to translate conscious feelings and desires into physical expressions—be it propitiatory ritual, hunting magic, or shamanistic art. All forms of creative (including religious, of course) arts develop mainly to serve as media of symbolic messages that are central to a given society. Art expresses sociocultural meanings and is, thus, conditioned by social and historical events. Artistic achievement, consequently, reflects the cultural idiom, or language. The earliest known art form—art of the Palaeolithic—had been probably developed in relation with the enactment of elementary forms of these early rituals, as well as with the conveyance of the mythic tradition. It is conceivable— and not more than a conjecture, for it still remains very speculative— that conscious representations of some rudimentary artistic forms and motifs, as well as the very beginnings of archaic magic and shamanism, predate the development of the spoken language. In other words, that man's ability and desire to depict his visual imagery were antecedent to the development of human speech.

Visual imagery (the image, pictographic metaphor) might have underscored the earliest mode of thinking, which eventually led to the power of the word (verbal metaphor) to stand for, or be the same as, the entity it represented. To know the true name of the deity meant to unconceal its divine essence. Thus, conceptualization was inseparable from visualization, which maintained an active connection between the "outer" and "inner" mind. The mind perceived concepts as visual images of objects and actions, even those representing more abstract ideas. Visual imagery appears to be a more effective method for exchanging information between the conscious and unconscious dimensions of the mind. It also predates the origins of language. Of course, conceptualization did not form in the same sense of meaning as we understand it today.

Here, again, the mythmaking mind exhibits a sort of consciousness of the relationship between its product and the phenomenon of language, though characteristically it can express this relationship not in abstract logical terms, but only in images. It transforms the spiritual dawn which takes place with the advent of language into an objective fact, and presents it as a cosmogonic process. . . . This emergence from the vague fullness of existence into a world of clear, verbally determinable forms, is represented in the mythic mode, in the imagist fashion peculiar to it, as the opposition between chaos and creation.[13]

Interestingly enough, Cassirer acknowledges the specious nature of an argument endeavoring to resolve the question of primacy between the metaphors of speech and the metaphors of myth. In essence, this is not a situation where the temporal issues of "before" and "after" enter into consideration, but rather "the logical relation between the forms of language and myth. . . ."

Language and myth stand in an original and dissoluble correlation with one another, from which they both emerge but gradually as independent elements. . . . [They stem from] the same impulse of symbolic formulation, springing from the same basic mental activity, a concentration and heightening of simple sensory experience.[14]

It seems, as Cassirer adduced, that the concept of godhead is defined primarily by linguistic categories and finds the formulation of its full qualitative aspect in language. Since one of the main attributes of speech is the tendency to fuse and generalize, inasmuch as to divide and demarcate,

the mythic mind finally reaches a point where it is no longer contented with the variety, abundance and concrete fullness of divine attributes and names, but where it seeks to attain, through the unity of the word, the unity of the God-idea. But even here man's mind does not rest content; beyond this unity, it strives for a concept of Being that is unlimited by any particular manifestation, and therefore not expressible in any word, not called by any name.[15]

Metaphor, Myth, and Transcendence

The transcultural myths of creation allude to the beginning of the world as being in chaos, where names for things did not exist on earth and the name for heaven was unknown. In ancient Egyptian cosmogony, gods had not existed before the time of creation, nor had the knowledge of names for objects. This amorphous condition prevailed until the demiurge bespoke his name and engendered his own creation through the intrinsic potency residing in the name; thus, becoming his own cause, *causa sui.* No other deities had preceded him, for only from this original power of utterance—contained in the demiurge—did gods, men, and all other things spring forth into being and concrete existence.

In the *Kabbalah,* the sound—that is, the quality (substance) and the form (structure)—of each letter of the Hebrew alphabet is thought to constitute the basic component of reality. This is not to be understood, in the sense conceptualized by Platonic doctrines, as merely symbolic of such an image. Hence, by the proper use of words, and the correct annunciation of names of objects and even of the spiritual entities, the initiated Kabbalist can manipulate the occult powers. The right pronunciation of the name of God, YHVH (rather than YAWEH), was always shrouded in the greatest secrecy. The Hebrew religious writings, *Kiddushim* (71a), inform us that in antiquity the learned and the wise teachers enlightened their deserving disciples by instructing them in the pronunciation of the divine name once every seven years.

According to the Tantric tradition, the annunciation of the name of god in Sanskrit, "as the primal language of the universe, will cause him to appear and his force to operate, since the name is the audible form of the god himself."[16] In the same cultural tradition, the phoneme AUM, or OM, as it is sometimes uttered, is the ultimate Word out of which the entire universe had come into being. Thus, conceptualization and utterance "unconceal" into Being. Through the act of naming (utterance), which contains inherent power within itself, man acquires intellectual and physical dominions, as it were, over the world, and subordinates it to his laws. We do not have to go beyond the New Testament to encounter recognizable parallels, wherein John (1:1-3) opens his Gospel with the well-known: "In the beginning was the Word, and the Word was with God, and the Word was God." Certain speech metaphors, such as the ritual cries, "Iacchos," in ancient Greece or the thrice-repeated "Hallelujah" of the Easter Hymn in our own times, are homophonically suited to arouse religious feeling, and their vagueness of meaning and efficacy for repetition add to this intrinsic quality. Unquestionably, the meanings conveyed by such utterances extend beyond the mere cognate sounds of verbal language, and the experience of the divine may be discovered through the forms of language and myth by reflective thought.

In his seminal work on *Divine Names: An Essay on Science of Religious Conception,* published in Germany in 1896 but little known in the English-speaking world, Usener[17] asserts that inquiries into mythology, being a study (*logos*) of the forms of religious concepts, are worth pursuing since only the development of mythic traditions lends itself to reconstructive interpretations, in lieu of determining the perplexing genealogies and supremacies in an endless web of divine beings, looming the labyrinthian pantheons of different religions. In the long process of the development of the human psyche, the mind has endured an arduous passage through the domains of "involuntary and unconscious conception." A wide disparity exists between a specific perception and general concepts—far greater then our language can evoke. Yet, it is language that is responsible for bridging this divide, just like it is language, again, that creates an expression, or an idiom applicable to many more situations than that for which it was originally intended. And there may come a rare moment when such an idiom begins to allude to a wide range of cases, which, in turn, are capable of merging into a new and different conceptual category, or class. However, by and large, the formulation of concepts seems to occur through the visual imagery and metaphors of the familiar. And what concerns are more familiar to men than those that deal with cultural myths?

We all know that mythology is an expression of a religious world-view, but it has also social functions. Through shamanistic imagery and rites, especially, it provides the individual with a sense of *numen* in relation to human existence and the universe, at large. The organized structure of the cosmos offers comprehensible images, which help define a person's place within it, thus, validating the social order and the very essence of society itself. Perhaps, more importantly, myths serve as guidelines for the individual, through the various crises and traumas arising from the need to conform to social mores, to lead a beneficial existence more or less in balance with the perennial cycles of the universe. The religious implications of such concerns with natural equilibria are well illustrated by the shamanistic system of the Desana Indians in the Vaupés territory of Colombian Amazon[18] and, through a diverse comparison, by their distant Palaeo-Asiatic relatives, the Ainus, in the northern islands of Japan.[19] It is important to bear in mind that myths not only create the expectancy of transcendence, but respond to the need for it, as well.

Hence, transcendence is manifest in many diverse symbolic forms, which are only metaphors for human desires and efforts to attain special goals. These symbols are the conveyors of messages from the unconscious to the conscious mind. Once comprehensive channels of communication have been established between the two realms of the mind, we reach what Jung calls "the transcendent function of the psyche," a highly desirable mental condition, allowing a person the fulfillment of all cherished aspirations and the realization of the full potential of his or her Self.

Nothing has a more direct link with the imagery created in our brain than dreams do. In fact, dreams possess the highest affinity for metaphors. Metaphor is the foodstuff and substance of dreams, which are, themselves, pictographic metaphors, only of the unconscious dimension. And since dreams find expressions in the recesses of our primordial thought patterns, they may "haunt" us for days at a time, as a result of the ongoing processes involved in "the transcendent function of the psyche." Human imagination plays a major role in the formations of myths and dreams, and it may be assessed that the psyche of the dreamer finds a metaphorical outlet in the content of the dream, inasmuch as the modal character of a culture "experiences" its metaphorical worldview through the myths.

The mythic imagery is derived from many sources, including the biophysical environment and common visionary experiences. Yet, the essential qualities of myths are contained in the metaphors, and one of mythology's primary tasks, as Campbell observed perceptively[20], may consist of attuning both the intellect and emotion to the phenomenon of transcendence; the second purpose may be to present the total cosmic schema as a numinous spectacle, inspiring bewilderment and awe. Since mythology is organized by metaphors, as well, and not by hard facts descriptive of place and time, such a cosmic paradigm does not reflect an actual place in a physical dimension, but projects a state of mind, a level of existence attainable by an individual.

The very ancient motifs in the language of the symbols of transcendence contain the recurrent theme of the shaman, who can be seen as an archaic guide to transcendence via the numerous ritual techniques of transformation.[21] Therefore, not uncommonly, transcendence is symbolized by a shaman. A Palaeolithic cave painting at Lascaux, France, depicts a reclining, ithyphallic, bird-masked[22] shaman, whose erect penis is interpreted, in scholarly literature, as a sign of entrancement.[23] Next to the masked shamanic figure, we see a staff surmounted by a bird, while an auroch, or a similar large mammal, is leaning over him. Some view the pictured animal as representing a sacrificial offering in a hunting ritual. The Siberian shamans are known to wear quite realistic bird costumes for the performance of their rites. Some of them even claim patrilineal descent from birds. Avian figures perched on the posts belonging to shamans' coffins are also known to occur in Siberia. These are quite reminiscent of the shaman's staff from the cave at Lascaux. Hence, the shaman's close association with a bird, implicit of ecstatic flights in which he moves about the universe in an avian-like fashion, transforms the bird-motif into a symbol of transcendence.

Metaphors, like myths, may be created and manipulated, through the process of ideation, to accommodate the ecclesiastical needs of every religious tradition. For example, in A.D. 431, the church council at Ephesus declared the secular Mary to have been a "God-bearer," or "Mother of God" *(Theotókos)*, drawing to a close the protracted question, scourging the mystical substance of early Christianity, as to whether Mary had, in fact, conceived through divine essence (breath), or had merely given birth, in the normal fashion, to a child who only later became the subject of entheogenesis, by acquiring the divine essence within, and becoming God-on-Earth during the sacramental rites in the Jordan River. Nestorius, the Bishop of Constantinople, was exiled to die in the arid regions of Egypt for refusing to accept the council's subjective reification of the religious metaphor of virgin birth into a concrete "historical" event. Similarly, the allegorical story of man's descent from the Garden of Eden, leaving behind the World Tree, was craftily elevated in its ranks and augmented into a piece of ancient history. While, in contrast, the actual event of the crucifixion was transformed, throughout Christendom, into a metaphor for salvation and the *a priori* reason for Christianity on earth.

Religious symbolism, divine epiphanies, and metaphors, however important in any given society, are functions of ethnic and regional differences. As such, they are conditioned by the very idioms of culture on which they exert vital impact. The actual value of metaphors, as media for spiritual messages in everyday life, may be illustrated by the following anecdote provided by a well-educated Druze, who chose this manner of response when asked about the calf-worship among his own people. Suppose, a complete stranger, never exposed to Christian tradition, entered a Catholic church and beheld all the religious art on display, with all the manifest scenes of crucifixion, saintly martyrdoms, and the symbolic lamb. Could he not arrive at a conclusion that the devout worshipped God in the form of a lamb, and placed great value on self-immolation and torture? Yet, neither a denial nor an affirmation would yield a completely true picture of this religious ideology and its mysticism. Inasmuch as the New Testament frequently alludes to the "lamb," such a stranger may receive the impression that the Christians supplicate to it, and if he were to query some nuns, might not he hear that they adore the lamb with their souls? How true, then, would it be to state plainly that Christianity is a heathen religion, worshipping the lamb? Would not reaching a conclusion unmindful of metaphors and based on literal inference only produce a disastrous distortion, devoid of any deep transcendental meaning?

The awareness of the sacred, which man had been capable of experiencing before the desacralization of nature and the cosmos began to permeate the empirical world, was filtered down to what we call the aesthetic experience, at the best, which, in itself, carries traces of a numinous sensation and sometimes even an appreciation, along with the other qualities for which we cherish a particular artistic manifestation. Thus, the psychological roots of art appreciation seem to be imbedded in religious experiences.

Visionary Experiences and Art

This is not the place to embark upon a lengthy dissertation on the causative and dynamic factors associated with the processes of creative expression. In other words, what makes art what it is? What we can do, here, is to comment on the effects of those experiences, transmitted by the artist, that are linked with our own and, thus, make them most valuable to us. They allow us to react by a pure act of imagination. The more ungarbled is the imagination, the purer the response; so it is with creativity. Art is an experience: the more enriching it is to be, the more personal it must remain.

If, in fact, an early mode of thinking consisted of "seeing" inside the head, then it could explain why a powerful image can still today communicate directly with us, by-passing the linguistic mode, and transmit a pictographic metaphor, that is, a visual image, which can internally excite our primeval mode of thinking and responding. Such an artwork is said to be endowed with a transporting quality. The significant aspect of art is to be realized in its function as a transcultural metaphor, a transporting idiom, opening up the doorways to visionary experiences of the primeval world. Through its ability to communicate by the use of metaphors and symbols, art can evoke impressions of the mythic reality. A genuine response to a transporting art work resembles a numinous sensation—a type of religious feeling. Hence, the visionary import of Classical Greek art stems from the artists' abilities to intimate the existence of primeval forms.

> The primeval is that which is most alive—in fact, it alone is truly alive. It is not the subjective talent of the [Greek] artist which gives the creations of Greek myth their incomparable vitality, quickening man's pulse as they have through the ages; but it is the appearance of the primeval world, which these creations have been able to evoke.[24]

The reasons for this evocation are to be sought in the viewer's subconscious, where this art echoes the archetypal imagery so well imbedded in the recesses of the mind. Classical art evokes a response of an emotionally familiar entity, enabling us to feel comfortable and psychologically secure. We seem to recognize the symbol in the stone façade, its secret meaning awaiting to be uttered by the frozen lips.

Hallucinogenic substances promoted, undoubtedly, the creations of many symbolic elements constructing the metaphors encountered in various mythologies and religions. The iconographic origins of some traditional art designs seem to be the result of hallucinogenic states. "We see these things when we drink *yajé!*" replied the Tukanoan Indians, when a field anthropologist queried them casually about this subject.[25] In ancient and aboriginal cultures, visions of color, luminosity, and inordinary forms have been produced regularly with the aid of botanic hallucinogens. Their likely roles in the emergence of art and in forming the basis for the general appeal of art, we can only begin to appreciate now. An entire iconographic corpus of designs comprised of hallucinatory images exists around the ritual experience of yajé preparation and trance. An interesting group of shamanistic pictorial metaphors is reproduced, in color, by Reichel-Dolmatoff in a book on the hallucinatory imagery of the Tukanoan Indians.[26] The compositions, created by several Amazonian natives and based on visions induced by the ritual consumption of the psychedelic yajé, encode profound mythic concepts relating to cosmic fertility, propagation of the clan, and Master of the Animals, to mention but a few. Among them are also to be found representations of shamanistic motifs, such as ecstatic flights, shamans, and their helping spirits. It is noteworthy to state that this hallucinatory imagery depicts neither hunting nor aggressive behavior, and it does not grant rewards (trophies) for acts of force. Consequently, we should use caution to avoid purely subjective interpretations of the numerous rock art scenes of hunting prey and other acts of violence, as projections of imagery seen in a shamanistic trance. Of course, it is recognized that trance-induced visions are not entirely free of psychological and cultural conditionings.

The influence of hallucinogenic plants on the art of an ancient people may be witnessed in the, so-called, sculpture of San Agustin, which was carved by artists who, in all likelihood, had experienced drug-induced states.[27] Amidst this preconquest stone statuary of the Magdalena highlands in southwestern Colombia, one finds lurid images of jaguars copulating with humans; rodents in sexual embrace with males, whose genitals are propped up by ropes encircling their waists. These are not graphic chapters from a *psychopathia sexualis*, but an elaborate syntax of shamanistic metaphors, describing certain cosmological analogues. Thus, the jaguar scene represents an avatar, and is symbolic of a merger with the animal's "life force." The sun, in a different example, stands for masculinity and power, while the moon for the female principle. The eagle connotes light, power, and fire, but in a visionary context it is a symbol of the spirit and ecstatic flight.

North of the tropics, in Texas, the rock art of the Indians identified with the Pecos River culture invoked a strong connection between shamanistic trance, based on the narcotic "mescal bean," a misnomer applied to *Sophora secundiflora*, and a rich language of metaphors.[28] The psychoactive seeds of the *Sophora* spp. are to be found almost at all levels of the archaeological debris on the floors of the Lower Pecos rock shelters. It is also possible that the Pecos River Style art was the work effected by participants in ecstatic visions, during or as an aftermath of shamanistic rituals, centered around the *Sophora* plant. This fact could suggest an alternate explanation, mainly, that the depicted "shamans" might have, in fact, represented spirits and supernatural beings encountered in the visionary quest, who, as Furst rightly points out, were often attributed with the characteristics of great shamans.[29] By the same token, the rich content of shamanistic metaphors among the Huichol Indians in western Mexico finds an expression through a unique ceremonial art idiom, known by the native term, *nearika*, which is composed of vibrantly colored yarns, where the strong hues have counterparts in the peyote visions.[30]

In the course of time, transporting devices used by the artists preempted, in some places, the need for hallucinogenic substances in the creation of visions, and, as a result, vision-inducing materials have come to form an intrinsic part of the religious art in many cultures. Gold and images adorned with jewels were essential not only at the altars, but later also extended to more secular surroundings. Each *sanctum sanctorum* and almost every mystery cult have had, at least, a small area reserved for a gold, and often jeweled, reliquary. Such treasures, in which a sparkling gem is the stone of fire, have been associated with the life-giving forces inherent in fire and light. The perennial flame at the altars of medieval Europe was transformed into candles burning in jeweled candlesticks. The product of the goldsmith's and the jeweler's craft, owing to the intrinsic nature of the raw materials, is one of the most vision-inducing, non-chemical, passive agents. Gold, because of its luminous aspect, Aldous Huxley believed, exerts a transporting influence upon the beholder, and once this quality is combined with the goldsmith's intricacy of design, the entire object acquires the power of a vision-inducing vehicle, that "of a genuine talisman."[31] Indeed, in the Vedic tradition of ancient India, gold possessed talismanic functions and ceremonial applications, as a purifying agent. By extension of its attributed relationship with the gods, gold was a symbol of life, as well as the human spirit. On account of its luminosity, gold represented light, or the solar entity, to be compared with fire in all its qualifying attributes, particularly, as they pertain to energy—brilliant, fiery, etc.—truth, status, kingship (sovereignty), and ritual purity.[32] To the shaman, however, gold was precious, not on account of its material worth, but because it was the locus of the revitalizing energy of the sun.

By analogy with plants, Huxley tells us, "precious stones are precious because they bear a faint resemblance to the glowing marvels seen with the inner eye of the visionary."[33] A carved inscription in the Angkor Temple of Ban Theat records with wonder the luminous adornment worn by a royal lady: "Sparkling with the fire thrown by the gems of her jewels." At the same time, the innate fascination with the transporting powers of the flame can compete with any jewel. "A flame," Huxley further asserted, "is a living gem." It is little wonder that the most transporting and awe-inspiring places of worship are situated in caverns or cavern-like surroundings, where the impact of the flame is to be felt the most, and the altar reliquary is brought to life shrouded in a mysterious shadow cast by the flickering flame.[34] Therefore, it is helpful to bear in mind that the reasons behind the abilities of the goldsmith and the jeweler to produce objects that could enhance the induction of visions are to be found in the intrinsic properties of the materials. The transmission of archetypal symbols is, thus, affected by technology and, as such, is influenced by culture change.

The use of multiplicity of vivid colors in decorating the wall reliefs of the ancient Egyptian temples must have produced a trancelike effect. In the temples of Abydos and Dendereh in Upper Egypt, I found myself increasingly aware of optic nerve stimulation, until, finally, I realized the incredible impact of so many vibrating colors on one's mental state and consciousness. Slight movements of the head, especially upward, causes the colors to vibrate, as far as the human eye is concerned. I could readily imagine a ceremonial procession of worshippers meandering inside the sanctuary, overwhelmed by the flame-illuminated, numinous colors, which seemed to be moving in the dark and coming at the gathering of the devout like a zooming kaleidoscope. And I could not overcome the feeling that this optical effect had been devised intentionally; it retained the echoes of more ancient, shamanistic, and Otherworldly experiences held significant by the Egyptian herbalist and the shaman-priest.

The city of Venice was nothing if not a tribute to humanity. What a splendid testimony is presented by the stately grandeur of the Basilica of San Marco! The gilded and colored pebbles, arranged into intricate compositions of most exquisite and overwhelming mosaic artwork, do not falter much in the shadows of the Egyptian temples. Huxley found in it the proper foodstuff for his impressions regarding the role of sparkling materials in the evocation of visionary experiences. The transporting effect, utilizing most skillfully the luminosity of gold, can hardly be matched in magnificence achieved by the builders of this basilica. The thirteenth-century mosaic scene, for example, showing the *Transportation of the Body of St. Mark*, which decorates the niche of the First Archway at the Portal of St. Alipius; the theme of the *Creation of the World* on the dome of the Atrium; or *Salomé's Dance* with the head of John the Baptist are intended to evoke mystical states of mind. Venice was not, by any means, the only city in Italy during that period to underscore visionary effects in its sacred architecture. The mystical Church of St. Anastasias in the noble city of Verona is just another example, among many, of the use of vivid colors to create a transporting experience intending to amplify the numinous presence.

No less effective, in a different sort of way, is the fifteenth-century painting created by the joint efforts of Antonio Vivarini and Giovanni d'Alemagna, *Enthroned Madonna and Four 'Dottori' of the Church*, in the Academy of Fine Arts in Venice. It blends the Medieval and Renaissance styles, on a grand scale, combining moderately heavy applications of paint and gild to elicit a mystical ambience, even in the eyes of those not steeped in the Christian ecclesiastical tradition. The manner of the painting is bold, and the perspective stylized. Yet, it is highly suggestive of deep spirituality, capable of moving the "soul," without a prerequisite for the understanding of its symbolic elements.

The use of prism and other types of glass, to manipulate light rays for visionary impact, is well exemplified by the fifteenth-century cross of St. Theodore, also in the Academy of Fine Arts, or by the numinous cathedrals of Chartres and Sens. While, still further back in time, the Celts bespoke high praises of glass, the Welsh cherished a magical land called *Ynisvitrin*, the Isle of Glass, and the Germanic tribes used *Glasberg*, Glass Mountain, as one of the names for the land of the dead. The importance of crystals to the cosmology—the shaman's, in particular—of the spirit world has been noted (see Chapter Four), while the extended identity of crystal to glass is known to have occasioned not too infrequently.

The elaborate symbolism of colors among certain Amazonian groups has already been discussed earlier in this book, as have the corresponding relationships formed by lines, energy, the cosmic principle of dimorphism, the hexagonal structure, and quartz crystals. The visionary experiences of certain patterns, colors, and intensities, such as the brilliance of gold, points to an early connection between psychotropic conditions and the development of art and metallurgy.[35] The knowledge of metals and alchemical transmutations—thus, the secret of immortality and eternal life—has always carried an aura of mystery. The conveyance of such knowledge was generally believed to be accompanied by an impending death. Each successive cycle of rebirth, or new life, was ushered in as a consequence of preceding death. To be sure, the symbol of resurrection is death itself. Thus, in ancient times, those possessed of this arcane knowledge occupied a privileged position in their world and, as a result, claimed a special status in the community. In fact, metalsmiths and shamans shared relatively kindred social ranks, with similar privileges and exercise of power. The importance of iron implements in the shaman's "toolkit" and on his vestments is a widespread occurrence. At the same time, the numerous shamanistic themes in the mythology of the smiths allude to more than a mere suspicion that both bodies have a single source.[36] The Yakuts possess a saying that pronounces the origins of both to be "from the same tree." Later on, when shamanistic practices subsided in favor of more rustic or agricultural modes of subsistence, the role of the metalsmith continued to carry with it many traits associated with shamanistic behavior. How strong was the relationship between shamanism and metallurgy? After all, was not the Great Shaman, Odin, a master metal-craftsman, and did not the Mesoamerican god, Quetzalcoatl, teach his people how to work metals?

Phosphenes and Shamanistic Symbolism

The neuronal system, which includes the cortical and subcortical ranges along with the network of retinal ganglions, generates so-called entopic forms. It appears that these neurally-induced light patterns in the brain, known as phosphenes, are common to all human beings and manifest themselves as pre-existing images. Analogues for phosphenes exist in nature, and some forms encountered in nature find corollaries with the imagery in the brain. Nature is not copied, just sometimes it reflects the neural phosphenes. These pre-existing shapes function as archetypes and are used in shamanistic art and systems of beliefs as prisms by which to view and organize This World, and to comprehend the path of the soul on its journey to the Beyond. Thus, not only the mental functions of the brain must find expressions, but other senses must find outlets, as well. Only then, the totality—the Gestalt—may become manifest as art. And most importantly, as Reichel-Dolmatoff notes perceptively,[37] the purpose of this art is not to create external impressions, but to direct the mind inward to abstract symbolism and metaphor. The metaphoric content of the shamanistic art is reinforced by the dreamlike quality of the state under which it is produced. The art is not intended to be an end in itself; only a channel for cultural ethos. As a result, substance is important, and not form; the expression of meaning, and not skill.

> Shamanistic art is not concerned with realistic representation but seeks the symbol or sign, its subject matter drawn from myth and magic. Suggestion and allusion are sufficient to evoke a particular concept. Of primary importance is the spiritual power concealed within the object. . . .To the Western viewer, shamanistic object may appear crude, primitive, misshapen, artless; to the shamanist it is an intimation of a higher reality, a transcendental world accessible only by mystical experience and magicoreligious techniques.[38]

Reichel-Dolmatoff notes an important consideration: "What we are inclined to call art and enjoy as an aesthetic impression, to the Indians is a more sober means of communication in which each shape, each colour, each sound, each combination or sequence expresses a deeply felt truth which must be perpetuated and propagated."[39] It becomes quite apparent that it is shamanistic experience which forms the basis for the Tukanoan aesthetic expression. Almost the entire corpus of their art motifs is derived from a common storeroom of phosphene designs. The drug-induced psychic voyage of the Desana initiate. . .

> is described as an ecstatic metamorphosis, a dream world of colors and shapes, projected by an intoxicated mind. . . .The entire transformative sequence is also comparable to the succession of neurological sensations perceived during an advancing state of drug-induced trance, and many of all these states and conditions have a strong sexual resonance.[40]

Such conditions can be triggered by certain exogenous stimuli. For example, the Desana compare sexual intercourse to a hallucinogenic experience, by claiming that during coitus they see *marari* and *nomeri*, luminous images perceived at the onset of all varieties of psychotropic trance.[41]

The geometric patterns of light, which appear during the initial stage of a yajé narcotic trance, become validated by the supernatural connotation of a hallucinogenic experience. These phosphenes, having counterparts in the physical reality, not only reinforce natural forms, but also assign to them specific symbolic associations (metaphors), and place them in corresponding social settings. Thus, a snail may represent a spiral, which, in turn, may symbolize incest, ritual contamination, a broader condition of social inequilibrium and dysfunction. It is, primarily, the shaman's task to forge cultural cohesion and find definitions for these symbols.[42] By incorporating the patterns seen in a trance into a menu of ornamental designs imbued with symbolic meaning, a geometric pattern, with neurophysiological origins, becomes transformed into a cultural metaphor, standing for a whole array of cultural norms and lore. It is here that we can witness best the communicative function of art, and its social importance.

Since one basis for the art is biochemical, it is possible to look for similar foundations beneath the universality of certain elementary patterns and art motifs, as a functional expression of corresponding biochemical and neurophysiological processes. Carl G. Jung, who observed the transcultural character of phosphene shapes effected by neural stimulation, pioneered the idea that certain archetypal symbols may originate in the personal experience of such luminous designs. It is this notion, particularly, that seems to be borne out by the Tukanoan Indians, who readily acknowledge that their source for the original designs is derived from hallucinatory imagery. Genuine archetypes do not have specific physical configurations, but are merely abstractions to be found within the person. Henceforth, the neurophysiological and biochemical impetus behind the origins of art must be recognized as being antecedent to the sociocultural foundations of aesthetic expressions.[43]

Shamanistic Parallels and Survivals

To the student of mythology and comparative religions, it becomes apparent quite soon, that there exist very powerful themes which occur, over and again, across boundaries of cultures and time. Such recurrent traits were labeled "elementary ideas" (*Elementargedanken*) by Adolf Bastian (1826-1905), for whom the chair of anthropology had been established at the University of Berlin. The cultural idiom, or metaphor, by which these "ideas" found expressions within their respective culture contexts, Bastian termed "folk ideas" (*Völkergedanken*). The product of integration of the mythic ideation into the social structure to form a modal character and worldview was referred to by Leo Frobenius (1873-1938) as a "monad" of culture. Oswald Spengler (1880-1936) applied these ideas, especially of "monads," very effectively in his notable achievement, *The Decline of the West*.

During the long course of history, the central elements of shamanism have retained their essential character across the many cross-cultural boundaries. Although their individual aspects may display varying and specific manifestations, the contingent elements submit to a basic general structure that affords shamanism its own unique quality. Each system of shamanistic beliefs emphasizes those traits which have proved to be functionally successful in its own cultural context, and idealogically meaningful to the community. The obvious congruence of these living nuclear traits, today, can be recognized in very remote places, spanning wide areas of the globe: northern Eurasia, including Hungary, the Steppe and Himalayan regions; the Americas; and, to a certain extent, Oceania, as well as Southeast Asia. Surprisingly, even in the Middle East some of these features have been integrated into the mystic ceremonies of the Sufi Dervishes. This compelling observation indicates rather convincingly that shamanism, as a belief system, contains elements which respond adaptively to certain fundamental needs of human beings. The parallels which occur in the structure and content of shamanistic motifs make up the many recurrent transcultural themes, as have already been discussed in the preceding chapters of this book. Among them, of course, there are ecstatic trances; soul-journeys; spiritual assistants and avatars; the World Tree, also known as the cosmic pillar, the world axis, or the "shaman's ladder," which, during the shaman's journey, leads through the multiple levels of the stratified cosmos.

The mask, the drum, and the dance (to mention only a select few) are features in the shaman's transpersonal experience of rapture, aimed at communication with the supernatural world. These items assist in his role as an intermediary between the unleashed (Dionysiac) forces of nature and the organized (Apollonian) community of men. The birth of Greek tragedy stems from the ritual drama associated with the cult of the dead, which, in turn, is connected with the shaman's activity as a psychopomp during the Bronze Age, or even earlier. The preoccupation with the dramatic, in the ancient Aegean, is well documented for Minoan Crete by the evidence of the construction of "theatral" areas and the creations of numerous frescoes depicting dramatic themes.

Not in too many places, today, is the metaphor of the dance evidenced more solemnly than in Java, particularly during the performance of the *Bedoyo Ketawang,* the most sacred Javanese ritual performance. The nine virgin dancers are vested with skirts adorned with gold designs representing the entire animal world, and their hair is styled into "the climbing lizard." The number nine, according to one account, represents the nine orifices of the body that need ideally to be mastered by mankind. At the same time, the continuous history of the Japanese theater, inclusive of the religious ceremonies and the secret traditions of Zeami and Zenchiku, based on the spiritual teachings of Zen, is richly embellished with documentations showing its development from "shamanistic rituals to contemporary pluralism."[44]

The most solemn, masked celebration, in the present day, which has retained many shamanistic features among the Kekchi and the Mopan Maya of the Toledo District in southern Belize, commemorates the killing of the sacred Deer, which was downed by the hunters after it had first managed to evade an attack by the dogs. It is obvious that this sacred Deer motif represents transcultural vestiges of the same religious metaphor—the quest for a sacred hallucinogenic plant—as can be encountered among the Huichols of the faraway western Sierra Madre in Mexico, as described by Peter Furst,[45] where the gathering of the divine cactus symbolizes the primordial hunt and the kill of the sacred Deer-Peyote.

At this point, as indicated by La Barre,[46] evidence suggests that the widespread interest in plant hallucinogens among the indigenous cultures of the New World is based on survivals of Eurasian shamanism from Palaeolithic-Mesolithic horizons. In turn, this archaic, Palaeo-Asiatic stratum of ecstatic shamanism had emerged from an ancient form based on the ritual use of the fly-agaric (Amanita muscaria), as was admirably shown by the pioneering ethnomycologist R. Gordon Wasson.[47] The ritual drug complex centered around the fly-agaric has survived, until this day, in the northern regions of Eurasia: Siberia, Scandinavia, and the Baltic area.

Archaeological evidence from Neanderthal sites (70,000–50,000 years ago) in Mesopotamia, more specifically in Iraq, is implicit about familiarity with the healing properties of certain plants. The floral varieties of plants found in the burial of an aged Neanderthal man, proved to be, through pollen analysis, of medicinal value that is still actively recognized throughout Southwest Asia. If it is kept in mind that large mammals, especially the apes, are aware of the healing qualities of some plants, we may want to conjecture that such knowledge was also available to not only the Neanderthal, but also to other species of the genus Homo. In considering the data, it should not be surprising if we are led to believe that the discovery of the psychoactive characteristics in certain botanic hallucinogens did not fall far behind in the exploratory steps of the floristic environment. However, one must heed the warning that not all shamanistic beliefs, at least among those observed today, are based on—or have been connected with—the use of hallucinogenic substances.

The ecstatic rapture transforms a person into a god, and in this state of ecstasy the essential knowledge of the divine can be attained. Henceforth, through this state of being a god, one can understand the mystery that is god. For, as the Tantric saying informs us: nādevo devam arcayet ("by none but a god shall a god be worshipped"). Perhaps, as our minds repose in the shadow of the Bodhi-tree (Tree of Enlightenment), we may be allowed to draw an inspiration from the metaphysical well of ancient Hindu wisdom, the *Chhāndogya Upanishad*, from around ninth century B.C. and realize that religious metaphors are created to remind humans of their potential spiritual transcendence, so that, paradoxically, through this experience they may no longer need such metaphors.

The religious objective, among others, of the early mystery rites had been to arouse two great mystical sensations—tragic pity (compassion, arising from the recognition of plight in shared human existence) and tragic terror (frenzy and rapture, associated with creation and destruction, alike). Hence, ancient drama, such as the Greek tragedy, which was an important socio-religious occasion enacted according to a specific formula during the Great Dionysia at Athens (examined by Aristotle in his *Poetics*), became a social metaphor for a mystical experience attainable through *katharsis* (in a Platonic sense)—a kind of metaphysical prototype of the human condition—allowing spiritual transformation through the participation in a shared ritual. Whether one looks at the process of culture history through the eyes of Bastian, Spengler, Frazer, or one of the modern anthropological theoreticians, it is obvious that religion is a fundamental "monadic" institution, found in the cultures of all peoples. The manipulations and epiphanies of religious systems, conditioned, as they are, by the ethnohistorical experience of the people, constitute the characteristic metaphors which make up the symbolic language and cognitive foodstuff of individual psychology and cultural ideology.

Shamanistic practices have not ceased, but by becoming modified, augmented, and transformed through religious syncretism continue to exert the impact of their efficacies by manifesting themselves in different modes, through which many societies today aspire to attain some of their cognitive ends. In its broadest dimension, shamanistic experience reaches far beyond any such phenomenon as common fakirism, magic, spiritualism, mysticism, or conventional religion. Yet, shamanism may encompass all of these, just as some of its elements may surface in any culture area, and at any point in culture history, traditional or modern, simple or complex. The entire nexus of shamanistic techniques, it must be remembered, depends on the successful manipulation of metaphors, whether applied to healing, initiations, or ecstatic journeys. Just as important, from a cultural perspective, are those shamanistic idioms and metaphors that are directed at reestablishing and maintaining a balanced relationship between nature and the community and at caring for the spiritual and physical welfare of its members. Once, again, the Desana can be called upon to provide a convenient example, demonstrating the organizational role of the shaman as an important mitigating agent in ecological and sociocultural equilibria. It is my belief that religious mores underscore the elementary units of social morality, conduct, and institutions, and that shamanism, as a religious metaphor, exhibits cultural traits that are well adapted to promote integrated relationships, on a social level, and transformative processes, on an individual. The probing into its practices delivers us at the threshold of more profound levels of the human mind. For does an essential difference, really, exist between Goethe's statement that "Everything transitory is but a metaphor," and Nietzsche's declaration that "Everything eternal is but a metaphor"? Perhaps, the answer may be found in the unitarian insight of one of Albion's own, who, in poetic, visionary revelation, avowed:

> If the doors of perception were cleansed, every thing would appear to man as it is, infinite.
>   William Blake, *The Marriage of Heaven and Hell*

Notes

Chapter 1—Introduction

1. Ian Hodder, "Archaeology in 1984," *Antiquity,* Vol. 58 (1984); p. 28.
2. Stephen Hawking, *A Brief History of Time. From the Big Bang to Black Holes.* New York: Bantam Books, 1988; p. 55.
3. Oswald Spengler, *Zur Weltgeschichte des zweiten vorchristlichen Jahrtausends* [*World History of the Second Millennium* B.C.], München, 1935. (English translation does not exist).
4. O. Spengler, *Zur Weltgeschichte des zweiten vorchristlichen Jahrtausends* [see note 3].
5. Hans G. Wunderlich, *The Secret of Crete.* New York: Macmillan, 1974. (Originally published in German, *Wohin der Stier Europa trug.,* 1972).
6. Vilmos Diószegi, "Shamanism," *Encyclopedia Britannica,* 15th ed.; pp. 1030–1033.
7. Mircea Eliade, *Shamanism: Archaic Techniques of Ecstasy.* Bollingen Series, 76. New York: Pantheon Books, 1964; p. 7.
8. Joseph Campbell, his different lectures and books, but particularly the various editions of the four-volume work *The Masks of God* (New York: Viking Press, 1959, revised ed. 1969; Penguin, 1976).
9. G. Reichel-Dolmatoff, *Amazoniam Cosmos: The Sexual and Religious Symbolism of the Tukano Indians.* Chicago: University of Chicago Press, 1971.

Chapter 2—Shamanism and Culture

1. Based on various reports, it would *appear* that Gurdjieff was born in at least two different places, at two different times, and his real name was not Gurdjieff.

2. On Gurdjieff's philosophy see his *Meetings with Remarkable Men,* various editions.
3. A. Watts, *In My Own Way. An Autobiography, 1915–1965.* New York: Vintage Books, 1973; p. 145.
4. I am not comparing Gurdjieff to a shaman, but merely wish to demonstrate a functional resemblance, and not a substantive one. Certain social needs, which in the past were fulfilled by the shamans, may become the concerns of clever individuals. These, in turn, seemingly contrive to offer desirable responses to the conditions in question. In other words, human societies have retained the requirements and needs that historically were satisfied by the shamans. Today, however, others may fill the void. The need still exists.
5. See, for example, Michael Ripinsky, "Middle Eastern Kinship as an Expression of a Culture-Environment System," *The Muslim World,* Vol. 58, no. 3 (1968), pp. 225–241; also "Cultural Idiom as an Ecologic Factor: Two Studies," *Anthropos,* Vol. 70, nos. 3–4 (1975); pp. 449–460.
6. Thomas Gregor, *Mehinaku. The Drama of Daily Life in a Brazilian Indian Village.* Chicago: University of Chicago Press, 1977; pp. 325, 328–330.
7. W. B. Seabrook, *Adventures in Arabia. Among the Bedouins, Druses, Whirling Dervishes, & Yezidee Devil Worshipers.* New York: Harcourt, Brace and Co., 1927; pp. 169, 177.
8. Jo Anne Van Tilburg, "Symbolic Archaeology on Easter Island," *Archaeology,* Vol. 40, no. 2 (1987); pp. 28, 30. For a discussion of the cultural role of *kava,* cf. Ron Brunton, *The Abandoned Narcotic. Kava and Cultural Instability in Melanesia.* Cambridge & New York: Cambridge University Press, 1989. For a comprehensive treatment of *kava,* and an extensive overview of research from several prespectives, see Vincent Lebot, Mark Merlin, and Lamont Lindstrom, *Kava. The Pacific Drug.* New Haven: Yale University Press, 1992.
9. The characteristic feature of Polynesian ecstatic religions is possession by supernatural entities, which, in turn, has produced vast numbers of healers among the sorcerors, medicine-men, priests, and other "inspired" individuals. As a result, it is difficult to regard shamanism, in form and in substance, as a true phenomenon in Polynesia.
10. Rudolf Otto, *The Idea of the Holy. An Inquiry into the Non-Rational Factor in the Idea of the Divine and Its Relation to the Rational.* 2nd edition. Trans. from German. London: Oxford University Press, 1950 (paper 1958).

11. J. Harrison, *Prolegomena to the Study of Greek Religion*. 3rd edition. Cambridge: Cambridge University Press, 1922 (reprinted New York: Meridian Books, 1960); p. 194.

12. The term *dervish* is applied to over thirty different Islamic mystic sects, stemming from Sufi ideology and thus sharing a common philosophy, inasmuch as diverse Christian orders refer to their members as monks. The dervishes are dispersed throughout the Muslim world, with their "monasteries" to be found in Turkey, Syria, Israel, Arabia, Egypt, and North Africa, as well as parts of Iran.

13. *Melewi* is an Arabic version of the Turkish *Mevlevi*.

14. This destruction need not be physical, but may be spiritual, psychological, or even intellectual. An old Arabian proverb has it: A cornered scorpion stings itself to death [an allegory for a perplexed man, a fool]; Allah laughs and lets him die.

15. G. Reichel-Dolmatoff, personal communication, December 28, 1990.

16. R. C. Zaehner, *Mysticism: Sacred and Profane. An Inquiry into some Varieties of Praeternatural Experience*. New York: Oxford University Press, 1961; p. ix. (Originally published Oxford: Clarendon Press, 1957).

17. R. C. Zaehner, *Mysticism: Sacred and Profane*; p. xii [see note 16].

18. R. C. Zaehner, *Mysticism: Sacred and Profane*; pp. xiii, 1 [see note 16]. The Huxley-Zaehner debate stands obviously unresolved, and it will remain in this status quo for a very long time, if, indeed, not forever. My concerns with such issues reflect long-standing interests in the phenomenology and philosophy of cultural metaphors.

19. In the opinion of many experts, which I share, the idea that the use of hallucinogenic agents represents a degenerate form ought to be rejected. G. Reichel-Dolmatoff (personal communication, December 28, 1990) not only disagrees strongly with Eliade, but believes that the use of hallucinogens, in a shamanistic context, reaches back to the Palaeolithic. It is appropriate to note here that Eliade, however significant his scholarly contributions, is somewhat outdated and, occasionally, reflects a subjective bias in the presentations of his material sources.

20. Mircea Eliade, *Shamanism: Archaic Techniques of Ecstasy*. Bollingen Series, 76. New York: Pantheon Books, 1964; pp. 72 ff., 344 ff., etc.

21. M. Eliade, *Yoga. Immortality and Freedom*. 2nd edition. Bollingen Series, 56. Princeton: Princeton University Press, 1970; Chapter 8, specifically pp. 306, 310, 312, 315–316, 318–341. (Originally published in Paris, 1954).

22. G. Reichel-Dolmatoff, personal communication, December 28, 1990.
23. I owe this observation to Professor Gérardo Reichel-Dolmatoff, who, in spite of serious illness, kindly sent me his comments from Bogotá, Colombia [see note 22].
24. C. Dawson, *Religion and Culture.* The Gifford Lectures, 1947. New York: Meridian Books, 1958; pp. 177, 179.
25. Wenceslas L. Sieroszewski, *Twelve Years among the Yakuts.* 1896; p. 639. (Original title *12 lat w kraju Jakutów.* Warsaw, 1900).
26. Although the studies of cultures and religions have considerably advanced since Dawson's times, his notion of the social position and import of shamanism can still be encountered today among quite a few specialists.
27. C. Dawson, *Religion and Culture;* pp. 39, 51, 54 [see note 24].
28. G. Reichel-Dolmatoff [see note 22]; also his various publications.
29. Åke Hultkrantz, "The Peril of Visions; Changes of Vision Patterns among the Wind River Shoshoni," *History of Religions,* Vol. 26, no. 1 (1986); pp. 34–46.
30. In his highly informative book, *Hallucinogens and Culture* (Novato, Calif.: Chandler & Sharp, [1976] 1982; p. 4), Peter T. Furst writes:

>   Now, as we know from ethnology, the symbolic systems or religions of hunting peoples everywhere are essentially shamanistic, sharing so many basic features over time and space as to suggest common historical and psychological origins. At the center of shamanistic religion stands the personality of the shaman and the ecstatic experience that is uniquely his, in his crucial role as diviner, seer, magician, poet, singer, artist, prophet of game and weather, keeper of the traditions, and healer of bodily and spiritual ills.

31. Louise Bäckman and Åke Hultkrantz, *Studies in Lapp Shamanism.* Stockholm Studies in Comparative Religion, 16. Stockholm: Almqvist & Wiksell International, 1978; pp. 27–28.
32. M. Ripinsky, "Middle Eastern Kinship as an Expression of a Culture-Environment System," and "Cultural Idiom as an Ecologic Factor: Two Studies" [see note 5, for both].
33. L. Bäckman and Å. Hultkrantz, *Studies in Lapp Shamanism;* p. 28 [see note 31].
34. Knud Rasmussen. *The Intellectual Culture of the Iglulik Eskimos.* Reports of the Fifth Thule Expedition, 1921–24, Vol. 7. no. 1. Copenhagen: Glydendalske Boghandel, Nordisk Forlag, 1929.

35. M. Ripinsky, "Cultural Idiom as an Ecologic Factor: Two Studies;"
p. 453 [see note 5]. The attempt, on the part of some (e.g., Marvin
Harris), to explain the original significance of *taboo*, primarily in
ecological terms, suffers from simplistic rationalism: adaptive
impracticalities within culture-environment systems need not be
expressed in normative, proscriptive metaphors guarding against
such traits. For example, if herding of pigs proved to be inefficient
and undesirable, this fact alone does not constitute, necessarily,
an adequate reason for making the pig a taboo animal. A taboo
behavior is better explained by taking into account the cultural
attitudes, of the people concerned, towards nature and the universe
in general, and not merely their practical needs.

Not every animal possesses a sacred character, and not every
sacred animal elicits the same type of response and treatment on
the part of man. To compare one species with another by noting
performance similarities in the ritual life of the community
amounts, in effect, to a comparison of individual culture traits out
of their functional context. For it is not the intrinsic significance
of the animal category which, in itself, is so important as is the
socio-religious (-symbolic) aspect that it represents.

The totemic relationships between people and animals do not
always afford ready clues to the latter's position in human society:
Totemic alliances with the animal world are manifested at different
levels at different times and are subject to variable influences, such
as culture contact. Therefore, to argue, as some do, for the prohi-
bition against the pig as an ecological strategy in line with the
migratory pattern of the nomadic life is to take too narrow a view
of the total range of conditions (symbolic inclusive). By the same
token, the environmental consideration, which suggests that the
pig was not herded because it was not adapted to the arid climate,
cannot be viewed seriously, either. If the pig had not found an
ecological niche in such a region, it would have been quite unlikely
for a taboo to be placed on an animal that does not have its habitat
there. And if the pig could be found in that environmental zone,
then the questions of climate and biological adaptation become
trivial and irrelevant. An indigenous variety of wild pig is still
thriving in southern Mesopotamia (Iraq) today, and even hunted for
sport by the marsh-dwelling Arab tribes in the Tigris-Euphrates
delta, even though the animal's meat is taboo for the Muslim [M.
Ripinsky, "Conoscenza dei Ma'dan," *Rivista di Etnografia*, Vol. 20
(1966); pp. 11–39].

Natural resources are but "cultural appraisals." Put otherwise,
it matters little what resource can be *potentially* exploited; what

matters instead is the willing *recognition* of such a potential by a given culture, and the ethos attributing a cultural value to such a resource. Throughout history, there have always been societies that did not exploit all the resources available to them, without placing some in the category of taboo.

36. Alfred Kroeber, *Handbook of the Indians of California.* Berkeley: California Book Co., 1953; pp. 669–670.

37. Gérardo Reichel-Dolmatoff, *Shamanism and Art of the Eastern Tukanoan Indians, Colombian Northwest Amazon.* Institute of Religious Iconography, State University of Groningen. Leiden: E.J. Brill, 1987; pp. 8, 9.

38. G. Reichel-Dolmatoff, *Shamanism and Art of the Eastern Tukanoan Indians;* p. 11 [see note 37].

39. G. Reichel-Dolmatoff, *Shamanism and Art of the Eastern Tukanoan Indians;* pp. 19, 9 [see note 37].

40. Leo Sternberg, "Die Religion der Giljaken," *Archiv für Religionswissenschaft,* Vol. 8 (1905); pp. 273, 456–458. Abstract of a Russian work on the Gilyaks, by a Dr. Seland or Seeland in *Archiv für Anthropologie,* Vol. 26 (1900); p. 796. J. Batchelor, *The Ainu and Their Folk-lore.* London, 1901; p. 479.

41. Oswald Menghin, "Der Nachweis des Opfers im Altpaläolithikum," *Wiener Prähistorischer Zeitschrift* (1926); pp. 14 ff. A. Gahs, "Kopf-, Schädel- und Langknochenopfer bei Rentiervölkern," *Festschrift: Publication d'hommage offerte au P. W. Schmidt.* Vienna: Mechitharisten-Congregations-Buchdruckerei, 1928; pp. 231 ff. A. J. Hallowell, "Bear Ceremonialism in the Northern Hemisphere," *American Anthropologist* (1926); pp. 87 ff. Uno Holmberg (later Uno Harva), "Über die Jagdriten der nördlichen Völker Asiens und Europas," *Journal de la Société Finno-Ougrienne,* Vol. 41, no. 1 (1925–1926); pp. 1–53 [Helsinki]. Lothar Friedrich Zotz, *Die schlesischen Höhlen und ihre eiszeitlichen Bewohner.* Breslau, 1937; and *Die Altsteinzeit in Niederschlesien.* Leipzig, 1939. Wilhelm Koppers, "Künstlicher Zahnschliff am Bären im Altpaläolithikum und bei den Ainu auf Sachalin," *Quartär* (1938); pp. 97 ff. Herbert Kühn, "Das Problem des *Ur*-monotheismus."

42. Emil Bächler, *Das alpine Paläolithikum der Schweiz.* Basel, 1940. The three caves excavated by Bächler, in the Swiss Alps, were Wildkirchi (1903–1908), 7,000 feet above sea level; Drachenloch (1917–1922), 8,000 feet; and Wildermannlisloch (1923–1927), 7,000 feet.

43. Joseph Campbell, *The Masks of God: Primitive Mythology.* Revised edition. New York: Penguin Books, [1969] 1976; p. 335.

44. Contrariwise, Roy A. Miller, (*Japanese and the Other Altaic Languages*. Cambridge: Cambridge University Press, 1971), basing his argument on phonological, morphological, and lexical grounds, proposes an affinity of the Japanese language with other Altaic languages.

    The Ainus have been classified traditionally as belonging to the Palaeo-Siberian Culture Area (the far northeast corner of Asia), together with six other ethnic groups—all shamanistic. They are the Asiatic Eskimos, Chukchees, Yukaghirs, Lamuts, Koryaks, and Kamchadals.

45. This observation draws attention to the existence of some features in the Ainu ceremonial life which resemble certain ones in Shinto. It is not to be understood as a simplistic comparison between the two religions.

46. It is very probable that the Brahmins had once been a special group of magi (cf. Chapter Three), who, like their counterparts in other cultures, had strong ties with Master of the Animals. As such, the Brahmin-priestly caste would have had strong mythico-ritual reasons to preserve an interest in Shiva-Paśupati, the Herdsman of Living Creatures. In the Indo-Iranian plateau, high social rank was, and still is, indicated by animal ownership, e.g., the name Zarathuštra (the suffix "-uštra" referring to Bactrian camel herds).

    The Sanskrit text of the *Linga Purāna* (2.9.12–13) states that "All beings, from the Creator to lifeless matter, are known as the animals (*paśu*), or 'the herd' of the wise God of gods who causes the world to move. Being their lord, the all-powerful Rudra [Shiva's incarnation as Fire] is known as the Herdsman" Paśupati, who is responsible for the generation of all living forms, and for making them bound by natural laws. In the *Śatapatha Brāhmana* (1.7.4.1–3) and the *Aitareya Brāhmana* (3.33), Rudra conceded to be born as Lord of the Animals. In the latter, Rudra is called Paśupati (the "Herdsman"), who stands for the embodiment of the ritual sacrifice, the destructive element Fire, and the bestower of life. Through the sacrificial flame the mortal offering becomes transformed into a divine essence. For comments and translations of Sanskrit passages, see Alain Daniélou, *Hindu Polytheism*. Bollingen Series, 73. New York: Bollingen Foundation/Pantheon Books, 1964; pp. 205, 208–209, and ff.

47. According to one tradition, Iphigenia, who had escaped at Aulis the sacrificial knife by the hand of her father, Agamemnon, found shelter in Tauris, Chersonese (Crimea), and there she received divine instructions from Athena to establish a sanctuary to Artemis in Brauron, by the eastern shores of Attica.

Iphigenia's name implies "she who grants healthy children," indicating an association with some aspect of a Mycenaean Mother-Goddess. It is not to be precluded that her cultic presence at Brauron may antedate the subsequent arrival of Artemis, who very plausibly succeeded in displacing Iphigenia and taking over, as her own, the precinct of the cult. Iphigenia's alleged tomb, on the grounds of the sanctuary, was the object of profound reverie and considered to be common knowledge in ancient Greece. In a play by Euripides, the goddess Athena informs Iphigenia that "There you shall die, and be entombed."

48. The existence of analogous rites, practiced in Larissa and Demetrias, are implied by the word *nebeïein*, "to play the fawn."

49. Robert Graves, *The Greek Myths*. 2 vols. Revised edition. Harmondsworth: Penguin Books, 1960; Vol. 1: § 22.1.

50. Plutarch, *Greek Questions* 39.

51. James B. Harrod, *The Tempering Goddess: A Phenomenological and Structural Analysis of the Britomartis-Diktynna-Aphaia Mythologem*. Unpublished doctoral dissertation, 1974. I am indebted to Dr. Harrod for the kindness in supplying a copy of his dissertation while I was in Greece working on the book manuscript, and for the exchange of useful information through personal communication.

According to L. R. Farnell, (*Cults of the Greek States*. Oxford, 1896–1909), Britomartis-Diktynna was a variant of Artemis in her aspect as being "a matriarchal, chthonic, orgiastic" Mother-Goddess. I, for one, find it hard to accept such a contention about this dual-phased, and frequently triple-phased, goddess. To me, Britomartis and Artemis represent disparate cultural influences, characterizing divinities with different functional attributes, although undoubtedly both of them relate to untamed nature and wild things.

52. Michael Harner, *The Way of the Shaman*. New York: Bantam Books, 1982; pp. 34–37. The author is a recognized authority on shamanistic religion, and heads the Foundation for Shamanic Studies in Norwalk, Connecticut.

53. G. Reichel-Dolmatoff, *Beyond the Milky-Way: Hallucinatory Imagery of the Tukano Indians*. Latin American Studies, 42. Latin American Center, University of California, Los Angeles, 1978.

54. W. F. Jackson Knight, "Maze Symbolism and the Trojan Game," *Antiquity*, Vol. 6 (1932); pp. 445–448, 450 n3.

55. For example, cf. J. Campbell, *The Masks of God: Primitive Mythology*; p. 65 [see note 43].

56. For a translation of the Egyptian text see Joseph Kaster (ed. & trans.), *The Literature and Mythology of Ancient Egypt*. London: Allen Lane, 1970; p. 83.

57. G. Reichel-Dolmatoff, *Shamanism and Art of the Eastern Tukanoan Indians;* p. 12 [see note 37].
58. Willy Schulz-Weidner, "Shamanism," *Encyclopedia of World Art,* Vol. 13. New York: McCraw-Hill, [1967]; col. 2.
59. Harold P. Cooke, *Osiris. A Study in Myths, Mysteries, and Religion.* London, 1931; p. 43.
60. G. Reichel-Dolmatoff, *Shamanism and Art of the Eastern Tukanoan Indians;* p. 3 [see note 37].
61. Compare the White Old Man, a deity of fertility and herds, with the Celtic Mother-Goddess of fertility and cattle, and a source of sovereignty.
62. Walther Heissig, *The Religions of Mongolia.* Trans. from German. London: Routledge & Kegan Paul, 1980; p. 77.
63. Wilhelm Schmidt, *Der Ursprung der Gottesidee. Eine historisch-kritische und positive Studie.* 12 vols. Münster in Westfalia: Aschendorff, 1912–1955.
64. Serge Sauneron, *The Priests of Ancient Egypt.* Trans. from French. New York: Grove Press, 1960; p. 34.
65. S. Sauneron, *The Priests of Ancient Egypt;* p. 34 [see note 64].
66. S. Sauneron, *The Priests of Ancient Egypt;* p. 35 [see note 64].
67. *Journal des Savants* (1899); pp. 401–414.
68. M. Murray, "Ritual Masking." [In]: *Melanges Maspero.* Cairo: L'Institut Français d'Archéologie Orientale, 1934.
69. Heinrich Schäfer, *Principles of Egyptian Art.* Oxford: Clarendon Press, [1919] 1974; p. 122.
70. S. Sauneron, *The Priests of Ancient Egypt;* p. 34 [see note 64].
71. Arlene Wolinski, "Egyptian Masks: The Priest and His Role," *Archaeology,* Vol. 40, no. 1 (1987); pp. 22–29.
72. Marija Gimbutas, "Figurines of Old Europe (6500–3500 B.C.)." [In]: *Les Religions de la Prehistoire.* Actes du Valcamonica Symposium, 1972. Capo di Ponte (Brescia): Centro Camuno di Studi Preistorici, 1975; pp. 122–125.
73. E. Comsa, "Typologie et Signification des Figurines Anthropomorphes Neolitiques du Territoire Roumain." [In]: *Les Religions de la Prehistoire;* pp. 143–152 [see note 72].
74. M. Gimbutas, "Figurines of Old Europe (6500–3500 B.C.)"; p. 124 [see note 72].
75. Weston La Barre's important considerations, formulated in an article "Old and New World Narcotics: A Statistical Question and an Ethnological Reply," [*Economic Botany,* Vol. 24, 1970; pp. 368–372), brought up interesting facts regarding the connection between hallucinogens and culture. In a later article, "Hallucinogens and the Shamanic Origins of Religion," [In: Peter T. Furst (ed.), *Flesh*

of the Gods. Ritual Use of Hallucinogens. New York: Praeger/
London: George Allen & Unwin, 1972], La Barre demonstrated the
important role played by hallucinogens in the development of
shamanism and, by extension, religion. Also his major study on
The Peyote Cult has already undergone five editions and has become
a classic (5th ed. Norman: University of Oklahoma Press, 1989).
Many valuable contributions are to be found in P. T. Furst (ed.),
Flesh of the Gods (ibid.). In his other book, *Hallucinogens and
Culture* (Novato, Calif.: Chandler & Sharp, 1976), Furst writes:
"Often, though not always or everywhere, the shaman's ecstatic
dream has involved the use of some sacred hallucinogenic plant
believed to contain a supernatural transforming power. . . (p. 4).

Michael J. Harner's introduction to *Hallucinogens and
Shamanism*, edited by M. J. Harner (London & New York: Oxford
University Press, [1973] 1981), contains the following on the use
of psychotropic substances in shamanism: "The use of hallucinogenic agents to achieve trance states for perceiving and contacting
the supernatural world is evidently an ancient and widespread
human practice. . . . The theoretical literature has largely overlooked
the fact that even the 'classic' shamanism often involved the use
of hallucinogen" (pp. xi, xiv).

Marlene Dobkin de Rios, who is not new to the study of the
anthropology of sacred plants, makes an important statement in
the very first paragraph of the introduction to her informative book,
Hallucinogens: Cross-Cultural Perspectives (Albuquerque: University of New Mexico Press, 1984; reprinted Bridport, Dorset: Prism
Press/Garden City Park, N.Y.: Avery Publishing Group, 1990):

> It is my firm conviction, based on more than fifteen years
> of specialized study of hallucinogens and culture, that
> these substances have played more than a minor role in
> structuring the lives, beliefs, hopes, and values of large
> numbers of people. Members of preindustrial societies in
> many cultures with varying epistemological perspectives
> have always incorporated mind-altering plants into facets
> of daily activity. The economic behavior, the social
> organization, and the belief systems of some societies, for
> example, have been affected by the use of mind-altering
> plants (p. 3).

Also cf. Michael Ripinsky-Naxon, "Hallucinogens, Shamanism,
and the Cultural Process: Symbolic Archaeology and Dialectics,"
Anthropos, Vol. 84 (1989); pp. 219–224: "Present-day studies offer

substantial support favoring strong Palaeolithic and Mesolithic roots for the use of psychotropic plants among the Old World and New World shamans. This is not only witnessed in the ethnographic present, but, indeed, the aboriginal religions in the New World can be viewed as the archaeological present of the Mesolithic horizon" (p. 220).

76. M. Eliade, *Yoga. Immortality and Freedom;* p. 338 [see note 21]; and his *Shamanism;* p. 401 [see note 20].
77. Weston La Barre, "Hallucinogens and the Shamanic Origins of Religion." [*In*]: P. T. Furst (ed.), *Flesh of the Gods;* p. 272 [see note 75].
78. For an excellent discussion on the significance of the head and the horns, see the relevant sections in Richard B. Onians, *The Origins of European Thought about the Body, the Mind, the Soul, the World, Time, and Fate.* 2nd edition. Cambridge & New York: Cambridge University Press, 1988.
79. Franco Cardino, *Europe 1492.* New York & Oxford: Facts on File, 1989; p. 172. I am indebted to Professor G. Reichel-Dolmatoff for this reference.
80. I owe this observation to the kindness of Professor G. Reichel-Dolmatoff (personal communication, December 28, 1990).
81. P. T. Furst, "West Mexican Tomb Sculpture as Evidence for Shamanism in Prehispanic Mesoamerica," *Antropologica,* No. 15 (1965); p. 54, fig. 32 [Caracas].
82. P. T. Furst, "West Mexican Tomb Sculpture as Evidence for Shamanism in Prehispanic Mesoamerica" [see note 81].
83. P. T. Furst ["West Mexican Art: Secular or Sacred?" (*In*): *The Iconography of Middle American Sculpture.* New York: The Metropolitan Museum of Art, 1973; p. 105, fig. 2] describes a life-size, single-horned effigy head from Colima, which, with its prominent protrudence, makes a good case for shamanism. Such uni-horns have connections with supernatural and shamanic powers the world over, and not just in North and Middle America. In addition to those mentioned above, "To wit, the Chinese and Japanese figure of 'Hermit Single-Horn.'"
84. P. T. Furst, "West Mexican Art: Secular or Sacred?"; pp. 115, 117 [see note 83].
85. Richard B. Onians, *The Origins of European Thought about the Body, the Mind, the Soul, the World, Time, and Fate* [see note 78].
86. G. V. Ksenofontov, *Legendy i rasskazy o shamanach u Yakutov, Buryat i Tungusov.* Moscow: Izdatel'stvo Bezbozhnik, 1930 (2nd edition). Trans. from Russian into German as *Schamanengeschichten aus Siberien [Legends of Siberian Shamans].* Munich: Otto Wilhelm Barth-Verlag, 1955; pp. 160–161.

87. Freerk C. Kamma, *Religious Texts of the Oral Tradition from Western New-Guinea*. Part A: The Origin and Sources of Life. Religious Texts Translation Series, 3. Leiden: E.J. Brill, 1975; pp. 25 and 29. For a comprehensive survey covering the broad field of Melanesian religion, cf. G. W. Trompf, *Melanesian Religion*. Cambridge: Cambridge University Press, 1990.

88. W. Heissig, *The Religions of Mongolia*; pp. 21, 22, 16 [see note 62]. A most valuable study, albeit not available to me at the time of writing this book, is Tore Ahlbäck and Jan Bergman (eds.), *The Saami Shaman Drum*. Based on papers read at the Symposium on the Saami Shaman Drum held at Åbo, Finland: Donner Institute for Research in Religious and Cultural History, 1991 (distributed by Almqvist & Wiksell International, Stockholm).

89. V. Diószegi, "Shamanism," *Encyclopedia Britannica*, 15th edition; p. 1032.

90. S. M. Shirokogoroff, *Psychomental Complex of the Tungus*. London: Kegan Paul, Trench, Trubner, 1935; pp. 326–327, 329.

91. M. Eliade, *Shamanism*; pp. 222–223 [see note 20].

92. G. Reichel-Dolmatoff, *Shamanism and Art of the Eastern Tukanoan Indians*; p. 22 [see note 37].

93. G. Reichel-Dolmatoff, "Some Source Materials on Desana Shamanistic Initiation," *Antropologica*, Vol. 51 (1979); pp. 33–34 [Caracas]. Johannes Wilbert, "The Calabash of the Ruffled Feathers." (In): *Stones, Bones, and Skin. Ritual and Shamanic Art*. Edited by *Artscanada*. Toronto; The Society for Art Publications (an Artscanada Book), 1977; p. 92.

94. G. Reichel-Dolmatoff, *Shamanism and Art of the Eastern Tukanoan Indians*; p. 10 [see note 37].

95. W. B. Seabrook, *Adventures in Arabia*; p. 279 [see note 7].

96. S. Ostrander and L. Schroeder, *Psychic Discoveries Behind the Iron Curtain*. New York: Bantam Books, 1971; p. 249.

97. Marcel Granet, "Remarques sur le taoïsme ancien," *Asia Major*, Vol. 2 (1925); p. 149 [Leipzig]. Also his *Danses et légendes de la Chine ancienne*, Vol. 1. Paris, 1926; pp. 239 ff. On Yü's dance, cf. Wolgang Eberhard, *Lokalkulturen im alten China*. Pt. 1: Leiden, 1942; pp. 362 ff; Pt. 2: Peking, 1942; pp. 52 ff.

98. Henri Maspero, *Les Religions chinoises*. (Mélanges posthumes sur les religions et l'histoire de la Chine, I). Paris, 1950; pp. 34, 53–54. And his *La Chine antique*. Paris, 1927; pp. 195 ff.

99. Jan J. M. de Groot, *The Religious System of China*, Vol. 6. Leiden, 1910; pp. 1212 ff.

100. For the relevant texts see Berthold Laufer, *The Prehistory of Aviation*. Anthropological Series, Vol. 18, no. 1. Chicago: Field Museum of Natural History, 1928; pp. 19 ff.

101. M. Eliade, *Shamanism*; p. 450 [see note 20].
102. Jan de Groot, *The Religious System of China*, Vol. 6; pp. 1205, 1209 ff. [see note 99].
103. L. C. Hopkins, "The Bearskin, Another Pictographic Reconnaisance from Primitive Prophylactic to Present-day Panache: A Chinese Epigraphic Puzzle," *Journal of the Royal Asiatic Society*, Pts. 1–2, (1943); pp. 110–117. See also his "The Shaman or Chinese *Wu*: His Inspired Dancing and Versatile Character," *Journal of the Royal Asiatic Society*, Pts. 1–2 (1945); pp. 3–16.
104. This conclusion had first been reached, apparently, by William Watson, "A Grave Guardian from Ch'ang-sha," *British Museum Quarterly*, Vol. 17, no. 3 (1952); pp. 52–56. Alfred Salmony arrived at the same conjecture (independently?) in his book, *Antler and Tongue: An Essay on Ancient Chinese Symbolism and Its Implications*. Ascona, 1954. Robert Heine-Geldern, reviewing Salmony's book in *Artibus Asiae*, Vol. 18 (1955); pp. 85–90, not only agrees with him on this point, but alludes to Watson's earlier article, as well.
105. Berthold Laufer, *Chinese Clay Figures*. Anthropological Series, Vol. 13, no. 2. Chicago: Field Museum of Natural History, 1914; esp. pp. 196 ff. and pls. 15–17.
106. Jan de Groot, *The Religious System of China*, Vol. 6; pp. 1235, 1239 [see note 99].
107. W. Heissig, *The Religions of Mongolia*; pp. 59 and 8–9 [see note 62].
108. Jarl Charpentier, *Vilhelms av Ruysbroeck resa genom Asien 1253–1255*. Stockholm, 1919; pp. 258–259.
109. W. Heissig, *The Religions of Mongolia*; pp. 9–10 [see note 62].
110. C. Damdinsürüng, Mongol texts edited in *Corpus Scriptorum Mongolorum*. Vol. 14. Ulan Bator: Institute of Language and Literature, 1959; p. 130. [Cited in Heissig, p. 108 (see note 62)].
111. Standish O'Grady, *Silva Gadelica*. London: Williams & Norgate, 1892; Vol. 1, pp. 233–237; Vol. 2, pp. 255–259.
112. Jean Markale, *Celtic Civilization*. Paris: Payot, 1976; p. 24.
113. J. Markale, *Celtic Civilization*; p. 33 [see note 112].
114. Alwyn Rees and Brinley Rees, *Celtic Heritage*. London: Thames and Hudson, 1961; p. 76.
115. Walter L. Brenneman, Jr., "Serpents, Cows, and Ladies: Contrasting Symbolism in Irish and Indo-European Cattle-Raiding Myths," *History of Religions*, Vol. 28, no. 4 (1989); p. 346.
116. W. J. Brenneman, Jr., "Serpents, Cows, and Ladies" [see note 115 p. 346].
117. A. Rees and B. Rees, *Celtic Heritage*; p. 76 [see note 114].

118. W. J. Brenneman, Jr., "Serpents, Cows, and Ladies;" p. 346 [see note 115].
119. The Central Asian khans, too, had their power and sovereignty validated by a heavenly being (tngri). In fact, by assuming political authority, the khans were believed to fulfill tngri's will (cf. J. P. Roux, "L'Origine céleste de la souveraineté dans les inscriptions paléo-turques de Mongolie et de Sibérie." La regalità sacrà. [The Sacral Kingship]. Leiden: E. J. Brill, 1959; p. 231–241).
120. W. J. Brenneman, Jr., "Serpents, Cows, and Ladies;" p. 343 [see note 115].
121. Michael J. Harner, The Jívaro. People of the Sacred Waterfall. Garden City, New York: Doubleday, Natural History Press, 1972; pp. 111, 117.
122. Irving Goldman, The Cubeo. Indians of the Northwest Amazon. Illinois Studies in Anthropology, 2. Urbana: University of Illinois Press, 1963; p. 263.
123. V. Diószegi, "Shamanism;" p. 1031 [see note 89].
124. For example, G. Reichel-Dolmatoff, personal communication, December 28, 1990; also his various publications.
125. The shaman's attitude towards the physico-biotic environment is but a reflection of his cultural worldview. These ecological concerns define the complex interactions between culture and nature. Through hunting and gathering, for example, the human species influences the biological selection of other species, modifying inadvertently the ecological conditions. At the same time, the ecology of human disease, like malaria, shows a correlation with the politico-economic events in human societies. In today's world, in particular, when the face of the earth can be modified beyond recognition and repair, the protection and conservation of nature are tied up with the demographic problems of growth, distribution, and basic human needs [M. Ripinsky, "Geography: A Personal Statement," Newsletter of the Association of Pacific Coast Geographers, (Winter, 1967); p. 10].
126. G. Reichel-Dolmatoff, Shamanism and Art of the Eastern Tukanoan Indians; pp. 2, 7, 10 [see note 37, also note 23]. The shaman's concern with "healing" imbalance in nature and society is aptly reflected in the English term "dis-ease," that is, lack of ease, synchronization, or balance.
127. Gerald Weiss, "Shamanism and Priesthood in Light of the Campa Ayahuasca Ceremony." (In): M. J. Harner (ed.), Hallucinogens and Shamanism; p. 41 [see note 75].
128. "To shamanize" is a literal translation of the Mongol word bögele, derived from böge, shaman, which seems to be related to the old

Mongolian title *bägi* [cf. W. Heissig, *The Religions of Mongolia*; p. 12 (see note 62)].

129. S. Ostrander and L. Schroeder, *Psychic Discoveries Behind the Iron Curtain*; p. 249 [see note 96].

130. V. Diószegi, "Shamanism"; p. 1031 [see note 89].

131. Possession and shamanic ecstasy are different, indeed. A shamanic journey differs from spirit possession by the shaman's relations with the helping spirits. In the latter instance, i.e., possession, the practitioner is taken over by a foreign spirit and surrenders to the will of the intrusive entity. His or her part is passive in such an encounter. Possession, on its own merits alone, does not constitute a shamanic journey.

> Generally shamanism co-exists with other forms of magic and religion. . . . By virtue of this fact, though the shaman is, among other things, a magician, not every magician can properly be termed a shaman. The same distinction must be applied in regard to shamanic healing; every medicine man is a healer, but the shaman employs a method that is his and his alone. . . . Hence any ecstatic cannot be considered a shaman; the shaman specializes in a trance during which his soul is believed to leave his body and ascend to the sky or descend to the underworld. . . . To be sure, shamans are sometimes found to be "possessed," but these are exceptional cases for which there is a particular explanation. [M. Eliade, *Shamanism: Archaic Techniques of Ecstasy*; pp. 5–6 (see note 20)].

132. S. Ostrander and L. Schroeder, *Psychic Discoveries Behind the Iron Curtain*; pp. 245–246 [see note 96].

133. M. Ripinsky, "Middle Eastern Kinship as an Expression of a Culture-Environment System"; p. 225 [see note 5], although it addressed specifically a different problem in social organization.

Chapter 3—Substance and Function of Shamanism

1. On the etymology of this word, see Berthold Laufer, "Origin of the Word Shaman," *American Anthropologist*, Vol. 19 (1917); pp. 361–371. Also N. D. Mironov and S. M. Shirokogoroff, "Śramana-Shaman: Etymology of the Word 'Shaman,'" *Journal of the Royal Asiatic Society* (North-China Branch, Shanghai), Vol. 55 (1924); pp. 105–130.

2. Weston La Barre, *The Ghost Dance. The Origins of Religion.* London: George Allen & Unwin, 1972; p. 161.
3. Mircea Eliade, *Shamanism: Archaic Techniques of Ecstasy.* Bollingen Series, 76. New York: Pantheon Books, 1964; pp. 7n, 8.
4. Louise Bäckman and Åke Hultkrantz, *Studies in Lapp Shamanism.* Stockholm Studies in Comparative Religion, 16. Stockholm: Almqvist & Wiksell International, 1978; pp. 10–11.
5. Åke Hultkrantz, *The Religions of the American Indians.* Berkeley: University of California Press, 1973; pp. 85–86. (Originally published in Swedish, 1967).
6. V. Diószegi, "Shamanism," *Encyclopedia Britannica,* 15th edition; p. 1031.
7. Thomas Gregor, *Mehinaku. The Drama of Daily Life in a Brazilian Indian Village.* Chicago: University of Chicago Press, 1977; pp. 335–336.
8. T. Gregor, *Mehinaku;* pp. 340–341 [see note 7, above].
9. A *yakapa* shaman may use smoke like a *yetamá*, the tobacco shaman. However, unlike the latter, who calls upon his spirits for assistance, a *yakapa* becomes possessed by them. He is intimately associated with the spirits, calling them his "pets." During his possession, the *yakapa* can accomplish non-ordinary deeds, including the finding of sorcerors and witchcraft-related objects. The term referring to such spirit possessions, *iyákene,* means "to metamorphize" and is used also to describe transformations of men into animals. A cognate of *yakapa* is the verb *yákapai,* with an associated meaning "to move erratically or frenetically" [T. Gregor, *Mehinaku;* pp. 340–1 (see note 7)]. Since the *yakapa* shamans are prone to spirit possessions, perhaps, in the past, they knew also ecstatic frenzies.

    The two kinds of *yetamá* shamans consist of the Master of the Breath and the Master of the Song. The former cures by blowing at his patients; the other with shamanistic songs (T. Gregor, *Mehinaku;* p. 333). Perhaps, originally, these two were only offshoots or marginally shamanistic. Only the *yakapa* becomes possessed, thus exhibiting traits of ecstatic shamanism.
10. T. Gregor, *Mehinaku;* p. 341 [see note 7].
11. T. Gregor, *Mehinaku;* p. 332 [see note 7].
12. Irving Goldman, *The Cubeo. Indians of the Northwest Amazon.* Illinois Studies in Anthropology, 2. Urbana: University of Illinois Press, 1963; pp. 261, 266.
13. I. Goldman, *The Cubeo;* pp. 264–265 [see note 12]. All the information on shamanism obtained by Goldman came from lay informants; the shamans refused to talk about these matters.

14. Knud Rasmussen, *The Intellectual Culture of the Iglulik Eskimos*. Report of the Fifth Thule Expedition, 1921–24, Vol. 7, no. 1. Copenhagen: Glydendalske Boghandel, Nordisk Forlag, 1929; pp. 118–119.
15. See note 14 above. Cf. also H. Ostermann, *The Alaskan Eskimos, as Described in the Posthumous Notes of Dr. Knud Rasmussen*. Report of the Fifth Thule Expedition, 1921–24, Vol. 10, no. 3. Copenhagen: Nordisk Forlag, 1952; pp. 97–99.
16. H. Hesse, *Siddhartha*. New York: New Directions, 1957; p. 144. Certain shamanistic notions have survived as inflections in the ideas of several modern philosophers, conveying a degree of aesthetic and philosophical appeal. Such ideas point to the existence of common elements, which form recurrent themes not only in shamanism, but extend and permeate into other cultural domains that no longer possess obvious shamanistic associations. These elements, nevertheless, have prevailed in the human psyche and its existential quest for meaning. So there exists a relationship today, as it did then, between a similar quest and a similar experience. This situation can be exemplified as much by the sufferings and visions of St. Teresa of Avila as by the plight of Fyodor Dostoyevsky. Not for a moment is it presumed that these individuals were shamans. However, they were undergoing, at least in part, transformative experiences that in some way could be described as shamanistic.

    Similarly, the issues raised here by the questions of disparity between wisdom and knowledge are not isolated presentiments among western writers. For example, the social commentator and playwright George Bernard Shaw alluded often to this problem. In one of his lighter allegories (*The Adventures of the Black Girl in Her Search for God*. New York: Dodd, Mead & Co., 1933; p. 23), dipped into Marxist ideology and intended as a manifesto against social mediocrity, Shaw poignantly notes, with the usual dose of cynicism, the gap separating the two.

    > "...I have spent twenty-five years studying their effects."
    > "Effects on what?" said the black girl.
    > "On a dog's saliva" said the myop.
    > "Are you any the wiser?" she said.
    > "I am not interested in wisdom" he replied: "in fact I do not know what it means and have no reason to believe that it exists. My business is to learn something that was

not known before. I impart that knowledge to the world, and thereby add to the body of ascertained scientific truth."

17. Weston La Barre, *The Ghost Dance*; p. 172 [see note 2].
18. Leo Sternberg, "Divine Election in Primitive Religion." *Congrès International des Américanistes*, Compte-Rendu de la XXI session, Pt. 2 (1924). Göteborg, 1925; pp. 475 ff.
19. This could possibly result from the confusion, in Celtic times, of the original attributes of the various archaic gods and spirits, and from occasionally apotheosizing a tutelary spirit of the Otherworld.
20. Leo Sternberg, "Divine Election in Primitive Religion"; p. 482 [see note 18].
21. Leo Sternberg, "Divine Election in Primitive Religion"; pp. 485 f., 487 [see note 18]. Sternberg received this information from his Buryat student, A. N. Mikhailof, a participant in shamanic ceremonies.
22. M. Eliade, *Shamanism: Archaic Techniques of Ecstasy*; p. 76 [see note 3].
23. G. Reichel-Dolmatoff, "Some Source Materials on Desana Shamanistic Initiation," *Antropologica*, Vol. 51 (1979); p. 54 [Caracas].
24. M. Eliade, *Shamanism: Archaic Techniques of Ecstasy*; p. 81 [see note 3].
25. Leo Sternberg, "Divine Election in Primitive Religion"; p. 480 [see note 18].
26. Gérardo Reichel-Dolmatoff, *Shamanism and Art of the Eastern Tukanoan Indians, Colombian Northwest Amazon*. Institute of Religious Iconography, State University of Groningen. Leiden: E.J. Brill, 1987; pp. 8 & 2.
27. Michael J. Harner, *The Jívaro. People of the Sacred Waterfall*. Garden City, New York: Doubleday, Natural History Press, 1972; p. 154.
28. Francis Huxley, *Affable Savages. An Anthropologist among the Urubu Indians of Brazil*. New York: Viking Press, 1957; pp. 191–193.
29. G. V. Ksenofontov, *Legendy i rasskazy o shamanach u Yakutov, Buryat i Tungusov*. Moscow: Izdatel'stvo Bezbozhnik, 1930 (2nd edition). Trans. from Russian into German as *Schamanengeschichten aus Siberien [Legends of Siberian Shamans]*. Munich: Otto Wilhelm Barth-Verlag, 1955; pp. 211–212.
30. G. V. Ksenofontov, *Legendy i rasskazy*; pp. 211–212 [see note 29].
31. K. Rasmussen, *Across Arctic America*. New York: G. P. Putnam's Sons, 1927; pp. 82–84. For a more recent study on this aspect of the Eskimo culture, cf. Daniel Merkur's published doctoral dissertation, *Becoming Half Hidden: Shamanism and Initiation*

among the Inuit. Stockholm Studies in Comparative Religion, 24. Stockholm: Almqvist & Wiksell International, 1985.

32. K. Rasmussen, *Across Arctic America*; pp. 82–84 [see note 31].
33. Peter H. Knudtson, "Flora, Shaman of the Wintu," *Natural History*, Vol. 84 (May, 1975); p. 6, 17. The Wintu were a part of the Wintun Indian nation, which inhabited the area stretching along the western side of the Sacramento River, around Mount Shasta, and reaching to the San Francisco Bay. Prior to 1870, the Wintun numbered 12,000; according to the 1970 census, they have been reduced to 1,165.
34. G. Reichel-Dolmatoff, "Some Source Materials on Desana Shamanistic Initiation;" pp. 29–30 [see note 23]. For an interesting discussion of river symbolism among the Desana, see Note 43 in Notes and Comments to Text II, in the above article. This work is particularly invaluable since it offers a direct glimpse into the world of shamanistic metaphors in the form of two texts dictated by a Desana shaman. Text I describes the first experience undergone by an initiate, while Text II treats, in detail, many shamanistic practices, relating them in a shamanistic idiom.
35. G. Reichel-Dolmatoff, "Some Source Materials on Desana Shamanistic Initiation"; p. 51, 52, 54 [see note 23].
36. G. Reichel-Dolmatoff, "Some Source Materials on Desana Shamanistic Initiation"; pp. 53–54 [see note 23].
37. G. Reichel-Dolmatoff, "Some Source Materials on Desana Shamanistic Initiation". p. 53 [see note 23].
38. M. Eliade, *Shamanism: Archaic Techniques of Ecstasy*; p. 352 [see note 3]. Cf. also V. Diószegi, "Shamanism," *Encyclopedia Britannica*, 15th ed.; p. 1034.

> . . .The intermediaries between men and the gods (especially the Sangiang) are the *balian* and the *basir*, priestess-shamaness and asexual priest-shaman (the term *basir* means "unable to procreate, impotent"). The latter are true hermaphrodites, dressing and behaving like women. . . .We here have a ritual androgyny, a well-known archaic formula for the divine biunity and the *coincidentia oppositorum*. Like the hermaphroditism of the *basir*, the prostitution of the *balian* is similarly based on the sacred value of the "intermediary," on the need to abolish polarities" (Eliade, *ibid.*; p. 352).

The elements of androgyny, for example, are also contained in the powerful Hindu god Vishnu. In his feminine incarnation as

Mohinī, the Enchantress (Lust), the deity's purpose is to entice and misguide the antigods in order to obstruct their acquisition of the divine ambrosia of immortality [*Mahābhārata* (1.18–19), *Bhāgavata Purāna* (8. 9–10, 12), *Padma Purāna* (3. 10), *Rāmāyana* (1. 45)]. Râdhâ, an *avatara* (epiphany, manifestation) of Vishnu, is the most beloved wife of Krishna. Note the transexual characters of the gods. Vishnu unites the polarities of sexes by manifesting either aspect. Krishna, on the other hand, loves the female counterpart of Vishnu. On the discussion of sexual metaphors in Hindu mythology, cf. Wendy Doniger O'Flaherty, *Women, Androgynes, and Other Mythical Beasts*. Chicago: University of Chicago Press, 1980. For examples of transexual roles in other native cultures, cf. Will Roscoe, *The Zuni Man-Woman*. Albuquerque: University of New Mexico Press, 1991.

39. Joan Halifax, *Shamanic Voices. A Survey of Visionary Narratives*. New York: E. P. Dutton, 1979; pp. 22, 27, 28.

40. G. Reichel-Dolmatoff, "Some Source Materials on Desana Shamanistic Initiation"; pp. 53, 54 [see note 23].

41. See Robert Graves, *What Food the Centaurs Ate*. Steps: Cassell & Co., 1958, for a very stimulating discussion on this subject.

42. *Webster's New Collegiate Dictionary* lists "an incarnation in a human form" as a second definition of avatar. Thus, an animal spirit with a human body would be an avatar (e.g., were-wolf, were-jaguar may function as the shaman's helpers). The word has entered into a broader usage denoting a shaman's animal counterpart, and occasionally it appears in this context in professional literature. However, the original meaning of avatar denoted a divine incarnation, specifically of the Hindu gods Vishnu, Shiva, and Brahma.

The mythical histories of India, the *Purânas*, glorify the Hindu trinity (*trimûrti; tri* = three, *mûrti* = aspect) of Vishnu, Shiva, and Brahma. The *Purânas* met with wide popular acceptance, owing to their less perplexing religious symbolism and easier understanding than one encounters when dealing with the *Vedas*. These stories form the repository of the Hindu folk beliefs, elaborating upon the traditional Epics of India. The concept of the divine essence to be found in man was popularized by the worship of the *Avatāras*. Their adventures and stories of demon-conquests are described in the mythical histories.

In one of the Avatāras of Vishnu, the god is manifest as a fish, a symbol of the beginning of the material existence of man, and as a carrier of the eggs of the man-to-become. In another, Vishnu becomes a tortoise, symbolizing the physical vitality of man, together with his acute desires emanating from the watery abyss of Infinity. In a third Avatāra, Vishnu is a boar, signifying the physical struggle, on the part of a mammal, to dominate the earth. The fourth transformation is into a Man-Lion (were-lion), combining both the animal and the human principles, as well as the fonts of consciousness. And so forth, through the many spiritual and social stages of development. It is interesting to note the similarities between the Avatāras of Vishnu and the forms of shamanistic transformations encountered on soul-journeys. Man-eagle, man-jaguar, or man-lion are common manifestations during shamanic trance.

43. Initiatory ordeals of the shamanistic type are to be found, for example, among the Druzes, an Islamic ethno-religious sect. Before a Druze male can be considered a mature member of his community, and earn the right to be instructed in the religous mysteries of his people, he must submit to the *agons* of initiation. These consist of three successive stages—hunger, thirst, and temptation—corresponding to both physical trepidations and that of the spirit:

    After a fast lasting three days and two nights, the neophyte is lured with the most delicious and savory repast. The Druze elders, *akils* (a status acquired by passing through the initiation, rather than by mere age), feast before his eyes, but, on the third night he is left alone, trusted not to succumb to all that banquet food.

    The next stage, occurring after an interval of several days or so, consists of water deprivation for three days, during which horseback riding excursions into the desert may take place under the hot sun. Again, on the third night, a performance similar to the previous one is enacted, wherein the neophyte abstains from indulging in any kind of refreshments. He may, however, display strength of character by playing with a goblet containing cool liquid, but never allowing it to touch his lips.

    The final phase tests against incontinence, mainly, the will power to confront sexual temptation. An alluring, naked damsel—not a Druze—entices the novice. She is deemed expert in Ovid's art and has instructions to resort to all modes of approach and method of seduction to win over the neophyte, who, on the other hand, must withstand her erotic advances. If he fails, the girl is entitled to an additional reward. If she fails, then the novice qualifies to enter the portals. There the "inner mysteries," which to this day have remained solemnly veiled before the intrusive eyes of the uninitiated, will be revealed.

44. D. Magarshak, "Introduction" to Fyodor Dostoyevsky, *The Idiot*. Harmondsworth: Penguin Books, 1955.

45. Nicholas Humphrey, *Consciousness Regained. Chapters in the Development of Mind*. Oxford & New York: Oxford University Press, 1983; p. 86. The author, however, concedes that some psychologists may not share his view on this point.
46. St. Teresa, quoted by G. Bataille in *Eroticism*. Calder, 1962.
47. The Seri people, speaking different dialects, are not members of a single tribe. They form a confederacy of tribes, sharing a common geographical locality. In 1930, they numbered about 200.
48. A. L. Kroeber, *The Seri*. Southwest Museum Papers, No. 6. Los Angeles: Southwest Museum, 1931 (reprinted 1964); pp. 4, 13, 14.
49. The Garifuna are descendents of African slaves who had survived Spanish shipwrecks in the seventeenth century. They reached the English-occupied St. Vincent Island, where they had assimilated with the indigenous Carib Indian population. However, in 1797, as a result of an uprising, two thousand of them were forced by the British to abandon the island for the shores of Central America. For a general discussion of Garifuna culture history see Nancie L. Gonzalez, *Sojourners of the Caribbean. Ethnogenesis and Ethnohistory of the Garifuna*. Urbana & Chicago: University of Illinois Press, 1988.

    The Belizean Garifuna inhabit, primarily, the Stann Creek District, with their religious centers in the town of Dangriga and Hopkins village on the southern coast, which I visited in the beginning of 1991 and then, again, in the summer of 1992. Their belief system is derived from *Aygnan*, the original cult of Island Carib. The techniques employed by the Garifuna spirit mediums (*buyai*) resemble closely those found today on some Caribbean islands, where the mediums attribute malevolent conditions, such as sickness and witchcraft, to the temperings of their foes' supernatural beings.
50. Byron Foster (*Heart Drum. Spirit Possession in the Garifuna Communities of Belize*. Benque Viejo del Carmen [Belize]: Cubola Productions, 1986; p. 11) defines *dugu* as "the cult of the dead," but perhaps, more appropriately, *dugu* ought to be thought of as the cult of the ancestors.
51. B. Foster, *Heart Drum*; p. 14 [see note 50].
52. For the significance of the rattle during a healing ritual, compare its symbolic function among the Warao of Venezuela and that of the shaman's stick rattle among the Desana.
53. M. Eliade, *Shamanism: Archaic Techniques of Ecstasy*; p. 138 [see note 3].
54. Michael Harner, *The Way of the Shaman*. New York: Bantam Books, 1982; p. 29–30. Also cf. his "The Sound of Rushing Water." (*In*):

M. J. Harner (ed.), *Hallucinogens and Shamanism*. New York: Oxford University Press, [1968] 1973; pp. 15–16. And his "The Sound of Rushing Water," *Natural History*, Vol. 77, no. 6 (1968); p. 28.

55. In connection with the role of the horse and ascent-journeys, I am reminded of a description offered by Herodotus regarding the Ossetes, vigorous horsemen in the Caucasus, whose custom it was at funerals to bespeak long oratories about the deceased's horseback journey to the realm of his worthy ancestors.

The burials of prominent Scythians with their horses, undoubtedly for a similar purpose, are documented only too well by archaeological finds. The prophet Muhammed's ascent to heaven on a white horse has been discussed elsewhere in this book.

56. *Excerpta de legationibus* (p. 142.19–22). (In): *Excerpta Historica*, edited by C. de Boor. Berlin, 1903.

57. G. Reichel-Dolmatoff, *Shamanism and Art of the Eastern Tukanoan Indians*; p. 8 [see note 26]. Also his "Some Source Materials on Desana Shamanistic Initiation"; p. 30 [see note 23].

58. James G. Frazer, "On Certain Burial Customs as Illustrative of the Primitive Theory of the Soul," *Journal of the Royal Anthropological Institute*, Vol. 15 (1885); pp. 64–101.

59. Religions based on the Principle of Duality, such as Gnosticism, Manichaeism, and Zoroastrianism, espouse the parallel and simultaneous existence of antipodal Worlds—the spiritual (Upper) belonging to god; and the physical (Lower) to satanic elements. These two Worlds engage in an inveterate power struggle, keeping the universe in balance.

60. G. Reichel-Dolmatoff, *Shamanism and Art of the Eastern Tukanoan Indians*. Colombian Northwest Amazon; p. 12 [see note 26].

61. G. Reichel-Dolmatoff, *Shamanism and Art of the Eastern Tukanoan Indians*. Colombian Northwest Amazon; p. 12 [see note 26].

62. G. Reichel-Dolmatoff, *Shamanism and Art of the Eastern Tukanoan Indians*. Colombian Northwest Amazon; p. 11 [see note 26].

63. Ward Rutherford, *Shamanism. The Foundations of Magic.* Wellingborough: Aquarian Press, 1986; p. 125.

64. Å Hultkrantz, "A Definition of Shamanism," *Temenos*, Vol. 9 (1973); pp. 28, 31.

65. Johan Reinhard, "Shamanism and Spirit Possession." (*In*): John Hitchcock and Rex Jones (eds.), *Spirit Possession in the Nepal Himalayas*. Warminster: Aris and Phillips, 1975; pp. 12–18.

66. M. J. Harner, Introduction to the section on Hallucinogens and Shamanism: The Question of a Trans-cultural Experience. (*In*): M. J. Harner (ed.), *Hallucinogens and Shamanism*; p. 153 [see note

54]. Claudio Naranjo, "Psychological Aspects of the *Yagé* Experience in an Experimental Setting." *(In)*: M. J. Harner (ed.) *ibid.*; p. 190.

67. Kenneth M. Kensinger, *"Banisteriopsis* Usage Among the Peruvian Cashinahua." *(In)*: M. J. Harner (ed.), *Hallucinogens and Shamanism;* p. 12n [see note 54].

68. C. Naranjo, "Psychological Aspects of the *Yagé* Experience in an Experimental Setting." *(In)*: M. J. Harner (ed.), *Hallucinogens and Shamanism;* p. 190 [see note 54]. Also, in the Introduction to the above volume, M. J. Harner writes:

> There can be little doubt that the use of the more powerful hallucinogens tends to strongly reinforce a belief in the reality of the supernatural world and in the existence of a disembodied soul or souls. An intriguing possibility is that hallucinogenic experiences may have also played a role in the innovation of such beliefs. This is an important question which clearly deserves comprehensive cross-cultural and inter-disciplinary research *(ibid.,* p. xiv).

69. Janet Siskind, "Visions and Cures among the Sharanahua." *(In)*: M. J. Harner (ed.), *Hallucinogens and Shamanism;* p. 29 [see note 54]. M. J. Harner, Introduction to a section on Cultures Undergoing Westernization. *(In)*: M. J. Harner (ed.), *ibid.*; p. 52.

70. M. J. Harner, Introduction to the section on Primitive World: the Upper Amazon. *(In)*: M. J. Harner (ed.); *Hallucinogens and Shamanism;* p. 6 [see note 54].

71. H. Munn, "The Mushrooms of Language." *(In)*: M. J. Harner (ed.), *Hallucinogens and Shamanism;* p. 92. [see note 54].

72. H. Munn, "The Mushrooms of Language." *(In)*: M. J. Harner (ed.), *Hallucinogens and Shamanism;* p. 122 [see note 54].

73. Claude Lévi-Strauss, "The Effectiveness of Symbols." *(In)*: C. Lévi-Strauss, *Structural Anthropology.* New York: Basic Books, 1963; pp. 198 & 199.

74. M. Eliade, "Shamanism." *(In)*: Vergilius Ferm (ed.), *Ancient Religions.* New York: Citadel Press, 1965; 306–307 (originally published as *Forgotten Religions,* 1950). Also Eliade's *Shamanism: Archaic Techniques of Ecstasy;* pp. 23–32 [see note 3].

75. J. Campbell, *The Masks of God: Primitive Mythology.* Revised edition. New York: Penguin Books, [1969] 1976; p. 253.

Chapter 4—The Psychotropic Universe

1. Michael Ripinsky-Naxon, "Hallucinogens, Shamanism, and the Cultural Process: Symbolic Archaeology and Dialectics," *Anthropos*, Vol. 84 (1989); p. 222.

2. M. Eliade, *The Forge and the Crucible*. 2nd edition. Chicago: University of Chicago Press, 1962 (Phoenix edition, 1978). G. Reichel-Dolmatoff, "Things of Beauty Replete with Meaning— Metals and Crystals in Colombian Indian Cosmology." (In): *Sweat of the Sun. Tears of the Moon: Gold and Emerald Treasures of Colombia*. Los Angeles: Natural History Museum of Los Angeles County, 1981; pp. 18, 20–21.

3. Several individuals observed the shamanistic aspects of goldwork in the New World. See Richard Schultes and Alec Bright, "Ancient Gold Pectorals from Colombia: Mushroom Effigies?" (In): *Sweat of the Sun. Tears of the Moon*; pp. 37–43 [see note 2]. And G. Reichel-Dolmatoff, "Things of Beauty Replete with Meaning—Metals and Crystals in Colombian Indian Cosmology," pp. 17-33 [see note 2]; also his *Goldwork and Shamanism. An Iconographic Study of the Gold Museum*. Bogotá.

4. See Å. Hultkrantz in Louise Bäckman and Åke Hultkrantz, *Studies in Lapp Shamanism*. Stockholm Studies in Comparative Religion, 16. Stockholm: Almqvist & Wiksell International, 1978; p. 12.

5. See the Soviet ethnologist, A, F. Anisimov, "Cosmological Concepts of the Peoples of the North." (In): Henry N. Michael (ed.), *Studies in Siberian Shamanism. Translations from Russian Sources*, 4. Arctic Institute of North America. Toronto: University of Toronto Press, 1963; p. 160.

6. Hence, a soul of a scholar or a hero may subsequently end up in the body of a degenerate or a bandit, and a soul of a good-hearted person in that of an evil incarnate, and so forth. At the end of the world, divine justice awaits all souls, which will be evaluated solely on their merits. The trial determines whether it will be heaven or hell.

7. The mountain Druzes believe that during a time when their mortality rate exceeds the birth rate, the "disembodied" souls "fly off" to the highlands of western China (!?), where they become incarnated into Chinese-Druze babies. It is a belief, commonly held among them, that the latter are meant to arrive, one day, with a helping hand in the Druze conquest of the world. Apparently, no one has ever seen individuals belonging to this ethnic group.

   W. K. Seabrook (*Adventures in Arabia. Amone the Bedouins, Druses, Whirling Dervishes, & Yezidee Devil Worshipers*. New

York: Harcourt, Brace and Co., 1927; pp. 215, 217), a keen observer, visiting the mountain Druzes in the first quarter of this century, offered this apt description: "They seem to me as they have been from the time of the Crusades—unconquered still—the proudest and most hospitable and at the same time the fiercest and most warlike little feudal aristocracy on the face of the earth." Of course, much has changed since the above lines were written, but I can personally bear witness to their profuse hospitality, fierceness, warlike disposition, and a "feudal" structure.

8. W. K. Seabrook, *Adventures in Arabia;* p. 194 [see note 7].
9. Thomas Gregor, *Mehinaku. The Drama of Daily Life in a Brazilian Indian Village.* Chicago: University of Chicago Press, 1977; pp. 333, 349, 325–326.
10. Irving Goldman, *The Cubeo. Indians of the Northwest Amazon.* Illinois Studies in Anthropology, 2. Urbana: University of Illinois Press, 1963; pp. 259–260.
11. Irving Goldman, *The Cubeo;* pp. 262–263, 266 [see note 10].
12. Napoleon A. Chagnon, *Yǫnomamö. The Fierce People.* Case Studies in Cultural Anthropology. New York: Holt, Rinehart, and Winston, 1968; pp. 48–49, 52.
13. G. M. Vasilevich, "Early Concepts about the Universe among the Evenks (Materials)." (*In*): Henry N. Michael (ed.), *Studies in Siberian Shamanism;* p. 68 [see note 5].

The Norse tradition that recounts Odin's offering himself in sacrifice to himself loses, thus, much of its strangeness. It is not much else than a variant of the transculturally encountered myth of transformation. In this particular account, the god Odin, by his own hand, hangs for nine days and nine nights (the recurrent significance of the number 9, or 3 x 3) from the World Tree (*Yggdrasil*), which represents the junction to the Otherworlds. During this transformational process, very much in shamanistic order, he acquires *nine* magical chants.

14. A. F. Anisimov, "Cosmological Concepts of the Peoples of the North"; pp. 165–166, 184–185 [see note 5].
15. A. F. Anisimov, "Cosmological Concepts of the Peoples of the North"; pp. 166–168 [see note 5].
16. G. Reichel-Dolmatoff, *Shamanism and Art of the Eastern Tukanoan Indians. Colombian Northwest Amazon.* Institute of Religious Iconography, State University of Groningen. Leiden: E. J. Brill, 1987; pp. 10–11.
17. G. Reichel-Dolmatoff, *Shamanism and Art of the Eastern Tukanoan Indians;* p. 3 [see note 16].

18. G. Reichel-Dolmatoff, *Shamanism and Art of the Eastern Tukanoan Indians*; pp. 16, 21–22, 24; pls. 35a–b [see note 16].
19. Claudio Naranjo, "The Psychological Aspects of the *Yagé* Experience in an Experimental Setting." *(In)* M. J. Harner (ed.), *Hallucinogens and Shamanism.* London & New York: Oxford University Press, [1973] 1981; pp. 182–183.
20. For example, see A. K. Coomaraswamy, "Symbolism of the Dome," *Indian Historical Quarterly*, Vol. 14 (1938); pp. 1–56. O. J. Brendel, *Symbolism of the Sphere. A Contribution to the History of Earlier Greek Philosophy.* Leiden: E. J. Brill, 1977. Seyyed H. Nasr, *An Introduction to Islamic Cosmological Doctrines. Conceptions of Nature and Methods Used for Its Study by the Ikewān al Safā', al Bīrunī, and Ibn Sīnā.* Cambridge: Harvard University Press, 1964. On the Dome of the Rock, specifically, see the popular, yet encompassing, introduction to the subject by Jerry M. Landay, *et al., Dome of the Rock.* New York: Newsweek, 1972.
21. For an interesting and learned study on this subject see Richard J. Clifford, *The Cosmic Mountain in Canaan and the Old Testament.* Harvard Semitic Monographs, 4. Cambridge, Mass.: Harvard University Press, 1972. For the more vague, yet, intriguing aspect of this question in the ancient Nile Valley, cf. the erudite John A. Wilson, "Egypt." *(In)*: H. and H. A. Frankfort, J. A. Wilson, T. Jacobsen, and W. A. Irwin, *The Intellectual Adventure of Ancient Man. An Essay on Speculative Thought in the Ancient Near East.* Chicago: University of Chicago Press, 1946; pp. 31–61. Also cf. the stimulating Mircea Eliade, *The Sacred and the Profane. The Nature of Religion.* New York: Harcourt, Brace, and Co., 1959; esp. Chapter I.
22. Gérardo Reichel-Dolmatoff, *The Sacred Mountain of Colombia's Kogi Indians.* Iconography of Religions, Vol. 9, part 2. Leiden: E. J. Brill, 1990.
23. G. Reichel-Dolmatoff, "Things of Beauty Replete with Meaning— Metals and Crystals in Colombian Indian Cosmology"; pp. 24–25, 28 [see note 2].
24. Peter T. Furst, "Myth in Art: A Huichol Depicts His Reality," *Los Anseles County Museum of Natural History Quarterly*, Vol. 7, no. 3 (1968–69); pp. 16–17.
25. P. T. Furst, "Myth in Art: A Huichol Depicts His Reality;" p. 20 [see note 24].
26. What exactly Freerk Kamma (*Religious Texts of the Oral Tradition from Western New-Guinea.* Part A: The Origin and Sources of Life. Leiden: E. J. Brill, 1975; pp. 12–14) means by the phrases "shaman-istic practitioners" and the confusing "shamanistic medicine-men"

is not altogether certain. Neither is it clear from his terminology whether he uses these designations to imply a classic or peripheral form of shamanism, nor, for that matter, whether he simply has in mind just ordinary "medicine men," i.e., those limited only to administering cures.

27. F. Kamma, *Religious Texts of the Oral Tradition from Western New-Guinea*; pp. 14–17 [see note 26].

28. N. A. Chagnon, *Yąnomamö*; pp. 44–45, 48 [see note 12].

29. Francis Huxley, *Affable Savages. An Anthropologist among the Urubu Indians of Brazil*. New York: Viking Press, 1957; pp. 212–214, 216.

30. G. Reichel-Dolmatoff, "Some Source Materials on Desana Shamanistic Initiation," *Antropológica*, Vol. 51 (1979); pp. 34–35 [Caracas].

31. A. F. Anisimov, "Cosmological Concepts of the Peoples of the North"; pp. 160–161, 164–165, 167–168 [see note 5]. Also cf. G. M. Vasilevich, "Early Concepts about the Universe among the Evenks (Materlals)"; p. 48 [see note 13].

32. E.g., among the Tungus, Buryat, Dayak, Pomo, Arawakan, Carib. Åke Hultkrantz in L. Bäckman and Å. Hultkrantz, *Studies in Lapp Shamanism*; pp. 12–13, 14 [see note 4]. M. Eliade, *Shamanism: Archaic Techniques of Ecstasy*. Bollingen Series, 76. New York: Pantheon Books, 1964; pp. 265 f, Cf. also the Old Testamement, for a description of a celestial ladder in Jacob's visionary dream.

33. Y. D. Profyeva, "The Costume of an Enets Shaman." [*In*]: Henry N. Michael (ed.), *Studies in Siberian Shamanism*; p. 150 [see note 5].

34. Åke Hultkrantz in L. Bäckman and Å. Hultkrantz, *Studies in Lapp Shamanism*; p. 14 [see note 4].

35. A. F. Anisimov, "Cosmological Concepts of the Peoples of the North"; pp. 202 ff. and his "The Shaman's Tent of the Evenks and the Origin of the Shamanistic Rite"; pp. 86 ff., 98, 112 [see note 5 for both]. V. Diószegi, "The Origin of the Evenki Shamanistic Instruments (Stick, Knout) of Transbaikalia," *Acta Ethnographica*, Vol. 17, nos. 3–4 (1968); pp. 298 f.

36. On the cosmological significance of the numbers 7 and 9, see Wilhelm Schmidt, *Der Ursprung der Gottesidee. Eine historisch-kritische und positive Studie*. 12 vols. Münster in Westfalia: Aschendorff, 1912–1955; Vol. 9, pp. 91 ff., 423, etc. Also Uno Harva, *Die religiösen Vorstellungen der altaischen Völker*. Folklore Fellows Communications, 52, 125. Helsinki: Academia Scientiarum Fennica, 1938; pp. 51 f., etc.

37. The hexagonal star, composed of two inverted triangles and sometimes referred to as the Star of David or the Star of Solomon,

is most likely of ancient Mesopotamian origins. It found its way to the West, along with the doctrines of the Kabbalah.

38. This can be inferred from, among others, the yarn paintings, nearikas, made by Ramón Medina Silva, alluding to "five" as being the number of years required for the souls to journey in the Lowerworld, and for the shaman's soul to transform into a rock crystal. For the descriptions and color reproductions, see P. T. Furst, "Myth in Art: A Huichol Depicts His Reality"; pp. 19, 20 [see note 24].

39. Lehtisalo, *Entwurf einer Mythologie der Jurak-Samojeden.* Mémoires de la Société Finno-Ougrienne. Helsinki, 1924; p. 67, 77 ff., 102, 147.

40. V. M. Mikhailowski, "Shamanism in Siberia and European Russia: Being the Second Part of *Shamanstvo*," *Journal of the Royal Anthropological Institute,* Vol. 24 (1894); p. 84. [Trans. from Russian].

41. Kai. Donner, *La Sibérie. La Vie en Sibérie, les temps anciens.* Paris, 1946; p. 223.

42. Toivo Immanuel Itkonen, *Heidnische Religion und späterer Aberglaube bei den finnischen Lappen.* Mémoires de la Société Finno-Ougrienne, 87. Helsinki, 1946; pp. 149, 159.

43. A. V. Anokhin, *Materialy po shamanstvu u altaitsev, sobranniye vo vremia puteshestvy po Altayu v 1910–1912 gg. po porucheniyu Russkovo Komiteta dla Izuchenia Srednei i Vostochnei Asii.* [*Materials on Shamanism among the Altaic People, Collected during...1910–1912...*]. Leningrad, 1924; p. 9.

44. On the symbolism of the menorah, cf. L. Yarden, *The Tree of Light. A Study of the Menorah—The Seven Branched Lampstand.* Ithaca, New York: Cornell University Press, 1971.

45. Among the Western Tukanoan shamans, quartz crystal is the most precious possession, the most important power object, engulfed in rich lore. Crystals, with special significance attached to them, are inherited from father to son, and the shamans store these prized items in special woven boxes [G. Reichel-Dolmatoff, "Desana Shaman's Rock Crystals and the Hexagonal Universe," *Journal of Latin American Lore,* Vol. 5, no. 1 (1979); pp. 17–18].

46. Aldous Huxley, *Heaven and Hell.* New York: Harper Colophon Books, 1963; p. 103 (bound together with *The Doors of Perception*).

47. See, G. Reichel-Dolmatoff, "Things of Beauty Replete with Meaning—Metals and Crystals in Colombian Indian Cosmology"; p. 23 [see note 2].

48. A. Huxley, *Heaven and Hell*; pp. 96, 103 [see note 46].

49. A. Huxley, *Heaven and Hell*; pp. 96, 97, 98 [see note 46].

50. Jerome Meyer Levi, "*Wii'ipay*: The Living Rocks—Ethnographic Notes on Crystal Magic among Some California Yumans," *Journal of California Anthropology*, Vol. 5, no. 1 (1978); pp. 42, 49.
51. Michael Harner, *The Way of the Shaman*. New York: Bantam Books, 1982; p. 140.
52. Irving Goldman, *The Cubeo*; p. 264 [see note 10].
53. M. Harner, *The Way of the Shaman*; pp. 139-140 [see note 51].
54. P. T. Furst, "Myth in Art: A Huichol Depicts His Reality"; pp. 17, 19 [see note 24].
55. G. Reichel-Dolmatoff, "Desana Shaman's Rock Crystals and the Hexagonal Universe;" pp. 118–119 [see note 45]. And his "Things of Beauty Replete with Meaning—Metals and Crystals in Colombian Indian Cosmology"; pp. 23-24 [see note 2].
56. G. Reichel-Dolmatoff, "Desana Shaman's Rock Crystals and the Hexagonal Universe"; p. 119 [see note 45]. And his "Things of Beauty Replete with Meaning—Metals and Crystals in Colombian Indian Cosmology"; p. 29 [see note 2].
57. G. Reichel-Dolmatoff, "Desana Shaman's Rock Crystals and the Hexagonal Universe;" pp. 119–120, 123 [see note 45].
58. G. Reichel-Dolmatoff, "Things of Beauty Replete with Meaning—Metals and Crystals in Colombian Indian Cosmology"; p. 28 [see note 2].
59. G. Reichel-Dolmatoff, "Desana Shaman's Rock Crystals and the Hexagonal Universe"; p. 127 [see note 45].
60. G. Reichel-Dolmatoff, "Some Source Materials on Desana Shamanistic Initiation"; pp. 51–52, especially, p. 51 for the quotation [see note 30].
61. W. B. Seabrook, *Adventures in Arabia*; p. 256 [see note 7].
62. K. Rasmussen, *The Intellectual Culture of the Iglulik Eskimos*. Report of the Fifth Thule Expedition, 1921–1924, Vol. 7, no. 1. Copenhagen: Glydendalske Boghandel, Nordisk-Forlag, 1929.

Chapter 5—The Ritual Drug Complex

1. G. Reichel-Dolmatoff, "The Cultural Context of an Aboriginal Hallucinogen: *Banisteriopsis Caapi*." (*In*): Peter T. Furst (ed.). *Flesh of the Gods. The Ritual Use of Hallucinogens*. New York: Praeger, 1972; p. 104.
2. M. J. Harner, Preface to *Hallucinogens and Shamanism*, edited by M. J. Harner. London & New York: Oxford University Press, [1973] 1981; p. vii.

3. M. Eliade, *Shamanism: Archaic Techniques of Ecstasy.* Bollingen Series, 76. New York: Pantheon Books, 1964; p. 401.

4. For a discussion of the adaptive mechanism of kinship system, from which the passage below is quoted, see Michael Ripinsky, "Middle Eastern Kinship as an Expression of a Culture-Environment System," *The Muslim World*, Vol. 58, no. 3 (1968); pp. 225–241.

> A system can be considered functionally adapted if it is capable of yielding an optimum result, for a specific purpose, under a given set of conditions. In this respect, if viewed teleologically, kinship system is adaptive, and it is this very property which allows it a change of attitude in the relations with its cultural, social, and physical environments. (p. 225).

5. G. Reichel-Dolmatoff, *Shamanism and Art of the Eastern Tukanoan Indians. Colombian Northwest Amazon.* Institute of Religious Iconography, State University of Groningen. Leiden: E. J. Brill, 1987; pp. 5 & 7. Also his "Some Source Materials on Desana Shamanistic Initiation," *Antropologica*, Vol. 51 (1979); p. 29 [Caracas].

6. G. Reichel-Dolmatoff, *Shamanism and Art of the Eastern Tukanoan Indians;* pp. 11, 13, 16, 21 [see note 5].

7. Michael J. Harner, *The Jívaro. People of the Sacred Waterfall.* Garden City, New York: Doubleday, Natural History Press, 1972; p. 134.

8. M. J. Harner, *The Jívaro;* pp. 135–136 [see note 7].

9. M. J. Harner, *The Jívaro;* pp. 136–137 [see note 7].

10. M. J. Harner, *The Jívaro;* p. 153 [see note 7].

11. G. Reichel-Dolmatoff, "Some Source Materials on Desana Shamanistic Initiation;" pp. 50–51, 53 [see note 5].

12. M. Ripinsky-Naxon, "Hallucinogens, Shamanism, and the Cultural Process," *Anthropos*, Vol. 84 (1989); p. 221.

13. In initiatory experiences, the neophytes are frequently thought of as having died, or as souls of the dead.

14. G. Reichel-Dolmatoff, "Some Source Materials on Desana Shamanistic Initiation"; pp. 32, 33 [see note 5]. For a fuller discussion of the *Virola* snuff see Reichel-Dolmatoff, *The Shaman and the Jaguar. A Study of Narcotic Drugs among the Indians of Colombia.* Philadelphia: Temple University Press, 1975; pp. 20ff. Also Richard Schultes, "A New Narcotic Snuff from the Northwest Amazon," *Harvard University Botanical Museum Leaflets*, Vol. 16, no. 9 (1954); pp. 248–250.

15. Valery Havard, "Food Plants of the North American Indians," *Bulletin of Torrey Botanical Club*, Vol. 22, no. 3 (1895); and "Plant Foods of the North American Indians," *Bulletin of Torrey Botanical Club*, Vol. 23, no. 2 (1896) [Lancaster, Penn].

16. David P. Barrows, *The Ethno-Botany of the Coahuilla Indians of Southern California*. Chicago: University of Chicago Press, 1900; pp. 75, 80 (Reprinted, with additional contributions and a Coahuilla Bibliography, by the Malki Museum Press, Morongo Indian Reservation, Banning, California, [1967] 1977).

17. Lowell J. Bean and Katherine Siva Saubel, *Temalpakh (from the Earth). Cahuilla Indian Knowledge and Usage of Plants*. Banning, Calif.: Malki Museum Press, Morongo Indian Reservation, 1972; pp. 60–62. Katherine Saubel is a native Cahuilla Indian, specializing in the traditional uses and ceremonial plant lore of her people. Lowell Bean is an anthropologist, with strong interests in native American ethnobotany.

18. William D. Strong, *Aboriginal Society in Southern California*. University of California Publications in American Archaeology and Ethnology, Vol. 26. Berkeley: University of California, 1929; pp. 173 ff.

19. Alfred L. Kroeber, *Handbook of the Indians of California*. Bulletin of the Bureau of American Ethnology, 78. Washington, D.C.: Smithsonian Institution, 1925; pp. 669–672.

20. G. Reichel-Dolmatoff, *Shamanism and Art of the Eastern Tukanoan Indians*; pp. 13–14 [see note 5].

21. R. Gordon Wasson, "The Divine Mushroom of Immortality." (*In*): P. T. Furst (ed.), *Flesh of the Gods*; pp. 197–198 [see note 1].

22. R. G. Wasson, "The Divine Mushroom of Immortality." (*In*): P. T. Furst (ed.), *Flesh of the Gods*; p. 196 [see note 1]. For an extraordinary account of a healing ceremony under the influence of the sacred psilocybin mushroom, see R. G. Wasson, *et al.*, *Maria Sabina and her Mazatec Mushroom Valeda*. New York: Harcourt Brace Jovanovich, 1975. This publication includes separate musical scores and four audio cassettes.

23. Roberto Escalante, "Ethnomycological Data of the Matlatzincas." Paper presented at the 72nd Annual Meeting of the American Anthropological Association, New Orleans, 1973.

24. Peter T. Furst, *Hallucinogens and Culture*. Novato, Calif.: Chandler & Sharp, [1976] 1982; p. 85.

25. Probably the most outstanding synthesis written on the peyote ceremonial is to be found in Weston La Barre, *The Peyote Cult* (5th ed., enlarged. Norman: University of Oklahoma Press, 1989). This important work is amended with extensive, additional bibliog-

raphies, and discussions of peyote studies from 1941 to 1988, and includes references to other psychotropic plants, as well. For a documentary treatment, see O. C. Stewart, *Peyote Religion. A History.* Norman: University of Oklahoma Press, 1987. One of the best ethnographic studies of peyotism consists of Lumholtz, *Unknown Mexico* (2 vols. New York, 1902).

26. P. T. Furst, *Hallucinogens and Culture;* p. 113 [see note 24].
27. Carl Lumholtz, *Unknown Mexico,* Vol. 2; pp. 127, 129–135 [see note 25].
28. P. T. Furst, *Hallucinogens and Culture;* pp. 113, 114, 116–117 [see note 24]. Weston La Barre, *The Peyote Cult;* pp. 32–33 [see note 25].
29. Johannes Wilbert, *Tobacco and Shamanism in South America.* New Haven, Conn.: Yale University Press, 1987; pp. 143, 172.
30. Thomas Gregor, *Mehinaku. The Drama of Daily Life in a Brazilian Indian Village.* Chicago: University of Chicago Press, 1977; p. 334.
31. V. N. Basilov, "Chosen by the Spirits." (*In*): Marjorie Mandelstam Balzer (ed.), *Shamanism: Soviet Studies of Traditional Religion in Siberia and Central Asia.* Armonk, N.Y.: M. E. Sharpe, 1990; pp. 3–48.
32. Those largely responsible for our modern understanding of psychotropic flora are the eminent Richard E. Schultes and Albert Hofmann. See, for example, their invaluable, joint publications, *The Botany and Chemistry of Hallucinogens.* 2nd edition. Springfield, Ill.: Charles C. Thomas, 1979; and *Plants of the Gods: Origins of Hallucinogenic Use.* New York: McGraw-Hill, 1980.
33. M. Ripinsky-Naxon, "Hallucinogens, Shamanism, and the Cultural Process"; p. 221 [see note 12].
34. A. H. Der Marderosian, H. V. Pinkley, and M. F. Dobbins IV, "Native Use and Occurrence of N,N-dimethyltryptamine in the Leaves of *Banisteriopsis rusbyana," American Journal of Pharmacy,* Vol. 140 (1968); pp. 137–147.
35. Claudio Naranjo, *The Healing Journey. New Approaches to Consciousness.* New York: Pantheon Books, 1973; p. 125.
36. Frank Barron, Murray E. Jarvik, and Sterling Bunnell, Jr., "The Hallucinogenic Drugs," *Scientific American,* Vol. 210, no. 4 (1965); pp. 29 ff.
37. Barry L. Jacobs, "How Hallucinogenic Drugs Work," *American Scientist,* Vol. 75 (July-August, 1987); pp. 387–390.
38. Torald Sollmann, *A Manual of Pharmacology and Its Applications to Therapeutics and Toxicology.* 8th edition. Philadelphia & London: W. B. Saunders, 1957; pp. 381, 394.
39. See, for example, Michael J. Harner, "The Role of Hallucinogenic Plants in European Witchtcraft." (*In*): M. J. Harner (ed.), *Hallucinogens and Shamanism* [see note 2].

40. Richard E. Schultes, "An Overview of Hallucinogens in the Western Hemisphere." (*In*): P. T. Furst (ed.), *Flesh of the Gods*; pp. 15 ff. [see note 1].

41. Albert Hofmann, *Die Erforschung der Mexikanischen Zauberpilze und das Problem ihrer Wirkstoffe*. Basel: Basler Stadtbuch, 1964; pp. 141–156.

42. Conrad H. Eugster, "Isolation, Structure, and Syntheses of Central-active Compounds from *Amanita muscaria* (L. ex Fr.) Hooker." (*In*): Daniel H. Efron (ed.), *Ethnopharmacologic Search for Psychoactive Drugs*. U.S. Public Health Service Publication, No. 1645. Washington, D.C.: U.S. Government Printing Office, 1967; pp. 416–418, 441. Peter G. Waser, "The Pharmacology of *Amanita muscaria*." (*In*): D. H. Efron (ed.) [see above]; pp. 419–439, 441. See also his "Pharmakologische Wirkungsspektren von Halluzinogenen," *Bull. Schweiz. Akad. Med. Wiss.*, Vol. 27 (1971); pp. 39–57.

43. R. Gordon Wasson, "Fly Agaric and Man." (*In*): D. H. Efron (ed), *Ethnopharmacologic Search for Psychoactive Drugs*; pp. 405–414 [see note 42].

44. R. G. Wasson, *Soma and the Fly-Agaric: Mr. Wasson's Rejoinder to Professor Brough*. Cambridge, Mass.: Botanical Museum of Harvard University, 1972; p. 12. For C. Eugster's findings, see main text, *supra*, and note 42, above.

45. J. Wilbert, *Tobacco and Shamanism in South America*; p. 148 [see note 29]. On the ritual use of tobacco among the ancient Maya, see Francis Robicsek, *The Smoking Gods. Tobacco in Maya Art, History, and Religion*. Norman: University of Oklahoma Press, 1978. On the introduction of tobacco, as a new culture trait, into Siberian shamanism, cf. V. N. Basilov, "Chosen by the Spirits." (*In*): Marjorie Mandelstam Balzer (ed.), *Shamanism: Soviet Studies of Traditional Religion in Siberia and Central Asia*. Armonk, N.Y.: M. E. Sharpe, 1990; pp. 3–48.

46. This symptom indicates an affinity with tobacco amblyopia.

47. J. Wilbert, *Tobacco and Shamanism in South America*; pp. 133–148 [see note 29].

48. Gerald Oster, "Phosphenes," *Scientific American*, Vol. 222, no. 2 (1970); p. 83, 84, 85. See also Klaus F. Wellmann, "Rock Art, Shamans, Phosphenes, and Hallucinogens in North America," *Bollettino del Centro Camuno di Studi Preistorici*, Vol. 18 (1981); p. 99 [Capo di Ponte].

49. M. Knoll and J. Kugler, "Subjective Light Pattern Spectroscopy in the Encephalographic Frequency Range," *Nature*, Vol. 184 (1959); pp. 1823–1824. G. Oster, "Phosphenes"; p. 83; also K. Wellmann,

"Rock Art, Shamans, Phosphenes, and Hallucinogens in North America"; pp. 99 ff. [see note 48 for the last two].

50. G. Reichel-Dolmatoff, "Some Source Materials on Desana Shamanistic Initiation"; pp. 42, 54 [see note 5].

51. G. Reichel-Dolmatoff, *Shamanism and Art of the Eastern Tukanoan Indians*; p. 14 [see note 5].

52. G. Reichel-Dolmatoff, *Shamanism and Art of the Eastern Tukanoan Indians*; pp. 15, 17, 18 [see note 5].

53. Rhoda Kellogg, M. Knoll, and J. Kugler, "Form-Similarity between Phosphenes of Adults and Pre-School Children's Scribblings," *Nature*, Vol. 208 (1965); pp. 1129–1130. Also cf. G. Oster, "Phosphenes"; pp. 82–87 [see note 48].

54. G. Reichel-Dolmatoff, "The Cultural Context of an Aboriginal Hallucinogen: *Banisteriopsis caapi*." (*In*): P. T. Furst (ed.), *Flesh of the Gods*; pp. 84–113 [see note 1].

55. Guy Murchie, *The Seven Mysteries of Life. An Exploration into Science and Philosophy.* Boston: Houghton Mifflin Co., 1981; p. 237.

Chapter 6—The Botanic Experience

1. This is not, by any means, an implication that narcotic substances are advisable to use, but only an address to the specialists for more concerted efforts in this area of research.

2. Giorgio Samorini, "Etnomicologia nell'arte rupestre Sahariana," *B.C. Notizie*, Vol. 6, no. 2 (April, 1989); p. 18. (Notiziario del Centro Camuno di Studi Preistorici). For photographs see also Jean-Dominique Lajoux, *Tassili n'Ajjer. Art rupestre du Sahara préhistorique.* Paris: Editions du Chêne, 1977; pp. 56 and 59. I am greatly indebted to G. Samorini for his selfless generosity in sharing with me much valuable information on this topic, as well as his photographic and written materials, during my 1989 visit to the Camunian Center in the Italian Alps, and afterwards through copious personal correspondence.

    On the climatic and chronological notes on the African Sahara of the post-Pleistocene (the "Round Head") period, characterized by a microlithic industry of the Mesolithic hunters, who developed finer and more skillful techniques of stone tool manufacture, see Michael Ripinsky, "The Camel in Dynastic Egypt," *Journal of Egyptian Archaeology*, Vol. 71 (1985); p. 135.

3. G. Samorini, "Etnomicologia nell'arte rupestre Sahariana"; p. 20 [see note 2]. For a very recent discussion, not available to me in time,

see Samorini, "The Oldest Representations of Hallucinogenic Mushrooms in the World (Sahara Desert, 9000–7000 B.P.)," *Integration*, Nos. 2–3 (1992); pp. 69–78 [Germany].

4. Emmanuel Anati, *Origini dell'Arte e della Concettualità*. Milano. Jaca Book, 1989; pp. 187 and 188, fig. 126. I wish to express my gratitude to Professor and Mrs. Anati for the gracious hospitality extended to us at the Camunian Center for Prehistoric Studies, in 1989.

5. Mauro S. Hernández-Pérez, "Vorbericht über die Erforschung der Felsbindkunst in der Provinz Alicante," *Madrider Mitteilungen*, Vol 24 (1983); pp. 35, fig. 1; and p. 36.

6. A. Beltrán, "L'Art Prehistorique Espagnol: Nouveaux Horizons et Problemes. Etat de la question," *Bollettino del Centro Camuno di Studi Preistorici*, Vol. 24 (1988); p. 34, fig. 25.

7. M. S. Hernández-Pérez; p. 36, and fig. 2 on p. 37 [see note 5].

8. S. Gitti, G. Samorini, *et al.*, "Contributo alla Conoscenza della Micoflora Psicotropa del Territorio Bresciano," *Natura Bresciana*, Vol. 20; p. 125. (Ann. Mus. Civ. Sc. Nat., Brescia).

9. The Indo-European characteristics in Monte Bego rock art were recognized by Roland Dufrenne, "Intérpretation des gravures rupestres de la Vallée des Merveilles à la lumière de la tradition védique," *Bollettino del Centro Camuno di Studi Preistorici*, Vol. 22 (1985); pp. 110–116.

Giorgio Samorini (personal communication) conjectures the occurrence of *Amanita muscaria* in Monte Bego art motifs and intimates a corollary for this region between the presence of the fly-agaric mushroom and the divinity, Soma, of the Vedas.

Using the hypothesis of the Indo-European fonts intrinsic in the designs ornamenting the menhirs of Valcamonica and Valtellina, as suggested by Anati [*Arte preistorici in Valtellina*. Archivi, Vol. 1. Capo di Ponte: Centro Camuno di Studi Preistorici, 1968; pp. 25 ff.; "Origine e significato storico-religioso delle statue-stele," *Bollettino del Centro Camuno di Studi Preistorici*, Vol. 16 (1977); p. 51; and *Le statue-stele della Lunigiana*. Milano: Jaca Book, 1981; p. 69]. Mario Piantelli draws a comparison between the decorations on these menhirs and the Vedic concepts encountered in the socio-religious contexts of the *Puruṣasūkta* (e.g., *Rigveda*, 10.90). For example, the eighteenth century, multi-brachiated figures, depicting the cosmic aspects of Krishna and Vishnu-Krishna in the miniature painting style from the Rajastan district, are inferred by Piantelli ["L'Interpretazione di Uno Schema Iconografico Complesso Rinvenibile nelle Stele Monumentali Camune e Valtellinesi: Appunti per un'Ipotesi," *Bollettino del Centro Camuno di Studi Preistorici*, Vol. 20 (1983); pp. 33–54] to represent a phenomenological continuity with certain design patterns shown on the Valcamonica and Valtellina stelae of the third millennium B.C., such as the characteristic large figures with many spider-like arms (p. 37). However, his comparisons of universal archetypal motifs, such as concentric circles and spirals, with the much later Indian esoteric schemata of the cosmic being (pp. 40–41) represent feeble attempts that distort otherwise interesting, if controversial, ethnohistorical speculations.

Half a century earlier, Dorothea Chaplin (*Matter, Myth and Spirit*. London: Simpkin, Marshall, Ltd., 1935) had proposed a correlation between the mythologems encountered in the ancient religions of India and that of another Indo-European culture, the Celts.

10. See, for example, G. Samorini, "Sulla presenza di funghi e piante allucinogene in Valcamonica," *Bollettino del Centro Camuno di Studi Preistorici*, Vol. 24 (1988); pp. 132–136.

11. G. Samorini, personal communication, 17 July, 1989.

12. E. Süss, *Le Incisioni Rupestri della Valcamonica*. Cologno Monzese: Arti Grafiche Torri, 1985; pp. xviii–xix, fig. 2.

13. Cf. Ausilio Priuli, *Incisioni Rupestri nelle Alpi*. Ivrea (Italy): Priuli & Verlucca, 1983; fig. 9. Also cf. E. Anati, *Capo di Ponte*. Studi Camuni, 1. Capo di Ponte (Brescia): Centro Camuno di Studi Preistorici, 1987; p. 15, fig. 8; and E. Süss, *Le Incisioni Rupestri della Valcamonica*; p. 39, fig. 54 [see note 12].

14. Not only the term "mycology," but also the word "fungus" is derived from a Greek cognate. The first, as is apparent, comes from a word denoting "mushroom"; the second from the word *sphonggos*, which was generally applied to the mycoflora, owing to the similarity in appearance shared by sponges and a botanic group, such as the Ascomycetes.

15. In the Museum of Argos, a town which had given its name to the Argive Plain and was made the capital of Peloponnese by the Romans, I discovered, in 1989, two small ceramic mushrooms (case 10, No. c.503), apparently found in that region, albeit undocumented. They appear to be from the Mycenaean (Helladic) period. During the same time, in the Museum of Nauplion, also in the Peloponnese, I came across four ceramic mushrooms and two vessels decorated with opium pods. Although the Nauplion items were uncatalogued and I could obtain no information on their provenance, I suspect them to date to the same period as the objects in the Argos Museum, exept that the pottery vessels with pods decorations, may come from the latter part of that era.

16. Cf. Bogdan Rutkowski, "Minoan Sacred Emblems." (In): *Antichità Cretesi*. Studi in Onore di Doro Levi. 2 vols. Catania: Instituto di Archeologia, Università di Catania, 1977–78; Vol. 1. Although Rutkowski makes no such inference in his article, nonetheless, Fig. 6-b resembles easily a hallucinogenic mushroom; Fig. 6-c can be a flatened mushroom or, perhaps, a flatened poppy flower; Fig. 6-d seems to be a poppy or an opium pod rising, symbolically, between the horns of a bull.

17. National Archaeological Museum in Athens, Inv. No. 484.

18. Michael Ripinsky-Naxon, "Hallucinogens, Shamanism, and the Cultural Process: Symbolic Archaeology and Dialectics," *Anthropos*, Vol. 84 (1989); p. 221.

19. R. Gordon Wasson, "The Wasson Road to Eleusis." (In): R. G. Wasson, A. Hofmann, and C. A. P. Ruck, *The Road to Eleusis. Unveiling the Secret of the Mysteries*. Chapter One. New York: Harcourt Brace Jovanovich, 1978; p. 21. Also cf. R. G. Wasson, S. Kramrisch, J. Ott, and C. A. P. Ruck, *Persephone's Quest. Entheogens and the Origins of Religion*. New Haven: Yale University Press, 1986.

20. Reid W. Kaplan, "The Sacred Mushroom in Scandinavia," *Man*, Vol. 10, no. 1 (1975); pp. 72–79.

21. J. P. Taavitsainen, "Recent Rock Painting Finds in Finland," *Bollettino del Centro Camuno di Studi Preistorici*, Vol. 16 (1977); pp. 152–153.

22. The Hunnic "mushroom" finds from: (1) Rumania include: a cauldron fished out from the Desa Lake in the Oltenia region; a fragment discovered in the mud of Lake Hotărani, also Oltenia region; another smaller fragment from the same region; and still another fragment unearthed in the eastern coast of Lake Motiştea in Boşneagu, district Calărăşi. (2) The Hungarian finds comprise: a cauldron found at the foot of a burial mound in Törtel, county Pest; another cauldron pulled out of a peat bog at Kurdcsibrák, in the Kapos River valley, county Tolna; and a third one from Bántapuszta, near Várpalota, county Veszprém. (3) The relic from Czechoslovakia consists of a cauldron bronze handle, like the others, decorated with mushrooms, and comes from Benešov (Bennisch), near Opava. (4) The Soviet Union yielded, among others, a cauldron from Shestachi, Moldavian SSR; another cauldron from Ivanovka, gubernie Ekaterinoslav; a fragment, similar to those mentioned above, from Narindzhan-baba, Kara-Kalpak ASSR.

On the whole, the Huns were not very capable metal workers, and their castings of large bronze vessels were, generally, products of inferior quality.

23. E. I. Spasskaia, *"Mednye kotly rannikh kochevnikov Kazakhstana i Kirgizii"* ["Cauldrons of Early Nomads in Kazakhstan and Kirghizia"], *Uchenie Zapiski Alma-Atinskogo Gosudarstvennogo Pedagogicheskogo Instituta,* 11 (1956); pp. 166–167 [Alma Ata].

24. Otto J. Maenchen-Helfen, *The World of the Huns. Studies in Their History and Culture.* Berkeley: University of California Press, 1973; pp. 329–330. See also Joachim Werner, "Beiträge zur Archäologie des Attila-Reiches," *Abhandlungen der Bayerischen Akademie der Wissenschaften* (Philosophisch-historische Klasse), N.F., Vol. 4:38:a–b (1956); p. 59 [Munich], who for purely stylistic reasons, thus different from the sacred character ascribed by Maenchen-Helfen, had identified the handle designs as mushrooms.

25. László, *Acta Archaeologica Hungarica,* Vol. 34 (1955); pp. 89, 249–252.

26. *Jordanis Romana et Getica,* edited by Th. Mommsen. Berlin, 1882; p. 162. (Quoted in O. J. Maenchen-Helfen, *The World of the Huns;* p. 268 [see note 24]). On haruspices in Central Asia cf. C. R. Bawden, "On the Practice of Scapulimancy among the Mongols," *Central Asiatic Journal,* Vol. 4 (1958).

27. O. J. Maenchen-Helfen, *The World of the Huns;* p. 269 [see note 24].

28. Adam Kamieński Dłużyk, *"Dyarusz więzienia moskiewskiego, miast i miejsc."* ("A Diary of Muskovite Captivity, Towns and Places"). (*In*): Rev. A. Maryanski (*ed.*), *Warta.* Poznań [Posen], 1874; pp. 378–388, specifically p. 382. There seems to have been no contemporary edition of the Diary, which, after more than two hundred years, was included in a collection of articles edited by a Polish clergyman.

29. R. Gordon Wasson, *Soma: Divine Mushroom of Immortality.* New York: Harcourt Brace Jovanovich, 1969; p. 11.

30. L. G. Czigány, "The Use of Hallucinogens and the Shamanistic Tradition of the Finno-Ugrian People," *Slavonic and East European Review,* Vol. 58, no. 2 (1980); p. 216.

31. J. Balázs, "A magyar samán reülete" [in Hungarian, with German summary], *Ethnographica,* Vol. 65, nos. 3–4 (1954); pp. 416–440. Reprinted in German as "Über die Ekstase des ungarischen Schamanen." (*In*): Vilmos Diószegi (*ed.*), *Glaubenswelt und Foklore der Sibirischen Völker.* Budapest, 1963; pp. 57–83. (See also the English version entitled *Popular Beliefs and Folklore Tradition in Siberia.* Trans. from Hungarian. Uralic and Altaic Series, 57. Bloomington: Indiana University/The Hague: Mouton, 1968).

32. R. G. Wasson, *Soma: Divine Mushroom of Immortality;* p. 35 [see note 29].

In 1398, Bartholomaeus Anglicus had used the phrase "frogge stole," in his *De Proprietatibus Rerum*, to describe the mushroom, and in 1526, the name "tode stole" appeared in *The Grete Herball*, in reference to any fungus of the larger variety. In England of Shakespeare's days, it was believed that toads were poisonous, allegedly establishiqg a correlation between "toad-stool" (the fungus) and "toad" (the amphibian). A more recent analysis of the fly-agaric, was believed, albeit erroneously, to disclose the presence of bufotenin, a psychoactive alkaloid present in the skins of certain psychotropic frogs of the *Bufo* spp.

33.   The varieties of forms and smells generated by mushrooms—some of which can grow as much as six inches an hour—gave rise to a rich anthropomorphic name-lore. For instance, the "earth-star," *Geaster fornicatus* invokes precisely such an image; while a semi-sacred mushroom found in New Guinea grows in the shape and size of a phallus, covered by a reflexed indusium with the appearance of a foreskin and, in some situations, growing a coat of slime over the cap. Its countenance is poignantly captured by the name, *Phallus indusiata*. In Bordeaux, members of a new religious order, calling themselves "Our Lady of the Tears," battered the Abbé almost to death in their belief that he had been responsible for the malicious spread of fungi "of obscene shapes which emitted such appalling odors. . ." in the garden of the founder of the sect. The mushroom for which the Abbé was attacked is known as *Phallus impudicus*.

34.   Since the appearance of R. G. Wasson's *Soma: Divine Mushroom of Immortality*, different writers have published a divergence of postulates and hypotheses, some new and others not, concerning the identification of the Vedic *Soma* and the Avestan *Haoma*. In the main, they try to disagree with Wasson's conclusions, but fail to do so convincingly. Some are unsuccessful in properly accounting for, while others ignore completely, the significance of the psycho-tropic urine—something that rightly is very fundamental to a segment of Wasson's theory. In fact, we are presented with inapt research and forced reasoning by a few who thrive on controversy rather than profoundness. For the more important examples, see: G. L. Windfuhr, "Haoma/Soma: The Plant," *Acta Iranica*, Vol. 25 (1985); pp. 699–726, where the author naively equates Soma with *Panax gingseng*. See also David S. Flattery and Martin Schwartz, *Haoma and Harmaline. The Botanical Identity of the Indo-Iranian Sacred Hallucinogen "Soma" and Its Legacy in Religion, Language, and Middle Eastern Folklore.* Berkeley: University of California Press, 1989; who identify Haoma (?) with the plant *Peganum harmala*.

35. M. Eliade, *Shamanism. Archaic Techniques of Ecstasy.* Bollingen Series, 76. New York: Pantheon Books, 1964; p. 401.
36. Although very close to Italy, Monte Bego is within the borders of France. It displays, however, stronger links, both past and present, with the "Alpine cultures" than with those of Gaul or France. Prior to First World War, this area was part of Italy.
37. R. Dufrenne, "Interprétation des gravures rupestres de la Vallée des Merveilles à la lumière de la tradition védique"; p. 110–116 [see note 9].
38. R. G. Wasson, *Soma: Divine Mushroom of Immortality*; p. 10 [see note 29].
39. To connect some of the northern Greek populations, e.g., the Thracians, with the Indo-Aryans would make for an attractive, if speculative, hypothesis.
40. The Vedic text: "ruvati bhimo vrsabhas tavisyaya srnge sisano harini vicaksanah a yonim somah sukrtam ni sidati gavyayi tvag bhavati nirnig avyayi" (*Rigveda*, 9.70.7).
41. R. G. Wasson, *Soma: Divine Mushroom of Immortality*; p. 19 [see note 29].
42. R. C. Zaehner, *Mysticism: Sacred and Profane. An Inquiry into some Varieties of Praeternatural Experience.* New York: Oxford University Press (Galaxy Book), 1961; p. xii.
43. Richard E. Schultes, "An Overview of Hallucinogens in the Western Hemisphere." (*In*): Peter T. Furst (ed.), *Flesh of the Gods: The Ritual Use Hallucinogens.* New York: Praeger, 1972; pp. 3–54.
44. J. M. Adovasio and G. S. Fry, "Prehistoric Psychotropic Drug Use in Northeastern Mexico and Trans-Pecos Texas," *Economic Botany*, Vol. 30, no. 1 (1976).
45. P. T. Furst, "West Mexican Art: Secular or Sacred?" (*In*): *The Iconography of Middle American Sculpture.* New York: The Metropolitan Museum of Art, 1973; pp. 105, 120, 121; figs. 3, 18.
46. P. T. Furst, *Hallucinogens and Culture.* Novato, Calif.: Chandler & Sharp, [1976] 1982; p. 9.
47. P. T. Furst, "West Mexican Art: Secular or Sacred?" (*In*): *The Iconography of Middle American Sculpture*; p. 123; figs. 19–21 [see note 45].
48. Dr. Doris Heyden, personal communication, March, 1988, to whom I am grateful for exchanging information, as well as for her thoughtfulness in providing me with a personally typed list of some of the ethnopharmacologically important plants in pre-hispanic Mexico, during our meeting at Universidad Nacional Autonoma de Mexico, D.F., on the occasion of the 11th Annual Ethnobiology Conference.

49. P. T. Furst, *Hallucinogens and Culture*; pp. 134–135 [see note 46].
50. Carl Lumholtz, *Unknown Mexico*. 2 vols. New York, 1902.
51. P. T. Furst, "West Mexican Art: Secular or Sacred?"; pp. 102–103 [see note 45].
52. Stefan A. de Borhegyi, "Miniature Mushroom Stones from Guatemala," *American Antiquity*, Vol. 26 (1961); pp. 498–504.
53. R. Gordon Wasson, "The Magic Mushroom," *Life Magazine*, May 13, 1957 [New York]. Also R. G. Wasson and Valentina P. Wasson, *Mushrooms, Russia and History*. New York: Pantheon Books, 1957.
54. *Uxbenka* ("Ancient Place") was discovered by the archaeological community in 1984, after several reports of looting had been received by the authorities. The site is situated in the rain forested foothills of the Maya Mountains—fifteen kilometers east of the Guatemalan border, seven kilometers past the Mopan Maya village of San Antonio, and half a kilometer before reaching the more remote and smaller settlement of Santa Cruz. *Uxbenka* was partially excavated by an American archaeologist, whose native house was burned down during the night by the discontented villagers of Santa Cruz. The excavation, on the whole, does not appear to have produced a very rewarding outcome.
55. P. T. Furst, "West Mexican Art: Secular or Sacred?"; pp. 98–133 [see note 45]. Also his "Hallucinogens in Precolumbian Art." (*In*): Mary E. King and Idris R. Traylor, Jr. (eds.), *Art and Environment in Native America*. Texas Tech University Museum Special Publication, No. 7. Lubbock: Texas Tech Press, 1974; pp. 55–101.
56. P. T. Furst, *Hallucinogens and Culture*; p. 81 [see note 46].
57. R. Gordon Wasson, "The Role of 'Flowers' in Nahuatl Culture: A Suggested Interpretation." *Harvard University Botanical Museum Leaflets*, Vol. 23, no. 8 (1973); p. 324.
58. Dr. D. Heyden, personal communication, Mexico City, March, 1988. For a very useful work on this subject, also cf. Doris Heyden, *Mitologia y Simbolismo de la Flora en el Mexico Prehispanico*. 2nd edition. Mexico City: Universidad Nacional Autonoma de Mexico, 1985.
59. P. T. Furst, *Hallucinogens and Culture*; p. 74 [see note 46]. For an interesting analogy in the Dionysiac phenomenology cf. Robert Graves, *What Food the Centaurs Ate*. Steps: Cassell & Co., 1958.
60. Weston La Barre, "Old and New World Narcotics: A Statistical Question and an Ethnological Reply," *Economic Botany*, Vol. 24 (1970); pp. 368–373. Also cf. R. G. Wasson, *Soma: Divine Mushroom of Immortality*; pp. 80–92 [see note 29].
61. Both vessels are in The Metropolitan Museum of Art (Acc. no. 64.228.2 and no. 63.226.8) and were donated by Nathan Cummings.

See Alan R. Sawyer, *Ancient Peruvian Ceramics. The Nathan Cummings Collection*. New York: The Metropolitan Museum of Art (distributed by New York Graphic Society, Greenwich, Connecticut), 1966; pp. 46, 47; figs. 64, 65.

62. Christopher B. Donnan, *Moche Art of Peru. Pre-Columbian Symbolic Communication*. Los Angeles: Museum of Cultural History, University of California, 1978; pp. 34–35; fig. 59.

63. For examples of this type of architectural device, see C. B. Donnan, *Moche Art of Peru*; p. 81; fig. 138 [see note 62].

64. This example is illustrated in Elizabeth P. Benson, *The Mochica. A Culture of Peru*. New York: Praeger, 1972; p. 99, fig. 5–5.

65. Compare this habit of sucking coca leaves to the use of the *kat* bush (*Catha edulis*), a stimulant offering a mild kick, without intoxication. The *kat* is packed into one cheek and gnawed slowly. It has a slightly bitter taste, with its small, red leaves tasting best. One should swallow only the plant's juices, drinking water often. It grows on the mountains in Yemen, whose inhabitants spent, around 1964, three-fourths of their earnings on the daily supplies of this plant's leaves, which competes with coffee as Yemen's leading cash crop.

66. E. P. Benson, *The Mochica*; p. 68, and fig. 3–25 for an illustration of the item [see note 64].

67. E. P. Benson, *The Mochica*; pp. 58–59 [see note 64].

68. Nonetheless, the "bone tray and tubes" found in Huaca Prieta, coastal Peru, by Junius Bird of the American Museum of Natural History, lack proof positive to be unquestionably classified as snuffing implements.

69. P. T. Furst, *The Flesh of the Gods*; p. 65 [see note 43]. Also his *Hallucinogens and Culture*; pp. 152–165 [see note 46].

70. For illustrations of the latter two see E. P. Benson, *The Mochica*; pp. 60, fig. 3–16; 93, fig. 4–18 [see note 64].

71. E. P. Benson, *The Mochica*; p. 32; fig. 2–8 [see note 64].

72. For illustrations of these examples see E. P. Benson, *The Mochica*; figs. 5–17, 5–19 [see note 64].

73. J. Pérez de Barradas, *Orfebrería Prehispánica de Colombia: Estilo Calima*. Madrid: Gráficos Jura, 1954.

74. André Emmerich, *Sweat of the Sun and Tears of the Moon*. Seattle: University of Washington Press, 1965; pp. 76–77; 186, note IX.2.

75. R. G. Wasson and V. P. Wasson, *Mushrooms, Russia and History*; pp. 258–259 [see note 53]. In addition to the above book by the Wassons, A. Emmerich also credits Gordon F. Ekholm as another source for this information obtained in a private communication of July, 1963.

76. P. T. Furst, "Hallucinogens in Precolumbian Art"; pp. 55–102 [see note 55].
77. Richard E. Schultes and Alec Bright, "Ancient Gold Pectorals from Colombia: Mushroom Effigies?" (In): *Sweat of the Sun, Tears of the Moon: Gold and Emerald Treasures of Colombia*. Los Angeles: Natural History Museum of Los Angeles County, 1981; pp. 38, 42. Also cf. R. E. Schultes and A. Hofmann, *The Botany and Chemistry of Hallucinogens*. 2nd edition. Springfield, Ill.: Charles C. Thomas, 1979; and cf. R. E. Schultes and A. Hofmann, *Plants of the Gods: Origins of Hallucinogenic Use*. New York: McGraw-Hill, 1980.
78. *Genesis*, ii.8; *Psalm*, civ.14.
79. Aldous Huxley, *Heaven and Hell*. New York: Harper Colophon Books, 1963; p. 104. (Bound together with Huxley's *Doors of Perception*).
80. A. Huxley, *Heaven and Hell*; p. 104 [see note 79].
81. M. Ripinsky-Naxon, "Hallucinogens and Culture Change: Dialectics and the New Archaeology." 10th Annual Conference of the Society of Ethnobiology, held at the Florida State Museum, University of Florida, Gainsville, March 5–8, 1987.
82. M. Ripinsky-Naxon, "Systematic Knowledge of Herbal Use in Ancient Egypt and Greece: From the Divine Origins to *De Materia Medica*." Paper delivered at the 11th Annual Conference of the Society of Ethnobiology, held at Universidad Nacional Autonoma de Mexico, Mexico City, March 9–12, 1988. Also "Hallucinogens, Shamanism, and the Cultural Process;" p. 221 [see note 18].

Chapter 7—The Power of Metaphors

1. Plato, *Sophist*; 266c, Loeb Library edition.
2. Plato's conceptions regarding the hierarchies of reality are treated by R. Schaerer, *La question platonicienne* (Neuchâtel, 1938); and in *Dieu, l'homme et la vie d'après Platon* (Neuchâtel, 1944).
3. Plato, *Republic*; 476c, 597a; Loeb Lib. ed.
4. Plato, *Timaeus*; 47bc, Loeb Lib. ed.
5. Plato, *Republic*; 603c, Loeb Lib. ed.
6. Plato, *Republic*; 596a–597e, Loeb Lib. ed.
7. Plato, *Timaeus*; 28a–29a, 37c; Loeb Lib. ed.
8. Jacob Bronowski, *The Origins of Knowledge and Imagination*. Silliman Memorial Lectures. New Haven, Conn.: Yale University Press, 1978; pp. 11, 18.

9. Ernst Cassirer, *Language and Myth*. New York: Harper and Brothers, 1946; pp. 57, 83–84.
10. Jacob Bronowski, *The Origins of Knowledge and Imagination*; esp. Chap. 2 [see note 8].
11. E. G. Wolff, *Aesthetik der Dichtkunst*. Zürich, 1944; pp. 19 ff.
12. For an erudite discussion of the Cartesian dilemma, see Gilbert Ryle, *The Concept of Mind*. Chicago: University of Chicago Press, 1984.
13. E. Cassirer, *Language and Myth*; p. 81 [see note 9].
14. E. Cassirer, *Language and Myth*; p. 88 [see note 9].
15. E. Cassirer, *Language and Myth*; p. 73 [see note 9].
16. Joseph Campbell, *The Masks of God: Primitive Mythology*. Revised ed. New York: Penguin Books, [1969] 1976; p. 86.
17. Usener, *Götternamen. Versuch einer Lehre von der religiösen Begriffsbildung*. Bonn, 1896; pp. 321, 330.
18. G. Reichel-Dolmatoff, *Shamanism and Art of the Eastern Tukanoan Indians, Colombian Northwest Amazon*. Institute of Religious Iconography, State University of Groningen. Leiden: E. J. Brill, 1987; pp. 1–12. Also his "Rock Paintings of the Vaupés: An Essay in Interpretation," *Folklore Americas*, Vol. 27, no. 2 (1967); pp. 107–112.
19. See the various literature on Ainu religion, including the classic work by J. Batchelor, *The Ainu and Their Folk-lore*. London, 1901; and the more recent D. L. Philippi, *Songs of Gods, Songs of Humans*. Princeton: Princeton University Press, 1979.
20. Joseph Campbell, *The Inner Reaches of Outer Space. Metaphor as Myth and as Religion*. New York: Harper & Row, 1988; pp. 12, 18, 20–21.
21. Joseph L. Henderson, "Ancient Myths and Modern Man." [In]: Carl G. Jung, et al., *Man and His Symbols*. Garden City, N.Y.: Doubleday & Co., 1964; p. 151.
22. See J. Campbell's discussion of the bird-shaman in *The Symbol without Meaning*. Zürich: Rhein-Verlag, 1958.
23. This is a good example of how the depiction of a biophysical condition, such as an erection, functions as a metaphor, at least among its interpreters, of a transcended state in consciousness.
24. Walter F. Otto, *Dionysos. Myth and Cult*. Bloomington & London: Indiana University Press, 1965; p. 120.
25. G. Reichel-Dolmatoff, *Beyond the Milky Way. Hallucinatory Imagery of the Tukano Indians*. Los Angeles: UCLA Latin American Center Publications, 1978; p. 15.
26. G. Reichel-Dolmatoff, *Beyond the Milky Way*. esp. Pls. I, III, V, VII, and p. 148 [see note 25].

27. For a discussion of the San Agustin culture and its art phenomenon, see G. Reichel-Dolmatoff, *San Agustin. A Culture of Colombia*. New York: Praeger, 1965. Also a more recent review article by Suzan Mazur, "Visions of the Alto Magdalena," *Archaeology*, Vol. 42, no. 6 (1989); pp. 28–35.

28. W. W. Newcomb (*In*): Forrest Kirkland and W. W. Newcomb, *The Rock Art of Texas Indians*. Austin: University of Texas Press, 1967; p. 79.

29. Peter T. Furst, "Shamanism, the Ecstatic Experience, and Lower Pecos Art. Reflections on Some Transcultural Phenomena." (*In*): Harry J. Shafer (ed.), *Ancient Texans. Rock Art and Lifeways along the Lower Pecos*. Published for the Witte Museum of the San Antonio Museum Association. San Antonio: Texas Monthly Press, 1986; p. 211.

30. P. T. Furst, "Myth in Art: A Huichol Depicts His Reality," *Los Angeles County Museum of Natural History Quarterly*, Vol. 7, no. 3 (1968–69); pp. 16–17.

31. Aldous Huxley, *Heaven and Hell*. New York: Harper Colophon Books, 1963; pp. 107–108. (Bound together with *The Doors of Perception*).

32. Jan Gonda, *The Functions and Significance of Gold in the Veda*. Orientalia Rheno-Traiectina, 37. Leiden: E. J. Brill, 1991.

33. A. Huxley, *Heaven and Hell*; p. 104 [see note 31].

34. A. Huxley, *Heaven and Hell*; p. 108 [see note 31].

35. A. Huxley, *Heaven and Hell*; pp. 107–108 [see note 31].

36. For an interesting discussion of the relationship between shamans and smiths see Mircea Eliade, *The Forge and the Crucible*. 2nd ed. Chicago: University of Chicago Press, 1962 (Phoenix Edition, 1978).

37. G. Reichel-Dolmatoff, *Shamanism and Art of the Eastern Tukanoan Indians*; pp. 17–18 [see note 18].

38. Willy Schulz-Weider, "Shamanism," *Encyclopedia of World Art*, Vol. 13. New York: McGraw-Hill, 1967; cols. 2–3.

39. G. Reichel-Dolmatoff, *Shamanism and Art of the Eastern Tukanoan Indians*; p. 14 [see note 18].

40. G. Reichel-Dolmatoff, "Some Source Materials on Desana Shamanistic Initiation," *Antropologica*, Vol. 51 (1979); p. 54.

41. G. Reichel-Dolmatoff, "Some Source Materials on Desana Shamanistic Initiation;" p. 42 [see note 40, above].

42. G. Reichel-Dolmatoff, *Beyond the Milky Way*; pp. 31, 151 [see note 25].

43. G. Reichel-Dolmatoff, *Shamanism and Art of the Eastern Tukanoan Indians*; pp. 14, 15, 17, 18 [see note 18].

44. Benito Ortolani, *The Japanese Theatre. From Shamanistic Ritual to Contemporary Pluralism*. Handbuch der Orientalistik, V. Abt., 2 Bd. Leiden: E. J. Brill, 1990.

45. P. T. Furst, "West Mexican Art: Secular or Sacred?" (In): *The Iconography of Middle American Sculpture*. New York: The Metropolitan Museum of Art, 1973; pp. 115–116.

46. Weston La Barre, *The Peyote Cult*. 5th edition, enlarged. Norman: University of Oklahoma Press, 1989.

47. R. G. Wasson, *Soma. Divine Mushroom of Immortality*. New York: Harcourt Brace Jovanovich, 1969. Also his "What Was the Soma of the Aryans?" (In): P. T. Furst (ed.), *Flesh of the Gods. The Ritual Use of Hallucinogens*. New York: Praeger, 1972; pp. 201–213.

Bibliography

Adovasio, J. M., and G. S. Fry, "Prehistoric Psychotropic Drug Use in Northeastern Mexico and Trans-Pecos Texas," *Economic Botany*, Vol. 30, no. 1 (1976).

Ahlbäck, Tore, and Jan Bergman (eds.), *The Saami Shaman Drum*. Based on papers read at the Symposium on the Saami Shaman Drum held at Åbo, Finland, on the 19th–20th of August, 1988. Scripta Instituti Donneriani Abonensis, 14. Åbo, Finland: Donner Institute for Research in Religious and Cultural History, 1991 (distributed by Almqvist & Wiksell International, Stockholm).

Anati, Emmanuel, *Capo di Ponte*. Studi Camuni, 1. Capo di Ponte (Brescia): Centro Camuno di Studi Preistorici, 1987.

———. *Origini dell'Arte e della Concettualità*. Milano: Jaca Book, 1989.

Anisimov, A. F., "The Shaman's Tent of the Evenks and the Origin of the Shamanistic Rite." (*In*): Henry N. Michael (ed.), *Studies in Siberian Shamanism*. Translations from Russian Sources, 4. Arctic Institute of North America. Toronto: University of Toronto Press, 1963.

———. "Cosmological Concepts of the Peoples of the North." (*In*): Henry N. Michael (ed.), *Studies in Siberian Shamanism*. Translations from Russian Sources, 4. Arctic Institute of North America. Toronto: University of Toronto Press, 1963.

Anokhin, A. V., *Materialy po shamanstvu u altaitsev, sobranniye vo vremia puteshestvy po Altayu v 1910–1912 gg. po porucheniyu Russkovo Komiteta dla Izuchenia Srednei i Vostochnoi Asii* [Materials on Shamanism among the Altaic People, Collected during... 1910–1912...]. Leningrad, 1924.

Artscanada (Editors of), *Stones, Bones and Skin: Ritual and Shamanic Art*. Toronto: The Society for Art Publications (an Artscanada Book), 1977.

Bäckman, Louise, and Åke Hultkrantz, *Studies in Lapp Shamanism*. Stockholm [University] Studies in Comparative Religion, 16. Stockholm: Almqvist & Wiksell International, 1978.

Balázs, János, "A magyar samán rēülete," *Ethnographica*, Vol. 65, no. 3–4 (1954); pp. 416–440 [in Hungarian, with a German summary]. Reprinted in German as "Über die Ekstase des ungarischen Schamanen." (*In*): Vilmos Diószegi (ed.), *Glaubenswelt und Folklore der Sibirischen Völker*. Budapest, 1963. (English version entitled *Popular Beliefs and Folklore Tradition in Siberia*. Trans. from Hungarian. Uralic and Altaic Series, 57. Bloomington: Indiana University/The Hague: Mouton, 1968].

Balzer, Marjorie Mandelstam (ed.), *Shamanism: Soviet Studies of Traditional Religion in Siberia and Central Asia*. Armonk, N.Y.: M. E. Sharpe, 1990.

Barron, Frank; Murray Jarvik; and Sterling Bunnell, Jr., "The Hallucinogenic Drugs," *Scientific American*, Vol. 210, no. 4 (1964); pp. 29 ff.

Barrows, David Prescott, *The Ethno-Botany of the Coahuilla Indians of Southern California*. Chicago: University of Chicago Press, 1900. (Reprinted with additional contributions and a Coahuilla Bibliography, Banning, Calif.: Malki Museum Press, Morongo Indian Reservation, [1967] 1977).

Basilov, V. N., "Chosen by the Spirits." (*In*): Marjorie Mandelstam Balzer (ed.), *Shamanism: Soviet Studies of Traditional Religion in Siberia and Central Asia*. Armonk, N.Y.: M. E. Sharpe, 1990.

Batchelor, Rev. J., *The Ainu and Their Folk-lore*. London, 1901.

Bawden, C. R., "On the Practice of Scapulimancy among the Mongols," *Central Asiatic Journal*, Vol. 4 (1958).

Bean, Lowell J., and Katherine Siva Saubel, *Temalpakh (from the Earth)*. *Cahuilla Indian Knowledge and Usage of Plants*. Banning, Calif.: Malki Museum Press, Morongo Indian Reservation, 1972.

Beltrán, Antonio, "L'Art Prehistorique Espagnol: Nouveaux Horizons et Problemes. Etat de la Question," *Bollettino del Centro Camuno di Studi Preistorici*, Vol. 24 (1988); pp. 13–44 [Capo di Ponte].

Benson, Elizabeth P., *The Mochica: A Culture of Peru*. New York: Praeger, 1972.

Bianchi, Ugo, *The Greek Mysteries*. Institute of Religious Iconography, State University of Groningen. Leiden: E. J. Brill, 1976.

Borhegyi, Stefan A. de, "Miniature Mushroom Stones from Guatemala," *American Antiquity*, Vol. 26 (1961); pp. 498–504.

Boylan, Patrick, *Thoth: The Hermes of Egypt*. London, 1922.

Brenneman, Jr., Walter L., "Serpents, Cows, and Ladies: Contrasting Symbolism in Irish and Indo-European Cattle-Raiding Myths," *History of Religions*, Vol. 28, no. 4 (1989); pp. 340–354.

Bronowski, Jacob, *The Origins of Knowledge and Imagination*. Silliman Memorial Lectures. New Haven: Yale University Press, 1978.

Brunton, Ron, *The Abandoned Narcotic. Kava and Cultural Instability in Melanesia*. Cambridge: Cambridge University Press, 1989.

Budge, E. A. W., *The Divine Origin of the Craft of the Herbalist*. London: The Society of the Herbalists, 1928.

Campbell, Joseph, *The Masks of God: Primitive Mythology*. Revised edition. New York: Penguin Books, 1976.

————. *The Inner Reaches of Outer Space: Metaphor as Myth and as Religion*. New York: Harper & Row, 1988.

Cassirer, Ernst, *Language and Myth*. Trans. from German. New York: Harper and Brothers, 1946. (Reprinted, New York: Dover Publications, 1953).

Chagnon, Napoleon A., *Yąnomamö: The Fierce People*. Case Studies in Cultural Anthropology. New York: Holt, Rinehart, & Winston, 1968.

Chaplin, Dorothea, *Matter, Myth and Spirit*. London: Simpkin, Marshall, Ltd., 1935.

Charpentier, Jarl, *Vilhelms av Ruysbroeck resa genom Asien 1253–1255*. Stockholm, 1919.

Comsa, Eugen, "Typologie et Signification des Figurines Anthropomorphes du Territoire Roumain." *Les Religion de la Prehistoire*. Actes du Valcamonica Symposium, 1972. Capo di Ponte (Brescia): Centro Camuno di Studi Preistorici, 1975.

Conrad, Jack R., *The Horn and the Sword: The History of the Bull as Symbol of Power and Fertility*. New York: E. P. Dutton, 1957.

Cooke, Harold P., *Osiris: A study in Myths, Mysteries, and Religion*. London, 1931.

Czigány, L. G., "The Use of Hallucinogens and the Shamanistic Tradition of the Finno-Ugrian People," *Slavonic and East European Review*, Vol. 58, no. 2 (1980); pp. 212–217.

Daniélou, Alain, *Hindu Polytheism*. Bollingen Series, 73. New York: Bollingen Foundation/Pantheon Books, 1964.

Dawson, Christopher, *Religion and Culture*. The Gifford Lectures, 1947. New York: Meridian Books, 1958.

Der Marderosian, A. H.; H. V. Pinkley; and M. F. Dobbins IV, "Native Use and Occurrence of N,N-dimethyltryptamine in the Leaves of *Banisteriopsis rusbyana*," *American Journal of Pharmacy*, Vol. 140 (1968); pp. 137–147.

Diószegi, Vilmos, "Shamanism," *Encyclopedia Britannica*, 15th edition; pp. 1030–1033.

————. "Problems in Mongolian Shamanism," *Acta Ethnographica*, Vol. 10, nos. 1–2 (1961); pp. 195–206.

———. "The Origin of the Evenki Shamanic Instruments (Stick, Knout) of Transbaikalia," *Acta Ethnographica*, Vol. 17, nos. 3–4 (1968); pp. 265–311.

———. (ed.), *Popular Beliefs and Folklore Tradition in Siberia*. Trans. from Hungarian. Uralic and Altaic Series, 57. Bloomington: Indiana University / The Hague: Mouton, 1968.

Dobkin de Rios, Marlene, *Hallucinogens: Cross-Cultural Perspectives*. Bridport, Dorset: Prism Press/Garden City Park, N.Y.: Avery Publishing Group, 1990. (Originally published Albuquerque: University of New Mexico Press, 1984.)

Donnan, Christopher B., *Moche Art of Peru: Pre-Columbian Symbolic Communication*. Los Angeles: Museum of Cultural History, University of California, 1978.

Donner, Kai., *La Sibérie: La Vie en Sibérie, les temps anciens*. Paris, 1946.

Dufrenne, Roland, "Intérpretation des gravures rupestres de la Vallée des Merveilles à la lumière de la tradition vedique," *Bollettino del Centro Camuno di Studi Preistorici*, Vol. 22 (1985); pp. 110–116 [Capo di Ponte].

Eberhard, Wolfram, *Lokalkulturen im alten China*. Part I: *Die Lokalkulturen des Nordens und Westens*. Leiden, 1942. Part II: *Die Lokalkulturen des Südens und Ostens*. Peking, 1942.

Edsman, Carl-Martin (ed.), *Studies in Shamanism*. Based on papers read at the Symposium on Shamanism held at Åbo on the 6th–8th of September, 1962. Scripta Instituti Donneriani Aboensis, 1. Stockholm: Almqvist & Wiksell, 1967.

Eliade, Mircea, *The Sacred and the Profane. The Nature of Religion*. New York: Harcourt, Brace and Co., 1959.

———. *The Forge and the Crucible*. 2nd edition. Chicago: University of Chicago Press, 1962. (Phoenix edition, 1978).

———. *Shamanism: Archaic Techniques of Ecstasy*. Bollingen Series, 76. New York: Pantheon Books, 1964.

———. "Masks: Mythical and Ritual Origins," *Encyclopedia of World Art*, Vol. 9. New York & London: McGraw-Hill, 1964; cols. 521–525.

———. "Shamanism." (*In*): Vergilius Ferm (ed.), *Ancient Religions*. New York: Citadel Press, 1965. (Originally published as *Forgotten Religions*. New York: Philosophical Library, 1950).

———. *Yoga: Immortality and Freedom*. 2nd edition. Bollingen Series, 56. Princeton: Princeton University Press, 1970. (Originally published as *Le Yoga. Immortalité et Liberté*. Paris, 1954).

———. *A History of Religious Ideas*. Vol. I: From the Stone Age to the Eleusinian Mysteries. Chicago: University of Chicago Press, 1978.

Emmerich, André, *Sweat of the Sun and Tears of the Moon: Gold and Silver in Pre-Columbian Art*. Seattle: University of Washington Press, 1965.

Escalante, Roberto, "Ethnomycological Data of the Matlatzincas." Paper presented at the 72nd Annual Meeting of the American Anthropological Association, held in New Orleans, 1973.

Eugster, Conrad H., "Isolation, Structure, and Synthesis of Central-active Compounds from *Amanita muscaria* (L. ex Fr.) Hooker." (*In*): Daniel H. Efron (ed.), *Ethnopharmacologic Search for Psychoactive Drugs.* U.S. Public Health Service Publication, No. 1645. Washington, D.C.: U.S. Government Printing Office, 1967.

Farnell, L. R., *Cults of the Greek States.* 3 vols. Oxford: Clarendon Press, 1896–1909.

Flattery, David Stophlet, and Martin Schwartz, *Haoma and Harmaline: The Botanical Identity of the Indo-Iranian Sacred Hallucinogen "Soma" and Its Legacy in Religion, Language, and Middle Eastern Folklore.* University of California Publications in Near Eastern Studies, 21. Berkeley: University of California Press, 1989.

Foster, Byron, *Heart Drum: Spirit Possession in the Garifuna Communities of Belize.* Benque Viejo del Carmen (Belize): Cubola Productions, 1986.

Frazer, James George, "On Certain Burial Customs as Illustrations of the Primitive Theory of the Soul," *Journal of the Royal Anthropological Institute,* Vol. 15 (1885–1886).

Freud, Sigmund, *The Future of an Illusion.* Newly trans. and edited by James Strachey. New York: W. W. Norton & Co., 1961.

———. *Civilization and Its Discontents.* Newly trans. and edited by James Strachey. New York: W. W. Norton & Co., 1962.

Furst, Peter T., "West Mexican Tomb Sculpture as Evidence for Shamanism in Prehispanic Mesoamerica," *Antropologica,* No. 15 (December, 1965); pp. 29–80 [Caracas].

———. "Myth in Art: A Huichol Depicts His Reality," *Los Angeles County Museum of Natural History Quarterly,* Vol. 7, no. 3 (1968–1969); pp. 16-25. (Also, UCLA Latin American Center Reprint Series, 11).

———. (ed.), *Flesh of the Gods: The Ritual Use of Hallucinogens.* New York: Praeger, 1972.

———. "West Mexican Art: Secular or Sacred?" (In): *The Iconography of Middle American Sculpture.* New York: The Metropolitan Museum of Art, 1973.

———. "Hallucinogens in Precolumbian Art." (*In*): Mary E. King and Idris R. Traylor, Jr. (eds.), *Art and Environment in Native America.* Texas Tech University Museum Special Publications, No. 7. Lubbock: Texas Tech Press, 1974; pp. 55–101.

———. *Hallucinogens and Culture.* Novato, Calif.: Chandler & Sharp, [1976] 1982.

————. "Shamanism, the Ecstatic Experience, and Lower Pecos Art. Reflections on Some Transcultural Phenomena." (In): Harry J. Shafer (ed.), Ancient Texans: Rock Art and Lifeways along the Lower Pecos. Published for the Witte Museum of the San Antonio Museum Association. San Antonio: Texas Monthly Press, 1986.

Giedion, Siegfrid, The Eternal Present: The Beginnings of Art. London: Oxford University Press / New York: Bollingen Foundation, 1962.

Gimbutas, Marija, "Figurines of Old Europe (6500–3500 B.C.)." Les Religions de la Prehistoire. Actes du Valcamonica Symposium, 1972. Capo di Ponte (Brescia): Centro Camuno di Studi Preistorici, 1975.

Gitti, S., G. Samorini, et al., "Contributo alla Conoscenza della Micoflora Psicotropa del Territorio Bresciano," Natura Bresciana, Vol. 20 (1983); pp. 125–130 [Ann. Mus. Civ. Sc. Nat., Brescia].

Goldman, Irving, The Cubeo: Indians of the Northwest Amazon. Illinois Studies in Anthropology, No. 2. Urbana: University of Illinois Press, 1963.

Gonda, Jan, The Functions and Significance of Gold in the Veda. Orientalia Rheno-Traiectina, 37. Leiden: E. J. Brill, 1991.

Gonzalez, Nancie L., Sojourners of the Caribbean. Ethnogenesis and Ethnohistory of the Garifuna. Urbana & Chicago: University of Illinois Press, 1988.

Granet, Marcel, "Remarques sur le taoïsme ancien," Asia Major, Vol. 2 (1925); pp. 145–151 [Leipzig].

————. Danses et légendes de la Chine ancienne. 2 vols. Paris, 1926.

Graves, Robert, What Food the Centaurs Ate. Steps: Cassell & Co., 1958.

————. The Greek Myths. 2 vols. Revised edition. Harmondsworth: Penguin Books, 1960.

Graziosi, Paolo, Palaeolithic Art. New York: McGraw-Hill, 1960.

Gregor, Thomas, Mehinaku: The Drama of Daily Life in a Brazilian Indian Village. Chicago: University of Chicago Press, 1977.

Groot, Jan J. M. de, The Religious System of China. 6 vols. Leiden, 1892–1910.

Halifax, Joan, Shamanic Voices: A Survey of Visionary Narratives. New York: E. P. Dutton, 1979.

Hallowell, A. J., "Bear Ceremonialism in the Northern Hemisphere," American Anthropologist, Vol. 28 (1926); pp. 1–175.

Harner, Michel J., The Jívaro: People of the Sacred Waterfall. Garden City, N.Y.: Doubleday/Natural History Press, 1972.

————. (ed.), Hallucinogens and Shamanism. New York & London: Oxford University Press, [1973] 1981.

————. "The Sound of Rushing Water." (In): M. J. Harner (ed.), Hallucinogens and Shamanism. New York & London: Oxford University Press, [1973] 1981. [Originally, published under the same title in Natural History, Vol. 77, no. 6 (1968); pp. 28-33, 60–61].

―――. "The Role of Hallucinogenic Plants in European Witchcraft." (*In*): M. J. Harner (ed.), *Hallucinogens and Shamanism*. New York & London: Oxford University Press, [1973] 1981.

―――. *The Way of the Shaman: A Guide to Power and Healing*. New York: Bantam Books, 1982.

Harrison, Jane E., *Prolegomena to the Study of Greek Religion*. 3rd edition. Cambridge: Cambridge University Press, 1922.

―――. *Epilegomena to the Study of Greek Religion*. Cambridge: Cambridge University Press, 1921.

―――. *Themis: A Study of the Social Origins of Greek Religion*. 2nd edition. Cambridge: Cambridge University Press, 1927.

Harrod, James B., *The Tempering Goddess: A Phenomenological and Structural Analysis of the Britomartis-Diktynna-Aphaia Mythologem*. Unpublished doctoral dissertation in Religion. Syracuse University, 1974.

Hawking, Stephen, *A Brief History of Time From the Big Bang to Black Holes*. New York: Bantam Books, 1988.

Heine-Geldern, Robert von, "Review of *Antler and Tongue: an Essay on Ancient Chinese Symbolism and Its Implications*, by A. Salmony," *Artibus Asiae*, Vol. 18 (1955); pp. 85–90.

Heissig, Walther, *The Religions of Mongolia*. Trans. from German. London: Routledge & Kegan Paul, 1980.

Henderson, Joseph L., "Ancient Myths and Modern Man." (*In*): Carl G. Jung, *et al.*, *Man and His Symbols*. Garden City, N.Y.: Doubleday & Co., 1964.

Hernández Pérez, Mauro S., *et al.*, "Vorbericht über die Erforschung der Felsbindkunst in der Provinz Alicante," *Madrider Mitteilungen*, Vol. 24 (1983); pp. 32–45 [Mainz].

Hodder, Ian, "Archaeology in 1984," *Antiquity*, Vol. 58 (1984); pp. 25–32.

Hofmann, Albert, *Die Erforschung der Mexikanischen Zauberpilze und das Problem Ihrer Wirkstoffe*. Basel: Basler Stadtbuch, 1964.

Hopkins, L. C., "The Bearskin, Another Pictographic Reconnaisance from Primitive Prophylactic to Present-day Panache: A Chinese Epigraphic Puzzle," *Journal of the Royal Asiatic Society*, Pts. 1–2 (1943); pp. 110–117.

―――. "The Shaman or Chinese *Wu*: His Inspired Dancing and Versatile Character," *Journal of the Royal Asiatic Society*, Pts. 1–2 (1945); pp. 3–16.

Hultkrantz, Åke, "A Definition of Shamanism," *Temenos*, Vol. 9 (1973); pp. 25–37.

―――. *The Religions of the American Indians*. Trans. from Swedish. Berkeley: University of California Press, 1979.

————. "The Peril of Visions: Changes of Vision Patterns among the Wind River Shoshoni," *History of Religions*, Vol. 26, no. 1 (1986); pp. 34–46.

Humphrey, Nicholas, *Consciousness Regained: Chapters in the Development of Mind*. Oxford & New York: Oxford University Press, 1983.

Hurry, Jamieson B., *Imhotep: The Egyptian God of Medicine*. Oxford, 1926.

Huxley, Aldous, *Heaven and Hell*. New York: Harper Colophon Books, 1963. (Bound together with Huxley's *The Doors of Perception*).

Huxley, Francis, *Affable Savages: An Anthropologist among the Urubu Indians of Brazil*. New York: Viking Press, 1957.

Itkonen, Toivo Immanuel, *Heidnische Religion und späterer Aberglaube bei den finnischen Lappen*. Mémoires de la Société Finno-Ougrienne, 87. Helsinki, 1946.

Jacobs, Barry L., "How Hallucinogenic Drugs Work," *American Scientist*, Vol. 75 (July-August, 1987); pp. 386–392.

Kamieński Dłużyk, Adam, "Dyarusz więzienia moskiewskiego, miast i miejsc [1658]." ("A Diary of Muskovite Captivity, Towns and Places [1658]"). (*In*): Rev. A. Maryanski (ed.), *Warta*. Poznań [Posen], 1874; pp. 373–388. This publication consists of a collection of articles. The passage on the fly-agaric is on p. 382. Contemporary edition does not exist.

Kamma, Freerk C., *Religious Texts of the Oral Tradition from Western New-Guinea. Part A: The Origin and Sources of Life*. Religious Texts Translation Series, 3. Leiden: E. J. Brill, 1975.

Kaplan, Reid W., "The Sacred Mushroom in Scandinavia," *Man*, Vol. 10, no. 1 (1975); pp. 72–79.

Kaster, Joseph (ed. & trans.), *The Literature and Mythology of Ancient Egypt*. London: Allen Lane, 1970.

Kensinger, Kenneth M., "*Banisteriopsis* Usage among the Peruvian Cashinahua." (*In*): M. J. Harner (ed.), *Hallucinogens and Shamanism*. New York & London: Oxford University Press, [1973] 1981.

Kirkland, Forrest, and W. W. Newcomb, Jr., *The Rock Art of Texas Indians*. Austin: University of Texas Press, 1967.

Knight, W. F. Jackson, "Maze Symbolism and the Trojan Game," *Antiquity*, Vol. 6 (1932); pp. 445–458.

Knudtson, Peter H., "Flora, Shaman of the Wintu," *Natural History*, Vol. 84 (May, 1975); pp. 6–17.

Kroeber, Alfred L., *Handbook of the Indians of California*. Bulletin of the Bureau of American Ethnology, 78. Washington, D.C.: Smithsonian Institution, 1925. (Reprinted, Berkeley: California Book Co., 1953).

————. *The Seri*. Southwest Museum Papers, No. 6. Los Angeles: Southwest Museum, [1931] 1964.

Ksenofontov, G. V., *Legendy i rasskazy o shamanach u Yakutov, Buryat i Tungusov*. 2nd edition. Moscow: Izdatel'stvo Bezbozhnik, 1930. Trans. from Russian into German as *Schamanengeschichten aus Siberien* [*Legends of Siberian Shamans*]. München: Otto Wilhelm Barth-Verlag, 1955.

La Barre, Weston, "Old and New World Narcotics: A Statistical Question and an Ethnological Reply," *Economic Botany*, Vol. 24 (1970); pp. 368–373.

————. "Hallucinogens and the Shamanic Origins of Religion." [*In*]: P. T. Furst (ed.), *Flesh of the Gods: The Ritual Use of Hallucinogens*. New York: Praeger, 1972.

————. *The Ghost Dance: The Origins of Religion*. London: George Allen & Unwin, 1972.

————. *The Peyote Cult*. 5th edition, enlarged. Norman: University of Oklahoma Press, 1989.

Lajoux, Jean-Dominique, *The Tassili n'Ajjer. Art rupestre du Sahara préhistorique*. Paris: Editions du Chêne, 1977.

Laufer, Berthold, *Chinese Clay Figures*. Anthropological Series, Vol. 13, no. 2. Chicago: Field Museum of Natural History, 1914.

————. "Origin of the Word Shaman," *American Anthropologist*, Vol. 19 (1917); pp. 361–371.

————. *The Prehistory of Aviation*. Anthropological Series, Vol. 18, no. 1. Chicago: Field Museum of Natural History, 1928.

Lebot, Vincent; Mark Merlin; and Lamont Lindstrom, *Kava. The Pacific Drug*. New Haven: Yale University Press, 1992.

Lehtisalo, T., *Entwurf einer Mythologie der Jurak-Samojeden*. Mémoires de la Société Finno-Ougrienne, 53. Helsinki, 1924.

Leroi-Gourhan, André, *The Art of Prehistoric Man in Western Europe*. London: Thames and Hudson, 1968.

Levi, Jerome Meyer, "*Wii'ipay*: The Living Rocks—Ethnographic Notes on Crystal Magic among Some California Yumans," *Journal of California Anthropology*, Vol. 5, no. 1 (1978); pp. 42–52.

Lévi-Strauss, Claude, "The Effectiveness of Symbols." [*In*]: his *Structural Anthropology*. New York: Basic Books, 1963.

Maenchen-Helfen, J. Otto, *The World of the Huns: Studies in Their History and Culture*. Berkeley: University of California Press, 1973.

Marais, Eugène, *The Soul of the Ape*. New York: Atheneum, 1969.

Markale, Jean, *Celtic Civilization*. Paris: Payot, 1976.

Maspero, Gaston, *Journal des Savants*. Paris, 1899; pp. 401–414.

Maspero, Henri, *La Chine antique*. Paris, 1927.

————. *Les Religions chinoises*. (Mélanges posthumes sur les religions et l'histoire de la Chine I). Paris, 1950.

Mazur, Suzan, "Visions of the Alto Magdalena," Archaeology, Vol. 42, no. 6 (1989); pp. 28–35.

Mellaart, James, The Neolithic of the Near East. New York: Scribner's, 1975.

Merkur, Daniel, Becoming Half Hidden: Shamanism and Initiation among the Inuit. Stockholm [University] Studies in Comparative Religion, 24. Stockholm: Almqvist & Wiksell International, 1985.

Michael, Henry N. (ed.), Studies in Siberian Shamanism. Translations from Russian Sources, 4. Arctic Institute of North America. Toronto: University of Toronto Press, 1963.

Mikhailowski, V. M., "Shamanism in Siberia and European Russia: Being the Second Part of Shamanstvo," Journal of the Royal Anthropological Institute, Vol. 24 (1894); pp. 62–100, 126–158. [Trans. from Russian].

Miller, Roy A., Japanese and the Other Altaic Languages. Cambridge: Cambridge University Press, 1971.

Mironov, N. D., and S. M. Shirokogoroff, "Śramana-Shaman: Etymology of the Word 'Shaman'," Journal of the Royal Asiatic Society (North-China Branch, Shanghai), Vol. 55 (1924); pp. 105–130.

Movius, Jr., Hallam L., "The Mousterian Cave of Teshik-Tash, S.E. Uzbekistan, C. Asia," American School of Prehistoric Research Bulletin, 17 (1953); pp. 11–71.

Munn, Henry, "The Mushrooms of Language." (In): M. J. Harner (ed.), Hallucinogens and Shamanism. New York & London: Oxford University Press, [1973] 1981.

Murray, Margaret, "Ritual Masking." (In): Mélanges Maspero. Cairo: L'Institut Français d'Archéologie Orientale, 1934.

Naranjo, Claudio, The Healing Journey: New Approaches to Consciousness. New York: Pantheon Books, 1973.

———. "Psychological Aspects of the Yagé Experience in an Experimental Setting." (In): M. J. Harner (ed.), Hallucinogens and Shamanism. New York & London: Oxford University Press, [1973] 1981.

Nilsson, Martin P., Greek Folk Religion. Philadelphia: University of Pennsylvania Press, 1972. (Originally, published as Greek Popular Religion. New York: Columbia University Press, 1940).

O'Grady, Standish, Silva Gadelica 2 vols. London: Williams & Norgate, 1892.

Ohlmarks, Åke, Studien zum Problem des Schamanismus. Lund-Kopenhagen, 1939.

Onians, Richard B., The Origins of European Thought about the Body, the Mind, the Soul, the World, Time, and Fate. New Interpretations of Greek, Roman, and Kindred Evidence, Also of Some Basic Jewish and Christian Beliefs. 2nd edition. Cambridge & New York: Cambridge University Press, 1988.

Oster, Gerald, "Phosphenes," *Scientific American*, Vol. 222, no. 2 (1970); pp. 82–87.

Ostermann, H., *The Alaskan Eskimos, as Described in the Posthumous Notes of Dr. Knud Rasmussen*. Report of the Fifth Thule Expedition, 1921–24, Vol. 10, no. 3. Copenhagen: Nordisk Forlag, 1952.

Ostrander, Sheila, and Lynn Schroeder, *Psychic Discoveries behind the Iron Curtain*. New York: Bantam Books, 1971.

Otto, Rudolf, *The Idea of the Holy: An Inquiry into the Non-Rational Factor in the Idea of the Divine and Its Relation to the Rational*. 2nd edition. London: Oxford University Press, [1950] 1958.

Otto, Walter F., *Dionysos: Myth and Cult*. Bloomington: Indiana University Press, 1965.

Pérez de Barradas, Jóse, *Orfebrería Prehispánica de Colombia: Estilo Calima*. Madrid: Gráficas Jura, 1954.

Piantelli, Mario, "L'Interpretazione di Uno Schema Iconografico Complesso Rinvenibile nelle Stele Monumentali Camune e Valtellinesi: Appunti per un'Ipotesi," *Bollettino del Centro Camuno di Studi Preistorici*, Vol. 20 (1983); pp. 33–54 [Capo di Ponte].

Priuli, Ausilio, *Incisioni Rupestri nelle Alpi*. Ivrea (Italy): Priuli & Verlucca, 1983.

Prokofyeva, Y. D., "The Costume of an Enets Shaman." (*In*): H. N. Michael (ed.), *Studies in Siberian Shamanism*. Translations from Russian Sources, 4. Arctic Institute of North America. Toronto: University of Toronto Press, 1963.

Rasmussen, Knud, *Across Arctic America*. New York: G. P. Putnam's Sons, 1927.

––––––. *The Intellectual Culture of the Iglulik Eskimos*. Report of the Fifth Thule Expedition, 1921–24, Vol. 7, no. 1. Copenhagen: Glydendalske Boghandel, Nordisk Forlag, 1929.

Rees, Alwyn, and Brinley Rees, *Celtic Heritage*. London: Thames and Hudson, 1961.

Reichel-Dolmatoff, Gérardo, *San Agustin: A Culture of Colombia*. New York: Praeger, 1965.

––––––. "Rock Paintings of the Vaupés," *Folklore Americas*, Vol. 27, no. 2 (1967); pp. 107–112.

––––––. *Amazonian Cosmos: The Sexual and Religious Symbolism of the Tukano Indians*. Trans. from Spanish. Chicago: University of Chicago Press, 1971.

––––––. "The Cultural Context of an Aboriginal Hallucinogen: Banisteriopsis caapi." (*In*): P. T. Furst (ed.), *Flesh of the Gods: The Ritual Use of Hallucinogens*. New York: Praeger, 1972.

––––––. *The Shaman and the Jaguar: A Study of Narcotic Drugs among the Indians of Colombia*. Philadelphia: Temple University Press, 1975.

————. *Beyond the Milky Way: Hallucinatory Imagery of the Tukano Indians.* UCLA Latin American Studies, 42. Los Angeles: University of California, Latin American Center Publications, 1978.

————. "Desana Shaman's Rock Crystals and the Hexagonal Universe," *Journal of Latin American Lore,* Vol. 5, no. 1 (1979); pp. 117–128.

————. "Some Source Materials on Desana Shamanistic Initiation," *Antropológica,* Vol. 51 (1979); pp. 27–61 [Caracas].

————. "Things of Beauty Replete with Meaning—Metals and Crystals in Colombian Indian Cosmology." (In): *Sweat of the Sun, Tears of the Moon: Gold and Emerald Treasures of Colombia.* Los Angeles: Natural History Museum of Los Angeles County, 1981.

————. *Shamanism and Art of the Eastern Tukanoan Indians, Colombian Northwest Amazon.* Institute of Religious Iconography, State University of Groningen. Leiden: E. J. Brill, 1987.

————. *The Sacred Mountain of Colombia's Kogi Indians.* Iconography of Religions, Vol. 9, part 2. Leiden: E. J. Brill, 1990.

Reinhard, Johan, "Shamanism and Spirit Possession." (In): John Hitchcock and Rex Jones (eds.), *Spirit Possession in the Nepal Himalayas.* Warminster: Aris and Phillips, 1975.

Ripinsky, Michael, "Conoscenza dei Ma'dan," *Rivista di Etnografia,* Vol. 20 (1966); pp. 11–39 [Naples].

————. "Middle Eastern Kinship as an Expression of a Culture-Environment System," *The Muslim World,* Vol. 58, no. 3 (1968); pp. 225–241.

————. "Cultural Idiom as an Ecologic Factor: Two Studies," *Anthropos,* Vol. 70, nos. 3–4 (1975); pp. 449–460.

————. "The Camel in Dynastic Egypt," *Journal of Egyptian Archaeology,* Vol. 71 (1985); pp. 134–141.

Ripinsky-Naxon, Michael, "Hallucinogens and Culture Change: Dialectic and the New Archaeology," Paper presented at the Tenth Annual Conference of the Society of Ethnobiology, held at the Florida State Museum, University of Florida, Gainesville, March 5–8, 1987.

————. "Systematic Knowledge of Herbal Use in Ancient Egypt and Greece: From the Divine Origins to *De Materia Medica.*" Paper delivered at the Eleventh Annual Conference of the Society of Ethnobiology, held at Universidad Nacional Autonoma de Mexico, Mexico City, March 9–12, 1988.

————. "Hallucinogens, Shamanism, and the Cultural Process: Symbolic Archaeology and Dialectics," *Anthropos,* Vol. 84 (1989); pp. 219–224.

Robicsek, Francis, *The Smoking Gods: Tobacco in Maya Art, History, and Religion.* Norman: University of Oklahoma Press, 1978.

Róheim, Géza, *Children of the Desert: The Western Tribes of Central Australia.* Published posthumously. Edited by Werner Muensterberger. New York: Basic Books, 1974.

Rosenthal, Franz, *The Herb: Hashish versus Medieval Muslim Society.* Leiden: E. J. Brill, 1971.

Roux, J. P., "L'Origine céleste de la souveraineté dans les inscriptions paléo-turques de Mongolie et de Sibérie," *La regalità sacrà. (The Sacral Kingship).* Leiden: E. J. Brill, 1959.

Rutherford, Ward, *Shamanism: The Foundations of Magic.* Welling-borough: Aquarian Press, 1986.

Rutkowski, Bogdan, "Minoan Sacred Emblems." (In): *Antichità Cretesi*, Vol. 1. Studi in Onore di Doro Levi. 2 vols. Catania: Istituto di Archeologia, Università di Catania, 1977–78.

Saggs, H. W. F., *The Greatness that Was Babylon.* New York: New American Library, 1962.

Salmony, Alfred, *Antler and Tongue: An Essay on Ancient Chinese Symbolism and Its Implications.* Ascona, 1954.

Samorini, Giorgio, "Sulla presenza di funghi e piante allucinogene in Valcamonica," *Bollettino del Centro Camuno di Studi Preistorici*, Vol. 24 (1988); pp. 132–136 [Capo di Ponte].

———. "Etnomicologia nell'arte rupestre Sahariana," *B.C. Notizie*, Vol. 6, no. 2 (April, 1989); pp. 18–22 [Notiziario del Centro Camuno di Studi Preistorici].

———. "The Oldest Representations of Hallucinogenic Mushrooms in the World (Sahara Desert, 9000–7000 B.P.)," *Integration*, Nos. 2–3 (1992); pp. 69–78 [Germany].

Sauneron, Serge, *The Priests of Ancient Egypt.* Trans from French. New York: Grove Press, 1960.

Sawyer, Alan R., *Ancient Peruvian Ceramics: The Nathan Cummings Collection.* New York: The Metropolitan Museum of Art, 1966. (Distributed by New York Graphic Society, Greenwich, Connecticut).

Schäfer, Heinrich, *Principles of Egyptian Art.* Oxford: Clarendon Press, [1919] 1974.

Schmidt, Wilhelm, *Der Ursprung der Gottesidee: Eine historisch-kritische und positive Studie.* 12 vols. Münster in Westfalia: Aschendorff, 1912–1955.

Schultes, Richard Evans, "An Overview of Hallucinogens in the Western Hemisphere." (In): P. T. Furst (ed.), *Flesh of the Gods: The Ritual Use of Hallucinogens.* New York: Praeger, 1972.

Schultes, Richard E., and Alec Bright, "Ancient Gold Pectorals from Colombia: Mushroom Effigies?" (In): *Sweat of the Sun, Tears of the Moon: Gold and Emerald Treasures of Colombia.* Los Angeles: Natural History Museum of Los Angeles County, 1981.

Schultes, Richard E., and Albert Hofmann, *The Botany and Chemistry of Hallucinogens.* 2nd edition. Springfield, Ill.: Charles C. Thomas, 1979.

————. *Plants of the Gods: Origins of Hallucinogenic Use.* New York: McGraw-Hill, 1980.

Schulz-Weider, Willy, "Shamanism," *Encyclopedia of World Art*, Vol. 13. New York & London: McGraw-Hill, 1967; cols. 1–5.

Seabrook, W. B., *Adventures in Arabia: Among the Bedouins, Druses, Whirling Dervishes, & Yezidee Devil Worshipers.* New York: Harcourt, Brace and Co., 1927.

Shirokogoroff, S. M., *Psychomental Complex of the Tungus.* London: Kegan Paul, Trench, Trubner, 1935.

Siikala, Anna-Leena, *The Rite Technique of the Siberian Shaman.* Folklore Fellows Communications, No. 220. Helsinki: Academia Scientiarum Fennica (Finnish Academy of Sciences), [1978] 1987.

Siskind, Janet, "Visions and Cures among the Sharanahua." [*In*]: M. J. Harner (ed.), *Hallucinogens and Shamanism.* New York & London: Oxford University Press, [1973] 1981.

Smith, Philip E. L., *Food Production and Its Consequences.* Menlo Park, Calif.: Cummings Publishing Co., 1976.

Sollmann, Torald, *A Manual of Pharmacology and Its Applications to Therapeutics and Toxicology.* 8th edition. Philadelphia: W. B. Saunders, 1957.

Spasskaia, E. I., *Mednye kotly rannikh kochevnikov Kazakhstana i Kirgizii* ["Cauldrons of Early Nomads in Kazakhstan and Kirghizia"]. *Ucheniye Zapiski Alma-Atinskogo Gosudarstvennogo Pedago-gicheskogo Instituta, 11.* ["Scientific Proceedings of the Alma-Ata State Pedagogical Institute, 11"]. Alma-Ata, 1956.

Spengler, Oswald, *Zur Weltgeschichte des zweiten vorchristlichen Jahrtausends* [*World History of the Second Millennium B.C.*]. Munich, 1935. (English translation not available).

Sternberg, Leo, "Divine Election in Primitive Religion." *Congrès International des Américanistes*, Compte-Rendu de la XXI session, Pt. 2, 1924. Göteborg, 1925.

Stewart, Omer C. *Peyote Religion. A History.* Norman: University of Oklahoma Press, 1987.

Strong, William D., *Aboriginal Society in Southern California.* University of California Publications in American Archaeology and Ethnology, 26. Berkeley: University of California, 1929.

Süss, Emanuel, *Le Incisioni Rupestri della Valcamonica.* Cologno Monzese: Arti Grafiche Torri, 1985.

Taavitsainen, J. P., "Recent Rock Painting Finds in Finlandia," *Bollettino del Centro Camuno di Studi Preistorici*, Vol. 16 (1977); pp. 148-156 [Capo di Ponte].

Thompson, Charles J., *Alchemy: Source of Chemistry and Medicine.* Reprint. New York: Sentry Press, 1974. (Originally, published in 1897).

Trompf, G.W., *Melanesian Religion*. Cambridge: Cambridge University Press, 1990.

Ucko, Peter J., and Andrée Rosenfeld, *Palaeolithic Cave Art*. New York: McGraw-Hill, 1967.

Van Tilburg, JoAnne, "Symbolic Archaeology on Easter Island," *Archaeology*, Vol. 40, no. 2 (1987); pp. 26–33.

Vasilevich, G. M., "Early Concepts about the Universe among the Evenks (Materials)." *(In)*: H. N. Michael (ed.), *Studies in Siberian Shamanism*. Translations from Russian Sources, 4. Arctic Institute of North America. Toronto: University of Toronto Press, 1963.

Verdenius, W. J., *Mimesis: Plato's Doctrine of Artistic Imitation and Its Meaning to Us*. Philosophia Antiqua, 3. Leiden: E. J. Brill, [1949] 1972.

Walton, Alice, *Asklepios: The Cult of the Greek God of Medicine*. Ithaca: Cornell University Press, 1894.

Waser, Peter G., "The Pharmacology of *Amanita muscaria*." *(In)*: Daniel H. Efron (ed.), *Ethnopharmacologic Search for Psychoactive Drugs*. U.S. Public Health Service Publication, No. 1645. Washington, D.C.: U.S. Government Printing Office, 1967.

———. "Pharmakologische Wirkungsspektren von Halluzinogenen," *Bull. Schweiz. Akad. Med. Wiss.*, Vol. 27 (1971); pp. 39–57.

Wasson, R. Gordon, "Seeking the Magic Mushroom," *Life Magazine*, May 13, 1957 [New York].

———. *Soma: Divine Mushroom of Immortality*. New York: Harcourt Brace Jovanovich, 1969.

———. "The Divine Mushroom of Immortality." *(In)*: P. T. Furst (ed.), *Flesh of the Gods: The Ritual Use of Hallucinogens*. New York: Praeger, 1972; pp. 185–200.

———. "What Was the Soma of the Aryans?" *(In)*: P. T. Furst (ed.), *Flesh of the Gods: The Ritual Use of Hallucinogens*. New York: Praeger, 1972; pp. 201–213.

———. "The Role of 'Flowers' in Nahuatl Culture: A Suggested Interpretation," *Harvard University Botanical Museum Leaflets*, Vol. 23, no. 8 (1973); pp. 305–324.

Wasson, R. Gordon, and Valentina P. Wasson, *Mushrooms, Russia and History*. New York: Pantheon Books, 1957.

Wasson, R. Gordon, *et al.*, *Maria Sabina and Her Mazatec Mushroom Valeda*. New York: Harcourt Brace Jovanovich, 1975. (This publication includes separate musical scores and four audio cassettes).

Wasson, R. Gordon; Albert Hofmann; and Carl A. P. Ruck, *The Road to Eleusis: Unveiling the Secret of the Mysteries*. New York: Harcourt Brace Jovanovich, 1978.

Watson, William, "A Grave Guardian from Ch'ang-sha," British Museum Quarterly, Vol. 17, no. 3 (1952); pp. 52–56.

Weiss, Gerald, "Shamanism and Priesthood in Light of the Campa Ayahuasca Ceremony." (In): M. J. Harner (ed.), Hallucinogens and Shamanism. New York & London: Oxford University Press, [1973] 1981.

Wellmann, Klaus F., "Rock Art, Shamans, Phosphenes, and Hallucinogens in North America," Bollettino del Centro Camuno di Studi Preistorici, Vol. 18 (1981); pp. 89–103 [Capo di Ponte].

Wierciński, Andrzej, "On the Origin of Shamanism." (In): M. Hoppál and O. J. von Sadovszky (eds.), Shamanism: Past and Present. Budapest-Los Angeles: ISTOR Books, 1989.

Wilbert, Johannes, "The Calabash of the Ruffled Feathers." (In): Stones, Bones, and Skin: Ritual and Shamanic Art. Edited by Artscanada. Toronto: Society for Art Publications (an Artscanada Book), 1977; pp. 58–61.

———. Tobacco and Shamanism in South America. New Haven: Yale University Press, 1987.

Wolinski, Arlene, "Egyptian Masks: The Priest and His Role," Archaeology, Vol. 40, no. 1 (1987); pp. 22–29.

Wunderlich, Hans Georg, The Secret of Crete. New York: Macmillan, 1974. (Originally published in German, Wohin der Stier Europa trug, 1972).

Yarden, L., The Tree of Light: A Study of the Menorah—The Seven Branched Lampstand. Ithaca: Cornell University Press, 1971.

Zaehner, R. C., Mysticism: Sacred and Profane. An Inquiry into some Varieties of Praeternatural Experience. New York: Oxford University Press (Galaxy Book), 1961.

Index

A

Adaptation, cultural, 6, 23, 65, 68, 213 n.35, 238–239 n.4

Adrenal gland, 142

Aegean, ancient, 31, 34, 63, 205. *See also* Greece

Agriculture, 105, 106; origins of, 184. *See also* Cultivation

Ainus, 28, 194, 215 n.44 & n.45; bear cult of, 27, 29; hunting magic of, 27; language of, 29; religion of, 29; shaman-priest, Fig. 2.4

Alps, 27, 28, 154–155, 157

Altars, 28, 199–200

Altered states of consciousness, 18, 67, 90, 97, 101, 108, 144, 198; and drumming, 20

Amanita muscaria, 122, 147, 153–157, 161, 164–165, 173–175, 179–181, 206, 244 n.9; preparations of; and Soma; use in Lapland; use in Siberia. *See also* Fly-agaric; Plants and Mushrooms

Amazonian Indians, 67, 73, 78. *See also* listings by tribal names

Amur river, 27, 75

Anadenanthera spp., 178–179

Analogy (also Analogue), 96, 199; cosmological, 125

Anati, Emmanuel, 153, 244 n.9

Androgyny, 84, 111, 125, 227–28 n.38. *See also* Sexuality

Angakok (Eskimo, "shaman"), 63, 80

Anima/animus, 42, 109

Animals, 23–24, 110; game, 27; power, 86

Anisimov, A. E., 12, 25

Antipodes, 112, 124, 184. *See also* Worlds, antipodal

Antlers, 32, 44, 55. *See also* Horns

Aphrodite, 32, 111, 128

Archetypes, 51, 61, 143, 150, 202, 204

Arctic, 23, 28, 32, 66, 71, 73

Arctic sickness, 66, 103

Ariki (Polynesian, "shaman-chief"), 15–16

Art, 64, 131, 149, 176–179, 182, 188–191, 196–199, 201; ceremonial, 112–115, origins of, 150, 204; Palaeolithic, 191, 195; rock, 153, 161, 165, 168, 198–199, 244 n.9; shamanistic, 191, 202–204

Artemis (goddess) 215 n.47, 216 n.51; Brauronia, 32; bear cult of, 27, 32; as Horse-Goddess (Mistress of the Horses), 33; origins of name of, 32; as Polymastus and fertility deity, 32; and shamanism, 32; and totemism, 32; as Triple-Moon-Goddess, 32

Arthurian epics, 21, 93; of Sir Lancelot and sword bridge, 93, 120

Ascent-journeys, 55, 76, 85, 88, 124, 143, 159, 231 n.55. *See also* Ecstasy; Soul-journeys

Asia, 32, 107, 153, 164
Athens, 159–160
Atropa spp., 155
Australia, 23, 24, 90, 123; aborigines
  of, 67
Avatar, 43, 86, 109–110, 136, 178,
  199, 205, 228–229 n.42
Avesta, 165–166
Ayahuasca, 86, 97, 113, 135. *See
  also Banisteriopsis* spp.; Yajé
Ayami (Goldi, "female tutelary
  spirit"), 75–76
Axis mundi, 34, 50, 110, 112, 117,
  143, 172, 177
Aztecs, 99, 167, 169, 173–175

B
Bächler, Emil, 28
Bäckman, Louise, 12
Balance: cosmic and natural, 91, 93,
  127, 184, 194; between nature and
  culture (ecological), 28, 65, 207
Balázs, János, 163–164
Balian (priestess-shamaness), 227
  n.38
Balkans, 43, 44, 154
Banisteriopsis spp., 51, 78, 99–100,
  112, 132, 134, 142–143, 167, 178.
  See also Ayahuasca; Yajé
Barasana Indians, 112, 132
Barradas, José Perez de, 181–182
Basilov, V. N., 141
Basir (asexual shaman-priest), 84,
  227 n.38
Baudelaire, Charles, 50, 190
Bear cult, 27–28
Beauty and Harmony: among
  Navajo, 65; as Platonic image, 17,
  129; in Sufism, 17, 53
Beliefs: 55, 139; shamanistic, 23, 66,
  90, 106
Belize, 90, 173, 206, 230 n.49, 250
  n.54
Belladona, 155
Beltrán, Antonio, 153–154
Benson, Elizabeth, 177–179

Bible, The, 121, 122. *See also* Old
  Testament; Scriptures
Big (Great) Bear constellation, 32,
  49, 119
Bintliff, John, 7; hypothetical
  distinction of, 7, 8
Biunity. *See* Androgyny
Blake, William, 124; *The Marriage
  of Heaven and Hell*, 208
Bohr, Neils: Principle of
  Complementarity of, 190
Borneo, 84
Brahmins, 22, 31, 94, 215 n.46
Brain, as producer of seminal fluid,
  46; as seat of the soul, 46
Brazil, 72, 73, 78, 118, 135, 141
Breath-control, 54
Brenneman, Jr., W. J., 62
Britomartis-Diktynna (Cretan
  goddess), 33, 216 n.51
Bronowski, Jacob, 189, 190
Bronze Age, 157–158, 161, 205
Buddhism: Lamaist, 56; Tantric, 20;
  Tibetan, 20
Bufo toad, 98, 144, 179, 248 n.32
Bufotenin, 179, 248 n.32
Buryats, 62, 120

C
Cahuilla Indians, 136–137
Cakchiquel, 172
California, 81, 91, 103, 123, 124,
  136, 153
Camonica Valley, 1, 34, 154–157,
  244 n.9
Campbell, Joseph, 10, 37, 103, 104, 195
Cashinahua Indians, 97
Cassirer, Ernst, 190, 192
Castaneda, Carlos, 21, 99
Cathedrals: Chartres, 34, 201; Lucca,
  34; Sens, 201
Caves, 36, 70, 82, 87, 89
Celestial bride (also, Spouse), 76
Celts, The, 30, 54, 62, 85, 201; lore
  of, 110–111, 120; Irish, 59; rituals
  of, 33, 59–62

Center (archetypal, cosmic), 36, 112–115, 117, 129, 171
Central America, 92, 172, 183, 230 n.49
Central Asia, 71, 162, 205
Ceremony. *See* Ritual
Chants, 56, 137, 142 (chanting); as metaphor, 52; sacred, 24
Charon, 129
Chhāndogya Upanishad, 207
Chimpanzees, 185
China, 44, 54–55, 162
Chingis Khan, 57
Chrisophoros, Saint (Greek), 2,3
Christianity (also Christians), 20, 88, 195; Byzantine, 2, 44
Chukchees, 86, 163–164, 215 n.44
Church of the Holy Sepulcher, 114
Claviceps paspali and C. purprea, 160, 185–186. *See also* Ergot
Clitoris, 84, 125, 135. *See also* Vagina
Coahuilla Indians. *See* Cahuilla Indians
Coca, 85, 136, 177
Codex: *Badianus*, 167; *Borbonicus*, 174–175; *Durán*, 167; *Florentine*, 167
Cofan Indians, 143
Cognition (and cognitive process), 10, 39, 99; cognitive meanings, 65. *See also* Conception
Cohabition, sexual, 35–36, 79. *See also* Sexual union
Coleridge, Samuel Taylor, 113, 187
Colima culture, 43, 46, 168–170, 219 n.83; single-horned figures, 45
Colombia, 73, 83, 107, 115, 121, 126, 135, 181–183, 198
Colors, 51, 85, 97, 122–128, 135, 149, 150, 171, 198, 200–201, 203
Conception, 107, 190–191, 194; in science, 4, 5; shamanistic, 94, 99
Confucianism, 55
Consciousness, states of, 16, 19, 53, 90, 144. *See also* Altered states of

consciousness; Shamanic states of consciousness
Consort, 61, 76
Cornelius, Agrippa, 121
Cosmic Mountain, 114, 171 (sacred). *See also Axis mundi*
Cosmic Tree, 110, 121–122. *See also* World Tree
Cosmology, 135; Amazonian, 39; Celtic, 110; Coahuilla, 137; Desana, 125–127; Greek, 128–130; Kogi, 126, Mongol, 49; shamanistic, 123, 188, 201; Siberian, 119; Yąnomamö, 117
Cosmos, 105, 129, 171, 194, 205; macrocosm and microcosm, 96
Coto, Fray Tomás, *Vocabulario de la lengua Cakchiquel*, 172
Creation, 34, 37, 92, 96, 101, 184, 188, 193
Crete, ancient. *See* Minoan civilization
Crystal, quartz, 51, 90–91, 123–126, 139, 201, 237 n.45; hexagonal, 111, 115, 123, 125–126; symbolic of semen, 51
Cubeo Indians, 63, 73, 108–109, 124
Cultivation, origins of, 184–186. *See also* Agriculture
Cults: Arcadian, 32; Bull, 46; of the Dead, 205; Deer, 44; Deer Spirit, of Mehinaku, 14; Dionysiac, 31, 49; *Dugu* (Garifuna), 230 n.49 & n.50; of the Feather-Serpent, 99; hallucinogenic, 169; Jagyar, 99; Mesolithic and Neolithic, 55; Minoan, 7, 46; Mystery, 96, 160, 207; Orphic, 31, 91; Osirid, 37, 91; Peyote, 139, 169. *See also* Religion; Rituals
Culture: change, 99, 200; contacts, 78; growth, 8; history, 207
Culture-Environment system (interaction), 213 n.35, 222 n.125, 238 n.4
Curanderos, 70–71

Curing. *See* Healing
Cycles: of human life, 112; of
nature, 62, 105

D
Dance, 68, 90, 138, 142 (dancing),
156–157, 205; as ecstatic or
shamanistic technique, 31, 49,
52–54
Datura spp., 85, 134–137, 145, 155,
167–170, 178; sacred experience,
24
Dawson, Christopher, 20–22, 212
n.26; *Religion and Culture*, 20
Death-rebirth, 20, 35, 43, 60, 62, 76,
82–83, 87, 91, 112–113, 137, 143.
See also Initiation; Resurrection
Deer-Peyote, 206
Demeter (goddess), 146, 159–160
Deprivation, 18, 76, 82, 83, 142. *See
also* Ordeal
Dervishes, 205, 212 n.26; Howling,
17, 52; Whirling, 17–18, 52, 53,
128; mysticism of Whirling
Dervishes, 16–18, 53
Desana Indians, 51, 76, 83, 85, 94, 106,
123–127, 134–136, 149, 194, 203
Descartes, René: on mind-matter
dichotomy, 10, 190
Descent-journey, 63, 85, 94, 143,
159. *See also* Ecstasy; Soul-journey
Devils: Christian, 44; Olympian
gods as Christian, 16; Gnostic, 44
Dialectic: Marxist, 5, 225 n.16
Dichotomy, 10, 65, 190
Dimorphism, 51. *See also* Biunity;
Duality
ed-Din, Jelal (Sufi poet-philosopher),
17, 18
Dionysos (god), 31, 91, 146, 165, 174;
essence of, 49; paradox of
Dionysos, 37, 50
Diószegi, Vilmos, 10, 12, 50, 66, 70,
86; "Shamanism," 10
Dismemberment, 20, 31, 74, 76, 84, 89,
90, 184. *See also* Skeletonization

Disorder: female, 186; mental 68,
102–103, 169; pathological, 88. *See
also* Psychopathology;
Schizophrenia
Divination, 157, 162
DMT, 142
DNA, 36, 190
DOM, 142, 144
Dobkin de Rios, Marlene, 218 n.75
Dome, celestial, 171
Dome of the Rock, 88, 114
Dostoyevsky, Fyodor, 88, 225 n.16;
The Idiot, 88
Drama, 205, 207; as shamanistic
technique, 31, 73; as shamanistic
metaphor, 52
Dreams, 60, 80, 87–88, 90, 106, 108,
188, 195, 203; and culture, 37; and
Gurdjieff, 14; importance of: as
metaphors, 37; in shamanistic
trance, 76; and visions, 75
Drug ceremonial, 134, 167. *See also*
Ritual: drug complex
Drum, 90, 128, 142 (drumming),
156, 205; in Mongolia, 58; in
Papua, 49; used to induce SSC;
and World Tree, 46. *See also*
Shaman's appurtenances: drum
Drumstick, 92, 128, 156. *See also*
Shaman's appurtenances:
drumstick
Druzes, 15, 107–108, 196, 229 n.43,
233 n.7
Duality (also, Dualism), 51, 92, 231
n.59. *See also* Biunity; Dichotomy;
Dimorphism
Dugu ritual, 90, 230 n.50
Durán, Diego, *Codex Durán*, 167
Dynamics, cultural, 15, 22, 68
Dysfunction, social, 204. *See also*
Disorder

E
Earth-Goddess, 32, 60, 61
Easter Island, 15, 16; *ariki*, 15;
human sacrifice on, 16

Eastern Hemisphere, 44, 176. *See also* Old World
Ecstasy, 16–17, 21, 49, 52, 53, 58, 66–68, 77, 86, 88, 93, 96, 101, 105, 123, 159, 163, 195, 205–206, 223 n. 131; attribute of great ruler, 54; bestowing sovereignty, 54; ecstatic flights and journeys, 54–55, 60, 75–76, 82, 85, 92, 95, 119, 155, 159, 166–167, 178, 198, 207, 223 n.131; induced by chanting, drumming, or music, 50, 54; as shamanistic technique, 164; *See also* Rapture; Trance
Ecuador, 73, 78, 134–135, 143
Eden, Garden of, 82, 184, 196
Egypt (also Egyptians), 52, 200; ancient, 114, 176, 186–187, 192–193, 200; beliefs in ancient, 37, 40; use of animal masks in, 40–42; temples of, 200–201
Einstein, Albert, 4
Eleusinian Mysteries (also, Eleusis), 160–161, 186
Eliade, Mircea, 10, 20, 44, 50, 52, 54, 55, 70, 76, 84, 86, 91, 96, 103, 164, 211 n.19; *Shamanism: Archaic Techniques of Ecstasy*, 10, 11, 227 n.38
Emmerich, André, 182
Enema, tobacco, 141
Enlightenment: shamanistic, 74, 76, 82, 87, 91, 124
Entheoi, 54, 88, 96, 146
Entropy, 34, 92, 112
Epiphany, 43, 196, 207
Ergine, 160, 186
Ergonovine, 146, 160, 186
Ergot, 85, 146, 160–161, 185–186
Eroticism, 134, 229 n.43; animal, 23; in shamanism, 75, 77; in *wu* rituals, 55. *See also* Sexuality
Eschatology, 118, 184
Eskimos, 74, 81, 215 n.44
Eternal return, principle of, 24, 62, 112–113

Ethnohistory, 151, 167, 174
Etruscans, 35, 157
Eugster, Conrad H., 147
Eurasia, 28, 43, 45, 121, 205, 206
Europe, 43–44, 46, 63, 91, 101, 107, 164, 199; Land of the Horses, 33
Evans, Sir Arthur, 7–8
Evenks, 24–25, 63, 110, 119–120, 122; World Tree of, 24–25
Evolution, 36, 111, 188
Existence (Being), 36, 83, 101, 115, 118, 138, 190, 194–195; forms of, 39; human, 14, 64, 65; primeval, 16, 77; existentialism and, 95. *See also* Reality
Experience, 66, 88, 106, 143, 189–193, 197; ecstatic and shamanistic, 50, 53–54, 76, 87, 96, 103, 149, 168, 207; hallucinogenic and psychedelic, 19, 87, 99, 101, 106, 144, 149–151, 154, 174, 178, 203, 232 n.68; mystical and preternatural, 19, 54, 68, 70, 99, 105, 207; numinous and sacred, 8, 24, 193; religious and spiritual, 9, 20, 93, 107, 132, 178, 197; visionary, 18, 20, 53, 91, 93, 103–106, 120, 135, 146–147, 168, 197, 201

F
Fecundity, 61, 83, 126, 184, 186. *See also* Fertility
Fertility, 32, 60, 91, 111, 112, 135–136. *See also* Fecundity
Fibonacci of Pisa, Leonardo, 189
Finland (also, Fins), 28, 161, 163; lore of, 120
Fire (also, Flame), 126, 199–200, 215 n.46
Flute pipes, 31; in rainmaking ceremonies, 45
Fly-agaric, 85, 139, 142, 147, 163–165, 179, 206, 244 n.9, 247–248 n.32. See also *Amanita muscaria*

Fodor, Nandor. *See* Nandor, Fodor
Frazer, Sir James G., 40, 94
Freud, Sigmund, 4–5, 74, 77, 101,
    102, 142; on Eros and Thanatos, 5;
    Beyond the Pleasure Principle, 4
Furst, Peter T., 12, 45, 46, 115, 131,
    139, 170, 174, 179, 182, 199, 206,
    218 n.75; *Flesh of the Gods*, 218
    n.75; *Hallucinogens and Culture*,
    212 n.30, 218 n.75

G
Ganoderma lucidum (mushroom),
    166
Garifuna, 90, 230 n.49, n.50
Gems (also, Gemstones), 123, 200.
    See also Jewels, Precious stones
Gilyaks, 28, 72; bear cult of, 27;
    Master of the Animals, 27
Gimbutas, Marija, 44
God, 17–19, 50, 53, 88, 121, 128,
    138, 184, 192–193, 196; origins of
    the idea of, 40
Gods and Goddesses, 31, 61, 70, 130,
    141, 165, 184, 200; Celtic, 60–62,
    76, 92; Egyptian, 39, 192–193;
    fertility deities, 91; Greek, 16, 39,
    85, 128, 159, 216 n.47; Hindu, 94
    (Kali), 215 n.46 (Rudra), 227–229
    n.38, n.42 (Vishnu); Mongolian,
    58–59; Norse, 85; Pre-Columbian,
    91, 173, 202
Goethe, 207
Gold, 199–201; pectorals, 181–183
Goldi, 76
Goldman, Irving, 73
Granet, Marcel, 54
Graves, Robert, 157
Great Mother goddess, 36, 42, 60,
    64, 83, 115, 150; of the Animals,
    77; as *Magna Mater*, 5; as Mother-
    Creatrix, 94. *See also* Mother
    Goddess
Great Spirit, 80, 128
Greece (also Greeks), 2–3, 146;
    ancient, 8, 16, 27, 31, 32, 35, 85,

    95, 111, 128, 160, 193, 197, 215–16
    n.47; Bronze Age, 7, 157–158
Greek Orthodox Church, 2; and
    ancient religion, 2, Fig. 1.1; and
    shamanism, 2–3, 95
Gregor, Thomas, 14, 73
Groot, Jan de, 54
Guatemala, 172–173, 182
Gurdjieff, G. I., 13, 14, 52, 209 n.1,
    210 n.2 & n.4; and Karl Haushofer,
    13; and Adolf Hitler, 14; influence
    of, in America and Europe, 13; and
    D. H. Lawrence, 14

H
Hades, 159
Halifax, Joan, 84
Hallucinations, 21, 101, 138, 142,
    144, 163, 168, 176–177
Hallucinogenic substances (drugs,
    plants, etc.) *See* Hallucinogens
Hallucinogens, 9, 18, 20, 27, 44,
    61–62, 73, 77, 95–100, 105–106,
    131–135, 138, 144–145, 148, 154,
    162–163, 166–169, 173–174, 183,
    186, 198–199, 206, 211 n.19,
    217–19 n.75; preparation of, 85,
    112, 132; properties of, 98, 141; in
    shamanism, 9, 44, 62, 86. *See also*
    Avahuasca; Mescaline; Peyote;
    Plants and Mushrooms:
    hallucinogenic; Psychotropic
    substances
Haoma, 165, 248 n.34
Harmaline (alkaloid), 106, 113, 143
Harmine (alkaloid), 143
Harmony, 18, 53, 121, 129. *See also*
    Beauty and Harmony
Harner, Michael, 12, 34, 63, 78, 85,
    132, 218 n.75; *Hallucinogens and
    Shamanism*, 218 n.75, 232 n.68
Harrison, Jane, 16, 111
Hawking, Stephen, 4
Headband, as substitute for
    shaman's horns, 45–46
Healers, 16, 20, 55, 64, 65, 178

Healing, 68, 77, 78, 87, 89, 90, 105, 110, 138, 168, 207, 240 n.22
Heidegger, Martin, 36
Heima salicifolia, 173–174
Heisenber, Werner, 3, 8, 188; Uncertainty Principle of, 4, 8, 190
Hemp, 85
Hereafter, 39, 96, 110, 115, 150
Hermaphroditism. *See* Androgyny
Herodotus, 37
Hesse, Hermann, 18; *Siddhartha*, 75
Hexagon, 83, 121, 125–127, 201. *See also* Universe: hexagonal
Heyden, Doris, 174
Historia Norwegiae, 97
Hofmann, Albert, 146
Holy, idea of the, 16; manifestation of God, 19, 40
Hominids, 36, 185; hominization, 2
Homo sapiens, 8
Horns, 31–32, 44–46, 115, 124, 219 n.83. *See also* Antlers
Huichol Indians, 45, 46, 115, 117, 121, 124–125, 139–140, 169, 174, 199, 206
Hultkrantz, Åke, 12, 22, 23, 70, 96
Humphrey, Nicholas, 89
Hungary, 161, 162, 205
Huns, 93, 161–163, 246 n.27
Hunters and Hunting, 23, 27, 28, 43, 61, 77, 127, 168, 185, 243 n.2; and biological selection, 222 n.125; primordial, 206; prohibitions against totem animals, 25
Huxley, Aldous, 19, 123, 184, 199–201, 211 n.18; *The Doors of Perceptions*, 18, 19
Hyoscyamus niger, 155

I

Idealogy, religious, 42, 73
Idiom, 194, 197; cultural, 68, 191, 196; mythico-religious, 10, 50, 70
Igjugarjuk (an Eskimo shaman), 74, 80–81

Image (also, Imagery), 193, 197–198; archetypal, 106, 198; involuntary mental, 34; mythic, 195; Platonic, 17, 101, 189; shamanistic, 194, visual, 189, 191, 194. *See also* Phosphenes
Imago mundi, 61, 106, 125–126. *See also* Archetypes
India, 14, 21, 31, 94, 164; ancient, 31, 92, 199; legends of, 20
Indo-Europeans, 30, 54, 61, 91, 154, 164–165, 244–45 n.9
Initiate, 132, 134, 137, 149. *See also* Neophyte
Initiation, 20, 62, 72, 76, 81–83, 84, 86, 89, 91, 94, 123, 126–127, 136–137, 207, 229 n.43. *See also* Dismemberment; Neophyte; Ordeal; Skeletonization
Inner personal crisis (IPC), 60–62, 71, 74, 89, 103–104, 133
Intoxication, 61, 134, 163–164. *See also* Hallucinogens; Trance
IPC. *See* Inner personal crisis
Iphigenia, 215–16 n.47
Irtysh-Ob rivers, 163, 165
Islam, 87, 229 n.43
Italy, 35, 64, 154, 157, 201, 248 n.36. *See also* Venice; Verona

J

Jaguar-shaman, 63, 109
Japan, 20, 28, 44, 194, 205–206; language of, 29, 215 n.44
Jerusalem, 88, 114
Jewels, 199–200. *See also* Gems; Precious Stones
Jívaro Indians, 63, 73, 78, 91, 96, 99, 124, 133–134
John of Patmos, Saint, 138; *Book of Revelations*, 122
Jones, Flora (a Wintu shamaness), 82
Judaeo-Christian, 94, 114, 127
Jung, Carl G., 36, 86, 104, 149, 194, 204

K

Kabbalah (Kabbalists), 54, 193
Kafka, Franz, 37
Kakaram (Jivaro, "outstanding killers"), 63, 133
Kalmucks, 314
Kamchadals, 163, 215 n.44
Kamieński Dłużyk, Adam, 163
Kant, Immanuel, 188, 190; and forms of sensibilities, 95
Katha Upanishad, 93
Kava (Piper methysticum), 16, 210 n.8; ingestion of, 16
Kensinger, Kenneth, 97
Kiddushim, 193
Kinalik (an Eskimo shamaness), 81
King, as cosmic fertilizer, 61–62
Knight, W. Jackson, 35
Knoll, Max, 149, 150
Knowledge, 64, 68, 75, 78–79, 81–82, 85, 87, 105–106, 132–133, 186, 188, 190, 202, 206, 225 n.16
Koch-Grünberg, Theodor, 31
Kogi Indians, 114–115, 126
Koran. See Quran, The
Koryaks, 163, 235 n.44
Kroeber, Alfred L., 24, 89, 137
Ksenofontov, G. V., 46, 79
Kykeon, 360, 186

L

La Barre, Weston, 12, 44, 70, 75, 206, 217–18 n.75; Peyote Cult, 218 n.75, 240 n.25
Labyrinth, 33–36, 92, 112, 150. See also Maze
Lady of Wild Things, 31, 33. See also Mistress of the Animals
Lamuts, 215 n.44
Language, 99–101, 187–195, 207
Lapps (also, Lapland), 46, 97, 120, 163
Lascaux, 70, 195
László, 162
Lebhar na Huidre, 60
Lévi-Strauss, Claude, 6, 102

Linga Purāna, 215 n.46
Ling-chih mushroom, 55, 166
Lophophora williamsii, 142, 168–169. See also Peyote
Lowerworld, 34–35, 60, 76, 94, 110, 112–113, 117–120, 137, 184. See also Otherworld, Underworld
LSD, 142–144, 146, 160, 167
Luiseño Indians, 137; puberty rites of, 24; daturs drinking by, 24
Lumholtz, Carl, 170

M

Mabinogion, 30
Maenchen-Helfen, Otto, 161, 162
Magic, 20, 107, 207; black or evil, 73, 108; Chinese, 54; hunting, 9, 23, 55, 61, 102, 191; of numbers, 121. See also Numbers; Rituals: hunting
Magic plants and mushrooms. See Hallucinogens; Plants and Mushrooms; Psychotropic substances
Mahābhārata, 94
Malekula island (Melanesia), 34–35, 95
Manchuria, 46, 58
Mandala, 34, 36
Mara'akáme (Huichol, "shaman"), 115, 124
Marais, Eugène, 5; The Soul of the Ape, 5
Mariette, Auguste, Dendera IV, 41
Markale, Jean, The Celtic Civilization, 60
Masks, 40–44, 46, 156, 171, 205
Maspero, Gaston, 41
Master of the Animals, 9, 20, 24, 25, 27, 29, 30–31, 40, 43, 77, 111, 119–120, 139, 198, 215 n.46; womb-like longhouse of, 27
Materialism, cultural, 5, 107; dialectic, 107; scientific, 101
Matlatzinca Indians, 76, 139, 184
Matsyendranath, 20

Maugham, W. Somerset, 93; *The Razor's Edge*, 93
Mayas, 99, 140, 171–173, 183, 206; Kekchi, 206; Mopan, 206; archaeological site, 250 n.54
Mazatec Indians, 138
Maze, 34, 92. See also Labyrinth
Mead (fermented drink), 61, 85
Medicine men, 16, 65, 66, 70, 186
Mehinaku Indians (Upper Xingu), 72–73, 108, 141; belief system 14; creation of new cults, 14–15; visionary experience, 15
el-Melewi, Sheikh Shefieh, 18, 128
Menorah, 122
Mescal bean, 168, 199. See also *Sophora secundiflora*
Mescaline, 19, 123, 142–143, 145, 184. See also Peyote
Mesmer, Anton, 101–102
Mesoamerica, 70, 99, 109, 115, 168, 170–171; iconography of, 170
Mesolithic, 55, 111, 219 n.75
Metal and Metallurgy, 105–107, 122, 201–202; metal smith, 202. See also Gold
Metaphor, 43, 65, 68, 83, 85, 111, 114, 121, 135, 139, 187, 190–191, 194–199, 202–203, 205; chanting as, 52; cultural, 2, 6, 112, 150, 197, 211 n.18; dance as, 52; drama as, 52; drumming as, 52; existential, 11; in hunting rituals, 23; of language and speech, 102, 192–193; mask as, 42; myth as, 52, 192; of procreation, 51; religious, 70, 107, 120, 196, 206–207; sexual, 228 n.38; shamanistic, 2, 49, 125, 198
Metaphysics, Gurdjieff's, 14; Heidegger's, 36; Plato's, 17, 37
Mexico, 43, 71, 98–99, 115, 121, 139, 168–169, 172–174, 184, 199, 206
Michael, H. N., *Studies in Siberian Shamanism*, Fig. 2.2
Middle America. See Mesoamerica
Middleworld, 119–120

Minoan(s), 7–8, 179; Crete, 7, 33, 35, 46, 159, 205; decipherment of language of, 8
Minotaur, 33, 35, 43
Mistress of the Animals (and Wild Things), 31, 33, 63, 120
Mochica, 176–180
Monad, of culture, 204, 207
Mongolia (also, Mongols), 39–40, 46, 56–59, 62–63, 92–93, 114, 119, 162
Morning glory, 167, 173–174. See also *Rivea corymbosa*
Mother Earth, 91, 184
Mother Goddess, 35, 55, 62, 216 n.47 & n.51. See also Great Goddess
Mousterian: remains, 28
Muensterberger, Werner, 102
Muhammed, the Prophet, 87–88, 114, 231 n.55
Mundari: animal eroticism, 23; magic and the supernatural, 23; relationship to animals, 23; shaman, 23
Munkácsi, B. *Collection of Vogul Heroic Songs*, 163
Munn, Henry, "The Mushrooms of Language," 99, 101, 103
Murchie, Guy, 150
Murray, Margaret, 41
Mushrooms. See Plants and Mushrooms
Music, 122; sacred, 45, 49–50, 64, 138; as shamanistic technique, 31, 93
Muslims, 88, 114, 213 n.35. See also Islam
Mycenae (city), 157, 159
Mystics and Mysticism, 15, 70, 74, 148, 207; ascetic, 6, 87; adepts, 13, 21; Christian, 17, 19, 52; classic, 18; Sufi, 18, 53, 128; Tantric, 135; transcultural, 19
Myths, 42, 109–110, 132, 190, 192–197; as fundamental response, 10; Hindu, 227–28 n.38; and

individual, 37; as metaphor, 37, 52;
Papuan origin, 49; sacred, 64; Vedic,
154, 165; Yąnomamö origin, 110

N

Nandor, Fodor (Nijinsky's
biographer), 52–53; Between Two
Worlds, 52
Naranjo, Claudio, 113, 143
Natemä (hallucinogenic drink), 78
Natural selection, 184, 222 n.125
Nature: cycles of, 62, 105; forces of,
56
Navajo, 65, 171
Nayarit culture, double-horned
figurines in, 45
Neanderthal man, 27, 28, 206; and
bear cult, 28
Neolithic, 42, 43, 55, 85, 185–186
Neophyte, 66, 76, 82–83, 87, 90,
122, 126, 132, 137, 229 n.43. See
also Initiation
New Guinea, 49, 117, 248 n.33
New Testament, 122, 193, 196
New World, 44, 70, 139, 151,
166–168, 170, 179, 183, 206. See
also Western Hemisphere
Ngadju-Dayak, 84
Nicotiana spp., 141, 148, 173, 183
Nietzsche, 207
Nijinsky (Russian dancer), 52–53
Nile, The, 40; White, 23; Valley, 40
Nivkhs, 110
Noiaidi (Lapp, "shamans"), 63
Norsemen, 85
North Africa: Algeria, 152–153;
Libya, 153; Neolithic, 153; Sudan,
186
North American Indians, 64, 97,
136–137
Northwest Coast Indians (Pacific),
24; shaman's mask of, Fig. 2.3
Numbers, mystical significance of,
49, 121–122, 126–127, 166, 234
n.13
Numen, 54, 194

O

Ob-Ugrians, 163
Odin, 59, 82, 85, 202, 234 n.13
Ohimarks, Åke, 103
Old Testament, 94, 122
Old World, 44, 85, 151, 155, 174,
179. See also Eastern Hemisphere
Olmecs, 99
Oneness, 16, 17. See also Unity;
Wholeness
Opium, 85, 159–160, 245–46 n.15 &
n.16
Ordeal, 20, 71, 74, 77, 80–82, 93.
See also Initiation
Osiris, 37, 39–40, 91; as ruler of the
dead, Fig. 2.5
Ostrander, Sheila, 52, 67
Ostyaks, 163–164
Otherworlds, 15, 24–25, 34–37,
49–50, 61–62, 64–65, 67, 74,
76–77, 86, 92, 94–96, 110, 112,
117–118, 123, 127–128, 133, 137,
176, 178, 184, 188. See also
Lowerworld; Middleworld;
Upperworld
Otto, Rudolf, 16

P

Palaeolithic, 43, 69, 211 n.19, 219
n.75; hunters, 127; Lower, 28;
Middle, 28; Upper, 27, 28, 42, 111
Pan (deity), 31; as devil, 44
Panaeolus mushroom. 154–155, 177
Panama, 107, 181–183
Paradigm, cosmic, 34, 92, 118, 126,
129, 195; divine, 106, 121
Paśupati, 215 n.46; as Lord of (herd)
Animals, 31; sexual energy of, 31
Payés (Tukano, "shamans"), 78
Payute Indians, 136
Penis, 125, 135. See also Phallicism
Perception (cognitive), 107, 124, 187,
191, 194; of cosmos, 104; in
science, 4–5
Persephone, 159, 161
Personality, 86, 104

Perspectives: in behavioral and cultural sciences, 5

Peru, 97, 135, 143, 176–180

Peyote, 21, 85, 115, 117, 142–146, 167–169, 174, 177–178, 240–41 n.25; ceremony, 139–140. *See also Lophophora williamsii;* Mescaline; Plants and Mushrooms; Psychotropic substance

Phallicism (also Phallus), 51, 84, 121, 136, bone as phallic metaphor, 136. *See also* Penis

Phenomenology, 4; religious, 14, 18, 70; shamanistic, 9, 22, 71, 174; of symbolic forms, 187 ff.

Phosphenes, 91, 148–150, 202–204

Picietl (tobacco), 167

Pineal gland, 144

Plains, The (American), 168, 170

Plants and Mushrooms: ancient ceramic mushrooms, 245 n.15; divine, 105, 106; hallucinogenic, 122, 134, 143, 152–153, 157–159, 163, 171–173, 180–182; Hunnic finds of mushrooms, 246 n.22; magical and sacred, 21, 33, 87, 122, 138–139, 161, 167, 169, 177, 179, 240 n.22; medicinal, 110; mushroom stones, Fig. 3.2, 99, 101; mushrooms in Vinča culture, 44. See also *Amanita muscaria;* Hallucinogens; Psychotropic substance; *Psylocibe* mushroom

Plato, 129, 188–189; images of, 17, 189; World-soul, 129; *Phaedo*, 37

Poland, 29–30, 181

Polaris (also Polar Star), 49, 114, 119

Polarity, 228 n.38. *See also* Biunity; Dimorphism

Polynesia, 15, 210 n.9

Poppy, 159–160

Porta, Giovanni Batista, 64; *Naturall Magick*, 64

Possession, 55, 64, 67, 72, 86, 87, 90, 108, 223 n.131, 224 n.9; in Polynesia, 16

Power, of evil, 56; feminine, 62, 111; mystical, 123; objects, 91, 123; occult and preternatural, 31, 139, 193; psychic and spiritual, 15, 52–53; shamanistic, 54–55, 63, 79, 109, 124

Pragmatism, material, 156; social, 5, 9

Precious stones, 123, 184, 200. *See also* Gems; Jewels

Pre-Columbian (also, Prehispanic), artifacts, 107; figurines, 43, 45, 169, 172–173, 176–178, Fig. 4.1; gold pectorals, 181–183

Priests, 16, 65, 67, 157, 162, 177; ancient Egyptian, 41–42; Christian, 41; priest-shaman, 84; Shinto, 44; Vodoun, 70

Process, 6, 85, 189; cosmic, 107, 192; creation, 134; cultural, 22; historical, 70; infinite, 36; natural, 64, 125; ontogenetic, 83; psychocultural, 70, 71; scientific, 4; supernatural, 64

Prophets, Hebrew, 40

Psilocin (alkaloid), 142, 146

Psilocybe mushroom, 85, 99, 139, 142, 146, 153–155, 173–174, 177, 183–184. *See also* Plants and Mushrooms

Psilocybin (alkaloid), 142–143, 146

Psychedelics, 20. *See also* Hallucinogens

Psychoactivity, 99, 106, 134, 141–145, 167, 179

Psychology, crowd, 14, 18

Psychopathology, 73, 104. *See also* Disorders, mental; Schizophrenia

Psychopomp, 2, 31, 37, 43, 45, 65, 95. *See also* Shaman: as psychopomp

Psychotropic substances (drugs, plants, etc.), 21, 44, 61, 64, 77, 85, 151, 155, 161, 167–168; Upper Palaeolithic beginnings for use of, 44. *See also* Hallucinogens; Plants and Mushrooms

Pueblo Indians, 40, 169–170;
  mandala in art of, 34
Purkinje, Johannes, 148
Puul (Cahuilla, "shaman"), 137
Pythagoras, 129; philosophy of, 121

Q
Quartz. *See* Crystal, quartz
Quest, existential: for meaning, 105
Quran, The, 87–88

R
Rapture, 50, 86–88, 93, 177,
  205–206. *See also* Ecstasy
Rasmussen, Knud, 24, 74, 80, 81,
  128; *Across Arctic America*, 80
Rasputin, 52
Rattle, 90, 112, 119. *See also*
  Shaman's appurtenances: rattle
Razor's edge, 93, 120.
Reality, 83, 84, 111–113, 133,
  187–188, 190–191, 193; archetypal,
  111; existential and transcendental,
  9, 65, 119; metaphysical, 37, 65;
  mythic, 197; Otherworldly, 69, 96;
  See also Existence
Rees, Alwyn and Brinley, 61
Reichel-Dolmatoff, Gérardo, 22, 39,
  50, 65, 76, 94, 111, 131, 135, 137,
  149, 198, 202–203, 211 n.19;
  Amazonian Cosmos, 12
Reinhard, Johan, 97
Religion, 70, 75, 105, 151, 198, 207;
  Ainu, 215 n.45; Ainu and Shinto,
  some similarities between, 29;
  Celtic, 59–62; Chinese, 54;
  creation of basic forms in, 16;
  Egyptian (ancient), 37, 39–40,
  41–42; Hebrew, 60; Greek Bronze
  Age, 7; Huichol, 115; Islamic, 60,
  88; Kogi, 115; Mystery, 146, 186,
  229 n.43; Native American 44;
  North American, 70; pantheistic,
  95; Polynesian ecstatic, 16, 210
  n.9; shamanistic, 56, 86; Shinto,
  215 n.45; and social order, 22;

South American, 70; as trans-
  formational process, 107;
  Tukanoan, 111, 138; Zoroastrian,
  166
Resurrection, 39, 76, 135, 166
Rhythm, 36, 50, 90; as technique of
  ecstasy, 53; trance-inducing, 17
Rigveda, 164–165
Ripinsky, Michael M., "Cultural
  Idiom as an Ecologic Factor," 213
  n.35, 245 n.15; "Middle Eastern
  Kinship as an Expression of a
  Culture-Environment System,"
  238–39 n.4
Ripinsky-Naxon, Michael, 52,
  156–157, 165, 173, 176–177, 200,
  207, 211 n.18, 216 n.51, 230 n.49,
  234 n.7; "Hallucinogens,
  Shamanism, and the Cultural
  Process," 218–19 n.75; *The Nature
  of Shamanism*, 9
Rites of passage, 132. *See also*
  Ritual
Ritual, 133, 191; Celtic, 33, 59–62;
  drug complex and use, 131–132,
  151, 154, 162, 169, 172, 176, 183,
  206; Egyptian (ancient), 41–42;
  fertility, 43; Garifuna (*dugu*), 90;
  Greek (ancient), 32; hunting, 23,
  24, 43, 157; Javanese, 205; marriage,
  65; mating, 33; Maya, 99;
  menstrual, 126; of Mother Earth,
  91; puberty, 24, 137; purification,
  94; Seri, 89; shamanistic, 32, 51,
  56, 76, 91, 136, 206; Shintoist, 44;
  techniques of, 14; totemic, 32;
  women exchange, 27; *wu*, 55. *See
  also* Cults
Rivea corymbosa, 173–174. *See also*
  Morning glory
Robicsek, Francis, *The Smoking
  Gods*, 140, 183
Rock art. *See* Art, rock
Rock of the Moriah, 88, 114.
Róheim, Géza, *Children of the
  Desert*, 102

Round Head period, 152–153, 243
n.2
Rufaim, 17, 52. *See also* Dervishes:
Howling
Rumania, 43, 161, 162
Russia (also Russians), 28, 44, 52,
62, 67
Ruysbroeck, Vilhelms av, 56

S
Sacrament, 17, 196
Sacred Deer, 124, 206
Sacrifice, 62, 91, 110, 128, 177, 184;
among Celts, 92; on Easter Island,
16; of goats on Naxos and Syros 2;
among Tukanoans, 27
Sahagún, Fray Bernardino de,
Florentine Codex, 167
Sahara, 153, 181, 243 n.2
Šaman (Tungus-Mongol, "shaman"), 69
Samana (Pali, "beggar monk"), 69
Samorini, Giorgio, 153–155, 244 n.9
Samoyeds, 62, 119, 163
San Pedro cactus, 177–178
Sanskrit, 193, 215 n.46
Sartre, Jean-Paul, *Being and
Nothingness*, 95
Sauneron, Serge, 41–42
Scandinavia, 161, 206
Schizophrenia, 68, 104, 144. *See also*
Disorder: mental; Psychopathology
Schmidt, Father Wilhelm, 40; *The
Origins of the Idea of God*, 127
Schroeder, Lynn, 52, 67
Schultes, Richard Evans, 145, 167,
173, 183
Science, 64, 190; Scientific
Revolution, 101
Scriptures, 184. *See also* Bible
Seabrook, W. B. (American traveler),
15
Secret History of the Mongols, 57
Seizure, epileptic, 87–88, 103, 176;
convulsive fits, 168. *See also*
Shamanic illness
Semen, 46, 51, 125, 136

Seri Indians, 86, 89–90, 230 n.47
Serotonin, 142–146
Sex: change, 84; and religion, 77
Sexual(ity), 31, 35, 51, 60, 77, 89,
135, 150, 203, 228 n.38, 229 n.43;
bond, 75; qualities of numbers,
121; and shamanism, 75, 77; union
(intercourse), 35, 60, 61, 81, 85,
149, 203; between shamans and
spirits, 76, 77, 198–199. *See also*
Androgyny; Biunity; Cohabition;
Eroticism; Hermaphroditism;
Transexuality
Shaman(s), 24–25, 44, 52–55, 59, 61,
63, 67–68, 70, 73, 82–84, 91–92,
96, 103–104, 107–109, 118, 134,
138–140, 154–156, 161, 169, 177,
186, 195, 199, 200, 202–204, 223
n.131; Ainu (shaman-priest), Fig.
2.4; Altaic, 91, 119, 122, 129; as
animal spirit, 43; Biak (New
Guinea), 117; Buryat, 50, 62, 76;
Cahuilla, 136–137; combat
between, 63, 73; compared to
spiritual master, 21; Cubeo, 63;
Desana, 119, 123, 125–127; Dolgan,
120; Eskimo, 18, 63, 74, 80, 93;
Evenk, 63, 110, 119; Gilyak, 66;
Goldi, 75; as harmonizer of social
and natural dysfunctions, 9, 65,
207–208; as healer, 9, 65, 77;
Huichol, 115, 124; Hunnic,
162–163; Jívaro, 124; Karagss, Fig.
2.6; Lapp, 30, 63, 97, 122; Malay,
109; as Master of Animals, 43;
Mongol, 57, 66; Ostyak, 122; -priest,
186, 200; as psychopomp, 9, 31, 37,
95, 117, 129, 205; the role of, 9,
20, 22, 41, 62, 65; Samoyed, 62;
Siberian, 50, 87, 195; selection of,
71–72; South American, 113;
techniques of, 21, 54, 65, 86, 164,
207; tent of Evenk, Fig. 2.2;
terminology, 69; tobacco-, 140–141,
148, 224 n.9; Tukanoan, 27, 39, 40,
65, 78, 95; Tungus, Fig. 2.7, 50, 62,

78–80; Ugrian, 121, 164; Ugrian-Ostyak, 91; Uralo-Altaic, 85; Wintu, 81–82; Yakut, 21, 46, 76, 120; Yaqi, 21; Yuman, 124. *See also* Shamaness; Shamanism

Shamaness, 33, 62, 76, 77, 81, 82; Celtic, 60. *See also* Shaman

Shamanic calling, 66, 71, 75, 89, 90, 102

Shamanic flights and journeys. *See* Ecstasy: ecstatic flights and journeys; Soul-journey

Shamanic illness, 66, 72, 79, 87, 90, 103. *See also* Seizure

Shamanic states of consciousness (SSC), 10, 25, 37, 49, 65, 74, 85–86, 88, 91–93, 96–97, 104, 142–143

Shamanism, 24, 52, 62, 67–68, 70–72, 79, 92, 96, 102, 105–107, 140, 151, 191, 207; as adaptive mechanism, 9, 65, 68; ancient, 10; Arctic, 103; Celtic, 30, 62; character of, 22; Chinese, 54, 55; classic, 10; as cultural process, 9; definitions, 69–71; and ecstasy, 44, 206; function of, 56; and hallucinogens, 9, 44, 62, 86, 103, 106, 132, 166, 217–218 n.75; Hungarian, 163; and hunting societies, 39, 43; Indo-European, 30, 54; Manchu, 56; Mongolian, 39, 56–59; Mundari, 23; mythic origins of, 132; Nepalese, 97; North American, 73; origns of, attributed, 39; and patriarchy, 40; Seri, 89–90; Siberian, 56, 73, 110, 139, 163; and sky-gods, 40; survivals of, 32, 204–208; recurrent themes in, 20, 40, 62, 71, 99, 104, 110–111, 116, 178, 195, 202, 204–205, 225 n.16; as religious metaphor, 207; Tungus, 56; in Vinča culture, 44. *See also* Shaman(s)

Shaman's appurtenances, 46–49, 51;

drum, 47, 50, 52, 56, 92, 119–120, 128; drumstick, 46–47, 50, 120, 128; flute, 45; headband, 45, 46; horns, 44, 115, 156, 219 n.83; mask, 42, 44, 46, 155–156; ornaments, Fig. 2.7; rattle, 50, 51, 119; staff, 40; vestments, Figs. 2.6 & 2.7, 50, 55, 122, 155, 195, 202; whistle, 45

Shaw, George Bernard, *The Adventures of the Black Girl in Her Search for God*, 225 n.16

Shintoism, 20, 29

Shirokogoroff, Sergei, 77

Shiva-Paśupati, 31, 215 n.46

Shoshoni Indians, visionary quests of, 22

Siberia, 13, 27, 28, 46–47, 62–63, 66, 69, 72, 75–76, 79, 84, 86, 91, 95, 97, 110, 122, 162–165, 195, 206

Sibero-Tungusic tribes, 46

Sieroszewski, Wenceslas L., 21; *Twelve Years among the Yakuts*, 21

Skeletonization, 20, 76, 79, 80, 171, 184. *See also* Initiation

Sky-gods, 40, 60, 127

Smith, The (also, Smithy), 61

Snuff, hallucinogenic, 73, 110, 135–136, 178–179

Soma, 155, 164–166, 244 n.9; identity in *Rigveda*, 164

Songs (singing), 52. *See* Chants

Sophora secundiflora, 168, 170, 199. *See also* Mescal bean

Sorceress, ecstatic techniques of Chinese, 54

Sorceror and Sorcery, 56, 66, 70, 73, 109, 155, 169

Soul, 24, 27–28, 53, 73, 82, 92, 95, 107–110, 115–118, 124, 133–134, 137, 233 n.6; according to Herodotus, 37; in shamanism, 37; theory of, 94; transmutation of, 17

Soul-journey, 24–25, 37, 39–40, 50, 54, 74, 77, 82, 85, 88, 92, 120, 128,

137, 205. *See also* Ecstasy: ecstatic
flights and journeys
South America, 70, 90, 92, 109, 115,
121, 123, 135, 142, 167, 173, 186
South American Indians, 141. *See
also* listings by tribal names
Soviet Union, 52, 66, 161
Space, existential, 126; sacred,
113–114, 129
Spain (also, Spaniards), 141, 153
Spengler, Oswald, 7, 8, 204; *The
Decline of the West*, 8, 204
Sperm, archetypal, 62. *See also*
Semen
Spirals, 34–36, 112, 150, 244 n.9
Spirit, 34–35, 50, 56, 66, 72, 73, 76,
83, 86, 92, 108, 116–118, 128, 133,
199, 200; ancestral, 39, 45, 56, 90,
110; animal, 25–26, 39, 91, 156;
divine, 92; female, 75, 77, 95;
guardian, helpers, and familiars,
25, 39, 57, 62, 74–75, 78, 80, 81,
89, 90, 109–110, 122–124, 137, 156,
198, 205, 223 n.131; of
Lowerworld, 37; Nature, 42;
phallic forest, 27; transformation
of, 42; tutelary, 76, 77; World, 72,
85, 124
Spouse, spiritual, 86. *See also*
Celestial bride
Sramana (Sanskrit, "an ascetic"), 69
SSC. *See* Shamanic states of
consciousness
Stag, 32
Sternberg, Leo, 75–77
Studies, cultural, 5–8
Styx river, 128–129
Sufis and Sufism, 16, 53, 166, 205.
See also Dervishes
Sun-Father, 40, 125
Sun-penis, 125, 136
Süss, Emanuele, 156
Sweden, 161
Sword bridge. *See* Razor's edge
Symbolism, 107, 176, 196;
cosmological, Fig. 2.6, 113, 120; of

shaman's rattle, 51; sexual, 51, 60,
85, 106, 134; shamanistic, 27, 135,
202. *See also* Metaphors; Symbols
Symbol, 62, 89, 112, 113, 150,
189–190, 195, 197–200, 204;
nonverbal, 2; of transformation, 51;
verbal, 2. *See also* Archetypes;
Metaphors; Symbolism

T
Taboo, 213 n.35
Tao (Taoists), 54, 55
Tankas (Tibetan), 34
Tantrism, 20, 135, 193, 206
Tassili n'Aijer (Algeria), 152–153
Tembé Indians, 78
Teonanacatl ("flesh of the gods"), 99,
174
Teresa of Avila, Saint, 88–89, 225
n.16
Testes, 51
Texas, 153, 168, 199
Thule Group, 13
Tietäjä (Finnish, "shaman"), 72
Toad, Fig. 3.2, 247 n.32. See also
Bufo toad
Toadstool, 99, 164, 247 n.32
Tobacco, 136, 140–141, 167, 173, 183;
drinking tobacco water, 134; enema,
141; smoking, 72, 78, 141, 148, 224
n.9. See also *Nicotiana* spp.
Totemism, 23–25, 39, 40, 109–110,
213 n.35
Trance, 17, 37, 49, 50, 52–54, 63,
73–78, 85–87, 90, 93–94, 96–97,
99, 104, 108–109, 113, 132–133,
137, 141–142, 164, 178, 198, 203,
205. *See also* Altered states of
consciousness; Ecstasy; SSC
Transcendence, 21, 82, 192, 194–195,
207
Transexuality. *See* Androgyny;
Biunity; Hermaphroditism
Transformation, 14, 67, 83–84,
105–112, 124, 138, 178, 195, 203;
shamanistic, 43, 96, 126–127, 135

Transmutation, 93, 133, 202. *See also* Transformation
Transubstantiation, 139
Trinity, divine: Christian, 17
Trois Frères, 70
Tukano Indians. *See* Tukanoan
Tukanoan Indians, 39, 50–51, 65, 77–79, 94–96, 110–111, 131–133, 132, 143, 192, 203. *See also* Shaman: Tukanoan
Tulayev (a Siberian shaman), Fig. 2.6
Tungus, 48, 50, 58, 62, 74, 79, 120
Tunnel, 133; as entrance to Lowerworld, 34
Turks (also, Turkey), 44, 52

U
Ugrians, 50, 163
Uncertainty Principle, 4, 8. *See also* Heisenberg, Werner
Underworld, 37, 39, 43, 94, 159, 161, 172, 179. *See also* Lowerworld
Ungnadia speciosa, 168
Unity, 15, 16, 24, 84, 104; Negative, in Sufism, 53; Positive, in Sufism, 53; spiritual, 17. *See also* Oneness; Wholeness
Universal categories, 6
Universe, 24, 105–106, 111–113, 115, 117, 119, 130, 189, 193–194; hexagonal, 126
Upperworld, 76, 112–114, 119, 172, 184. *See also* Otherworld
Ur-religion, 9, 151
Uralic tribes, 69, 79
Urine, 147
Urubu Indians, 73, 78–79, 118–119
Usener, *Divine Names*, 193
Uterus (also, *utero*), 51, 94, 135. *See also* Womb
Uwišin (Jívaro, "shamans"), 63, 133

V
Valcamonica. *See* Camonica Valley
Vagina, 51, 60, 135; vaginal orifice, 83; vaginal passage, 133. *See also* Clitoris

Vanaprasthas, 21
Vedas, 31, 164–166, 199, 244 n.9, 248 n.34
Venezuela, 51
Venice, 200–201. *See also* Italy
Venus (planet), 119, 171
Verona, 201. *See also* Italy
Villanovan culture, 157
Vinča culture, 43, 44, 154, 161
Virola tree, 135–136, 178–179
Visions, 24, 60–62, 66, 74, 76, 78, 80–81, 90, 96, 101, 105, 113, 123, 133, 135, 137–139, 148, 177, 184, 198–200; Beatific, 19; drug-induced, 9, 97–99, 199; quest of, among Shoshoni, 22
Visualization (and visual imagery), 39, 191; by Mehinaku, 15
Voguls, 164

W
Walbiri, 24
Warao Indians, 51
Waser, Peter G., 147
Wasson, R. Gordon, 138, 164–165, 172–174, 206, 248 n.34; *Soma*, 147, 164; and V. Wasson, *Mushroom, Russia and History*, 164, 182
Watts, Alan, 14
Weber, Max, *The Religion of India*, 94
Western Hemisphere, 45, 85, 141–142, 148, 151, 166, 176. *See also* New World
Whistles, used in shamanic healing and soul retrieval, 45
Wholeness, 16. *See also* Oneness; Unity
Wilbert, Johannes, 12, 51, 148; *Tobacco and Shamanism in South America*, 140, 183
Wintu Indians, 81–82, 103, 227 n.33
Wisdom, 61, 68, 75, 87, 207, 225 n.16
Witchcraft, 145, 155

Womb, 36, 51, 83, 111, 125–126;
mystical return to, 36. *See also*
Eternal return; Uterus
World Tree, 24–25, 92, 110, 114, 120,
172, 196, 205, 234 n.13; and
drums, 46
World, antipodal, 10, 95, 103, 112,
133, 231 n.59; botanic, 184;
cosmic, 120–121; preternatural,
127, 134, 184; -spirit, 24, 141. *See
also* Antipodes
Worldview, 11, 70, 96, 99, 101, 104,
106–107, 115, 119, 130, 194, 195,
204, 222 n.125
Wrangham, Richard, 185
Wu, Emperor, 55, 166
Wu and *Wu*-ism, 54–56; Chinese
term for shaman, sorceress,
55
Wunderlich, Hans Georg, 8; *The
Secret of Crete*, 8

X
Xibalbá, 172
Xingu (in Amazon), 14, 72, 108
Xochipilli (Aztec, "God of Flowers"),
173–174

Y
YHVH (also, YAWEH), 193
Yajé (also *Yagé*), 51, 85, 91, 113,
134–136, 198, 203. See also
Ayahuasca; Banisteriopsis spp.
Yąnomamö Indians, 24, 108, 110,
117–118
Yakuts, 46, 77, 114, 122, 202
Yavi (Cubeo, "jaguar-shaman"), 63
Yee (Desana, "shaman," "jaguar"), 135
Yenisei river, 63, 122, 163, 165
Yetamá (Mehinaku, "tobacco
shaman"), 72, 141, 224 n.9
Yoga, 20; techniques of, 14
Yogins, 14, 54
Yü (Chinese ruler), 54
Yucatan, Fig. 3.2
Yukaghirs, 163, 215 n.44
Yuman Indians, 124
Yuraks, 46, 92; Yurak–Samoyed, 121

Z
Zaener, R. C., 19–20, 211 n.18;
Mysticism: Sacred and Profane, 19
Zarathuštra, 215 n.46
Zeus, 32, 128, 159
Zoroastrians, 165–166
Zuñi Indians, 170